Rhetoric and Communication

A Volume in Honor of

**Professors Karl R. Wallace,
Marie Hochmuth Nichols, and Richard Murphy**

RHETORIC AND COMMUNICATION

Studies in the University of Illinois Tradition

Edited by
Jane Blankenship
and
Hermann G. Stelzner

Published for the Department of Speech Communication by the
UNIVERSITY OF ILLINOIS PRESS
Urbana Chicago London

EDITORIAL BOARD

Jane Blankenship
University of Massachusetts

Wayne Brockriede
University of Colorado

Roger E. Nebergall
University of Illinois

Robert L. Scott
University of Minnesota

Hermann G. Stelzner
University of Massachusetts

Library of Congress Cataloging in Publication Data

Main entry under title:

Rhetoric and communication.

"A volume in honor of professors Karl R. Wallace,
Marie Hochmuth Nichols, and Richard Murphy."
   Included bibliographical references.
   1. Oral communication—Addresses, essays, lectures.
I. Blankenship, Jane. II. Stelzner, Herman Georg,
1931-   III. Wallace, Karl Richards, 1905-1973.
IV. Nichols, Marie Hochmuth. V. Murphy, Richard,
1903-   VI. Illinois. University at Urbana-Champaign.
Dept. of Speech Communication.
PN4121.R437   808   75-37621
ISBN 0-252-00566-X

Contents

Preface:
Professors Wallace, Nichols, Murphy
and the Illinois Tradition

ROGER E. NEBERGALL AND JOSEPH W. WENZEL

KARL WALLACE was born in Hubbardsville, New York, on November 10, 1905. He died at Amherst, Massachusetts, on October 16, 1973. He received a B.A. in 1927, an M.A. in 1931, and a Ph.D. in 1933, all at Cornell University. He taught at Iowa State College from 1933 to 1936, and at Washington University (St. Louis) from 1936 to 1937. At the University of Virginia he was Chairman of the School of Speech from 1937 to 1944 and of the School of Speech and Drama from 1944 to 1947. He was Head of the Department of Speech and Theatre at the University of Illinois from 1947 until his retirement in 1968. After his retirement, he taught at the University of Massachusetts until his death.

MARIE HOCHMUTH NICHOLS was born on July 13, 1908, at Dunbar, Pennsylvania. She received an A.B. degree in 1931, an M.A. in 1936 from the University of Pittsburgh, and a Ph.D. in 1945 from the University of Wisconsin. She also studied at the University of Illinois. She taught at Mt. Mercy College from 1935 to 1939. She has taught at the University of Illinois since 1939. She has been a visiting professor at the University of Hawaii and the University of Southern California.

RICHARD MURPHY was born in Marienville, Pennsylvania, on September 12, 1903. He received a B.A. in 1927, an M.A. in 1928, and a Ph.D. in 1938, all at the University of Pittsburgh. He also studied at Cornell University, the State University of Iowa, and the University of Edinburgh, Scotland. He taught at the University of Pittsburgh from 1927 to 1935, at Cornell University from 1935 to 1936, and at the University of Colorado from 1936 to 1945. He taught at the University of Illinois from 1945 until his retirement in 1971.

This volume of essays has been prepared as a tribute to three distinguished professors who led the study of rhetoric and public address at the University of Illinois during a period of twenty years. Karl R. Wallace, Marie Hochmuth Nichols, and Richard Murphy, by example as well as precept, inspired their students with a spirit of scholarship that we have here called "the Illinois Tradition." A "tradition," we suppose, must be compounded of a body of knowledge and experience, a motivating spirit, and a certain historical continuity. On these grounds it seems entirely appropriate to speak of an Illinois tradition. This volume is an effort by students and friends to recall that tradition, to thank those who were so much responsible for it, and to express through these essays their continuing indebtedness.

The spirit of the Illinois tradition cannot really be captured in a few paragraphs. Probably each student touched by it would express the feeling differently: some would speak of dedication to original research, others of the importance of teaching skill in public utterance; some would stress the advancement of rhetorical theory, some the uses of rhetorical criticism, and still others the study of the history of rhetorical practice. The program of study that Wallace, Nichols, Murphy, and their colleagues created at Illinois was a rich and rounded one. Its central tenets were these: that rhetoric in its most useful sense embraces the whole rationale of influential discourse; that rhetoric is an essential dimension of human social action; and that the study of rhetorical theory, practice, and criticism has an important place in liberal education. Thus grounding the study of rhetoric in the tradition of Western humanism, Wallace, Nichols, and Murphy maintained in their teaching a clear vision of the large social purposes of rhetorical studies.

As is true of any such historical phenomenon, one cannot point precisely to a time or place where the Illinois tradition may be said to have begun. Perhaps as good a time as any would be the year 1947 when Karl Wallace came to the University of Illinois from the University of Virginia, where he had been Chairman of the School of Speech and Drama, to serve as the first head of the newly formed Department of Speech. Prior to that time, work in speech had been offered in a separate division of the Department of English, under the supervision of Wayland Maxfield Parrish.

Already at Illinois and ready to move from the Division of Speech to the new department were Marie Hochmuth and Richard Murphy. Hochmuth had joined the faculty in 1939, coming from Mt. Mercy College. Murphy had arrived in 1945, from the University of Colorado. For more than twenty years, these three scholars were at the center of teaching and research in rhetoric and public address.

They were joined by many others, of course. Some of these were in theatre and in speech and hearing science, and their labors brought those areas to full development and eventual department status. Others made their contribution along with Wallace, Nichols, and Murphy in rhetoric and public address. Otto Dieter, whose service at Illinois dated from 1938, was an active force in the tradition until his death in 1968. So was Ray Nadeau who came to Illinois in 1950, taught here for fourteen years until he left to become department head at Purdue, and returned on a part-time basis to teach seminars from 1968 to 1970. Other colleagues included Lee Hultzén, Kenneth Burns, Halbert Gulley, King Broadrick, Henry Mueller, as well as many others, some of whom have contributed to this volume. But the three scholars to whom this volume is dedicated were central to the Illinois tradition. Moreover, they were the pre-eminent members of the faculty in their field. Throughout the fifties, when one thought of the Department of Speech at Illinois, one immediately thought of Wallace, Nichols, and Murphy. They were, in varying degrees, near the peaks of their careers; and their careers exemplified the highest type of service by academic persons. All three were leaders in professional associations; all were scholars who helped to shape a discipline; and all were teachers dedicated to creating a climate of learning in which new scholarship could emerge and mature.

Professors Wallace, Nichols, and Murphy were among the most active members of the Speech Association of America, later to become the Speech Communication Association. Both Wallace and Nichols served as president of the association and Murphy was a member of its administrative council. Each of the three served a term as editor of the *Quarterly Journal of Speech*. In addition to service on numerous committees and boards, each of the three was called upon for special tasks. Karl Wallace edited the SAA-sponsored *History of Speech Education in America* and Marie Nichols edited volume III of *A History and Criticism of American Public Address*, both of which remain required reading for serious scholars in rhetoric and public address. Richard Murphy served as editor of "Shop Talk," when everyone began his reading of the *Quarterly Journal of Speech* at the back. Without actually checking old programs, one suspects that there were few conventions of the association in the fifties and sixties without at least two of the three on a program. Because they believed in their professional association as a community of scholars, they were often called upon to speak "for the good of the order," and we are all in their debt for much good speaking.

Wallace, Nichols, and Murphy were humanist-scholars, too; they were among the group of serious scholars who helped the speech communication profession, in its formative years, to grow from a collection of teachers of public speaking into a substantial discipline concerned with the full range of scientific and philosophical inquiry into speech communication. In their several editorships and in their teaching they helped to shape the discipline. Perhaps their own works were an even greater influence, for they stand as models of rigorous scholarship. One cannot read their best works without being moved by their enthusiasm for learning and by their humane approach to rhetoric as a means to better understanding of the human condition.

Karl Wallace will probably be remembered best for two strands of his work. The first is his series of writings on Francis Bacon which reveals the depth and subtlety of a philosophical mind grappling with human communication and human nature. Had Wallace lived longer we would probably have been blessed with a third book on Bacon to add to that impressive body of work.

The second strand of Wallace's work continues to influence teachers and scholars from primary grades through graduate schools; it is his concern for understanding and managing practical discourse in public affairs. In his essay on "Rhetoric, Politics, and the Education of the Ready Man," Wallace wrote of politics as the indispensable art of human cooperation and of rhetoric as the indispensable handmaiden. Characteristically, his closely reasoned analysis was placed within a broad humanistic perspective:

> If rhetoric teaches nothing else, she requires that her student make up his mind, that he take decision only after search and full inquiry, that he speak from his convictions with all the skill he can acquire. The student of rhetoric learns, also, that he has no monopoly on ability, privilege, and skill. When opinion encounters opinion, each ably presented and strongly high-lighted, he learns that agreement amid difference is found in a shadowland where the light is more or less strong, and its illuminating signs marked "probably" and "possibly" rather than "certainly" and "exclusively," a territory in which persons can meet for common action and still preserve their dignity and worth. Gradually he learns that in a commonwealth of mutual deference, integrity and self-respect are shared.[1]

Through a life-long series of essays, such as "Rhetoric and Advising"[2] and "The Substance of Rhetoric: Good Reasons,"[3] Wallace continued to clarify the functions of rhetoric as it serves the political person in common social relations. Throughout, he was motivated by the belief, expressed in his last book, "that to establish control over speech and language behavior is to better the human condition in all of its essential aspects."[4]

The central focus of Marie Hochmuth Nichols's work has been in applying the methods of rhetorical analysis and criticism to the body of public utterance that illuminates social and political history. To that end she has contributed to the enlargement of rhetorical theory and criticism, for example, in introducing the works of Kenneth Burke and I. A. Richards to a wider readership through the pages of the *Quarterly Journal of Speech*. Her critical study of Lincoln's First Inaugural is often cited as a model of rhetorical criticism. In a series of lectures at the Annual Conference on Speech Education at Louisiana State University in 1959, Mrs. Nichols explained the rationale that has motivated her work: "I find considerable humanizing value in the examples of men in their moments of decision, exercising a judgment, moral, rational, imaginative, and in the finest tradition of the human spirit. . . . The study of rhetorical discourse yields scores of examples of men in their most manly occupation, that of making decisions which ennoble them, and, in general, give insight into our own lives."[5]

Richard Murphy also pursued an interest in the role of rhetoric in politics, especially in the methods of discourse that facilitate deliberation, decision-making, and problem-solving. A central problem for the political person, as Murphy expressed it, is "to strengthen methodologies which encourage fair and thorough investigation, free hearings, and just, efficient decision or solution."[6] As a teacher of argumentation, discussion, and parliamentary procedure, he sought to instill in his students a respect for free speech and the institutions that safeguard it. That concern found expression in widely read essays on "The Forensic Mind,"[7] "The Ethics of Debating Both Sides,"[8] and "Preface to an Ethic of Rhetoric."[9]

These, of course, are the public images of three leaders in their profession. Their students and colleagues who have been a part of the Illinois tradition have fond memories of a more private kind as well. In the more intense and personal contact on the Urbana-Champaign campus, Wallace, Nichols, and Murphy developed the climate of learning that Illinois graduates recall affectionately. Each was a scholar, but each was a person, memorable in a unique way. Every graduate student at Illinois during the years of their tenure brought away a vivid memory of each, an image unique to the individual but at the same time made common by shared experiences and recollections.

From graduate school days the present authors remember Wallace as the teacher who could demand, and get, more and better work from a student than the student ever imagined was possible. For a generation of Illinois graduates "Aristotle papers" had a special meaning, describing what was for many a first introduction into the world of meticulous and demanding scholarship. Wallace taught by example that rigor and humane understanding could complement each other to the advantage of both. Probably none of us, before taking the seminar on Aristotle, had ever spent three consecutive hours in such intense intellectual encounter. The routine was fairly regular: some volunteer would begin to read that week's paper, with frequent hopeful glances at Wallace. If the paper was pretty good, he would be rewarded with an occasional smile or a "yup, yup" with a sharp nod. But usually there came the moment when some difficult point was not quite mastered. Wallace would just perceptibly shift in his seat, square his shoulders, and look off at that spot near the ceiling where we were convinced he could see the whole Aristotelian corpus in large type. With everyone alert for one of his precise and probing questions, he would launch a discussion that gripped our attention for two or three hours.

We remember Karl Wallace in many roles that revealed his versatile and vibrant humanity. One of the present writers recalls the day (when he was barely past thirty) that he succumbed in three vigorous games of handball to Wallace (then nearing sixty), and then dragged himself to the showers while the great man went out to run a mile, just to round off his exercise! One recalls Wallace dancing expertly with a new faculty wife and putting her completely at ease at the president's reception. One recalls Karl and Dorothy at one of their splendid parties, where the newest graduate student was made to feel welcome in a department led by warm and caring people. In every human way, as in every academic way, Karl Wallace was a rare person.

When former students return to the department's corner of Lincoln Hall, they find much that has changed. One familiar sight will please them, however: as always, the door stands open at Marie Hochmuth Nichols's office. More than any other faculty member, Mrs. Nichols came to be loved for giving of herself to students. She is always available to talk to a student or a colleague, most often about that person's concerns, but sometimes too about her own current work. As graduate students we all learned that if one wanted a break from routine or a stimulating half-hour of conversation, one could always count on Marie Nichols to be caught up with some new idea and anxious to talk about it. No one can say how much the morale of a generation of graduate students came to depend on those occasions when we could entice her to leave the office and join a group for coffee and talk. No doubt we all came to appreciate, and feel some twinge of conscience about, the magnitude of her gift of those hours. For we saw the lights burning in her office every evening and nearly every weekend, as she did the work that had been put aside for us during the day.

Mrs. Nichols's classes were as stimulating as her conversation. She has read so much, explored so many interconnections, that her students find new avenues to ideas constantly suggested to them. Probably dozens of dissertations sprang from hints dropped casually in her classes in American public address and in modern rhetorical theory. Nor did her contribution end there, for she directed those dissertations with patience, skill, and an amazing willingness to accommodate student needs. Even today one is not surprised to see on her busy desk—amid the manuscripts of her own writing, the parts of dissertations, the scholarly books and journals—a paper from some former student who seeks her criticism. Regardless of the press of other business, Mrs. Nichols will read it with care and return it with encouragement.

Richard Murphy remains a part of the Lincoln Hall scene although he has retired from active teaching. On his visits to the office we may still look forward to a lively discussion of the latest public issue, especially if it touches on civil liberties or freedom of speech. Murphy had a way of putting students and colleagues in touch with public affairs, and of relating our professional concerns to the current issues. Long before consumerism became fashionable, Murphy's offer of a group subscription to *Consumer Reports* was an annual event. He had an impact on the world beyond the campus, for he was frequently asked to teach short courses for businessmen and union leaders, especially on discussion and parliamentary procedure. The high point of his public service came in 1970 when he served as parliamentarian to the Constitutional Convention of the State of Illinois.

Thinking of Murphy reminds graduates in the Illinois tradition of his brilliant, pungent wit, which in a seminar could lay bare an inanity or expose a contradiction while still leaving its source alive and functioning. Murphy was the supreme debater and the graduate student was assumed to be his equal in the management of ideas. The genuine gift, of course, was in making it appear at least that the student could manage that. But also, the graduate student remembers books. Books filling bookcases, piled on the desk, on the floor, on every chair, and on every surface that could hold them. But they were used, neither decoration nor discard, and the student marveled at Murphy's ability to locate quickly the exact book the student wanted, complete with comment on its publishing history, errata, and availability and price on the used book market.

The Illinois tradition is thus a compound of private memories entwined with the public images of Wallace, Nichols, and Murphy. We know them as dedicated professionals and disciplined scholars, but we have been touched by them most deeply as teachers and friends. In the essays which comprise this volume, one will find students of the three differing in specific ways with positions that Wallace, Nichols, and Murphy have taken. Doubtless some of those differences are due to developments in the field, but more are attributable to the quality of education that the three provided. Wayne Brockriede commented on that circumstance in a recent letter:

> . . . to be true to the liberalizing education we received we had no choice but to pursue ideas where they led us, to make judgments as good as we could make, and to make them after the most rigorous research, thinking, and arguing we could muster. The legacy they leave us is not the positions they have taken in the course of their own productive careers, but rather the tradition of taking scholarship seriously, of grappling with ideas rigorously, of giving as much of self to students as they could, and of all the other aspects of the teacher-scholar that connote a humane but hardheaded way of dealing with people and with ideas.

By the substance of Wallace, Nichols, and Murphy's teaching we have not invariably been persuaded; by the spirit of their teaching we have been enriched and inspired. With this volume, we honor the Illinois tradition established by Karl Wallace, Marie Nichols, and Richard Murphy. Those of us who were schooled in it, and who have the privilege of remaining a part of it, strive to build in a manner worthy of their foundations.

1. Donald C. Bryant, Ed., *The Rhetorical Idiom* (Ithaca, N.Y.: Cornell University Press, 1958), pp. 91–92.

2. Karl Wallace, "Rhetoric and Advising," *Southern Speech Journal,* 29 (Summer, 1964), 279–287.

3. Karl Wallace, "The Substance of Rhetoric: Good Reasons," *Quarterly Journal of Speech*, 49 (October, 1963), 239–249.

4. Karl Wallace, *Understanding Discourse* (Baton Rouge: Louisiana State University Press, 1970), p. vi.

5. Marie Hochmuth Nichols, *Rhetoric and Criticism* (Baton Rouge: Louisiana State University Press, 1963), p. 10.

6. Richard Murphy, "The Forensic Mind," *Studies in Speech and Drama in Honor of Alexander M. Drummond* (Ithaca, N.Y.: Cornell University Press, 1944), p. 469.

7. *Ibid.*

8. Richard Murphy, "The Ethics of Debating Both Sides," *The Speech Teacher*, 6 (January, 1957), 1–9.

9. Richard Murphy, "Preface to an Ethic of Rhetoric," in Bryant, *The Rhetorical Idiom*, pp. 125–143.

PART I
Communication and Rhetorical Study:
The Humanistic Perspective

The Fourth *Stasis* in Greek Rhetoric

RAY D. DEARIN

Near the end of his definitive work on the *Attic Orators*, R. C. Jebb comments on the growth of rhetorical theory in the Hellenistic period following Aristotle. After explaining the development of two schools of rhetorical thought, the "practical" and the "philosophical," Jebb identifies succinctly the place of Hermagoras in the history of rhetoric:

> Hermagoras now worked up the treatises both of the Practical and of the Philosophical Rhetoric into a new system. His object was practical; but he followed the philosophers in giving his chief care to the province of Invention. Erring on the side of too much subtlety, he founded a Rhetoric which, as distinguished from the Practical and the Philosophical, may be called the Scholastic. For Greek oratory this could do little directly. But for Roman oratory Hermagoras and his followers did very much what the school of Isokrates had done for Athens.[1]

This passage has three insights that are central to a proper understanding of rhetorical developments in the transitional period from Aristotle to Cicero and the *auctor ad Herennium*. First, Hermagorean rhetoric was developed in a Hellenistic environment, following in the wake of the great flowering of Attic oratory in the fifth and fourth centuries B.C., and was influenced both by the sophistical and by the philosophical traditions. Second, Hermagoras was to have his greatest influence on the Romans. Third, his impact on them was enormous.

These three points, if kept clearly in mind, shed light on a problem that has perplexed many students of Latin rhetoric. Briefly stated, the problem is this: in Hermagoras' system of rhetorical invention, as it can be reconstructed from quotations by other writers, there were four *stases*, or "issues," on which a dispute turned: στοχασμός (Latin, *coniectura*); ὅρος (Latin, *definitiva* or *proprietas*); κατα συμβεβηκός or ποιότης (Latin, *generalis* or *qualitas*); and μετάληψις (Latin, *translativa* or *translatio*).[2] This quadripartite division was retained by many Latin rhetoricians following Hermagoras, but, for some reason, other writers dropped the fourth *stasis* in favor of a tripartite scheme.[3] To discover why this occurred is the purpose of this essay.

Hopefully, this effort to dispel some of the confusion surrounding the fourth *stasis*, the translative issue as it came to be called in Roman rhetoric, will lead to a heightened awareness that rhetorical theory is inevitably conditioned by culture and society. More is involved in this attempt than a mere inspection and notation of trivial classificatory schemes. My thesis is that Hermagorean rhetoric, conceived as it was in the Hellenistic milieu of the second century B.C., drew the four *stases* from earlier Greek thought and codified the practices of the Attic orators, but was modified when applied to Roman rhetorical needs. Specifically, this paper will suggest that the fourth *stasis*, which, in certain Latin treatises, was regarded as an extra-rational attempt to avoid trial on procedural grounds, had been in Greek oratorical practice an integral part of the rational inventive process.

This essay will first show how the *stasis* theory was treated in various Latin rhetorics. It will next explore the origins of the theory in earlier Greek philosophy and in oratorical practice. Finally, it will present some observations based on these findings which should clarify why many Latin writers omitted the fourth *stasis* or relegated it to a subordinate role.

I

In the first century B.C. the opposing views about the number of *stases* had already formed. They are apparent in two works otherwise remarkably similar, Cicero's *De Inventione* and the anonymous *Rhetorica ad Herennium*. Although the mature Cicero [*Orator* 15; *De Oratore*, II. xxiv. 26] later declared in favor of a three-fold system, the young Cicero, after discussing the conjectural, definitional, and qualitative *stases*, wrote in *De Inventione*:

> But when the case depends on the circumstance that it appears that the right person does not bring the suit, or that he brings it against the wrong person, or before the wrong tribunal, or at a wrong time, under the wrong statute, or the wrong charge, or with a wrong penalty, the issue is called translative because the action seems to require a transfer to another court or alteration in the form of pleading. There will always be one of these issues applicable to every kind of case; for where none applies, there can be no controversy. Therefore it is not fitting to regard it as a case at all.[4]

The author of the *ad Herennium* objected to the fourth category as a distinct type of issue. Following his teacher in recognizing only the conjectural, legal, and juridical issues,[5] he made transference (*translatio*) one of the six subtypes of the legal issue (his term for the definitional issue).[6] Cicero credits Hermagoras with being the inventor of the fourth issue, "not that orators did not use it before his day—many did use it frequently—but because earlier writers of text-books did not notice it nor include it with the issues."[7] And he may have the teacher of the *auctor* in mind, along with others, when he says: "Since [Hermagoras'] invention of the term many have found fault with it, not misled by ignorance, I think, for the case is perfectly plain, so much as they have been kept from adopting it by a spirit of envy and a desire to disparage a rival."[8] We need not take seriously Cicero's reasoning as to why some theorists did not adopt the translative issue. Indeed, in later years he accepted a three-part system in his *Orator* and *De Oratore*. The significant point is that other writers were aware of Hermagoras' four-part scheme. Some merely chose to omit the fourth *stasis*, or to treat it as a subsidiary element in their systems.

In the sixth chapter of the third book of his *Institutio Oratoria*, written near the end of the first Christian century, Quintilian summarizes the views of earlier thinkers concerning *stases*. After mentioning the categories used by Archedemus, Pamphilus, Apollodorus, Theodorus, Posidonius, Cornelius Celsus, Cicero, Patrocles, Marcus Antonius, Verginius, Athenaeus, Caecilius, Theon, and Aristotle, Quintilian states: "Hermagoras is alone in thinking that there are four, namely *conjecture, particularity, competence,* and *quality.*"[9] Here the fourth issue is called, in Butler's translation, *competence.* One sees what has become of this *stasis* in Quintilian's system as he explains: "I used to follow the majority of authorities in adhering to three *rational bases*, the *conjectural, qualitative* and *definitive*, and to one *legal basis*. These were my *general bases*. The *legal basis* I divided into five species, dealing with the *letter of the law and intention, contradictory laws*, the *syllogism, ambiguity* and *competence.*"[10] Thus, Quintilian, like the writer to Herennius, makes μετάληψις a subcategory of the "legal" issue. But he goes even further to separate it entirely from the rational *stases* (bases):

> It is now clear to me that the fourth of the *general bases* may be removed, since the original division which I made into *rational* and *legal bases* is sufficient. The fourth therefore will not be a *basis*, but a kind of *question*; if it were not, it would form one of the *rational bases*. Further I have removed *competence* from those which I called *species*. For I often asserted . . . that the *basis* concerned with competence hardly ever occurs in any dispute under such circumstances that it cannot more correctly be given some other name, and that consequently some rhetoricians exclude it from their list of *bases*.[11]

Having made a clear division between the *stases* and legal questions, Quintilian then explains that questions of "competence" are often resolved by reference to one of the other "issues." Suppose, for example, this assertion should be made: "You ought to demand the return of a deposit not before the praetor but before the consuls, as the sum is too large to come under the praetor's jurisdiction." "The question then arises," says Quintilian, "whether the sum is too large, and the dispute is one of fact."[12] The conjectural issue arises here.

Legal interpretations also come into play in questions of competence. In such cases the dispute no longer turns on the original question at issue, but on one that is, so to speak, "one step removed." Thus, "in cases of *competence* it is not the question concerning which the advocate argues that is involved, but the question on account of which he argues."[13] Quintilian exemplifies this point: " 'You have killed a man.' 'I did not kill him.' The *question* is whether he has killed him; the *basis* is the *conjectural*. But the following case is very different. 'I have the right to bring this action.' 'You have not the right.' The question is whether he has the right, and it is from this that we derive the *basis*."[14] The Roman rhetorician thus explains at length why "It is ... to *kinds of causes*, not to *bases* that the term *competence* applies...."[15] In so doing, he makes *translatio* into a technical matter of proper legal procedure rather than one of the main *stases* on which a controversy turns.

Although the *auctor ad Herennium*, the mature Cicero, and Quintilian favored a tripartite division of *stases*, many later writers followed Hermagoras in adhering to the quadripartite system. Among them were Hermogenes,[16] Aurelius Augustine, Julius Victor, Cassiodorus, Alcuin, and Clodianus. One of the best surviving sources of pure Hermagorean rhetoric is the little tractate of Aurelius Augustine, *De Rhetorica*, a product of the fourth or fifth century A.D. Concerning the division of *stases*, Augustine states: "Rational or logical questions ... are made in four ways. In them these things are asked: (1) Whether or not something is? (*an sit*), (2) What it is? (*quid sit*), (3) Of what quality it is? (*quale sit*), and (4) Whether or not it should be brought to trial? (*an induci in iudicium debeat*)."[17] After noting the contention that surrounded the fourth issue, Augustine invokes the authority of Hermagoras: "But the authority of Hermagoras far surpasses all others and he holds that it is a type of question, and an especially necessary type, and one which is often resorted to in public matters...."[18] That the authority of Hermagoras over four hundred years after his death was sufficient to justify the writer's inclusion of the fourth *stasis* testifies to his great influence. Nevertheless, Augustine feels obliged to comment further on this *stasis*:

> ... I recognize that nothing is of more interest to those threatened with a trial than to avoid a trial, furthermore, that the avoidance of a trial has some semblance of a trial. For if a legal matter were handled in this way that whenever anyone did not wish his case to be tried, this would be within his power, there would be no investigation; at the present time, however, since those always arise who would prevent a trial, that contention itself in which one party demands a hearing and the other makes an objection against it, constitutes a question; this type of

controversy Hermagoras calls *metalepsis* (transference). A few of our men have called it *reprehensio*, many have termed it *translatio*, both for good reasons. Those who have called it *reprehensio* did so obviously because at the very moment when the case is brought into court, it is laid hold of again and, so to speak, pulled back; those who have called it *translatio* did so because the defendant does not preclude court action altogether but, in order to free himself from the present conditions of the action, he transfers the trial to another kind of court, either now in session or to be convened in the future.[19]

These comments reveal that Augustine does not differ strenuously with Quintilian over the meaning of the fourth *stasis*. Both understand it to refer to procedural questions of correct judicial action. Even though Augustine accepts the authority of Hermagoras and lists it among the *rational stases*, he clearly views it differently from the other three. For him, it appears to be a way of avoiding trial while seeming to meet the primary accusation of the prosecutor head on.

From this cursory treatment of how various Latin writers dealt with the fourth *stasis*, one point is clear: whether they accepted or rejected it, the influence of Hermagoras compelled them to take it into account. As R. G. Collingwood has said, "An intense polemic against a certain doctrine is an infallible sign that the doctrine in question figures largely in the writer's environment and even has a strong attraction for himself."[20] The influence of Hermagoras seems to explain why some theorists retained *translatio*. Why others rejected it can perhaps best be understood after a study of the pre-Hermagorean origins of the theory of *stasis*.

II

Modern scholars have contributed greatly to our understanding of the theory of *stasis*. In particular, American scholars such as Otto A. L. Dieter and Ray Nadeau, relying heavily upon certain German scholars, especially Georg Thiele and Dieter Matthes, have labored diligently to uncover the meaning and origins of *stasis*.[21] In a 1950 article Dieter observes, "In Pre-Aristotelian Greek thought, in Aristotle's physical philosophy and in the *metaphysical* rhetoric of Post-Aristotelian Peripatetics of the Third Century before Christ, [*stasis*] was the rest, pause, halt, or standing still, which inevitably occurs between opposite as well as between contrary 'moves,' or motions."[22] The four Hermagorean *stases*, Dieter explains, correspond closely to Aristotle's four categories of physical changes: *Being, Quantity, Quality,* and *Place.*[23] Explaining how the *stasis* system functions in rhetorical invention, Dieter writes:

In Stasis I, unqualified Being, or the subject's actual existence, is challenged, controverted, and rejected; there is no agreement whatever between the speakers on the subject and the area of dispute is consider-able. In Stasis II, the subject's actuality or actual *Being* is admitted, or waived, but its quantification, or *Being-in-Quantity*, is checked, "re-torted" and denied and the area of disagreement is more limited. In Stasis III, the subject's *Being* and *Quantity* are admitted, or waived, but its qualitative *Being*, i.e., *Being-in-Quality*, is "arrested, re-directed, and repelled" and the extent of the dispute is correspondingly restricted. In Stasis IV, the subject's *Being*, *Quantity*, and *Quality* are admitted, or waived; its *Being-in-Place* only, is "not allowed to pass," but "re-turned" and "hurled back."[24]

To exemplify how a charge may be stasiated and rebuffed by an answer in the fourth category, Dieter cites this response: "It *is not in Place for you* to take this action, or to bring this charge *at this time*, or *in this court*, or *in this manner*, etc."[25] Here it is obvious that the fourth category, *Place*, is re-stricted in no literal sense to the idea of location (for example, the proper court), though the underlying tenor of the idea might have originally been physical.[26] Rather, the term refers to the *appropriateness* of the action that is being taken. Its appropriateness may be questioned on any one of a number of grounds (wrong prosecutor, improper court, incorrect legal procedure, and so forth).

Nine years after the publication of Dieter's article, Nadeau suggested that the four rhetorical *stases* developed from the four steps used by the Peripa-tetics and the Stoics in studying matter, and from the Aristotelian system set forth in the *Topics* for stating propositions.[27] It is significant that both Dieter and Nadeau find the origins of the *stasis* theory in some four-fold system of classification. Cicero's statement (*De Inventione*, I. xi. 16) that Hermagoras was thought to be the originator of the fourth *stasis*, then, simply indicates that he was the first to employ it in a system of rhetorical *stases*.

Although Hermagoras was probably the first to offer a full-blown quadri-partite system of *stases*, the roots of such a system are certainly in earlier Greek theory. In the *Rhetoric* Aristotle asserted that rhetorical proofs should bear directly upon the "question in dispute," which will fall under one of four heads: "(1) If you maintain that the act *was not committed*, your main task in court is to prove this. (2) If you maintain that the act *did no harm*, prove this. If you maintain that (3) the act was *less* than is alleged, or (4) *justified*, prove these facts, just as you would prove the act not to have been committed if you were maintaining that."[28] But, again, Hermagoras seems to have been the first to present the four-part *stasis* system as a method of rhetorical invention.

The concern of modern scholars with the meaning of *stasis* and with its origins in earlier Greek thought has tended to draw attention to the philologi-cal aspects of the concept rather than to its usage in oratorical practice. To be sure, writers on *stasis* sometimes employ brief illustrations from the early

Attic orators. Thus, Kennedy parenthetically cites this example of the fourth *stasis* as an instance where the competence of the prosecutor is denied: "(perhaps, as Aeschines alleged of Timarchus, the prosecutor has lost his civil rights)."[29] Concerning the four *stases*, Kennedy also says, "All can be found in the Attic orators, and their possibilities were hardly unappreciated by logographers."[30] And Nadeau comments that "Various forms of stasis can certainly be seen in pre-Hermagorean practice—for example, in the speeches of Lysias, Demosthenes, Aeschines, and others."[31] Because instruction in the art of rhetoric followed in the wake of practice,[32] a more thorough consideration of oratorical practice in Greece may shed additional light on *stases* in general and on the fourth *stasis* in particular.

A knowledge of the administration of justice in ancient Greece is necessary to the understanding of the fourth *stasis*. The great influence of the Attic orators and speechwriters on later rhetorical practice, and of the Athenian court system upon the judiciaries of the other Hellenistic city-states, makes a knowledge of Athenian justice particularly important.

According to Bonner and Smith, "there was general codification of the laws in Greece in the course of the seventh century."[33] Generally speaking, the Athenian judiciary developed from the Homeric *agora* into the Solonian *heliaea*, a popular appeals court. This latter court developed into the highly organized fourth-century dicasteries. In the fifth and fourth centuries B.C. distinctions between civil and criminal law had not been finely drawn. Moreover, in the courts there was much latitude open to pleaders in bringing suits and in discussing matters of jurisdiction. In no area of Athenian law was the complexity of legal procedure more pronounced than in the homicide laws and in the jurisdictional responsibilities of the various courts. Bonner describes the functions of the various homicide courts:

> In early times the distinction between different kinds of homicide were not drawn. The Areopagus, which was reputed to be the most ancient homicide court in Greece, tried all cases.
> But in Draco's code [621 B.C.] appears the classification of homicide as voluntary, involuntary, and justifiable. . . . In addition to the Areopagus there were four minor homicide courts. The court of the Palladium tried cases of involuntary homicide, while the court of the Delphinium tried cases of justifiable homicide. These courts, in all probability, were instituted to try homicides who took refuge in shrines, claiming justification. It was inconvenient to assemble the entire Areopagus, so a committee, or commission, of fifty-one Areopagites was sent out to try such cases. . . . A court at Phreatto . . . held sessions on the shore. It heard the plea of a man accused of another homicide while in exile for homicide. The accused made his plea from a boat moored off-shore in order that he might not pollute the soil of Attica. The fifth court, the Prytaneum, was a purely ceremonial court for the disposal of animals and objects that had caused the death of human beings.[34]

An understanding of the Greek laws and legal procedures leads to the realization that, for all practical purposes, the *issues* raised in court were often hopelessly intertwined with the judicial *processes* themselves. The interpretation of the central questions in a case of accidental homicide, for example, determined which court had jurisdiction over the matter. Moreover, the assignment of the case to a certain court had vital implications for the defendant. To illustrate, Antiphon's Second Tetralogy concerns the death of a boy accidentally killed by a javelin in a gymnasium. When the dead youth's father brings charges against the thrower of the javelin, the charge is accidental homicide, and the case comes before the court of the Palladium. Central to this case is the Greek notion of accidental homicide, which is a religious view of the death as a pollution. As Jebb points out, "Some person, or thing, must be answerable for that pollution, and must be banished from the State, which would else remain defiled."[35] In the case of the javelin-slaying, three different hypotheses about the cause of the impurity were possible. Perhaps, as the accuser alleges, the defendant is to blame, or the victim himself may have been negligent, and thus have caused his own death. Finally, the javelin could be considered the agent causing the pollution. If the latter interpretation prevailed, the case would have come under the jurisdiction of the Prytaneum, which was charged with the disposal of inanimate objects that had caused human deaths. One sees, therefore, that the issues raised in Greek forensic speeches were sometimes inseparable from legal questions regarding proper judicial form and procedure.

A good example of how the fourth *stasis* was used by the Greek orators appears in Antiphon's speech written for the defendant Helos, *On the Murder of Herodes*. The dispute turns on the case of Helos' companion Herodes, who was missing and presumed murdered during a sea voyage. The relatives of Herodes accuse Helos of the crime, but do not follow the usual procedure in laying the case before the Areopagus as a murder indictment. Instead, they bring him before an ordinary jury court and indict him as a "malefactor," a term usually reserved for thieves, housebreakers, and lesser criminals. The method chosen by the relatives was disadvantageous for the accused for several reasons: (1) trial before the Areopagus afforded the prisoner an option of withdrawing into exile before sentence;[36] (2) witnesses in trials before ordinary jury courts (dicasteries) were not required to take a solemn oath, as in the Areopagus;[37] and (3) if acquitted by the ordinary court, he might still be indicted for murder before the Areopagus.[38]

In the speech Antiphon's client raises several procedural questions that turn on what later rhetoricians were to call the *stasis* of objection, μετάληψις. Early in the speech, he attacks the uncommon legal maneuvers of his prosecutors:

See what they have done: first, they have caused this trial to take place in the very surroundings from which men accused of murder are excluded by public proclamation—*in the market-place*. Second, they have suggested a money-compensation, whereas the law decrees that a murderer shall give life for life. . . . Third, as you all know, all the law-courts judge murder-cases *in the open air*, with the sole object of safeguarding the jury from entering into the same building as the man whose hands are unclean, and of preventing the prosecutor from being under the same roof as the murderer.[39]

During the course of the oration, the defendant insists that the law against malefactors does not apply to him,[40] that the prosecutors are asking the jury to set their own "illegal invention" above the laws themselves,[41] and that he is placed in double jeopardy, since, if he is acquitted on this charge, he is still liable to face the Areopagus on a murder indictment.[42] He turns this last point into an argument for his acquittal. In his epilogue he says, "If you acquit me now, you can do with me as you wish on the future occasion; but if you condemn me, you will lose your power of even deliberating any further on my case."[43]

Antiphon's decision to stasiate his client's case largely on procedural grounds reveals two facts about forensic rhetoric in Athens at that time (419 B.C.). First, questions of legal form, the competence of the prosecutor, court jurisdictions, and so forth, were not simply delaying tactics or efforts to avoid a trial. On the contrary, such issues were substantive matters which involved the nature of the crime, degree of guilt, and the possibilities open to the defense in refutation of the charges themselves. Second, as a consequence, these questions were aspects of the *rational* inventive process of the rhetorician, and were closely bound up with the other *stases* of fact, definition, and quality.

Historians of rhetoric generally assume that at least some logographers examined the law and advised on the conduct of the case, in addition to performing the literary function of composing the speech. Certainly, Isaeus furnished legal advice on the intricacies of the heredity laws.[44] And Kennedy, relying on the authority of Thucydides, says that "Antiphon was the man most able to help anyone who consulted him about a case in the courts or the assembly; he was a complete legal advisor, not just a speech writer."[45] The nature of the Athenian judiciary illustrates why nice distinctions could not be drawn between the functions of the speechwriter as rhetorician and legal counselor.

In the forensic oratory of ancient Greece, therefore, the fourth *stasis* certainly involved substantive questions. Perhaps, as Jebb says, Aeschines was quibbling when he insisted in his oration, *Against Ctesiphon*, that "the proclamation should be made in the ekklesia, and could not lawfully be made in the theatre."[46] But, as we have seen, defendants who resorted to similar arguments in the law courts were not always trifling with technicalities. Often the answers to these fundamental questions constituted the rhetorical stance to be taken in denial of the charge.

III

On the basis of this study of *translatio* in the Latin rhetorics, and of its origins and development in pre-Hermagorean rhetorical theory and oratorical practice, one should be able to speculate with some assurance about the reasons why the fourth *stasis* seemed to Hermagoras and his followers to be coordinate with the other three, while some Roman theorists omitted it, others subordinated it to another *stasis*, and still others relegated it to a category of nonrational legal questions. The foregoing account of Athenian judicial procedure should, first of all, show that the fourth *stasis* was better adapted to Greek than to Roman forensic pleadings. Although Cicero accepts the translative issue in *De Inventione*, he explains that it is seldom used in Rome:

> In legal procedure at Rome there are many reasons why speeches involving transfers rarely are made. For many actions are excluded by the *exceptiones* (counter-pleas) granted by the praetor, and the provisions of our civil law are such that one who does not bring his action in the proper form loses his suit. Therefore such questions generally are disposed of *in iure* (before the praetor). For it is there that exceptions are requested and the right of action is granted, and the complete formula for the guidance of the trial of private (or civil) actions is drawn up. Pleas for transfer rarely come up in the actual trial and if they do they are of such a nature that they have little force in themselves, but are supported by the aid of some other issue. . . .[47]

And the writer to Herennius states that "transference," his subtype of the legal *stasis*, is used by the Greeks in the actual proceedings before the judges, whereas the Romans handle such matters before the magistrate's tribunal.[48] That these questions were usually settled before the beginning of the trial explains why some Roman theorists slighted the fourth *stasis* in their treatment of invention. The pervasive influence of Hermagoras explains why others retained it.

Another reason why the fourth issue was less esteemed in Rome than in Greece may lie in the growth of *declamatio* as a rhetoric of display. Kennedy suggests that, by putting the fourth *stasis* last, Hermagoras had "regarded it as a last resort and a kind of petty legalism."[49] Because it can be a very strong issue in actual practice, Kennedy concludes that Hermagoras "shows that he has rhetorical exercises rather than actual oratory in mind, for in declamation it is not an effective base of argument."[50] If Hermagoras in the second century B.C. already had an eye toward scholastic exercises, Roman writers after the development of the *controversiae* and *suasoriae* could also be expected to tailor their systems to suit imaginary speech occasions. Clearly, with the circumstances and setting of a fictitious courtroom speech already laid down, there was little need to rely upon *translatio* as a *status* or *constitutio*.

Perhaps the key to undertanding the evolution (or devolution) of the fourth *stasis* can be found in this idea: the *stasis* theory derived from, and was originally applied to, *forensic* discourse. Efforts to apply the system to deliberative and epideictic oratory have usually been less than successful. Moreover, when such success has come, it has almost always come at the expense of the fourth *stasis*.

"Ordinary deliberative and epideictic do not exhibit *stasis* in the strict sense, since they do not necessarily imply an opponent,"[51] writes Kennedy. In most deliberative or ceremonial speeches, more than two possibilities are open to the speaker in urging a course of action or in praising a man. It is instructive to remember this when reading Cicero or Quintilian. Lee Hultzén points out that "Cicero and Quintilian wrote in a situation in which forensic pleading was the principal field of the activity of the orator."[52] Both, however, attempted to apply the system to deliberative and epideictic oratory as well. Although Cicero does not illustrate how each issue applies to all three kinds of discourse, he says in Book II of *De Inventione*: "Every speech whether epideictic, deliberative or forensic must turn on one or more of the 'issues' described in the first book."[53] In the *Topica*, where he does not commit himself to a four-part system of *stases*, he explains:

> The same issues (*status*) come up in deliberative and encomiastic speeches. For when some one has given his opinion that certain things will happen, the opponents deny that this is true, basing their argument on the statement that these things cannot be done at all, or only with the greatest difficulty. And in this argument the conjectural issue arises. Or when there is some discussion about advantage, honour, or equity and their opposites, we have the issue of justification and definition. And the same holds true of encomiastic speeches. For one can deny that the deed which is being praised was done at all; or that it is at all praiseworthy, because it was immoral or illegal to do it.[54]

Here there is no mention of how *translatio* is to be applied to these other genres of discourse. In his *Institutes* Quintilian writes: "Some, it is true, have thought that [the issues] were peculiar merely to forensic themes, but their ignorance will stand revealed when I have treated of all three kinds of oratory."[55] Again, however, it is significant that Quintilian accepts only the issues of fact, definition, and quality. He is relieved of the burden of trying to fit the fourth issue into his scheme of analysis. The fourth *stasis* should be a reminder that the *stasis* theory was originally conceived with the rhetoric of the law courts in mind.[56]

Finally, it should be clear that the fourth *stasis* was, to the Romans (and, perhaps, to Hermagoras), a purely procedural matter. Nadeau says that in Hermagoras' day, "it was the typical and specific relational action to which speakers resorted in objections of all kinds not directly concerned with the 'case' itself."[57] Hultzén endorses Quintilian's distinction between the first three *stases* as rational and the fourth as a legal question on the basis that dealing with procedure is different from making judgments about the actual case.[58] As should be clear by now, however, such distinctions between the other three *stases* and the fourth could not be made in the law courts of ancient Greece. Indeed, questions concerning appropriate judicial action, court jurisdiction, and similar matters were integrally related to the facts about the alleged act, to its nature and quality, and to its degree of severity. Furthermore, investigations into the origins and development of the *stasis* theory in Aristotelian physics, and in Peripatetic and Stoic philosophy, give support to the assumption that the theory originated in a quadripartite rather than a tripartite system of classification. The conclusion seems sound, therefore, that the fourth *stasis* was in pre-Hermagorean thought and practice a coordinate member of the system of rational *stases*, but that the differences in the judicial procedures of Greece and Rome, together with the growth of *declamatio*, led many subsequent rhetoricians to omit it from their analyses, to subordinate it to one of the first three *stases*, or to assign it to a category of nonrational legal questions.

1. R. C. Jebb, *The Attic Orators from Antiphon to Isaeos* (New York: Russell and Russell, 1962), II, pp. 444–445.

2. George Kennedy, *The Art of Persuasion in Greece* (Princeton: Princeton University Press, 1963), pp. 307–308.

3. Seven of the ten rhetoricians in Karl Halm's *Rhetores Latini minores* (Leipzig: Teubner, 1863) who deal with *stases* retain the four-fold division, while three omit the fourth as a distinct *stasis* (*status*) or "issue."

4. Cicero, *De Inventione*, trans. H. M. Hubbell (Cambridge: Harvard University Press, 1960), I. viii. 10.

5. [Cicero], *Rhetorica ad C. Herennium*, trans. Harry Caplan (Cambridge: Harvard University Press, 1954), I. xi. 18.

6. *Ibid.*, I. xi. 19. See also Kennedy, *Art of Persuasion*, p. 307.

7. Cicero, *De Inventione*, I. xi. 16.

8. *Ibid.*

9. Quintilian, *Institutio Oratoria*, trans. H. E. Butler (Cambridge: Harvard University Press, 1963), III. vi. 56. But Quintilian had said earlier that Theodorus also recognized four: existence, quality, quantity, and relation (III. vi. 36).

10. *Ibid.*, III. vi. 66 (Butler translates *status* or *constitutio* as *basis*).

11. *Ibid.*, 67–68.

12. *Ibid.*, 70.

13. *Ibid.*, 72.

14. *Ibid.*, 73.

15. *Ibid.*, 75.

16. For a detailed treatment and translation of Hermogenes' treatise dealing with *stases*, see Ray Nadeau, "Hermogenes' *On Stases*: A Translation with an Introduction and Notes," *Speech Monographs*, 31 (November, 1964), 361–424.

17. Otto Alvin Loeb Dieter and William Charles Kurth, "The *De Rhetorica* of Aurelius Augustine," *Speech Monographs*, 35 (March, 1968), 100.

18. *Ibid.*, p. 101.

19. *Ibid.*

20. R. G. Collingwood, *The Idea of History* (Oxford: Clarendon Press, 1946), pp. 21–22.

21. Two of the standard works of German scholarship on *stasis* are Georg Thiele, *Hermagoras: ein Beitrag zur Geschichte der Rhetorik* (Strassburg: K. J. Trübner, 1893), and W. Jaeneke, *De statuum doctrina ab Hermogene tradita* (Leipzig: R. N. Bornen, 1904). For a more recent study, see Dieter Matthes, "Hermagoras von Temnos 1904–1955," *Lustrum*, 3 (1958), 58–214.

22. Otto Alvin Loeb Dieter, "Stasis," *Speech Monographs*, 17 (November, 1950), 369.

23. *Ibid.*, p. 357. See also Aristotle, *Physica*, trans. R. P. Hardie, and also R. K. Gaye, *The Basic Works of Aristotle*, ed. Richard McKeon (New York: Random House, 1941), 200. b. 33.

24. *Ibid.*, 358.

25. *Ibid.*

26. Concerning the relationship between the four rhetorical *stases* and Aristotle's physical categories, Nadeau writes: "Dieter . . . demonstrated that the stases of the . . . physical motions are *analogous* to the four rhetorical stases of Hermagoras and others. That there is anything more than an analogy between the physical and rhetorical stases Dieter does not suggest, and I can find no evidence that Hermagoras (or anybody else) used the physical stases as a basis for constructing a system of rhetorical stases." Ray Nadeau, "Some Aristotelian and Stoic Influences on the Theory of Stases," *Speech Monographs*, 26 (November, 1959), 248.

27. *Ibid.*, pp. 248–254. Quintilian (III. vi. 23ff.) had seen in the concept of *stasis* the influence of Aristotle's categories: substance, quantity, relation, and quality.

28. Aristotle, *Rhetoric*, trans. W. Rhys Roberts, *The Rhetoric and Poetics of Aristotle* (New York: Modern Library, 1954), 1417b 21–26. Although the first three of Aristotle's "disputed points" may be similar to the first three Hermagorean *stases*, there seems to be no connection of the fourth, *justice*, with μεταληψις.

In an article "*Stasis* in Aristotle's *Rhetoric*," *Quarterly Journal of Speech*, 58 (April, 1972), 134–141, Wayne N. Thompson states that "though Hermagoras and his successors may have secured a number of ideas from Aristotle, they were not indebted to the Stagirite for the full form of their systems or for many of the details."

29. Kennedy, *Art of Persuasion*, p. 306.

30. *Ibid.*

31. Nadeau, "Hermogenes' *On Stases*: A Translation with an Introduction and Notes," p. 374.

32. J. Walter Jones, *The Law and Legal Theory of the Greeks* (Oxford: Clarendon Press, 1956), p. 300.

33. Robert J. Bonner and Gertrude Smith, *The Administration of Justice from Homer to Aristotle* (Chicago: University of Chicago Press, 1930), I, 67.

34. Robert J. Bonner, *Aspects of Athenian Democracy* (New York: Russell and Russell, 1967), pp. 29–30.

35. Jebb, *The Attic Orators*, I, 53.

36. *Ibid.*, I, 58.

37. Kathleen Freeman, *The Murder of Herodes and Other Trials from the Athenian Law Courts* (New York: W. W. Norton, 1963), p. 85.

38. *Ibid.*, p. 63.

39. Antiphon, "On the Murder of Herodes," in *ibid.*, p. 65.

40. *Ibid.*

41. *Ibid.*, p. 66.

42. *Ibid.*, p. 82.

43. *Ibid.*, pp. 82–83.

44. Kennedy, *Art of Persuasion*, p. 127.

45. *Ibid.*, p. 130.

46. Jebb, *The Attic Orators*, II, 399.

47. Cicero, *De Inventione*, II. xix. 57–58.

48. [Cicero] , *Rhetorica ad Herennium*, I. xii. 22.

49. Kennedy, *Art of Persuasion*, p. 308. Kennedy's assumption that Hermagoras regarded the fourth *stasis* as less important than the others because he placed it last need not be accepted. If one follows Dieter's line of reasoning, the *stases* represent a progressive narrowing of the area of dispute. Dieter, "Stasis," p. 358. Thus, the fourth one is simply the most restricted, not necessarily the weakest.

50. *Ibid.*

51. Kennedy, *Art of Persuasion*, p. 311.

52. Lee S. Hultzén, "Status in Deliberative Analysis," *The Rhetorical Idiom: Essays in Rhetoric, Oratory, Language, and Drama Presented to Herbert August Wichelns*, ed. Donald C. Bryant (New York: Russell and Russell, 1966), p. 104; see also Donald Lemen Clark, *Rhetoric in Greco-Roman Education* (New York: Columbia University Press, 1959), p. 73.

53. Cicero, *De Inventione*, II. iv. 12.

54. Cicero, *Topica*, trans. H. M. Hubbell (Cambridge: Harvard University Press, 1960), xxv. 93–94.

55. Quintilian, *Institutio Oratoria*, III. vi. 3.

56. Modern writers have had no more success than the ancients in applying the fourth *stasis* to nonforensic oratory. Hultzén, "Status in Deliberative Analysis," uses the other three *stases* as tools in deliberative analysis. In a 1960 article James C. Backes tried to find illustrations of the four *stases* in Aristotle's *Rhetoric*. His illustrations of the fourth *stasis* in forensic rhetoric (*Rhetoric*, 1416a 31; 1373a 7) are clear, but his examples of how it appears in political speaking (*Rhetoric*, 1418b 6; 1418b 10) are confusing. These excerpts from the *Rhetoric* seem to apply to the disposition of arguments rather than to μετάληψις. James C. Backes, "Aristotle's Theory of Stasis in Forensic and Deliberative Speech in the *Rhetoric*," *Central States Speech Journal*, 12 (Autumn, 1960), 6–8.

57. Nadeau, "Some Aristotelian and Stoic Influences on the Theory of Stases," p. 253.

58. Hultzén, "Status in Deliberative Analysis," p. 103.

On Eloquence, Part 1st:
"The Literary Essays"
of Dr. David Skene and
the Scottish Rhetoric of Style

VINCENT M. BEVILACQUA

While it is now clear that students of eighteenth-century British rhetorical theory can accept with assurance that the observations on wit, humor, and ridicule which comprise the discourse *"On Eloquence, Part 1st"* contained in the "Literary Essays, [of] Dr. David Skene" (MS 475, University Library, King's College, Aberdeen) are not, as had previously been thought, the belletristic views of the physician Skene himself, neither must it be assumed that the brief discourse is the work of Dr. John Gregory, who, according to the recorded minutes of the Aberdeen Philosophical Society, responded on May 8, 1764, to the question "What are the distinguishing characteristics of Wit and Humour?" previously proposed by Gregory himself for consideration by the society.[1] For as a line by line collation of the so-called "Skene" discourse *"On Eloquence"* with George Campbell's *The Philosophy of Rhetoric* (1776) demonstrates, the "Skene" essay is in fact a verbatum account (abstract) of Book I, Chapter II, of *The Philosophy of Rhetoric*, "Of Wit, Humour, and Ridicule," an essay written some fourteen years earlier in 1750, delivered before the Philosophical Society in 1758, and subsequently published in essentially unaltered form in 1776.

Thus although the recently discovered "Skene" essay does not, as might have been anticipated, lend additional insight into either the intellectual origins of Campbell's own stylistic view of rhetoric or into the broader philosophical and literary climate of opinion which gave rise to that widely accepted belletristic view, inclusion in the collection of what appears to be a portion of Campbell's earlier Aberdeen discourse on "The Nature of Eloquence, its various species and their Respective ends" (proposed January 24, 1758, and delivered and recorded in the specified "Book of Discourse" on

March 8, 1758) does suggest that the Skene manuscript may indeed be of considerable value to modern students of eighteenth-century rhetorical thought insofar as it includes similar philosophical discourses presented by still other members of the society and recorded in the now lost "Book of Discourses," designated in the minutes of the society as one of three books to be kept as a substantive record of its proceedings and philosophical speculations.[2]

Yet in the case of Campbell on rhetoric in particular, and with respect to the widely pervasive Scottish concern for both the psychological origins and belletristic effects of wit, humor, and ridicule in general, the precise nature of the philosophical observations of the society regarding this distinctive "species of eloquence" must still remain largely unresolved. Hence, the historically perplexing question of the degree to which Campbell's *Philosophy of Rhetoric* was in effect a result of the common thought of his philosophical and academic peers at Aberdeen must likewise remain but tentatively resolved in favor of Campbell's originality. But more important still perhaps than either revealing the precise authorship of the several belletristic discourses delivered before the Society, or even of demonstrating the philosophical distinctiveness of Campbell's own rhetorical views, is the role of the Skene discourse *On Eloquence* as a yet further illustration of the popularly held, mid–eighteenth-century Scottish understanding of rhetoric as *stylistic adornment of discourse*. For the Skene essay provides still broader indication of that typically eighteenth-century view of the belles lettres in which rhetoric was taken to be the "art of eloquence": that is, as a "grand art of communication" distinguished by its concern for grace, elegance, and force of expression.[3]

Accordingly, it is the aim of this paper to suggest in what respect the Scottish rhetorics of Smith, Blair, Campbell, Gerard, and Beattie were in fact rhetorics of style or "eloquence" (in the broad, eighteenth-century meaning of the term), and thereby subsequently to explain Adam Smith's characteristically eighteenth-century conviction that stylistic embellishment and affective adornment of thought are the principal concerns of rhetoric and were historically so received by the best ancient and modern rhetoricians.

I

That George Campbell should in fact inaugurate both his early discourses on rhetoric before the Aberdeen Philosophical Society and his later *Philosophy of Rhetoric* with an examination of wit, humor, and ridicule as exemplary of rhetorical "eloquence in its largest acceptation" (rather than proceeding from an initial consideration of rhetorical "invention" and "disposition" in the traditional manner) reflects the popular Scottish conviction that a stylistic or ornamental function of rhetoric constitutes its distinguishing and proper concern.

Various prevailing, though not necessarily rhetorical, presuppositions common to the eighteenth-century intellectual milieu account in part for this conviction. Not the least of such presuppositions, it appears, was Shaftesbury's widely popular espousal in the *Characteristics* (1711) that the free use of "wit and humour" comprises a legitimate philosophical means by which to determine whether a "particular doctrine" (frequently a religious one) warrants a sober hearing; a measure which Bishop Berkeley later carried from Shaftesbury's tentative mere "test of gravity" to a fully warranted absolute "test of truth."[4] Indeed, as was generally acknowledged by eighteenth-century literators—and as Shaftesbury had prominently observed to his own philosophical purpose from the rhetorical works of Aristotle and Gorgias— " 'humour was the only test of gravity; and gravity of humour. For a subject which would not bear raillery was suspicious; and a jest which would not bear a serious examination was certainly false wit.' "[5]

Yet wit, humor, and ridicule were likewise widely received as legitimate concerns of rhetoric as well, largely by reason of their being both eloquent and ornamental modes of affective verbal expression—"the eloquence of conversation" as Campbell termed it. In this view, wit, humor, and ridicule were taken to be eloquent forms of thought and expression through which discourse could be adapted to the ends of moving the passions, enlightening the understanding, or influencing the will. That they often served the art of conversation, rather than more traditional modes of public address, did not render them unfit for consideration as species of rhetoric, since their ends, like the ultimate end of rhetoric, were to enhance that verbal and conceptual eloquence which affords affective stylistic expression and ultimately leads to persuasion.

Nor was such an ornamental and affective view of the rhetorical effect of wit, humor, and ridicule out of keeping with Thomas Reid's understanding that the proper province of rhetoric is "grace, elegance, and force in thought and in expression"; with James Beattie's belief that rhetoric concerns "words as they may be employed for [the purpose of] *ornament*"; with Robert Watson's view that rhetoric is that "art which delivers rules for the excellence and beauty of discourse"; or with Hugh Blair's conviction that "rhetoric serves to add the polish" to those substantive materials of discourse which are furnished by "knowledge and science."[6] For all such views reflect in common the widely accepted Scottish presupposition—prominently expressed by Adam Smith—that even among the ancients style, embellishment, and "the ornaments of language and expression" were the principal concerns of rhetoric; that traditional rhetorical invention was—in the classical world of Cicero and Quintilian and hence in the neo-classical world of Smith and Blair—"a slight matter" and clearly not an "earnest" concern of either rhetoric or theorists.

Such a stylistic understanding of rhetoric was, of course, not wholly out of keeping with the rhetorical tradition to which the mid—eighteenth-century Scottish rhetoricians were heir. Hence Campbell's inclusion of wit, humor, and ridicule as "rhetorical" modes of eloquent expression ornamental to thought is likewise not unexceptional. Indeed, that Campbell should characterize such traditional rhetorical devices of thought and expression as "eloquent"—and almost without exception employ the term "eloquence" synonymously with "rhetoric"—further suggests that wit, humor, and ridicule (like metaphor, simile, and metonymy) were taken by him to be artistic means of affective expression through which the psychological force of verbal discourse may be heightened beyond its common, merely grammatical or literal effect to a more eloquent ornamental or figurative effect. In short, for Campbell—as for George Jardine, professor of logic and rhetoric at the University of Glasgow from 1774 to 1824—the ultimate end of rhetoric was "eloquence," or grace and efficacy of expression; and all these devices of thought and language which lend such eloquence to verbal expression were taken thereby to be rhetorical.[7]

Little wonder then that despite the widely professed distrust of stylistic ornamentation historically expressed by rhetorical writers from Aristotle to Blair, the ornamental or stylistic capacity of rhetoric was frequently taken to be its distinguishing characteristic and primary concern. And little wonder that Campbell's close friend, James Beattie, believed *The Philosophy of Rhetoric* to be a work on style and criticism rather than one concerning the traditional art of persuasion.[8] Yet in mid—eighteenth-century rhetorical thought, several additional literary and philosophical presuppositions distinctive of the Scottish intellectual milieu account for the prevailing stylistic view of rhetoric and explain in part the distinctly "ornamental" orientation of the rhetorical works of Smith, Kames, Blair, Beattie, Gerard, and Priestley, while further explaining Campbell's inclusion of wit, humor, and ridicule as rhetorical forms of expression.

II

Doubtless such an ornamental view of rhetoric derived in large measure from the prevailing eighteenth-century presupposition that rhetoric is most properly to be considered as the communicative part of logic; that is, as the fourth of the four mental operations of invention, judgment, memory, and communication which then comprised logic. James Beattie, for example, professor of logic and moral philosophy at Marischal College, Aberdeen, from 1760 to 1797, held that "Logic consists of 4 Parts. viz: 1. The Art of Inventing, 2. of Judging, 3. of Retaining, [and] 4. Rhetoric, or the art of communicating."[9]

So, too, Alexander Gerard proposed that "the Fourth part of Logic is RHETORIC, taken in a more extensive sense indeed than it usually is. Its Business is to consider every thing that is related to the nature & use of those Signs by which we communicate our Sentiments to one another."[10] Yet what is more, for Beattie, rhetoric itself properly concerned "the art of conveying our thoughts to others by word and writing"; namely "words as they may be employed for *ornament* as well as for *necessary use*, and . . . those things [devices of style] that constitute Elegance of Language."[11]

Traditionally, of course, Scottish university students were "drilled in logic and rhetoric by analysis of Latin and Greek authors, and by handling simple and compound themes."[12] Yet in keeping with his own particular view, John Stevenson, professor of logic and belles lettres at the University of Edinburgh from 1730 to 1775, had long "endeavoured, by prelections on the most esteemed classics, ancient and modern, to instil into the minds of his pupils, a relish for works of taste, and a love of elegant composition"; most particularly by study of the rhetorical and poetical works of Aristotle and Longinus, and the critical discourses of Dryden, Addison, Bossu, Dacier, and Pope which he appended to his class on logic.[13] Likewise in their own academic lectures at Marischal College both Gerard and his student and successor Beattie devoted a portion of their lectures on moral philosophy to rhetoric, a subject which in their view embraced both universal grammar and composition, especially historical, poetical, philosophical, and rhetorical composition, the latter being taken to include the sermon, the popular essay, and the oration. So, too, Campbell devoted nearly three-quarters of his *Philosophy of Rhetoric* to those historically stylistic "essential" and "discriminating" properties which distinguish eloquence: perspicuity and vivacity, "qualities of Style strictly rhetorical" as he noted.[14]

Indeed, despite their avowed esteem for the rhetoricians of the ancient world—most especially Cicero and Quintilian with whom, as Beattie notes, "every scholar ought to be intimately acquainted"[15] —the rhetoricians of the late eighteenth century did not view rhetoric in a traditional or Ciceronian vein as a broad art of communication made up of five subordinate arts including invention, arrangement, style, memory, and delivery. They took rhetoric, rather, largely to concern language, style, and verbal embellishment; in short to concern *elocutio* or "eloquence," the third canon of rhetoric, and the only one, as Adam Smith noted, about which the ancients were especially "in earnest." Accordingly, even where other traditional offices of rhetoric were considered, as in the works of Smith and Blair, the examination was more to satisfy an historical expectation of the reader and to demonstrate the author's orthodox knowledge of traditional rhetoric than to develop a modern theory of "rhetoric" or eloquence as such; in effect to "serve as an apology" to academic tradition for not treating the subject as the ancients did.[16]

True invention, it was held, was the proper concern of empirical science; memory, the concern of pneumatology (psychology); and disposition, a "methodological" concern of the fourth part of logic, as in the vein of Isaac Watts's *Logick* (1725) and William Duncan's *The Elements of Logick* (1748). Hence among the Scottish rhetoricians, the ancient five-part system of rhetoric, while still providing many established insights into the grand art of persuasion, was examined in its historical form largely as an academic exercise, rather much "to gratify curiosity with respect to an artificial method," as Adam Smith observed regarding his own consideration of traditional logic.[17] Little wonder then, that in retrospect James Wodrow—librarian at Glasgow when Smith assumed the professorship of logic in 1751—characterized Smith's lectures on rhetoric as "a set of admirable lectures on language ([delivered by Smith] not as a grammarian but as a rhetorician) on the different kinds or characteristics of style," thus suggesting a less than distinctly five-part orientation to Smith's rhetorical theory.[18] Indeed, of all the major rhetoricians writing between 1748 and 1783 only Joseph Priestley devoted particular philosophical attention to the matters of rhetorical invention and disposition; and he was as much to illustrate the universality of the Hartleian doctrine of "the association of ideas" as to espouse the heuristic value of the ancient system of rhetorical invention.

So, too, Adam Smith's apparently traditional consideration of the topical system of judicial rhetoric was intended largely to "gratify curiosity" with respect to an artificial method of investigation. For surely he was not especially enthusiastic about such a system of invention, as is suggested by his slighting observation that "the rhetoricians divide all these topics [of judicial rhetoric] into many orders and classes. (These will be found in Quintilian by those who incline to read them. For my part I'll be at no further trouble about them at present.)"[19] Indeed, for Smith "the invention of arguments, or topics, and the composition or arrangement of them" were in rhetoric "very slight matters and of no great difficulty"—a view which he believed to be warranted by the long-standing opinion of both Cicero and Quintilian.[20] Stylistic directions concerning the ornaments of eloquence and expression, he proposed, were in fact the only "earnest" concern of the ancient rhetoricians.

III

Among the Scottish rhetoricians of the eighteenth century such a distinctly stylistic view of rhetoric was in turn likewise prompted by Bacon's widely accepted "Division of Logic into the Arts of Discovering, of Judging, of Retaining, and of Transmitting"; and his subsequent division of the "Art of Transmission" into the "Organ of Discourse" (philosophical grammar), the "Method of Discourse" (arrangement), and the

"Illustration of Discourse" (verbal "Adornment"), "that which is called Rhetoric." That the Scottish rhetoricians of the eighteenth century were enthusiastic Baconians is without question. Stevenson, we know, long taught the logic of Locke and Bacon in place of that of Aristotle and Ramus.[21] And in 1752 "by Order of the faculty" Alexander Gerard reorganized the philosophy curriculum at Marischal College in keeping with the substantive changes in moral philosophy necessitated by the adoption of Baconian inductive logic in place of the scholastic logic previously taught.[22]

But more important still, in such a distinctly Baconian milieu true invention was taken to be the proper concern of empirical science. Thus although a parallel mode of rhetorical "invention"—received as recollection of previously gathered subject matter—was proposed by Bacon himself, there was nonetheless a widely accepted distinction in mid–eighteenth-century philosophical thought between the scientific "*discovery of* Arts" by inductive examination and the rhetorical "*discovery of* Arguments" by topical recollection, very much as there was a parallel distinction between the largely investigative capacity of Baconian logic (the "Art of Inquiry or Invention") and the largely expressive capacity of Baconian rhetoric (the "Doctrine of Ornament in Speech"). In short, despite the respectability afforded rhetorical "invention" by Bacon himself having regarded it as a figurative mode of "discovery," true invention and discovery in the most literal sense was for the eighteenth century empirical and scientific, not rhetorical and recollective. Hence, even with respect to the "discovery" of "what to say" in a speech or an essay, empirical knowledge and direct examination of the subject itself (not a topical scheme of recollective invention) constituted the true source of the subject matter of verbal discourse; a view suggested by Blair's own endorsement of "knowledge and science" as the "body and substance of any valuable composition," and by Smith's rhetorical demand for direct rather than conjectural proofs.

Yet what is more, in such a Baconian frame of reference, while true invention was the extra-rhetorical concern of direct "scientific" inquiry, the "Art of Transmitting"—Bacon's theory of rhetoric as such—concerned largely the means of "producing and *expressing* to others those things which have been [previously] invented, judged, and laid up in the memory" and thus but await recollection or "rhetorical" invention and transmission.[23] Note, for example, that in this belief Gerard, like Beattie, divides the resulting forms of literary composition (the philosophical, historical, poetical, and rhetorical) after Bacon's own partition of knowledge into philosophy, history, and poetry, while further in the manner of Bacon distinguishing each of the species of rhetorical composition according to its particular appeal to the intellectual faculties of reason, memory, or imagination.[24]

Thus, although like his Scottish contemporaries Gerard understood rhetoric historically to include four of the five Ciceronian offices of rhetoric ("the Rules of Rhetoric explain . . . the means by which persuasion may be obtained & that whether they relate to the Subject, to the Disposition, or the Expression including Elocution, Pronunciation & Action"),[25] in his own conception of rhetoric and treatment of "eloquence" he proposes an essentially Baconian or stylistic view of the affective art of discourse. Note, for instance, Gerard's distinctly Baconian conviction that "Eloquence addresses itself immediately to the Passions & to the *Will*"; and note as well his further belief that invention is of two kinds, "the Invention of Arguments & that of Sciences: the former is not so properly Invention, as the recollecting [of] what was formerly known."[26]

In short, while Gerard's language often echoes the classical rhetorical tradition of the ancients, the theory of rhetoric resulting from his philosophical frame of reference was one in which the true "invention" or literal "discovery" of subject matter was regarded as extra-rhetorical, while the corresponding *art* of rhetoric (those rhetorical concerns truly distinctive of the theory of discourse) was taken to be the transmission and stylistic embellishment of previously discovered subject matter, a view which in effect ruled out all "topical" methods of "rhetorical" invention, including Bacon's own recollective scheme.

It is not without reason then that, in an intellectual climate of opinion in which the actual discovery of knowledge was taken philosophically to be the proper concern of empirical observation, the Baconian "Art of Transmitting" and its attendant regard for "Adornment of Discourse" was popularly taken to be the companion theory of rhetoric most suited to the new philosophical ideal of the Scottish Enlightenment—the Baconian "mode of discovery by Induction and Experiment," as Alexander Fraser Tytler characterized it.[27] Nor is it surprising that Scottish rhetoricians of the mid-eighteenth century should attend primarily to the transmission and affective expression of previously discovered subject matter according to established principles of style and human nature rather than to traditional systems of rhetorical invention.

Affective transmission was in fact the only view of rhetoric philosophically suited to the new Baconian mode of investigation, since the inventional systems of traditional rhetoric were widely regarded as inconsonant with the new experimental ideal (direct "knowledge of the nature of a Subject . . . is a much surer Guide for the mind to acquire proper Arguments than any Artificial Topics can be")[28] and the artificial figures and tropes of Renaissance and Ramian rhetoric were rejected as sources of false ornament. Thus while Bacon's view of transmission as "lively representation . . . by ornament of words" did not comprise the whole of the Scottish understanding of his rhetoric, the view did suggest that affective imagery and stylistic ornamentation were distinguishing concerns of Baconian rhetoric, or—as Peter Shaw translated Bacon's notion of rhetorical transmission—the "Doctrine of Ornament in Speech."[29] Indeed, although the Scottish rhetoricians of the eighteenth century may, like Shaw, have taken a broader and more orthodox view of rhetorical "ornament" than Bacon himself intended, it was in just such a largely stylistic fashion that Bacon's "Illustration of Discourse" was received by Campbell and his contemporaries.

IV

Yet in addition to the influence of Baconian premises, the path for an eighteenth-century stylistic view of rhetoric was also laid by Peter Ramus. For in effect the prevailing attenuation of the inventive capacity of rhetoric, as well as the parallel aggrandizement of the ornamental function of the art of transmission, was but a modern reiteration and further application of Ramus's long-established distinction between the properly investigatory function of scholastic logic and the largely ornamental capacity of Renaissance rhetoric. Doubtless the Ramian distinction was widely received in eighteenth-century Scotland. Thomas Ruddiman, for example, notes that even as late as Blair's day the "regular course" at the High School of Edinburgh required in the fifth year study of the "whole Rhetoric of Tulaeus [Talaeus]"; and so, too, at the University of Edinburgh students were instructed in the traditional "tropes and figoures" of rhetoric through study of the *Rhetorica* of Taleus, having previously mastered the *Dialectica* of Ramus.[30] This, of course, is not to say that the Scottish rhetoricians of the eighteenth century derived their stylistic notion of rhetoric either directly or entirely from a conscious acceptance of the Ramian stylistic tradition. It is, rather, only to suggest the lingering influence in the eighteenth century of a long-established rhetorical tradition in Scottish academic thought, which, together with Baconian influences and a stylistic interpretation of Cicero and Quintilian, could well have led the Scottish Augustans to the presupposition that historically the distinctive concern of rhetoric had in fact been that of style and embellishment.

In much the same manner the Scottish view of rhetoric as a verbal manifestation of the "various mental operations as they are expressed by the several modifications of speech and writing" as well as the companion view that rhetoric comprises "the best method of explaining and illustrating the various powers of the human mind"[31] also contributed in part to the establishment in the eighteenth century of a broad rhetoric of style. That is, since (according to Beattie) "Style may be defined, [as] That particular way in which a man chooses, or is accustomed to express his thoughts, by speech or writing,"[32] and further since a belletristic analysis of human nature was a distinguishing characteristic of eighteenth-century investigation in the vein of the Philosophical Society of Aberdeen, style or eloquence of expression was taken to be the one office of traditional rhetoric of greatest artistic and psychological latitude, and thereby as a key to the most subtle operations of the sensitive branch of human nature as those operations are reflected in human expression.

Such a method of psychological analysis by stylistic analysis was in fact the rhetorical mode of inquiry into human nature espoused by Smith and pursued after him by Blair. For Smith assumed that while recent discoveries in human nature explain various established precepts of rhetoric, so too the very principles of rhetoric—especially as they regard style or manner of expression—provide reciprocal insight into human nature as well. Indeed, Smith saw in the metaphor "lust of fame," for example, an imagined but natural transposition of the literal meaning of "lust" from a corporeal passion to a resembling, yet figurative, mental passion equally gross and indelicate; a figurative transposition which in his view revealed the psychological effect on human expression of man's native sense of resemblance, while demonstrating in turn the ultimate origin of rhetorical eloquence in human nature. Likewise, Smith observes that "when we say *the slings and arrows of adverse fortune*" there is suggested a natural resemblance "betwixt the crosses of bad fortune and the slings and arrows of an enemy" which reveals a natural inclination of the mind to perceive analogical relationships among things not generally connected; for Smith a native perceptive capacity of the mind which explains both the origin and efficacy of metaphor, simile, allegory, and like rhetorical expression.[33]

It was in fact in just such a belief that Campbell as well proposed that the "lights [insights into human nature] which the Poet and the Orator so amply furnish" would in turn add "both weight and evidence to all precedent [rhetorical] discoveries and rules."[34] So, too, it was by means of an essentially rhetorical view of human nature that Smith accounted for Addison's frequent but appropriate use of figurative language in terms of the "flowery modesty" of Addison's style and character. And in the psychological-rhetorical vein of Smith and Blair, Robert Burrowes presented an essay to the Royal Irish Academy in 1793 "*On* STYLE *in* WRITING, *considered with respect to Thoughts and Sentiments as well as Words, and indicating the Writer's peculiar and characteristic Disposition, Habits and Powers of Mind.*"[35]

But more important still, Campbell—like Smith, Kames, Blair, Gerard, Beattie, and Burrowes—recognized that the psychological insights into human nature provided by *stylistic* analysis of rhetorical expression (verbal "experiments of the mind") comprised the most intelligible and valuable "scientific" knowledge of human nature yet available to man. It was therefore owing in part to a prevailing belief in the psychological value of the study of rhetoric that there arose among Scottish rhetoricians of the period a corresponding conviction that historical matters of style constitute the one office of traditional rhetoric which reveals with greatest efficacy such subtle "operations of the imagination" as "increase our acquaintance with some of the most refined feelings which belong to our frame."[36]

Indeed, it was owing to just such a belief in the psychological value of the study of rhetorical style that Campbell began his *Philosophy of Rhetoric* with an examination of the affective manner in which wit, humor, and ridicule enhance rhetorical expression and thereby provide insight into human nature; and it was further the reason that Blair pursued Smith's vein of psychological (character) analysis in his own examination of the style of Joseph Addison. [37] It was, in short, by examining philosophically (empirically, introspectively) those accepted principles of style and human nature commonly held both to ensure eloquence of expression and to provide insight into the affective nature of man that the Scottish rhetoricians of the eighteenth century further encouraged that almost exclusively stylistic concern for rhetoric broadly characteristic of the period. Of the major rhetoricians of the day only Joseph Priestley devoted considerable philosophical analysis to the psychological bases of rhetorical invention and arrangement; although he, too, devotes nearly two-thirds of the *Lectures on Oratory and Criticism* (1777) to the psychological origins of rhetorical style in the association of ideas and the reciprocal illustration of that Hartleian doctrine in rhetorical eloquence.

V

So, too, the pervasive eighteenth-century concern for style as the distinguishing characteristic of the art of rhetoric arose from the prevailing conviction— implicit in both Smith and Blair—that style is in fact the common well-spring of the several belles lettres; that poetry, eloquence, history, and philosophical writing are not disparate forms of verbal discourse but related modes of expression commonly rooted in style. Note, for example, that in the belief that ornamental expression properly extends to "all species of writing in the sciences and in literature," Jean Henri Formey observed in his *Elementary Principles of the Belles Lettres* (1766) that "the *Belles-Lettres* may comprize human knowledge without exception, so far as the several branches of this knowledge are susceptible of being presented in an agreeable manner [style], and embellished with such ornaments, as respectively suit them."[38] And for Smith, as well, style of expression—taken to be a verbal manifestation of both the thought and character of its author—is the standard of judgment underlying his criticism of narrative, didactic, and rhetorical discourse, as well as forensic, epideictic, and deliberative public address. Little wonder then that

Robert Watson, Smith's successor at Edinburgh in 1752, should view rhetoric stylistically as that "art which delivers rules for the excellence and beauty of discourse."[39] And little wonder that it was an essentially stylistic view of rhetoric and the belles lettres which commonly engaged literators like Kames, Smith, Campbell, and Blair, and which further underlies their stylistic understanding of the traditional art of discourse.

Yet it was from the rhetorical works of the most eloquent ancients themselves—Cicero, Quintilian, Demetrius, Dionysius, and Longinus—that eighteenth-century literators like Adam Smith derived their belletristic "interpretation" of style as the primary concern of the ancient rhetoricians. Smith, as we know, held the literary works of Aristotle, Apthonius, Cicero (three editions of the *Opera*), Demetrius, Demosthenes, Dionysius, Hermogenes, Isaeus, Isocrates, Longinus, Lysias, and Quintilian (two editions) in his own personal library, and spent nearly all of his undergraduate years at Balliol College, Oxford (1740–46), in the systematic and thorough study of ancient language and literature.[40] It was indeed owing to Smith's close acquaintance with the literary works of the ancient—broadly reflected in his lectures on belles lettres—that Lord Kames encouraged Smith to deliver a course of lectures on "rhetoric" at the Philosophical Society of Edinburgh, to the considerable edification of such Scottish literators as Blair, Alexander Wedderburn (founder of the first *Edinburgh Review*), and Kames himself. Thus, while to present-day readers the rhetorical works of Cicero and Quintilian may suggest a "traditional" (five-part) rhetoric rather than a belletristic one, given the prevailing stylistic milieu suggested in this paper it is not entirely without explanation that Smith should believe that "Cicero, Quintilian, and all the best authors who treat of Rhetorical Composition, treat of the invention of arguments, or topics, and the composition or arrangement of them, as *very slight matters* and of no great difficulty, and never seem to be in earnest unless when they give us directions concerning the ornaments of language and expression."[41]

Nor was Smith's distinctly stylistic interpretation of the rhetorical concern of the ancient authors without evidence from the very ancients themselves. For although Smith would find in Cicero's youthful *de Inventione* the conclusion that invention "is the most important of all the divisions" of rhetoric, Smith would likewise find in the widely popular *Orator* the more mature conclusions that rhetorical invention and disposition "are not specially marked out for the highest praise, but are rather fundamental [necessary], and apart from that are shared in common with many other pursuits [are not distinctive of rhetoric alone]"; that rhetorical invention and arrangement (though "weighty") "require less art and labour" than the "all-important question of the manner [style] of presentation"; and that the "whole essence" of rhetoric is the embellishment of ideas.[42]

So, too, Smith could note in *de Orator* that "a style that is dignified and graceful" is the "essential concern of the orator" and that it is indeed with regard to matters of style and eloquence (not content or arrangement) that "science and philosophy must come to oratory."[43] Such a view of the stylistic importance of rhetoric to related studies was of course also held by Girolamo Fracastoro, an Italian humanist of the sixteenth century, and derived by him from the ancients. For, as Fracastoro himself proposed, it was in fact from the Ciceronian, rhetorical "master of eloquence" and from his "certain general art of eloquence" that "the other sciences and arts receive the particular kind of eloquence which they need."[44] And in Quintilian as well Smith would find the conclusion that "as all orators agree" it is the cultivation of an eloquent style which constitutes both the "chief object" and the "greatest difficulty" in the study of rhetoric, as well as the further conviction of Quintilian that the cultivation of such eloquence of expression was the chief rhetorical concern of Cicero: that for Cicero "while invention and arrangement are within the reach of any man of good sense, eloquence belongs to the orator alone, and consequently it was on the rules for the cultivation of eloquence that he expended the greatest care."[45]

Little wonder then—especially in light of Quintilian's own view of Cicero's primary rhetorical concern—that Smith should believe himself to be in the historical tradition of Cicero and Quintilian in his regard for style above all of the other offices of rhetoric, or that he should believe such a capital esteem for style to be the primary concern of the ancients as well as the primary concern of rhetoric itself. And hence it is not without reason that Smith should likewise conclude from Cicero and Quintilian that among modern rhetoricians the invention and disposition of "what to say" was in fact a "very slight matter" and that it was with "how best to say it" that the best ancient and modern rhetoricians were most earnestly concerned.

VI

Doubtless, of course, Scottish rhetoricians of the mid-eighteenth century were aware historically of the traditional five-part rhetoric proposed by the ancients and reiterated in their own day in such "classical" works as John Ward's *System of Oratory* (1759). Yet as has been suggested, various philosophical presuppositions common to the mid–eighteenth-century intellectual milieu resulted in an emphasis on style or rhetorical eloquence as the primary and most distinctive characteristic of the modern art of discourse. That such an emphasis is central to the major rhetorical works of the period is evident. And that such a concern for style should distinguish the rhetorical theory of the day is neither without explanation, nor, as has been suggested, without precedent. Accordingly, it is not especially remarkable that Smith should read

Cicero and Quintilian as rhetorical stylists; that Campbell should consider wit, ridicule, and humor as legitimate "rhetorical" concerns of the affective art of eloquence; or that Alexander Skene's manuscript abstract of Campbell's rhetorical views of wit, humor, and ridicule should long have been taken as Skene's very own. For it was an almost universal conviction among the rhetoricians of the mid–eighteenth century—one prompted by the ancients and corroborated by Ramus, Bacon, and the distinctly psychological view of the belle lettres characteristic of Scottish literary thought—that the distinguishing concern of rhetoric was in fact style, embellishment, and elegance of expression: in short rhetorical "eloquence" in its largest and historical acceptation.

1. "Original Minutes of the Philosophical Society of Aberdeen, 1758–1771," Aberdeen University Library MS. 539, Question 70.

David Skene was a founding member of the society as well as an esteemed Aberdeen physician.

According to the minutes of the society, members in attendance on the night of Gregory's Discourse on Wit included: "Dr. Gregory, President, Dr. Gerard, Dr. Campbell, Mr. Farquhar, Dr. George Skene, Mr. Gordon." "Original Minutes of the Philosophical Society of Aberdeen," May 8, 1764.

Rule 15 of the society specifies that "the President may propose some Question which he thinks proper for the Consideration of the Society, and if one third of the meeting consent it shall be entered into a Book in order to be discussed at some future Meeting." Rule 17 adds that: "The subject of the discourses and questions shall be philosophical. . . . And philosophical matters are understood to comprehend: every principle of science which may be deduced by just and lawful induction from the phenomena either of the human mind or of the material world; all observations and experiments that may furnish materials for such induction; the examination of false schemes of philosophy and false methods of philosophizing; the subserviency of philosophy to arts, the principles they borrow from it, and the means of carrying them to their perfection." "Original Minutes of the Philosophical Society of Aberdeen," Rules.

2. The nature and content of the Skene papers held in the Aberdeen University Library has been most fully reported by Professor Bernhard Fabian of the Englisches Seminar, Munster University ("David Skene and the Aberdeen Philosophical Society," *The Biblioteck*, 5 [1968], 81–99), to whom I am in considerable debt.

Compare the following on the nature of wit from Campbell with a parallel passage from the recently reported Skene essays: "To consider the matter more nearly, it is the design of wit to excite in the mind an agreeable surprise, and that arising, not from any thing marvellous in the subject, but solely from the imagery she employs, or the strange assemblage of related ideas presented to the mind" (*The Philosophy of Rhetoric*, ed. Lloyd F. Bitzer [Carbondale: Southern Illinois University Press, 1963], p. 8); "But to consider the Matter more nearly—Tis the design of Wit to excite in the Mind an agreeable Surprise, & that arising not from any thing marvellous in the Subjects, but solely in the Imagery she employs or the strange assemblage of similate Ideas presented to the Mind" ("*On Eloquence, Part 1st*," Aberdeen University Library MS. 475, p. 25).

Rule 16 of the society stipulates that "the Society shall have three Books, one to Record the Discourses, wherein every Discourse shall be recorded unless for special

Reasons the Author desire the Contrary and every Member shall record or Cause recorded his own Discourses. Another Book shall be kept for the Questions and a third for the Rules and Minutes of the Society and the Annual Accounts of the Society's Money." "Original Minutes of the Philosophical Society of Aberdeen," Rules. According to present knowledge, only the "third" book designated for rules and minutes is now extant.

Present on the night of Campbell's discourse *On Eloquence* were "Dr. Skene, President and all the Members except Mr. Trail." "Original Minutes of the Philosophical Society of Aberdeen," March 8, 1758.

3. Campbell, *Philosophy of Rhetoric*, p. xlix.

4. Regarding Shaftesbury on "raillery" as a "test" of gravity and a means of free expression, see Alfred O. Lovejoy, "Shaftesbury and the Test of Truth," *PMLA*, 60 (March, 1945), 129–156. Among the Scots, Kames, for example, held the truly grave to be immune from ridicule, thereby espousing an essentially Shaftesburian position in the controversy. Campbell cautiously maintains that ridicule is "fitter for refuting error than for supporting truth," and is properly leveled at the "absurd" (that which is contrary to common sense) rather than at the false. Campbell, *Philosophy of Rhetoric*, pp. 20–21, and "*On Eloquence*, Part 1st," p. 32.

5. Anthony Ashley Cooper, Lord Shaftesbury, "*Sensus Communis*: An Essay on the Freedom of Wit and Humour," (1709), in *Characteristics of Men, Manners, Opinions, Times* (London: John Darby, 1711), Treatise II, Sec. V.

As John Brown has suggested in his *Essays on the Characteristics* (London: C. Davis, 1752; 3rd ed. i. 9.), Shaftesbury extended to his own purpose the clearly more restricted passage he cites from the *Rhetoric* of Aristotle in which Gorgias is noted as proposing that "we must ruin our opponent's earnestness with our jocularity, and his jocularity with our earnestness" (*The Rhetoric of Aristotle*, trans. Lane Cooper [New York: Appleton-Century-Crofts, 1932], 1419b).

6. Thomas Reid, "Of the Improvement of Logic," in Henry Home, Lord Kames, *Sketches of the History of Man* (Edinburgh: W. Creech, 1778; 1st ed., 1774), III, 418; James Beattie, *Elements of Moral Science* (Philadelphia, Pa.: Mathew Carey, 1792–94; 1st Brit. ed., 1790–93), II, 226; Robert Watson, "Introduction to Logic & Rhetoric (1778)," St. Andrews University Library MS. Bc 6. W2, Pt.II, p. 1; Hugh Blair, *Lectures on Rhetoric and Belles Lettres* (London: Charles Daly, 1838; 1st ed., 1783), p. 3.

7. George Jardine, *Outlines of Philosophical Education, Illustrated by the Method of Teaching the Logic Class in the University of Glasgow* (Glasgow: Glasgow University Press, 1825), p. 239.

8. Beattie observes in a letter to Sir William Forbes, September 10, 1776, that on "certain topics of criticism" Campbell's *Rhetoric* is the "most ingenious performance" he has seen. William Forbes, *An Account of the Life and Writings of James Beattie, LL.D.* (London: E. Roper, 1824), I, 404.

9. James Beattie, "Observations on Logic: by Several Professors," Edinburgh University Library MS. Dk. 3. 2, p. 201.

10. "Lectures of Alexander Gerard. Written by Robert Morgan at Marischal College, Aberdeen, 1758–59," Edinburgh University Library MS. Dc. 5. 61, p. 625.

11. Beattie, *Elements of Moral Science*, II, 225, 226. Likewise, George Jardine took rhetoric to be one of the four "intellectual habits: of thinking, judging, reasoning, and communicating natural to man." Jardine, *Outline of Philosophical Education*, p. V. As the concern of "rhetoric" Beattie considers "tropes and figures," the composition of sentences, style, prose style (including historical, philosophical, and rhetorical composition), and poetry. Beattie, *Elements of Moral Science*, II, 226, *passim*.

12. James Coutts, *A History of the University of Glasgow* (Glasgow: James Maclehose, 1909), p. 109.

13. [Andrew Dalzel], "Account of the late Duke Gordon, M.A., including Anecdotes of the University of Edinburgh," *Scots Magazine*, 64 (January, 1802), 21–22. See also *Scots Magazine*, 65 (February, 1803), 76. Hugh Blair, of course, was a student in Stevenson's logic class in 1733 to 1734, and was highly regarded by Stevenson for an essay "On the Beautiful" which he composed as a class exercise and read publicly at Stevenson's request. John Hill, *An Account of the Life and Writings of Hugh Blair* (Philadelphia, Pa.: Humphreys, 1808), pp. 16–17.

14. Campbell, *Philosophy of Rhetoric*, p. 214.

15. James Beattie, "A Compendious System of Pneumatology Comprehending, Psychology, Moral Philosophy, & Logic. Taken at the Lectures of Mr. Js. Beattie P.P. at the Marischal College & University of Abdn. By J. Rennie. Anno. 1767," Glasgow University Library MS., p. 544. Beattie observes that in the "eighth and ninth books of Quintilian" may be found an account of all the traditional figures and tropes of rhetoric and hence he does not intend to elaborate on them. Beattie, *Elements of Moral Science*, II, 243.

16. Beattie, *Elements of Moral Science*, II, 320. Beattie refers here to his lectures on logic but holds the same view regarding the historical art of rhetoric.

17. Adam Smith, *Essays on Philosophical Subjects*, eds. Joseph Black and James Hutton (London: T. Cadell, Jr., and W. Davies, 1795), p. XVI.

18. William Robert Scott, *Adam Smith as Student and Professor* (Glasgow: Jackson, Son, 1937), pp. 51–52.

19. Adam Smith, *Lectures on Rhetoric and Belles Lettres*, ed. John M. Lothian (London: Thomas Nelson and Sons, 1963), p. 167. So, too, Smith considers the historical systems of figurative rhetoric a "very silly set of books and not at all instructive." *Ibid.*, p. 23.

20. *Ibid.*, p. 142.

21. *Scots Magazine*, LXV, 76.

22. Alexander Gerard, *Plan of Education in the Marischal College and University of Aberdeen, with the Reasons of It* (Aberdeen: James Chalmers, 1755), pp. 3–9. See also "The order of teaching in the Marischal College, &c.," *Scots Magazine*, 14 (December, 1752), 606.

23. Francis Bacon, *De augmentis scientiarum*, in *The Works of Francis Bacon*, eds. James Spedding, Robert Leslie Ellis, and Douglas Denon Heath (Boston: Brown and Taggard, 1860–64), IX, 60, 108. My italics.

24. "Lectures of Alexander Gerard . . . By Robert Morgan," MS. Dc. 5. 62, p. 1. Likewise Beattie divides rhetoric into philosophical, historical, rhetorical, and poetical composition and founds such composition on corresponding mental faculties. "Lectures of Prof. Alexander Gerard [sic], Marischal College, Aberdeen, 1753–60," Edinburgh University Library MS. Dc. 5. 117, pp. 377–383, 387. The lectures are in fact those of James Beattie.

25. "Lectures of Alexander Gerard . . . By Robert Morgan," MS. Dc. 5. 61, p. 631.

26. *Ibid.*, pp. 631–670.

27. Alexander Fraser Tytler, *Memoirs of the Life and Writings of the Honourable Henry Home of Kames* (Edinburgh: T. Cadwell and W. Davies, 1807), II, 126.

28. "Lectures of Alexander Gerard . . . By Robert Morgan," MS. Dc. 5. 61, p. 572.

29. Peter Shaw, *The Philosophical Works of Francis Bacon* (London: J. J. and P. Knapton, 1737), I, 150. Although Shaw's "sense translation" may take liberty with Bacon's philosophical meaning, it does provide contemporary insight into the way in which Bacon's "Illustration of Discourse" was understood in the eighteenth century.

30. George Chalmers, *The Life of Thomas Ruddiman* (London: John Stockdale, 1794), pp. 88–90; *University of Edinburgh Charters, Statutes, and Acts of the Town Council and the Senatus 1583–1858* (Edinburgh: Oliver and Boyd, 1937), pp. 111–112. The first English translation of Ramus' *Dialecticae Libri Duo*, for example, was published in 1574 by Roland McIlmaine of St. Andrews University. Another Scottish academician, Andrew Melville, principal of the University of Glasgow, knew Ramus personally and inaugurated a Ramian reform of academic studies at Glasgow in the sixteenth century. Melville used as textbooks in logic and rhetoric Ramus' *Dialectic* and Talon's *Rhetoric*. Among Beattie's contemporaries, Thomas Reid and William Barron both acknowledged Ramus as a reformer of Aristotelian and scholastic philosophy. See William Barron, *Lectures on Belles Lettres and Logic* (London: Longman, Hurst, Rees, and Orme, 1806), II, 517; and *The Works of Thomas Reid*, ed. Sir William Hamilton (Edinburgh: Maclachlan and Stewart, 1872), II, 689.

31. Reid, *Works*, II, 735. Speaking of George Jardine's approach to rhetoric after the manner of Stevenson and Smith; Dugald Stewart, "An Account of the Life and Writings of the Author," in Smith, *Essays on Philosophical Subjects*, p. XVI. Quoting Smith's former student Millar. In turn, such a rhetorical method of explanation and illustration "arises from an examination of the several ways of communicating our thoughts by speech, and from an attention to those literary compositions which contribute to persuasion or entertainment." *Ibid*.

32. Beattie, *Elements of Moral Science*, II, 253.

33. Smith, *Lectures on Rhetoric*, pp. 26, 25.

34. Campbell, *Philosophy of Rhetoric*, pp. xliii, li.

35. Robert Burrowes, "Polite Literature," *Transactions of the Royal Irish Academy*, 5 (1794).

36. Blair, *Lectures on Rhetoric and Belles Lettres*, p. 7.

37. Blair acknowledges that "on this head, of the General Characters of Style, particularly the plain and the simple, and the characters of those English authors who are classed under them, in this and the following lecture, several ideas have been taken from a manuscript Treatise on Rhetoric, part of which was shown to me, many years ago, by the learned and ingenious author, Dr. Adam Smith; and which, it is hoped, will be given by him to the public." *Ibid.*, p. 238.

38. Joseph Priestley, *Lectures on Oratory and Criticism*, trans. Sloper Foreman (London: F. Newbery, 1777), pp. 130–131, 1.

39. Robert Watson, "Introduction to Logic & Rhetoric," St. Andrews University Library Ms. Be 6. W2, Pt. II, p. 1.

40. Hiroshi Mizuta, *Adam Smith's Library: A Supplement to Bonar's Catalogue with a Check-List of the Whole Library* (Cambridge: Cambridge University Press, 1967).

41. Smith, *Lectures on Rhetoric*, p. 142. My italics.

42. Cicero, *De Inventione*, trans. H. M. Hubbell (London: William Heinemann, 1960), I. viii. 10; Cicero, *Orator*, trans. H. M. Hubbell (London: William Heinemann, 1962), xiv. 43–45, xvi. 51, xxxix. 136.

43. Cicero, *De Oratore*, trans. E. W. Sutton and H. Rackham (London: William Heinemann, 1959), xii. 54.

44. "Girolamo Fracastoro *Naugerius Sive De Poetica Dialogus*," trans. Ruth Kelso in *University of Illinois Studies in Language and Literature*, IX (August, 1924), 60–63.

45. Quintilian, *Institutio Oratoria*, trans. H. E. Butler (London: William Heinemann, 1966), viii. 13–17.

Development of the Concept of Analogy in Rhetorical Theory

JAMES S. MEASELL

The term "analogy" is used frequently in both scholarly works and daily discourse. The manifold meanings found in common usage contribute to confusion when they are used in scholarly works. Often, the problem is compounded because scholars employ the term without a clear definition and focus. Modern rhetoricians, for example, label as "analogy" figures of speech likened to simile and metaphor. They also identify analogy as a form of argument, usually inherently weak, which is founded upon resemblance or comparison.[1] In other disciplines, different significations of the term are found. The linguist sees analogy as a principle of consistency which dictates grammatical form.[2] The chemist and the biologist, respectively, use the term "analogous" to refer to compounds which exhibit structural identity and to refer to organs which exhibit functional similarity.[3] The modern social scientist regards "analogy" as a tentative relationship, which, when viewed in the context of a model, may be manipulated to generate hypotheses which are subjected to testing before reinsertion into the model.[4]

The purpose of this essay is to pinpoint the origins of, and subsequent developments in, the major meanings of the term "analogy," with particular attention to those contributions which are of interest to the rhetorician. Such an inquiry should make clear both the various meanings of the term and the assumptions underlying them. The modern rhetorician may then better understand the place of analogy in rhetorical theory. Further, the modern rhetorician may formulate hypotheses about the process of proof itself.

Etymologically, the word "analogy" is derived from the Greek $αναλογια$. This term denoted geometric proportion in mathematics, which was expressed by the formula a:b::c:d. This meaning, which first appeared in the now-lost treatises of Thales and Pythagoras, is known to us from the extant mathematical works of Euclid, Nicomachus, Iamblichus, and Proclus.[5] The four-part form for an $αναλογια$ in mathematics, denoting a strict *equivalence* of ratios, was appropriated by writers such as Plato and Aristotle, who utilized the same four-part form to posit *resemblances* of ratios.

Plato used αναλογια both to explain his cosmological theories and as an epistemological tool. In the *Timaeus*, Plato suggested that the Empedoclean elements—earth, air, fire, and water—were brought into harmony by God. This God "bestowed upon them as far as possible a like ratio one toward another—air being to water as fire to air [air:water::fire:air], and water being to earth as air to water [water:earth::air:water] ."[6] Plato's assumption that proportional structures are basic to reality influenced later writers who comprise that school of thought today known as Neoplatonism—Philo, Plotinus, and Proclus.[7] Plato also used αναλογια as an epistemological tool. In Book VI of the *Republic*, he argued that "the sun," a phenomenon in the visible world, was analogous to "the good," an entity of the intelligible world [sun:visible world::good:intelligible world].[8] The relations between the visible and the intelligible worlds were detailed further in the famous "Simile of the Divided Line." This is, in fact, a graphic representation of the analogical relations between the visible and the intelligible spheres. Behind these relations is an epistemological premise, namely, that one may come *to know* the intelligible world by cognizance of the visible world. This premise is of historical import, for Scholastic notions of the analogous knowledge of God were rooted in this Platonic conviction.[9]

Aristotle preserved the four-part form of αναλογια and used the term in virtually all of his works. In his biological works, Aristotle posited numerous "analogies of function" in which various organs in animals were compared to corresponding organs in man.[10] Of interest to the rhetorician is Aristotle's use of αναλογια in the *Poetics* and in the *Rhetoric*. The notion of "proportional metaphor" developed there is the foundation of the so-called figurative analogy. After defining metaphor as "giving a thing a name which belongs to something else," Aristotle indicated the four species of metaphor; following brief descriptions of the first three, the proportional metaphor was explained as follows:

> That from analogy [αναλογια] is possible whenever there are four terms so related that the second (B) is to the first (A), as the fourth (D) is to the third (C); for one may metaphorically put D in lieu of B and B in lieu of D. . . . Thus a cup (B) is in relation to Dionysius (A) what a shield (D) is to Ares (C). The cup accordingly will be metaphorically described as the "Shield of Dionysius" (D+A), and the shield as the "Cup of Ares."[11]

Although the primary function of a proportional metaphor is stylistic, it may also have value as proof. Aristotle noted that the mind of the hearer grasps the relation suggested in the metaphor and "seems to say, 'Yes, to be sure, I never thought of that.' "[12]

While the foundation of our notion of figurative analogy is in the Greek notion of αναλογια, the basis of the literal analogy is in the Greek concept of παραδειγμα. "Paradigms" were discussed briefly by Plato, who explained example as the comparing together in the mind of two things, one which is clear and one which is not. The comparison resulted in the less clear thing being made easier to apprehend because of its relation to the principles associated with the clearer thing.[13] Aristotle's analysis of "paradigms" dealt with both the psychological process and the logical construct. The psychological process involves sense perception, memory, and experience: "So out of sense perception comes to be what we call memory [retention in the soul], and out of frequently repeated memories of the same thing develops experience...."[14] Experience enables one to produce in the mind principles of universal application. Such principles arise "when from many notions gained by experience one universal judgment about a class of objects is produced."[15]

The logical construct of the rhetorical induction or "example" was detailed by Aristotle in the *Prior Analytics*:

> We have an "example" when the major term is proved to belong to the middle by means of a term which resembles the third. It ought to be known both that the middle belongs to the third term, and that the first belongs to that which resembles the third. For example, let A be evil, B making war against neighbours, C Athenians against Thebans, D Thebans against Phocians. If then we wish to prove that to fight with the Thebans is an evil, we must assume that to fight against neighbours is an evil. Evidence of this is obtained from similar cases, e.g., that the war against the Phocians was an evil to the Thebans. Since then to fight against neighbours is an evil, and to fight against the Thebans is to fight against neighbours, it is clear that to fight against the Thebans is an evil.[16]

Of the three types of examples in rhetoric outlined by Aristotle—the mention of actual past facts, the illustrative parallel, and the fable—the first, actual past facts or precedent cases, most closely corresponds to the modern notion of literal analogy.[17]

The Romans, Seneca the Younger and Quintilian, used prior experience to predict the unknown and called the process *analogia*. Quintilian's view is reminiscent of Plato's treatment of παραδειγμα: "But, in all these cases, we have need of a critical judgment, especially as regards analogy.... The essence of analogy is the testing of all subjects of doubt by the application of some standards of comparison about which there is no question, the proof that is to say of the uncertain by reference to the certain."[18]

In short, ancient contributions to the development of the concept of analogy in rhetoric are threefold. First, the mathematical notion of αναλογια, equivalence between ratios, was broadened to include resemblances of ratios, which Aristotle deemed useful in both style and proof. Second, the concept of direct resemblance was given a clearly articulated logical construct which served as the basis for subsequent theories of induction in both logic and rhetoric. Third, Roman works assimilated the Greek παραδειγμα under the label *analogia*. Thus, later writers were able to refer to both resemblances of ratios and direct resemblance as "analogy."

During the Middle Ages, Neoplatonist philosophers continued to use the four-part form of the Greek αναλογια to explain their cosmological theories.[19] Likewise, the concept continued to be an epistemological tool, especially for the Christian Neoplatonists, St. Augustine and Pseudo-Dionysius. They argued that God could be known via Creation. For example, "goodness" found in the world of man could be used to infer, by analogy, some knowledge about the ultimate goodness of God.[20] The Scholastic theologians, St. Anselm, St. Bonaventura, St. Thomas Aquinas, and Cardinal Cajetan, developed the theory of the analogous knowledge of God to its fullest extent.[21]

Grammarians and theorists of poetic and rhetoric in the Middle Ages seldom wrote of analogy. The grammarians mentioned the ancient dispute between the Analogists and the Anomalists, in which Quintilian had taken part.[22] Nowhere in the early rhetorics of style does one find a form of *analogia* used to refer to a figure or word or sentence.[23] Since the ancient works which influenced medieval writers on rhetoric and poetic contained few references to *analogia*, perhaps this is not surprising.[24]

During the English Renaissance, analogy was discussed by writers in philosophy, logic, and rhetoric. In rhetorical works, the term *analogia* was used only by two writers, both of the stylistic school,[25] Sherry and Puttenham.[26] In their works, "analogy" was not a kind of figure or trope, but was a quality of style best termed "appropriateness." Sherry, for instance, equated *analogia* with *proportio* and argued that style should be "in due proportion" to the office of the speaker or writer.[27] Other writers discussed figures and tropes such as *comparatio, similitudo*, and *parabole*.[28] These discussions tended toward illustration rather than definition, and the frequent "borrowing" among authors contributed to the confounding of terms. Angel Day, for instance, used the same illustrative example in his discussion of *comparatio* that Richard Sherry had used four decades earlier in his treatment of *similitudo*.[29] The Neo-Ciceronian writer Thomas Wilson treated *similitudo* under the canon of style in his *Arte of Rhetorique*, but he cut his discussion short, "because I have spoke of similitudes heretofore in the boke of Logique. . . ."[30] Perhaps Wilson recognized the dual role of resemblances in style and in proof. When Aristotle's *Rhetoric* became influential, theorists such as John Hoskins discussed under the heading "similitude" that which Aristotle had termed "proportional metaphor."[31] Neither the formulary nor the Ramistic rhetorics contained systematic treatments of *analogia, comparatio, similitudo,* or *parabole.* The Ramists included none of the terms in their lists of tropes and figures. Renaissance rhetoricians, in short, were working toward delineations of kinds of arguments and devices of style that were to be more cogently stated in eighteenth- and nineteenth-century works.

In the logical and philosophical treatises of the Renaissance, notions of *comparatio* and *similitudo* were first called "analogy." Ramus's term *comparata,* which denoted qualitative comparisons,[32] became synonymous with the term *similitudo* in the works of his successors.[33] Both terms eventually became allied with *analogia* in the works of later Ramists such as Thomas Granger and Franco Burgersdijck, who abandoned Ramus's rigid separation of disciplines and strict definitions of terms.[34] The Aristotelian notions of induction and example received considerable attention from the more "traditional" logicians, Thomas Wilson,[35] Thomas Blunderville,[36] Edward Brerewood,[37] and Robert Sanderson.[38] Although none of these writers used the term "analogy" to refer to example, their discussions preserved the precepts of induction and example as Aristotle had viewed them.

Induction was also of interest to the philosophers René Descartes and Francis Bacon. The former's *Discourse on Method,* which was the foundation of the *Port-Royal Logic,* both preserved the classical view of induction and postulated a "new logic" of scientific induction.[39] The writings of Francis Bacon, however, served to establish a philosophical basis for this scientific empiricism. In short, Bacon rejected the Aristotelian notion of induction wherein observations led directly to generalizations. He postulated a system in which the observations of the senses were tested and re-tested before a generalization was posited.[40] At the beginning of this process of scientific induction were the various "Prerogative Instances," one of which was "Instances Conformable, or of Analogy." Bacon defined "analogy" broadly and he used it to refer to resemblances in general. He argued that one should seek to detect the analogies and resemblances among things, for the apprehension of these was the start of scientific discovery: "Men's labour therefore should be turned to the investigation and observation of the resemblances and analogies of things, as well in wholes as in parts. For these it is that detect the unity of nature and lay a foundation for the constitution of science."[41]

At the close of the Renaissance, then, one finds the term "analogy" to have a multitude of significations, ranging from the narrow characterizations of the stylistic rhetoricians to the broader views of logicians and philosophers of science.[42] In the works of eighteenth- and nineteenth-century writers on rhetoric and logic the use of "analogy" to refer to resemblances in general became firmly established.

These rhetorical and logical theorists were strongly influenced by philosophical and theological works. Locke's *Essay Concerning Human Under-*

standing viewed "analogy" as an epistemological tool and established the value of analogy in obtaining probable knowledge when direct evidence was unobtainable.[43] Bishop Butler's *Analogy of Religion*, which received wide dissemination, was the touchstone of the so-called "Argument from Design," wherein the observable presence of an orderly world was held to imply the existence of an "orderer," God.[44] In his *Enquiry Concerning Human Understanding*, Hume saw analogy as likeness in general, and he argued that "all our reasonings concerning matters of fact are founded on a species of Analogy, which leads us to expect from any cause the same events [effects], which we have observed to result from similar causes."[45] The *Dialogues Concerning Natural Religion* contained his attack on the logical validity of analogy. His doubts sprang from the notion that "exactly similar" causes were impossible.[46] Despite the efforts of Reid and Stewart,[47] this distrust of the value of analogy took firm hold in the works of later logicians and rhetoricians.

Although the stylistic and classical rhetorics of the eighteenth and nineteenth centuries did not discuss analogy, the belletristic and the psychological-epistemological rhetorics dealt with analogy at length.[48] The belletristic rhetorics of Lord Kames and Hugh Blair mentioned analogy, and both viewed it as an intrinsic mental activity of man, based upon the association of ideas. Kames argued that analogy could be a sound form of reasoning, and he may also have had analogy in mind when he wrote of a figure "which, among related objects, extends the properties of one to another."[49] Blair explicitly viewed analogy or resemblance as basic to both figures of thought and figures of words.[50] Both George Campbell and Joseph Priestley argued against the worth of analogy in evincing proof, though they admitted the value of analogy as probable evidence and in refutation.[51] Their regard for analogy as a device of refutation probably grew from their admiration for Butler's *Analogy of Religion*.[52] The lone rhetorical theorist of the times who gave wholehearted support to analogy as a kind of argument was Archbishop Whately, who defined analogy as resemblance of ratios, the Aristotelian signification. Indeed, Whately differentiated sharply between direct resemblance and resemblance of relation and urged that the label "analogy" be applied only to the latter.[53] Unlike Campbell and Priestley, Whately was willing to regard analogy as a kind of argument.[54] Except for Whately's narrow definition, "analogy" in eighteenth- and nineteenth-century rhetorical theory meant resemblance in general, and most theorists considered analogy to be a form of inductive proof.

Logicians of this era generally regarded analogy as a useful kind of indirect evidence on questions of probability. The logical theories of Reid, Bentham, Condillac, Beattie, and Stewart all held this general view.[55] Aristotelian logical works usually discussed analogy or induction as a syllogistic process much like Aristotle's notion of example.[56]

Mill's monumental *System of Logic*[57] systematizes these logical theories. Although he seemed to favor the philosophical, inductive logical theories, Mill ranged freely over earlier logical theories in arriving at his definitions and precepts. His treatment of analogy is noteworthy because he brought the diverse directions of earlier thought together. After taking note of the confusion which had surrounded the term "analogy," Mill argued that analogy ought to be considered as a kind of inductive argument. He posited a general definition which included both direct resemblance and resemblance of relations: "Analogical reasoning . . . may be reduced to the following formula: Two things resemble each other in one or more respects; a certain proposition is true of the one; therefore it is true of the other."[58] Like Bacon, Mill prized analogy as a helpful instrument in scientific investigation, but, unlike most eighteenth- and nineteenth-century writers on logic and rhetoric, Mill did not question the value of analogy as evidence. Indeed, he noted that analogy, like any kind of argument or evidence, depends upon the material circumstances of the case or cases in question: "The circumstance in which the two cases resemble may be capable of being shown to be the material circumstance. . . ."[59] Certainly, Mill's *System of Logic* must be regarded as a watershed in the development of the concept of analogy both for its systematization of earlier positions and its general definition of analogy.

In recent years, the confusion Mill had hoped to correct has continued instead. Twentieth-century writers on rhetoric discuss the so-called literal and figurative modes of analogy. The former is characterized as a weak form of inductive proof used chiefly for clarification and illustration and the latter is regarded as a stylistic device. From time to time, theorists have argued that both literal and figurative analogies ought to be admitted to the citadel of logical proof,[60] but, judging from recent speech textbooks, the pleas have been largely ignored.[61]

Of more significance to the rhetorician may be the role that analogy, broadly viewed, holds in theories of concept formation and change, for it is within these constructs that the question of rhetorical proof may be approached with some exactitude. Wallace had this in mind when he suggested in his pioneer essay that "two properties of analogy, the familiarity of the model and the possibility of its extension, hold out much for rhetorical proof."[62] In *The New Rhetoric* of Perelman and Olbrechts-Tyteca, the authors suggest that analogies may effect transfers of value between their constituent elements, the *theme* and the *phoros*. In a four-part analogy A:B::C:D, A:B is the theme, or lesser known element, and C:D is the phoros or better known element.[63] The interaction between theme and phoros enables the unobservable or the unknown to become familiar via the observable and the known. The effect is more than mere "understanding," however, for transfers of value entail judgment on the part of the auditor and thus the establishment of belief. The transfer of value is made, argue the authors of *The New Rhetoric*, because the familiarity of the phoros of the analogy allows the recipient to view the theme in the context of the familiar setting of the phoros.[64]

Recent investigations by experimental psychologists in the areas of concept formation and concept utilization have yielded conclusions which support theoretical constructs similar to those noted above.[65] Conceptual behavior is related to perception, learning ability, and problem-solving ability, but the single most important factor in the acquisition of concepts seems to be verbal ability.[66]

What, then, is the place of analogy in modern rhetorical theory? Certainly, scholars must endeavor to use precise terminology when dealing with analogy. In light of Mill's definition of analogy, the literal/figurative dichotomy is no longer viable. The labels suggested by Ehninger and Brockriede—parallel case, collection of parallel cases, and analogy—are valuable since they refer to different species of the concept.[67] Further, speculative debate on the probative force of analogy ought to take second place to quantitative considerations of the role of analogy in concept formation and change. The existing literature on verbal concept formation seems to suggest that the selection of an analogy for rhetorical discourse quite probably belies both the epistemological assumptions and the cognitive structure of the rhetor. Thus, Scott's observation that rhetoric is epistemic[68] becomes more meaningful to the critic of discourse who investigates the efficacy of analogical inferences.

Although few studies have focused upon analogy and attitude change,[69] there seems to be evidence that various kinds of analogies do evince proof and act as corroborative support for other forms of proof. McCroskey and Combs found that messages which contained an analogy produced greater attitude change than those which did not. In discussing this result, they suggested that analogies produce sets of associations and that analogies "decrease 'selectivity' as an alternative to attitude change."[70] Thus, the probative force of analogical argument is predicated upon the conceptual behavior of the receiver. Both suggestions merit further inquiry, especially regarding the "sets of associations" and their subsequent role in attitude change. If, indeed, rhetoric deals with the "opinions of men," a deeper consideration of analogy on both practical and theoretical levels should provide the modern rhetorician with a greater understanding of the ways opinions are shaped and changed.

---

1. See, for example, George P. Baker and Henry B. Huntington, *The Principles of Argumentation* (Boston: Ginn, 1905), pp. 105–106; William Trufant Foster, *Argumentation and Debating* (2nd ed.; Cambridge: Riverside Press, 1936), p. 146; and A. Craig Baird, *Rhetoric: A Philosophical Inquiry* (New York: Ronald Press, 1965), pp. 64–66.

The most careful separation of the species of analogy is that of Douglas Ehninger and Wayne Brockriede; they write of proof by parallel case, collection of parallel cases, and analogy in *Decision by Debate* (New York: Dodd, Mead, 1963), pp. 139–144.

2. Donald A. Schon, *Invention and the Evolution of Ideas* (London: Tavistock Publications, 1963, 1967), p. 37ff.

3. Robert Oppenheimer, "Analogy in Science," *American Psychologist*, 11 (March, 1956), 127–136.

4. Ernest G. Bormann, *Theory and Research in the Communicative Arts* (New York: Holt, Rinehart and Winston, 1965), p. 101.

5. See Sir Thomas L. Heath, comm. and trans., *The Thirteen Books of Euclid's Elements* (2 vols.; Cambridge: Cambridge University Press, 1926), II, p. 293; Nicomachus of Gerasa, *Introduction to Arithemetic*, trans. Martin Luther D'Ooge (New York: Macmillan, 1926), pp. 264–265; Iamblichus, *On Nicomachus' Introduction to Arithemetic*, trans. Ivor Thomas in *Selections Illustrating the History of Greek Mathematics*, ed. Ivor Thomas (2 vols., Loeb Classical Library; Cambridge: Harvard University Press, 1951), I, pp. 111–113; and Proclus, *Commentary on Euclid*, in *Selections*, ed. Ivor Thomas, I, p. 147.

6. Plato, *Timaeus*, 32B, trans. R. G. Bury (Loeb Classical Library; Cambridge: Harvard University Press, 1952).

7. For a discussion of this tenet in Plato, see James F. Anderson, "Analogy in Plato," *Review of Metaphysics*, 4 (September, 1950), 113. For a thorough treatment of Neoplatonist adaptations of this tenet see Hampus Lyttkens, *The Analogy between God and the World: An Investigation of Its Background and Interpretation of Its Use by Thomas of Aquino* (Uppsala: Almqvist and Wiksells, 1952).

8. Plato, *Republic*, 508 C-D, trans. Paul Shorey (2 vols., Loeb Classical Library; Cambridge: Harvard University Press, 1946). See also Herman L. Sinaiko, *Love, Knowledge and Discourse in Plato: Dialogue and Dialectic in Phaedrus, Republic and Parmenides* (Chicago: University of Chicago Press, 1965), pp. 122–126.

9. Lyttkens, *Analogy between God and the World*, p. 27. See also R. J. Henle, *St. Thomas and Platonism* (The Hague: Martinus Nijhoff, 1956), pp. 324–327.

10. For example, *Historia Animalium* 488b29–33, 530b31–531a2; *De Partibus Animalium*, 655b2. For a comprehensive listing of these see Howard Raymond Delaney, "The Doctrine of Four-Term Analogy in Aristotle" (Ph.D. dissertation, St. Louis University, 1959), pp. 57–67; G. I. Muskens, *De Vocis αναλογιας significatione ac usu apud Aristotelem* (Groningen, Holland: J. B. Wolters, 1943), pp. 95–96; and James S. Measell, "Foundations of the Concept of Analogy in Greek Mathematics and Rhetoric" (M.A. thesis, University of Illinois, 1968), pp. 42–45.

11. Aristotle, *Poetica*, 1457b17–22, trans. Ingram Bywater (New York: Random House, 1954). See also *Rhetorica*, 1407a–1412a, trans. W. Rhys Roberts (New York: Random House, 1954).

12. Aristotle, *Rhetorica*, 1412a20–21.

13. Plato, *Statesman*, 278C, trans. Benjamin Jowett in *The Dialogues of Plato* (2 vols.; New York: Random House, 1937).

14. Aristotle, *Analytica Posteriora*, 100a3–6. See also *Metaphysica*, 980b27.

15. Aristotle, *Metaphysica*, 981a6–7.

16. Aristotle, *Analytica Priora*, 68b37–69a7. See also *Rhetorica.* 1393a25–1393b3.

17. G. E. R. Lloyd, *Polarity and Analogy: Two Types of Argumentation in Early Greek Thought* (Cambridge: Cambridge University Press, 1966), p. 406.

18. Quintilian, *Institutio Oratoria*, I, vi, 3, trans. H. E. Butler (4 vols., Loeb Classical Library; Cambridge: Harvard University Press, 1920). This passage may have been the

inspiration behind Bishop Joseph Butler's *Analogy of Religion* (1736), for he quotes it on the title page of the first edition. For Seneca the Younger's remarks on analogy, see *Ad Lucilium Epistulae Morales*, LXX, trans. R. M. Gummere (3 vols., Loeb Classical Library; Cambridge: Harvard University Press, 1925).

19. See, for example, Plotinus, *Enneads*, V, 5 and 9, VI, 2 and 7, trans. Stephen MacKenna (2nd ed. rev. by B. S. Page; London: Faber and Faber, 1957), and Proclus, *The Elements of Theology*, Props. 10, 11, 25, 100, 108, and 110, trans. E. R. Dodds (Oxford: Clarendon Press, 1933).

20. The biblical precept that God is to be understood from that which he has made (Romans 1:20) was discussed by St. Augustine in *On the Trinity*, XV, 20 and 39, trans. A. W. Hadden in *Basic Writings of St. Augustine*, ed. Whitney J. Oates (2 vols.; New York: Random House, 1948). See also Pseudo-Dionysius, *The Celestial Hierarchies*, III, trans. by editors of The Shrine of Wisdom (London: Unwin Bros., 1949).

21. James S. Measell, "Development of the Concept of Analogy in Philosophy, Logic and Rhetoric to 1850" (Ph.D. dissertation, University of Illinois, 1970), pp. 63–79.

22. For reference to this dispute, see Charisius, *Artis Grammaticae* in *Grammatici Latini*, ed. Henry Keil (7 vols.; Lipsiae: In Aedibus B. G. Teubneri, 1850–88), I, p. 116; Martionus Capella, *De Nuptiis Philologiae et Mercurii*, ed. Fransiscus Eyssenhardt (Lipsiae: In Aedibus B. G. Teubneri, 1866), p. 76; and Isidore of Seville, *Etymologiae*, in J. P. Migne, *Patrologia Latina* (221 vols.; Paris, 1844–1905), LXXXII, col. 104–105.

23. This conclusion is based upon my examination of the treatises in Carolus Halm's *Rhetores Latini Minores* (Lipsiae: In Aedibus B. G. Teubneri, 1850); The Venerable Bede's *De Schematibus et Tropis*, *De Arte Metrica*, and *De Orthographia*; and the twelfth- and thirteenth-century works discussed by Edmond Faral in *Les Arts Poetiques du XIIe et du XIIIe Siecle* (Paris: Librarie Ancienne Honore Champion, 1924).

24. The major influences were, of course, the works of Quintilian and Cicero and the *ad Herennium*, which was often ascribed to Cicero. Quintilian's remarks on analogy are few (see note 18) and neither the *ad Herennium* nor the rhetorical works of Cicero contain a form of *analogia*. See Kenneth Morgan Abbott, William Abbott Oldfather, and Vernon Canter, *Index Verborum in Ciceronis Rhetorica* (Urbana: University of Illinois Press, 1964).

25. I have here adopted as "trends" those suggested by Wilbur Samuel Howell in his *Logic and Rhetoric in England, 1500–1700* (Princeton: Princeton University Press, 1956), pp. 6–7.

26. Richard Sherry, *A Treatise of Schemes and Tropes*, ed. Herbert W. Hildebrandt (Gainesville, Fla.: Scholars' Facsimiles and Reprints, 1961), pp. 37, 90–91; George Puttenham, *The Arte of English Poesie*, eds. Gladys Willcock and Alice Walker (Cambridge: Cambridge University Press, 1936), pp. 155–156.

27. Sherry, *Treatise*, p. 37. Sherry's subordination of *analogia* under the heading of "proprietas" indicates his reliance upon Petrus Mosellanus for this view; see Petrus Mosellanus, *Tabulae, De Schematibus* (Lipsiae: n.p., 1532).

28. For treatments of *comparatio*, see Henry Peacham, *The Garden of Eloquence*, ed. William G. Crane (Gainsville, Fla.: Scholars' Facsimiles and Reprints, 1954), p. 156; Angel Day, *The English Secretarie* (London: Printed by P. S. for C. Burkie, 1599), p. 93; and John Hoskins, *Directions for Speech and Style*, ed. Hoyt H. Hudson (Princeton: Princeton University Press, 1935), p. 17. For *similitudo*, see Peacham, *Garden*, pp. 158–159; Hoskins, *Directions*, p. 10; and John Smith, *The Mystery of Rhetoric Unveiled* (10th ed.; London: Printed for R. Wilkin *et al.*, 1721), pp. 156–157. For *parabole*, see Sherry, *Treatise*, pp. 90–91, and Peacham, *Garden*, V, ii, recto [this page from the 1577 edition is not numbered in the facsimile reprint cited above].

29. Day, *English Secretarie*, p. 93; Sherry, *Treatise*, pp. 74–75.

30. Thomas Wilson, *The Arte of Rhetorique*, ed. Robert Hood Bowers (Gainesville, Fla.: Scholars' Facsimiles and Reprints, 1962), pp. 213–214.

31. Hoskins, *Directions*, p. 10.

32. Peter Ramus, *Dialectique* (1555), ed. Michel Dassonville (Geneve: Librairie Droz, 1965), p. 80.

33. See Dudley Fenner, *The Artes of Logike and Rethorike*, ed. Robert D. Pepper in *Four Tudor Books on Education* (Gainesville, Fla.: Scholars' Facsimiles and Reprints, 1966), p. 156, and Abraham Fraunce, *The Lawiers Logike* (London: William Haw, 1588), fol. 72.

34. Thomas Granger, *Syntagma Logicum, or, The Divine Logike* (London: William Jones, 1620), p. 146. See also Franco Burgersdijck, *An Introduction to the Art of Logick*, trans. anon. (London: T. Bollard, 1701), p. 78; this work appeared in 1668 under the title *Institutionem Logicarum Libri Duo*.

35. Thomas Wilson, *The Rule of Reason* (London: n.p., 1552), fol. 65.

36. Thomas Blundeville, *The Art of Logike* (English Linguistics, 1500–1800; Menston, England: The Scolar Press, 1967), pp. 149–151.

37. Edward Brerewood, *Elementa Logicae* (Londini: Joannem Raworth, 1638), p. 103.

38. Robert Sanderson, *Logicae Artis Compendium* (Oxoniae: M. Fletcher, 1741), p. 151; this work first appeared in 1618.

39. Howell, *Logic and Rhetoric*, p. 350.

40. Francis Bacon, *The Great Instauration*, in *The Works of Francis Bacon*, eds. and trans. James Spedding, Robert Leslie Ellis, and Douglas Denon Heath (14 vols.; London: Longman, 1858), IV, pp. 25–26.

41. Bacon, *Novum Organum*, in *Works*, IV, p. 167.

42. Measell, "Development of the Concept of Analogy in Philosophy, Logic, and Rhetoric to 1850," pp. 169–170.

43. John Locke, *An Essay Concerning Human Understanding*, Book IV, Ch. 16, Sec. 12, ed. A. D. Woozley (Cleveland: Meridian Books, 1964).

44. Bishop Joseph Butler, *The Analogy of Religion, Natural and Revealed, to the Constitution and Course of Nature* (London: James, John, and Paul Knapton, 1736). For a detailed study of Butler's influence, see Ernest C. Mossner, *Bishop Butler and the Age of Reason* (New York: Macmillan, 1936) and Robert H. Hurlbutt, *Hume, Newton, and the Design Argument* (Lincoln, Neb.: University of Nebraska Press, 1965).

45. David Hume, *An Enquiry Concerning Human Understanding*, Sec. IX, ed. Eugene Freeman (LaSalle, Ill.: Open Court, 1966).

46. David Hume, *Dialogues Concerning Natural Religion*, Part II, ed. Norman Kemp Smith (2nd ed.; New York: Social Sciences Publishers, 1948), p. 147.

47. See Thomas Reid, *Inquiry into the Human Mind*, in *The Works of Thomas Reid*, ed. Dugald Stewart (3 vols.; New York: E. Duychinck *et al.*, 1822), I, pp. 311–316; Reid, *Essays on the Intellectual Powers of Man*, in *Works*, I, pp. 369–372; and Dugald Stewart, *Works* (7 vols.; Cambridge: Hilliard and Brown, 1829), II, pp. 273–286.

48. Vincent M. Bevilacqua, "Philosophical Influences in the Development of English Rhetorical Theory: 1748 to 1783," *Proceedings of the Leeds Philosophical and Literary Society, Literary and Historical Section*, 12 (April, 1968), pp. 200–201.

49. Henry Home, Lord Kames, *Elements of Criticism*, ed. Abraham Mills (New York: Mason Bros., 1860), p. 365; see also Kames's *Sketches of the History of Man* (4 vols.; London: James Williams, 1774), III, pp. 133–134, and his *Essays on the Principles of Morality and Natural Religion* (Edinburgh: R. Fleming, 1751), esp. "Essay V. of Our Knowledge of Future Events."

50. Hugh Blair, *Lectures on Rhetoric and Belles Lettres*, Lects. XIV and XVII.

51. George Campbell, *The Philosophy of Rhetoric*, ed. Lloyd F. Bitzer (Carbondale: Southern Illinois University Press, 1963), pp. 53–54, and Joseph Priestley, *A Course of Lectures on Oratory and Criticism*, eds. Vincent M. Bevilacqua and Richard Murphy (Carbondale: Southern Illinois University Press, 1965), pp. 15–17.

52. Campbell, *Philosophy of Rhetoric*, p. 54 and Priestley, *Course of Lectures*, p. 15.

53. Richard Whately, *Elements of Rhetoric*, ed. Douglas Ehninger (Carbondale: Southern Illinois University Press, 1963), pp. 90–91.

54. *Ibid.*, pp. 434–439.

55. See Reid, *Works*, I, p. 369; Edward Bentham, *An Introduction to Logick, Scholastic and Rational* (Oxford: W. Jackson and J. Lister, 1773), p. 84; Etienne Bonnot De Condillac, *The Logic of Condillac*, trans. Joseph Neef (Philadelphia: n.p., 1809), pp. 130–134; James Beattie, *Elements of Moral Science* (2 vols.; Edinburgh: Archibald Constable, 1817), II, pp. 404–405; and Stewart, *Works*, II, p. 273.

56. William Duncan, *The Elements of Logick in Four Books* (London: R. Dodsley, 1752), pp. 373–374; Isaac Watts, *Logick* (London: John Clark and Richard Hett, 1725), pp. 7–8; and Richard Whately, *Elements of Logic* (3rd ed.; London: B. Fellowes, 1829), pp. 216–217.

57. John Stuart Mill, *A System of Logic* (1st ed. reprinted; New York: Harper and Bros., 1850).

58. *Ibid.*, pp. 332–333. The two things, of course, could be a pair of ratios.

59. *Ibid.*

60. See Gladys Murphy Graham, "Analogy—A Study in Proof and Persuasion Values," *Quarterly Journal of Speech*, 14 (November, 1928), pp. 534–542, and Karl R. Wallace, "On Analogy: Re-definition and Some Implications," in *Studies in Speech and Drama in Honor of Alexander M. Drummond*, ed. Herbert A. Wichelns, *et al.*, (Ithaca, N.Y.: Cornell University Press, 1944), pp. 412–426.

61. See, for example, John T. Wilson and Carroll C. Arnold, *Public Speaking as a Liberal Art* (Boston: Allyn and Bacon, Inc., 1964), p. 158; Wayne C. Minnick, *The Art of Persuasion* (2nd ed.; Boston: Houghton Mifflin, 1968), pp. 136–140; and Robert C. Jeffrey and Owen Patterson, *Speech: A Text with Adapted Readings* (New York: Harper and Row, 1971), pp. 271–272.

62. Wallace, "On Analogy," p. 423.

63. C. Perelman and L. Olbrechts-Tyteca, *The New Rhetoric: A Treatise on Argumentation*, trans. John Wilkinson and Purcell Weaver (Notre Dame, Ind.: Notre Dame University Press, 1969), p. 381.

64. *Ibid.*, p. 385.

65. For a summary of this literature, see Lyle E. Bourne Jr., *Human Conceptual Behavior* (Boston: Allyn and Bacon, 1966).

66. E. J. Archer, "On Verbalizations and Concepts," in *Categories of Human Learning*, ed. A. W. Melton (New York: Academic Press, 1964).

67. Ehninger and Brockriede, *Decision by Debate*, pp. 139–144.

68. Robert L. Scott, "On Viewing Rhetoric as Epistemic," *Central States Speech Journal*, 18 (February, 1967), pp. 9–17.

69. Bourne, *Human Conceptual Behavior*, pp. 125–126.

70. James C. McCroskey and Walter H. Combs, "The Effects of the Use of Analogy on Attitude Change and Source Credibility," *The Journal of Communication*, 19 (December, 1969), p. 338.

Language, Symbolism, and Criticism:
Paul Tillich's "Existentialist" Analysis

CAROLYN CASTLEBERRY DEILE

"The fact that there is so much discussion about the meaning of symbols going on in this country as well as in Europe," observes Paul Tillich, "is a symptom of something deeper. . . . It is a symptom of the fact that we are in a confusion of language in theology and philosophy and related subjects which has hardly been surpassed at any time in history."[1] Although Tillich never deals systematically with the theory of language and symbolism, he deals indirectly with it throughout his writings in relation to other major topics. It is the thesis of this study that a theory of language, symbolism, and criticism can be constructed from Tillich's writings, which have important implications for contemporary rhetorical theory and criticism.

A philosopher-theologian whom John Herman Randall, Jr., considers to be "by far the most persuasive exponent of the philosophy of existentialism,"[2] and whom Charles Hartshorne views as "one of the most creative contributors to metaphysical theory who have written during the past half century,"[3] Paul Tillich deserves to be related to rhetorical theory and criticism. In recent years, scholars have become increasingly interested in the potential contributions of the existentialist philosophers to the study of rhetoric.[4]

My purpose is to clarify Tillich's ideas regarding language, symbolism, and criticism, to organize them into a meaningful theoretical framework, and to suggest their relevance for rhetoric. I propose to begin with an examination of Tillich's theory of language and the philosophical assumptions upon which it is based; then to examine his theory of symbolism; and finally to determine his critical principles for evaluating symbols.

I

For Tillich, language is the defining feature of human existence: "Man is man through the power of the word."[5] His analysis of language parallels his tripartite dialectical analysis of the nature of man, in terms of essential being, existential being, and teleological being. Thus, it will be helpful to begin the analysis of his theory of language with an examination of the philosophical assumptions upon which it is based.

Essential being, the first stage in the analysis of man, is for Tillich an "image." It is not an actual stage of human development; it is present in all stages of man's development, but in existential distortion. Essential being "has potentiality, not actuality. It has no place, it is *ou topos* (utopia). It has no time; it precedes temporality."[6] But essentialism is the necessary starting point in the analysis of man, for structural analysis is possible only in the realm of essences. He explains this element of philosophical idealism in his thought: "I am epistemologically an idealist, if idealism means the assertion of the identity of thought and being as the principle of truth."[7] In other words, a correlation exists between the rational structure of the mind (*Geist*) and the rational structure of reality and, through language, the mind has the potential to grasp the rational structure of reality. But the correlation remains an image against which man's existential being stands in perpetual tension.

Existential being, the second element in the analysis, is the original fact of human existence. For the actualization of potentiality produces existential estrangement, and estrangement is the basic characteristic of the human condition, that is, estrangement from one's self, from other persons, from one's essence, and from truth. Tillich views existentialism (including depth psychology) as the analysis of the human predicament. Existentialism formulates the universally asked question of existence, and gives an analysis of what it means to exist. But it cannot provide answers. Whenever existentialists become constructive and give answers pointing to the possibility of transcendence, they are no longer functioning as existentialists, but rather as *theologians*. Hence, there is no "theistic" or "atheistic" existentialism or depth psychology:

> [Existentialism] develops the question implied in existence, but it does not try to give the answer, either in atheistic or in theistic terms. Whenever existentialists give answers, they do so in terms of religious or quasi-religious traditions which are not derived from their existentialist analysis. Pascal derives his answers from the Augustinian tradition, Kierkegaard from the Lutheran, Marcel from the Thomist, Dostoevski from the Greek Orthodox. Or the answers are derived from humanistic traditions, as with Marx, Sartre, Nietzsche, Heidegger, and Jaspers. None of these men was able to develop answers out of his questions. The answers of the humanists come from hidden religious sources. They are matters of ultimate concern or faith, although garbed in a secular gown. Hence the distinction between atheistic and theistic existentialism fails. Existentialism is an analysis of the human predicament. And the answers to the questions implied in man's predicament are religious, whether open or hidden.[8]

Because all existentialists do *in fact* provide answers they are theologians. For example, there is a religious dimension in Freud, for despite his existential view of man as infinite libido which can never be satisfied and which therefore produces the death instinct, he was convinced of the possibility of healing and of the fragmentary transcendence of existential distortion. In short, "if you speak of man's existential predicament as opposite to his essential nature, you must in some way presuppose an idea of his essential nature."[9]

The possibility of healing is the third aspect of Tillich's analysis. Healing means self-transcendence from existential distortion, or "salvation" in the sense of " 'healed' or 'whole,' as opposed to disruptiveness."[10] The consideration of "man's essential and existential nature points to his teleological nature."[11] Healing or transcendence always remains partial and fragmentary, for human existence remains a contradiction of essence, knowledge is always fragmentary, and truth is ambiguous.

Tillich's analysis of language parallels his tripartite analysis of man. Approaching language from the essentialist perspective, he defines "meaning" as a "correspondence between reality and the human spirit,"[12] and "language" as "the bearer of meaning."[13] The fundamental feature of human language is that it provides man with the potential "power of universals," or power of ideation. "Language, as the power of universals, is the basic expression of man's transcending his environment, of having a world. The ego-self is that self which can speak and which by speaking trespasses the boundaries of any given situation.[14] The universal structures, forms, and laws inherent in language give man a "world," in the sense of "a structured whole of innumerable parts" or "a unity in infinite manifoldness," as in the Greek *kosmos* and the Latin *universum.*[15] And it is that structured whole rather than his natural environment to which he responds and upon which he acts. For this reason, language serves as the foundation for human freedom. giving man the power to question, to deliberate and decide, to build theoretical and artistic structures, and to form interpersonal relationships and social organizations. Considered environmentally and in actuality, man participates in a very limited portion of reality, for his language system is a filter through which only certain features of reality penetrate. But considered potentially, "the universals make man universal; language proves that he is *microcosmos,*" and "this is the ontological basis for the assertion that knowledge is union and that it is rooted in the *eros* which reunites elements which essentially belong to each other."[16]

For confirmation of his view that man cannot be properly understood without both the essentialist and the existentialist interpretations of human nature, Tillich turns to the very nature of language: "In using universals, language is by its very nature essentialist, and cannot escape it. . . . Therefore, there is an essentialist framework in his mind. Existentialism is possible only as an element in a vision of the structure of being in its created goodness, and then as a description of man's existence within that framework. The conflicts between his essential goodness and his existential estrangement cannot be seen at all without keeping essentialism and existentialism together."[17] He argues further that the attempt of many modern existentialists and positivists to avoid any essentialist element is a logically impossible position, for "if they were to succeed in avoiding it completely, they must remain mute; they could no longer speak. Since every word expresses a universal, the radical existentialist is an illusion."[18]

From the existentialist perspective, language is viewed as the basis for the universal estrangement of man. While language is the foundation of human freedom, it is also the basis for his loss of freedom, for his freedom inevitably means the power to surrender his freedom and contradict his essential nature. Furthermore, language accounts for the subject-object split which man experiences in relation to his world, for "in transforming reality into meaning it separates mind and reality."[19] Four types of linguistic ambiguity result from the subject-object cleavage: (1) the ambiguity of poverty and abundance, that is, "the poverty in the midst of richness that falsifies that which is grasped through neglect of innumerable other possibilities";[20] (2) the limitation on universality inherent in every particular language system; (3) the unavoidable indefiniteness of language "because of the infinite distance between the language-forming subject (collective or individual) and the inexhaustible object (every object) it tries to grasp," causing language to betray the mind;[21] and (4) the anticommunicative possibilities of language—such as empty talk and the flight into silence, propaganda, contradiction, intoxication, and polemics—that arise from conscious and unconscious, personal and social sources. "Since language cannot penetrate to the very center of the other self, it is always a mixture of revealing and concealing."[22] And while these four distortions are based upon the subject-object split, the split is ambiguous, for "no language is possible without the subject-object cleavage" although "language is continuously brought to self-defeat by this very cleavage."[23]

But language has a third possibility, a possibility of healing. When ordinary language is transformed into symbolic language, it is "fragmentarily liberated from the bondage to the subject-object scheme," thereby "expressing the union of him who speaks with that of which he speaks in an act of linguistic self-transcendence."[24] When the word becomes a symbol (or Word) it fragmentarily overcomes linguistic distortion. Symbolic language is "beyond poverty and abundance. A few words become great words!"[25] It "transcends the particular encounter which it expresses in the direction of that which is universal, the Logos, the criterion of every particular logos."[26] The ambiguity of indefiniteness is overcome: "[It] does not try to grasp an ever escaping object but expresses a union between the inexhaustible subject and the inexhaustible object in a symbol which is by its very nature indefinite and definite at the same time. It leaves the potentialities of both sides of the symbol-creating encounter open—and in this sense it is indefinite—but it excludes other symbols (and any arbitrariness of symbolism) because of the unique character of the encounter."[27] Finally, the anticommunicative possibilities of language are transcended, for the symbol "reaches the center of the other one but not in terms of definitions or circumscriptions of finite objects or finite subjectivity (for example, emotions); it reaches the center of the other one by uniting the centers of the speaker and the listener in the transcendent unity."[28] When the ordinary language of signs is transformed into symbolic language, language becomes a form of healing. It becomes the medium for genuine dialogue.

Turning from the relation between language and man to the relation between language and culture, we find language viewed as the substructure of culture. First of all, the functions of culture are prefigured in the functions of language. The three functions of language—denotation, expression, and communication—can be distinguished but not separated, for all three are present to some extent in all meaningful discourse. The denotative or cognitive function is "its ability to grasp and communicate general meanings" and the expressive or aesthetic function is "its ability to disclose and to communicate personal states."[29] The basic unit of denotation is the concept, while the basic unit of expression is the image. The communicative function of language is operative even when nonverbal forms are substituted for language. Nonverbal forms serve a linguistic function because "they have meaning only in reference to words, to the spoken language."[30] There is no meaning apart from language, and anything which conveys meaning—be it a protest march, a tree, a painting, or a mathematical formula—is dependent upon language. Language is both a prerequisite of and a constituent feature in all other forms of communication. Communication, then, is the process by which signs and symbols, through their cognitive and expressive power, influence attitudes, values, beliefs, and action.

Language is the basic cultural creation. In sharp contrast with philosophers like Bergson and Whitehead who view language as an extension of the tool-making function of the intelligence which has developed according to the principles of evolutionary naturalism, Tillich sees even the use and production of tools as dependent upon language: "Man produces tools as tools, and for this the conception of universals is presupposed, i.e., the power of language. The power of tools is dependent on the power of language. Logos precedes everything. If man is called *homo faber*, he is implicitly called *anthropos logikos*, i.e., man who is determined by the logos and who is able to use the meaningful word."[31] On the other hand, he insists that in actuality language and technology must be viewed as the dual foundation of culture. Language and technology, providing the powers of apprehension and action, are the foundation for the general duality in all cultural creativity: "Beings 'receive each other' and, by doing so, change each other. They receive and react. In the realm of the organic, this is called stimulus and response; under the dimension of self-awareness, it is called perception and reaction; under the dimension of spirit, I suggest calling it *theoria* and *praxis*. The original Greek forms of the words 'theory' and 'practice' are used because the modern forms have lost the meaning and power of the ancient words."[32] In its denotative and expressive functions, language is the basic expression of *theoria*. The communicative function of language together with the tool-making function constitute the basic expression of *praxis*. Put in terms of a hypothetical conversation with Kenneth Burke, Tillich might respond to Burke's analysis this way: "Language is not only symbolic action (*praxis*)—it is also symbolic reception (*theoria*). Mr. Burke, you have left out half of life!"

Theoria is "the act of looking at the encountered world in order to take something of it into the centered self as a meaningful, structured whole."[33] The aesthetic image and the cognitive concept are the two modes by which we apprehend reality. They represent poles of a continuum, rather than separate and distinct types. The terms "image" and "concept" are very broad: "image" as the essence of all aesthetic creations and the expressive dimension of language, "concept" as the essence of all cognitive creations and the denotative dimension of language. The inner aim (*telos*) of the cognitive act is "truth," the bridging of the gap between subject and object, driving toward the concept which embraces all concepts. While the aesthetic act shares this end, its primary aim is "beauty" (in the sense of the unity of the good and the beautiful, *kalon k'agathon*), driving toward the image which encompasses all images. The cognitive act aims toward unity with the aesthetic act. Thus, the highest form of discourse represents a unity of dialectical validity and expressive adequacy.

Praxis includes "the whole of cultural acts of centered personalities who as members of social groups act upon each other and themselves."[34] Communication, as the basic form of *praxis*, is action which in the interpersonal realm is aimed at the actualization of human potentialities, and which in the communal realm is aimed at "justice," the social good. Personal growth demands interpersonal encounter: "Man actualizes himself as a person in the encounter with other persons within a community."[35] And such an encounter necessitates two-way communication: "A person-to-person relationship is actual through the word. One is related to a person in speaking to him, and one remains in relation to him only if he answers."[36] Dialogue, then, is merely another name for the moral act, for "the moral imperative is the command to become what one potentially is, a *person* within a community of persons."[37]

While Tillich's analysis of dialogue closely parallels that of Martin Buber in many respects, there is one decisive distinction. Unlike Buber, Tillich views community (*Gemeinschaft*) as necessarily implying an organizational and power structure.[38] Therefore, dialogue must also be viewed as the aim of persuasion directed toward the transformation of the political structure.

In its cognitive and aesthetic, personal and communal forms, culture is the structure for the dynamic actualization of reason. Ontological reason (*logos, Vernunft*) is "the structure of the mind which enables the mind to grasp and to transform reality."[39] It is both subjective and objective, theoretical and practical, cognitive and aesthetic, detached and passionate. Ontological reason is sharply distinguished from technical reason, the capacity for "reasoning," or what Aristotle meant by "deliberative reason." Deliberative reason is concerned only with the discovery of *means* for given ends. It can provide the basis for nothing more than a rhetoric of expediency. "While reason in the sense of Logos determines the ends and only in the second place the means, reason in the technical sense determines the means while accepting the ends from 'somewhere else.' "[40] Ontological reason unites the polarities of subjectivity and objectivity, of theory and practice, of image and concept, of passion and detachment, of structure and depth. But as actualized under the conditions of existence, the polarities become separated and thereby distorted. Existentially distorted reason can only be fragmentarily transcended through the apprehension of transcendent meaning embodied in symbolic forms.

The concept of transcendent meaning is the foundation for the theory of symbolism. Three structural components are involved in every actualization of meaning: subject matter or content, form, and substance or import. "Substance or import is grasped by means of a form and given expression in a content. Content is accidental, substance essential, and form is the mediating element."[41] The substance of meaning cannot become real and effective unless embodied in symbolic form. The function of symbolism is "the intuition of the forms of meaning filled with a living import, not the intuition of any sort of independent metaphysical essences."[42] Form and substance cannot be separated without the distortion of both elements.

The apprehension of transcendent meaning encompasses two elements: the intuitive or existential element, and the critical or ethical element. The intuitive element is experienced as the presence of unconditioned meaning here and now, while the critical element appears as the judging and transforming power of unconditioned meaning. In every actualization of transcendent meaning both elements are present, both the experience of meaning as being and as what ought to be. For "what is and what ought to be are united in the ground of all being."[43] When the intuitive element alone is operative, there results "a world-defying, static mysticism, without ethical dynamics and without a world-transforming will and power."[44] When the active element is operative in isolation, it results in "a world-controlling technical activism, without a spiritual substance and a world-transcending will and power."[45] The elements are interdependent, and the absence of one implies the distortion of the other.

Corresponding to these two elements in the experience of meaning are the two basic forms of symbolic expression—myth and cult. Symbols do not appear in isolation; a particular symbol is a part of a mythic or cultic nexus, and it must be understood in that context. The functions of reason, which separate and become distorted under the conditions of existence, are fragmentarily reunited in myth and cultic expression. "The union of the cognitive and aesthetic functions is fully expressed in mythology, the womb out of which both of them were born and came to independence and to which they tend to return."[46] And likewise; the union of personal and "communal functions is fully expressed in the cult community which is the mother of both of them and to which they try to return."[47] And finally, the separation of the intuitive and active elements is overcome: "In the relation of myth and cult no separation is even imaginable. Cult includes the myth on the basis of which it acts out the divine-human drama, and myth includes the cult of which it is the imaginary expression. It is, therefore, understandable that there is a continuous struggle for the reunion of theory and practice."[48] Myth and cult are the forms through which transcendent meaning is apprehended, and ontological reason actualized in culture. Myth and cult are necessary forms of expression "because existence resists conceptualization. Only the realm of essences admits of structural analysis."[49] They are "forms of the human consciousness which are always present. One can replace one myth by another, but one cannot remove the myth from man's spiritual life."[50] They may be couched in philosophical, scientific, artistic, political, economic, or ethical language, but they cannot be removed. Symbols, the building blocks of myth and cult, should be approached from this perspective.

II

Tillich maintains that the concept of the symbol has been lost in twentieth-century thought, and argues that the source of the problem is the disappearance of the distinction between sign and symbol, brought about with the help of medieval nominalism and contemporary analytic philosophy. Using the distinction of Martin Heidegger, his colleague at the University of Marburg, Tillich posits the distinction between sign and symbol: "Language grasps the encountered reality in terms of 'being at hand'—in the literal sense of being as an object for 'handling' or managing in order to reach ends (which may become means for other ends). This is what Heidegger has called *Zuhandensein* (being at disposal) in contrast to *Vorhandensein* (being in existence); the first form denotes a technical, the second a cognitive, relationship to reality."[51] The language of signs is the language of the ordinary technical encounter with reality, which encompasses all empirical facts and events and in which language is used as an object for manipulating or managing in order to reach desired ends. The symbolic-mythological language of spiritual experience uses the objects of ordinary experience and their linguistic expressions, but it uses them as symbols, that is, transcending the subject-object cleavage, rather than as signs, bound to the subject-object scheme. In prescientific modes of thought the sign-symbol confusion rests in using symbolic-mythological language to refer to the phenomena of ordinarily encountered reality. This category of linguistic misuse includes (1) sorcery, where language is used as a physical cause; (2) magic, where language is used as a psychic cause; and (3) suggestion, where language is used as an emotional cause. "These uses of the word are possible, but they eliminate the essence of the word, its quality as the bearer of meaning."[52] On the other hand, the sign-symbol confusion in contemporary thought more frequently rests in interpreting symbolic language as if it had the same type of referent as the language of ordinary technical experience. In identifying reality with empirical reality, positivists have given the term "symbolic" a connotation of non-real and have obscured the distinction between sign and symbol.

Tillich repeatedly emphasizes that when a person uses the phrase "only a symbol," he has completely misunderstood the meaning of symbol, confusing it with sign.[53] Symbols and signs have only one feature in common: they both "point beyond themselves to something else."[54] Although signs and symbols have this one point of identity they are substantively different. The basis for the difference in the two concepts resides in their differing relationships to that to which they point. Convention is the basis for the relationship between signs and their referents. For that reason, "the sign can be changed arbitrarily according to the demands of expediency."[55] Convention and expediency, as we shall see, are not part of the relationship of symbols with that to which they point.

It should be emphasized that symbolism is not bound to language, although language is both a prerequisite of and a constituent feature in all other media of symbolization. "*Verbum* is more than *oratio*. . . . [It] can be in everything in which the spirit expresses itself, even in the silent symbols of art, even in the works of the community and law."[56] Anything within the realm of human experience is a potential medium for symbolization. It should be emphasized that, for Tillich, the term "symbol" is not an entitative term. To raise the question, "What sort of entity is a symbol?" is to misconstrue the problem.

The first characteristic of the symbol decisively differentiates symbol from sign: symbols participate in the meaning and power of the reality to which they point. "The difference between symbol and sign is the participation in the symbolized reality which characterizes the symbol, and the non-participation in the 'pointed-to' reality which characterizes the sign."[57] The letters of the alphabet do not participate in the sounds which we may utter upon seeing the letters—being signs, the relationship is one of mere convention. On the other hand, a flag participates in the meaning and power of the group it represents; thus, persons who acknowledge it as a symbol view an attack upon the flag as an attack upon the very meaning of the group.

The second feature of the symbol is that it opens up dimensions of reality which are otherwise closed and which cannot be apprehended in any other way. A painting, for example, mediates a meaning which can be apprehended only through the experience of that particular painting. When a word becomes a symbol, it functions in the same way; it acquires imagery associated only with that particular word.

The third characteristic of the symbol, the counterpart of the second, is that it opens up "dimensions and elements of our soul [*Geist*] which correspond to the dimensions and elements of reality"[58] —dimensions within us of which we cannot become aware except through symbols. Hence, every symbol has a two-sided or double-edged function—opening up "reality in deeper levels and the human soul in special levels."[59] Stated another way, symbolic language has "an expressive power which points through the ordinary expressive possibilities of language to the unexpressible and its relation to us."[60] Apprehension of symbolic meaning is an act in which the whole existence of the person is involved, including his temporal, spatial, historical, psychological, sociological, and biological conditions.

Corresponding to the second and third characteristics of the symbol is the primary function of the symbol: the apprehension of transcendent meaning through symbolic forms produces existential knowledge, not knowledge in the sense of information, *episteme*, or *scientia*, but knowledge in the sense of "wisdom," "insight," *sapientia*, or *gnosis*. "It is the level of Being and truth as such before they split into subject and object; and, therefore, it has the character of a mystery."[61] Elsewhere, Tillich terms this dual function the "perceptibility" of the symbol: "this implies that something which is intrinsically invisible, ideal, or transcendent is made perceptible in the symbol and is in this way given objectivity."[62] This does not imply that the symbol produces objective knowledge; for by definition, transcendence implies knowledge of that which transcends the subject-object cleavage, and "a real symbol points to an object which can never become an object."[63] The perceptible element of the symbol is the imagery it evokes from the total personality. Through the expressive power of imagery, concepts become more than abstract, empty, powerless forms. They become a unity of universality and concreteness. They become symbols with transforming and healing power.

The imagery of the symbol is subject to continuous change. For "every period of human history expresses" its "encounter between the infinite in ourselves and in the whole universe in different images."[64] Furthermore, the uniqueness of every person guarantees a manifold of images perceived in every symbol. An image has two components, the actual fact and the reception of that fact, and the image "belongs both on the side of fact and on the side of reception."[65] No amount of critical or historical study can separate the two. The scholar cannot "divide the image and say, 'This aspect is reception of the fact, while this other aspect is actual fact,' for they cannot be separated. They belong together."[66] This does not mean that image and reality are incompatible terms. "Image is the way in which, in history, reality expresses itself and is handed down from one generation to the other."[67] Furthermore, for symbolic or mythical analysis, the image or impression created by the historical event or person is the decisive element. For example, in talking about Lincoln as a symbol for the American people, Tillich states that while "a living person stands behind" the symbol, "the decisive thing is how he impressed himself on the American people so that he could become a symbol."[68]

A fourth characteristic of symbols is that they cannot be invented, replaced, or produced intentionally. "They grow out of the individual or collective unconscious and cannot function without being accepted by the unconscious dimension of our being."[69] For this reason, a symbol cannot be replaced by another symbol. "Every symbol has a special function which is just it and cannot be replaced by more or less adequate symbols. . . . A symbolic word, such as the word 'God,' cannot be replaced. No symbol can be replaced when used in its special function."[70] It is for this reason that he emphasizes that the way to achieve dialogue among the world religions and political systems is not to relinquish one's religious and political symbols for the "sake of a universal concept which would be nothing but a concept."[71] A universal concept can be created, but a universal symbol cannot, and only a symbol has the healing and transforming power to overcome estrangement. Hence, the way to dialogue is "to penetrate into the depth" of one's own religious and political symbols. For in the depth of the symbol, there is a point at which the symbol itself loses importance, and "that to which it points breaks through its particularity, elevating it to spiritual freedom and with it to a vision of the spiritual presence in other expressions of the ultimate meaning of man's existence."[72] Universal meaning can only be approached indirectly through the particularity and dynamic power of the symbol.

The fifth and final characteristic common to all symbols follows as a consequence of the fourth. Like living beings, symbols are born, they grow, and they die—as distinct from signs which may be consciously invented and removed. Symbols are born within a group when the historical situation of the group is ready for them: "Out of the womb which is usually called today the 'group unconscious' or 'collective unconscious,' or whatever you want to call it—out of a group which acknowledges, in this thing, this word, this flag, or whatever it may be, its own being. It is not invented intentionally; and even if somebody would try to invent a symbol, as sometimes happens, then it becomes a symbol only if the unconscious of a group says yes to it."[73] A speaker, for example, may coin a phrase, but it does not become a symbol until it evokes a symbolic response. The speaker does not create the symbol; the speaker-audience transaction creates the symbol. Likewise, symbols cannot be destroyed or removed by human intent. They die when the "inner situation of the human group to a symbol ceases to exist."[74] Historical movements can be viewed in terms of the life cycle of the myth which propels them. A movement comes into existence with the birth of a new myth, it grows as more people respond to it, and it dies when it loses the power to produce response in the group.

The life of the symbol is accompanied by two tragically unavoidable tendencies—profanization and demonization—which pervert the transcendent character of symbolic meaning. "Profane" means "the resistance against self-transcendence under all dimensions of life."[75] Under the impact of profanization, the inexhaustible substance of meaning disappears, leaving the symbolic form empty. The symbol becomes an object. And despite its emptiness it is tenaciously maintained. The emptiness created by the profanization of symbols is all the more dangerous because it invites demonic invasions to fill the vacuum, as in the case of the emergence of Nazi Germany.

Demonization is the second way in which the transcendent character of symbolic meaning becomes perverted. Unlike the profane, the demonic does not resist self-transcendence, but rather it *identifies* itself with the transcendent. The demonic is the mythical expression for "the structural, and therefore inescapable, power of evil."[76] Tillich explains: "When we speak of 'the demonic' we mean more than failure and distortion, more than intentional evil. The demonic is a negative absolute. It is the elevation of something relative and ambiguous (something in which the negative and the positive are united) to absoluteness. The ambiguous, in which positive and negative, creative and destructive elements are mingled is considered sacred in itself, is deified."[77] A religious creed identified with the absolute, a political ideology identified with justice itself, a philosophical system identified with truth itself, an artistic style identified with beauty itself—all are examples of the demonization of symbolic forms. Transcendent meaning can only become actual through symbolic forms. But when the forms themselves are held to be transcendent, they become demonic. Because of the inevitable distortion of symbolic meaning through demonization and profanization, criticism remains a permanent necessity.

III

Signs and symbols cannot be understood or evaluated with the same critical tools. In this section we shall explicate the critical principles for evaluating symbols implicit in Tillich's writings. Throughout the discussion to follow it should be remembered that a symbol cannot be judged on a true-false continuum. Rather, it must be judged (1) on an authentic-inauthentic continuum with respect to its meaning, and (2) on an adequate-inadequate continuum with respect to its expressive and communicative power.

The literalistic interpretation of the symbol is profane because it attempts to objectify what cannot be objectified, reducing the symbol to an object; and it is demonic because it tries to raise the distorted objectification to the level of ultimacy. Hence, the first principle of criticism is the principle of deliteralization, that is, "the necessity of recognizing a symbol as a symbol and a myth as a myth."[78] The need for deliteralization is continuous, for the tendency to literalize is inherent in the subject-object cleavage of language. Symbolic language is necessary for the preservation of meaning, but it must be continually transcended and negated. To demonstrate Tillich's meaning let us use his example of the symbolic term "God." On the one hand, "God is no object for us as subjects. He is always that which precedes this division."[79] In other words, "God is a symbol for God."[80] But on the other hand, when we use the term we cannot avoid the subject-object split because "everything which becomes real to us enters the subject-object correlation,"[81] and the subject-object separation is necessary for both knowing and acting. For this reason, "atheism is the correct response to the 'objectively' existing God of literalistic thought,"[82] and "genuine religion without an element of atheism cannot be imagined."[83] For Tillich, there is no possible "atheism" in the popular conception of the term, and genuine atheism is prophetic criticism against literalistic distortions.

The literalistic distortion of symbols is manifested in all attempts to prove the "existence" of symbols and in the method of arguing to a conclusion. Apprehension of a symbol has the character of self-evidence or "existential truth," that is, "a truth which lives in the immediate self-expression of an experience."[84] Apprehension of a symbol is "not an act of cognitive affirmation within the subject-object structure of reality. Therefore, it is not subject to verification by experiment or trained experience."[85] If judged by the criteria of logic and adequacy of evidence, symbols can never be justified and are reduced to the absurd. Take, for example, all so-called arguments for the "existence of God": "Such a statement as 'a being, called God, does exist' is not an assertion of faith but a cognitive proposition without sufficient evidence. The affirmation and the negation of such statements are equally absurd. This judgment refers to all attempts that would give divine authority to statements of fact in history, mind, and nature."[86] Furthermore, he states: "God does not exist. He is being-itself beyond essence and existence. Therefore, to argue that God exists is to deny him."[87] Apprehension of a symbol is a matter of understanding verified by existential participation. And understanding and participation are interdependent. "There is no understanding . . . without participation; but without understanding the participation becomes mechanical and compulsory."[88] The first principle of criticism, then, is the protest against the literalistic perversion of genuine symbols.

The second principle of criticism is based upon the inevitable demonization of genuine symbols. This is the principle of prophetic protest "against every power which claims divine character for itself."[89] The critic must fight all claims to ultimacy: "no individual and no human group can claim a divine dignity for its moral achievements, for its sacramental power, for its sanctity, or for its doctrine. . . . It implies that there cannot be a sacred system, ecclesiastical or political; that there cannot be a sacred hierarchy with absolute authority; and that there cannot be a truth in human minds which is divine truth in itself. Consequently, the prophetic spirit must always criticize, attack, and condemn sacred authorities, doctrines, and morals."[90] The principle of protest points to a *self-critical* element involved in every genuine act of symbolic apprehension. In every authentic symbol "there is an element that judges the symbol and those who use it."[91] Every genuine symbol must include an element of self-negation: "That symbol is most adequate which expresses not only the ultimate but also its own lack of ultimacy."[92] Apprehension of symbolic meaning means intuiting in one's own symbols "the No of the Unconditional against every symbol."[93] The principle of protest does not accept any truth "as ultimate except the one that no man possesses it."[94] Any person, group, or idea which claims ultimacy for itself, lacking a principle of self-criticism, is self-destructive, destructive to others, and destructive to the pursuit of truth. It is the job of the critic to fight such claims to ultimacy in the name of the self-transcending and self-negating element of the authentic symbol.

The principle of protest includes the dialectic of tradition and reformation. Taken separately, each element becomes distorted: "the danger of tradition is demonic hubris; the danger of reformation is emptying criticism."[95] Hence, genuine criticism "does not come from outside but from the center of the tradition itself, fighting its distortions in the name of its true meaning. There is no reformation without tradition."[96] Thus, the critic of the symbol must be a part of the tradition; he must apprehend the genuine meaning of the symbol. He must perceive reformation as the permanent necessity against the demonization and profanization of genuine symbols. But the critic cannot depend upon any objective standards to guide him in a movement of reformation. It is always a matter of daring and risk: "it has no safe standards, no spiritual guaranties. It pushes forward, and it may find that it has merely forged ahead into the void and has missed its mark. And yet it cannot do other than venture and risk. . . . It denies the security of sacramental systems with inviolable forms, sacred laws, eternal structures. It questions every claim of absoluteness: it remains dynamic even if it tries to become conservative."[97] The risk of reformation may involve the disintegration of particular institutions and groups. But the risk involves the certainty that the dynamic essence of meaning "cannot be destroyed."[98] And it is the responsibility of the critic to take that risk.

The principle of prophetic protest cannot stand alone without becoming distorted and destructive. It is dependent upon the principle of form-creation. Meaning must have concrete embodiment in symbolic forms in order to retain its power. However, it is "not dependent on the special symbols in which it is expressed. It has the power to be free from every form in which it appears."[99] The relative truth of any genuine symbol in whatever form it may appear must be affirmed. The "no" of the principle of protest must be coupled with the "yes" of the principle of form-creation. Nels Ferre describes Tillich's critical dialectic: "Because his writings showed two faces, Tillich could state in his *Systematic Theology* both that incarnation . . . is indispensable to the Christian faith and also that incarnation, historically and factually speaking, is blasphemy and nonsense; or even, as he blandly told the Japanese Buddhists, that it was a matter of indifference to him as a Christian theologian whether Jesus ever lived. From within the concrete circle of faith the former statements are true and necessary, but all such statements are symbolic, lacking ultimacy. They are only analytically indispensable to the Christian faith, not historically or *in reality*."[100] Unless one recognizes the relativity of the symbols of his group, dialogue with other groups not sharing those symbols is impossible.

A symbol cannot be fought effectively on the basis of scientific or practical criticism. Myth and cult, of which a particular symbol is a part, are necessary forms of human consciousness and, therefore, necessary forms of expression: "An existential protest against myth and cult is possible only in the power of myth and cult."[101] To negate a symbol means to affirm another symbol. The principles of affirmation and negation must be kept together in the method of the critic:

> It is a general axiom concerning all being that the negative can manifest itself only in connection with something positive (as the lie can exist

only through the element of truth in it). According to this axiom, we must say that protest cannot exist without a "Gestalt" to which it belongs. The Gestalt embraces itself and the protest against itself; it comprises form and the negation of form. There is no "absolute" negation and there is no "absolute" protest—absolute in the literary sense of "absolved from any involvement." Negation, if it lives, is involved in affirmation; and protest, if it lives, is involved in form. . . . Its "No" would fall into nothingness without the creativity of its "Yes." [102]

The union of protest and creation implies that "the symbol is not simply rejected but criticized and by this criticism it is changed." [103] And the transformation of the symbol implies a transformation of the social group which affirms it. "A successful struggle for the purification of the symbols transforms them and creates a changed social group." [104] Even if the group rejects the judgment of the critic, it "does not remain the same as it was before. It may be weakened or it may be hardened in its demonic and profane traits; in either case it is transformed." [105] The critic's task is the preservation of the substance of meaning. Fulfilling that goal may necessitate the discovery of new symbolic forms. The twentieth-century movements of Naziism and Communism, for example, "transformed ordinary concepts, events, and persons into myths, and ordinary performances into rituals; therefore they had to be fought with other myths and rituals." [106] In short, effective criticism involves either the restoration of the genuine meaning of the symbol, or the discovery and communication of counter-symbols.

Authentic form-creation stands under the polar demand of form-affirmation and form-transcendence. When and to the extent that the principles are considered separately they are perverted. The principle of form-affirmation means that the structural demands of cultural forms must not be violated. For symbols emerge *through* cultural forms, not outside of them. Logical principles must be adhered to in the cognitive act, aesthetic rules in the artistic act. A symbolic document may emerge from a parliamentary debate, but the rules of parliamentary law must not be violated in the process. But at the same time the symbol transcends its form. The principle of form-transcendence means that the cultural form expresses transcendent meaning only "if there is an ecstatic, form-transcending quality in them," only if transcendent meaning "breaks into the finite forms and drives them beyond themselves." [107] When the principle of form-affirmation is effective apart from form-transcendence, symbols become empty, profane forms, as in legalism, conventionalism, aestheticism, and intellectualism. "A form which is too rigid to be transcended becomes by degrees more and more meaningless—though not wrong. It is first felt as a protection from transcendent interference, then as the embodiment of formal correctness, and last as empty formalism." [108] When, on the other hand, the principle of form-transcendence is alone effective, the symbol becomes demonic, and its adherents become fanatical and destructive: "[They are] driven to repress in everyone and every group that conscience of form which demands honest submission to the structural necessities of cultural creation. For example, they violate artistic integrity in the name of a sacred (or politically expedient) style; or they undercut the scientific honesty which leads to radical questions about nature, man, and history; or they destroy personal humanity in the name of a demonically distorted fanatical faith."[109] The critic must understand the structural demands of the particular cultural form if he is to even recognize the repressive effects of demonized symbols.

A fourth critical principle of symbolic forms is the principle of contemporaneity. Based upon the assumption of the inseparable unity of knowledge and situation, the principle of contemporaneity affirms that in every symbolic form "the eternal element must be expressed in relation to a 'present situation.' "[110] The "situation" of the present does not refer to a person's psychological state or a group's sociological condition. "Situation" refers "to the scientific and artistic, the economic, political, and ethical *forms* in which they express their interpretation of existence."[111] Meaningful symbolic forms must use the conceptual tools of the present situation; otherwise they have no power for transforming the present. The symbol once embodied in the term "sin," for example, has lost its genuine meaning and become moralistically distorted. To be effective today the symbol must be embodied in the terms of our own self-interpretation, terms such as "estrangement," "alienation," and "existential anxiety." The inseparable unity of knowledge and situation cannot be broken without destroying both knowledge and situation.

It should be noted at this point that contemporaneity does not refer to the popular communication of symbols, but refers to the adequacy of symbols themselves. Put in Platonic terms, dialectic is not rhetoric, and rhetorical effectiveness does not prove dialectical validity. Dialectical terms are themselves symbolic forms, a unity of concrete situation and transcendent meaning, of conceptual authenticity and expressive adequacy, and they can only be discovered and interpreted through existential participation in the situation.

The principle of contemporaneity encompasses the polar elements of verity and adaptation. If taken separately, verity becomes demonic absolutism and adaptation becomes emptying relativization. Affirmation of verity alone is a demonic perversion, for it destroys the dynamic element of truth and distorts the static element by raising the static element to the position of absolute validity. Affirmation of verity without adaptation "destroys the humble honesty of the search for truth, it splits the conscience of its thoughtful adherents, and it makes them fanatical because they are forced to suppress elements of truth of which they are dimly aware."[112] The element of adaptation, taken alone, produces an empty relativization and creates a vacuum to be filled by new demonic distortions. Adaptation without verity leaves the content "in continual danger of being surrendered for the sake of accommodation."[113] Without the corrective of criticism, the symbol "would lose itself in the relativities of the 'situation'; it would become a 'situation' itself—for instance, the religious nationalism of the so-called German Christians" during the Nazi era. [114] The critic must strive to preserve the dynamic tension of the polarity of verity and adaptation.

Although the process of adaptation to the present situation may be consciously and intentionally denied, it is never possible to completely escape the adaptive process. This necessity is rooted in the adaptive dynamics of language "since language is the basic and all-pervasive expression of every situation."[115] Hence, no historical movement that has fought "for verity as against accommodation" has "escaped the necessity of adaptation" itself. [116] A careful analysis of the language of such a movement will reveal that is has indeed adapted to its cultural-historical situation. The real problem of the claim to verity alone is the absence of its adaptation being a conscious and intentional process. Only when adaptation becomes a conscious process can it be subjected to rational criteria.

A final criterion in the evaluation of symbols is the principle of expressive adequacy. Symbols "must be criticized on the basis of their power to express what they are supposed to express." [117] " 'Adequacy' of expression means the power of expressing an ultimate concern in such a way that it creates reply, action, communication." [118] Symbols capable of expressing transcendent meaning so as to create reply, action, and communication are those which not only express conscious beliefs, values, and attitudes, but which also express unconscious drives and images. If the ultimate concern of someone "expresses itself in symbols which are adequate to his unconscious strivings, these strivings cease to be chaotic. They do not need repression, because they have received 'sublimation' and are united with the conscious activities of the person." [119] Expressive adequacy is possible only if the symbol is born out of the present cultural situation. From the point of view of the artist, expressive adequacy implies expressive honesty. An artistic style, for example, is dishonest if it is an imitation of a stylistic tradition. "An artistic style is honest only if it expresses the real situation of the artist and the cultural period to which he belongs." [120] The real situation is the existential depth of the present, which can only be grasped through participation. "The depth, the dynamic structure of a historical situation, cannot be understood by a detached description of as many facts as possible. It must be experienced in life and action. The depth of every present is its power to transform the past into a future." [121] For this reason, the expression of the present situation is a matter of risk and decision, which becomes symbolic only when it creates action, response, and communication.

The importance of expressive adequacy, both as a criterion for critical judgments and as a requirement for effective criticism, deserves emphasis. Adequate expression transforms what it expresses. "Expression gives life to what is expressed—it gives power to stabilize and power to transform." [122] Expressive forms which are not able to transform are inauthentic, whereas authentic expression has "critical and revolutionary" power. [123] Here lies the distinction between authentic art and propaganda: Authentic art is revelation and dishonest art is propaganda. [124] It is the task of the critic to distinguish between the two, for he is part of the "vanguard" which "precedes a great change in the spiritual and social-psychological situation." [125]

The method of the critic is dialectical. Tillich's dynamic dialectic is based on polarities, not antitheses, within one structure, each of which is necessary for the existence of the other and for the whole. The tension within polarities is a permanent, structural tension in life and history. The tension remains creative as long as the contrasting poles are kept together, but becomes destructive when they break apart. The task of the critic, then, is to maintain the unity of the dialectical polarities of the symbol—the polarities of expressive adequacy and conceptual validity, of form and meaning, of verity and adaptation, of tradition and reformation. But there can be no real synthesis of dialectical polarities, for "an absolute stage as the end of the dialectical process is a contradiction of the dialectical principle." [126] All synthesis remains symbolic, subject to the judgment of both Yes and No. The symbolic synthesis, fragmentary and transitory as it may be, is necessary for effective criticism. For a demonic or profane symbol can be fought effectively only on the basis of another symbol.

There are no objective or universal standards to guide the critic in this endeavor. The critic must be driven beyond all theoretical formulations, for it is "impossible to form useful universal concepts of cultural ideas" because abstraction destroys what is essential, [127] and "the standpoint of the systematic thinker belongs to the heart of the matter itself." [128] Interpretation cannot be performed in detachment. It demands a creative participation in the situation and an openness to the critical principles which emerge. And beyond this Tillich would remind us that criticism is an attitude of humility, an acceptance of ambiguity, and an act of courage.

1. Paul Tillich, *Theology of Culture*, ed. Robert C. Kimball (New York: Oxford University Press, 1959), p. 53.

2. John Herman Randall, Jr., "The Ontology of Paul Tillich," *The Theology of Paul Tillich*, eds. Charles W. Kegley and Robert W. Bretall (New York: Macmillan, 1952), p. 161.

3. Charles Hartshorne, "Tillich and the Nontheological Meanings of Theological Terms," *Paul Tillich: Retrospect and Future*, ed. T. A. Kantonen (Nashville and New York: Abingdon Press, 1966), p. 19.

4. Cf. Myrvin F. Christopherson, "Speech and the 'New' Philosophies Revisited," *Central States Speech Journal*, 14 (February, 1963), 5–11; Raymond E. Anderson, "Kierkegaard's Theory of Communication," *Speech Monographs*, 30 (March, 1963), 1–14; Robert L. Scott, "Some Implications of Existentialism for Rhetoric," *Central States Speech Journal*, 15 (November, 1964), 267–278; Michael Gilati, "A Rhetoric for the Subjectivist in a World of Untruth: The Tasks and Strategies of Soren Kierkegaard," *Quarterly Journal of Speech*, 54 (December, 1969), 372–380; Richard L. Johannesen, "The Emerging Concept of Communication as Dialogue," *Quarterly Journal of Speech*, 57 (December, 1971), 373–382.

5. Paul Tillich, *Systematic Theology* (Chicago: University of Chicago Press, 1951), I, 124.

6. *Ibid.*, II, 33.

7. Paul Tillich, *On the Boundary: An Autobiographical Sketch* (New York: Charles Scribner's Sons, 1966), p. 82.

8. Tillich, *Systematic Theology*, II, 27.

9. Tillich, *Theology of Culture*, p. 117.

10. *Ibid.*, p. 119.

11. *Ibid.*

12. Tillich, *Systematic Theology*, II, 68.

13. Tillich, *On the Boundary*, p. 83.

14. Tillich, *Systematic Theology*, I, 170–171.

15. *Ibid.*, p. 170. Cf. Paul Tillich, *Morality and Beyond* (New York: Harper and Row, 1963), pp. 19–20; Paul Tillich, *My Search for Absolutes* (New York: Simon and Schuster, 1967), pp. 72–76.

16. *Ibid.*, p. 176.

17. Paul Tillich, *Perspectives on 19th and 20th Century Protestant Theology*, ed. Carl E. Braaten (New York: Harper and Row, 1967), p. 245.

18. Paul Tillich, *Ultimate Concern: Tillich in Dialogue*, ed. D. Mackenzie Brown (New York: Harper and Row, 1965), p. 56.

19. Tillich, *Systematic Theology*, III, 69. Cf. *Ibid.*, II, 31.

20. *Ibid.*

21. *Ibid.*, p. 254.

22. *Ibid.*, p. 255.

23. *Ibid.*, p. 253.

24. *Ibid.*

25. *Ibid.*, p. 254.

26. *Ibid.*

27. *Ibid.*

28. *Ibid.*, p. 255.

29. *Ibid.*, I, 123.

30. Paul Tillich, *Biblical Religion and the Search for Ultimate Reality* (Chicago: University of Chicago Press, 1955), pp. 31–32.

31. Tillich, *Systematic Theology*, III, 61.

32. *Ibid.*, p. 62.

33. *Ibid.*

34. *Ibid.*, p. 65.

35. *Ibid.*, p. 308.

36. Tillich, *Biblical Religion and the Search for Ultimate Reality*, p. 31.

37. Tillich, *Morality and Beyond*, p. 19.

38. Tillich, *Theology of Culture*, pp. 198–199.

39. Tillich, *Systematic Theology*, I, 72.

40. *Ibid.*, p. 73.

41. Paul Tillich, *What Is Religion?*, ed. James Luther Adams (New York, Evanston, and London: Harper and Row, 1969), pp. 165–166.

42. *Ibid.*, p. 53.

43. Paul Tillich, "Vertical and Horizontal Thinking," *American Scholar*, 15 (Winter, 1945–46), 103.

44. *Ibid.*

45. *Ibid.*

46. Tillich, *Systematic Theology*, I, 91.

47. *Ibid.*, p. 92.

48. *Ibid.* Cf. *What Is Religion?*, pp. 101–121.

49. Paul Tillich, *The Courage to Be* (New Haven and London: Yale University Press, 1952), p. 127.

50. Paul Tillich, *Dynamics of Faith* (New York: Harper and Row, 1957), p. 50.

51. Tillich, *Systematic Theology*, III, 59. Cf. Martin Heidegger, *Being and Time*, trans. John Macquarrie and Edward Robinson (New York and Evanston: Harper and Row, 1962).

52. Tillich, *Biblical Religion and the Search for Ultimate Reality*, p. 32.

53. Paul Tillich, "Reply to Interpretation and Criticism," in *The Theology of Paul Tillich*, pp. 334–335. Cf. *Systematic Theology*, I, 131.

54. Tillich, *Theology of Cultures*, p. 54.

55. Tillich, *Systematic Theology*, I, 239. Cf. his *Dynamics of Faith*, p. 55.

56. Paul Tillich, *The Interpretation of History*, trans. N. A. Rasetzki and Elsa L. Talmey (New York and London: Charles Scribner's Sons, 1936), p. 238.

57. Tillich, *Theology of Culture*, pp. 54–55.

58. Tillich, *Dynamics of Faith*, p. 42.

59. Tillich, *Theology of Culture*, p. 57.

60. Tillich, *Systematic Theology*, I, 124.

61. Paul Tillich, *The Protestant Era*, trans. James Luther Adams (Chicago: University of Chicago Press, 1948), p. 65.

62. Paul Tillich, "The Religious Symbol," *Daedalus*, 88 (Summer, 1958), 3.

63. *Ibid.*, p. 5.

64. Tillich, *Perspectives on 19th and 20th Century Protestant Theology*, p. 101.

65. Tillich, *The Interpretation of History*, p. 165.

66. Tillich, *Systematic Theology*, III, 329.

67. *Ibid.*, II, 90.

68. Tillich, *Ultimate Concern*, p. 155.

69. Tillich, *Dynamics of Faith*, p. 43.

70. Tillich, *Theology of Culture*, pp. 57–58.

71. Paul Tillich, *Christianity and the Encounter of the World Religions* (New York: Columbia University Press, 1963), p. 97.

72. *Ibid.* Cf. Paul Tillich, *The Future of Religions*, ed. Jerald C. Brauer (New York: Harper and Row, 1966), pp. 52–63.

73. Tillich, *Theology of Culture*, p. 58.

74. *Ibid.*

75. Tillich, *Systematic Theology*, III, 87.

76. Tillich, *The Protestant Era*, p. xvi.

77. Tillich, *My Search for Absolutes*, pp. 132–133. Cf. his *On the Boundary*, pp. 79–80, and *What Is Religion?*, pp. 85–89.

78. Tillich, *Dynamics of Faith*, p. 50.

79. Tillich, *Theology of Culture*, p. 25.

80. Tillich, *Dynamics of Faith*, p. 46.

81. Tillich, *Theology of Culture*, p. 25.

82. Tillich, *On the Boundary*, p. 65.

83. Tillich, *Theology of Culture*, p. 25.

84. Paul Tillich, "Autobiographical Reflections," *The Theology of Paul Tillich*, p. 16.

85. Tillich, *Systematic Theology*, III, 131.

86. *Ibid.*

87. *Ibid.*, I, 204–205.

88. *Ibid.*, III, 194.

89. Tillich, *The Protestant Era*, p. 168.

90. *Ibid.*, p. 226.

91. Tillich, *Systematic Theology*, III, 206.

92. Tillich, *Dynamics of Faith*, p. 97.

93. Tillich, *What Is Religion?*, p. 97.

94. Tillich, *Dynamics of Faith*, p. 98.

95. Tillich, *Systematic Theology*, III, 183.

96. *Ibid.*, p. 184.

97. Tillich, *The Protestant Era*, p. 215.

98. Tillich, *Systematic Theology*, III, 185.

99. *Ibid.*, II, 165.

100. Nels F. S. Ferre, "Tillich and the Nature of Transcendence," *Paul Tillich: Retrospect and Future*, ed. T. A. Kantonen (Nashville and New York: Abingdon Press, 1966), p. 7.

101. Tillich, *Christianity and the Encounter of the World Religions*, p. 93.

102. Tillich, *The Protestant Era*, pp. 206–207.

103. Tillich, *Systematic Theology*, III, 206.

104. *Ibid.*, p. 139.

105. *Ibid.*, p. 213.

106. Tillich, *Christianity and the Encounter of the World Religions*, p. 93.

107. Tillich, *Systematic Theology*, III, 187.

108. *Ibid.*, p. 183.

109. *Ibid.*, p. 188.

110. Tillich, *The Protestant Era*, p. 214.

111. Tillich, *Systematic Theology*, I, 3–4 (italics added).

112. *Ibid.*, p. 3.

113. *Ibid.*, III, 186.

114. *Ibid.*, I, 5.

115. *Ibid.*, p. 7.

116. *Ibid.*, III, 186.

117. *Ibid.*, II, 152.

118. Tillich, *Dynamics of Faith*, p. 96.

119. *Ibid.*, p. 107.

120. Tillich, *Theology of Culture*, p. 48.

121. Tillich, *The Protestant Era*, p. 214.

122. Tillich, *Systematic Theology*, III, 198.

123. Tillich, *The Courage to Be*, p. 147.

124. Paul Tillich, "Existentialist Aspects of Modern Art," *Christianity and the Existentialists*, ed. Carl Michalson (New York: Charles Scribner's Sons, 1965), p. 147.

125. Tillich, *The Courage to Be*, p. 146.

126. Tillich, *The Protestant Era*, p. 42.

127. Tillich, *What Is Religion?*, p. 156.

128. *Ibid.*, p. 155.

Persistent Problems
in Rhetorical Criticism

MALCOLM O. SILLARS

In her lectures at Louisiana State University in 1959 Marie Hochmuth Nichols recognized that there was a need to find "an orderly methodology for the analysis of discourse."[1] Despite some notable efforts, including those of Professor Nichols herself, that need has not been met. There is, however, a substantial body of comment on the nature of rhetorical criticism from writers in the field of speech communication. In these statements a variety of critical approaches may be identified and differentiated by the issues which separate them.

Contemporary statements which define the approaches are usually considered to have begun in 1925. "In our own times, at least by 1925," Nichols notes, "rhetorical critics began to find their way. Herbert Wichelns' 'Literary Criticism of Oratory' in that year undoubtedly has had something to do with giving impetus to a more systematic approach to criticism and to what might be considered something of a critical movement among rhetoricians."[2]

Wichelns defined the essential nature of the rhetorical act and designated the elements and relationships which he believed explained rhetorical criticism. Although his study has been questioned on a number of points which forty-five years of experience with "The Literary Criticism of Oratory" should have revealed, it provided the first modern statement of some critical precepts which each later theorist could question and refine in the search for an approach to rhetorical criticism.

Although some attention was given in the next two decades to defining approaches to rhetorical criticism, the major thrust developed after World War II,[3] and can be dated roughly from 1948 with the appearance of *Speech Criticism* by Lester Thonssen and A. Craig Baird.[4] Five years earlier, in compiling the first two volumes of *A History and Criticism of American Public Address*, William Norwood Brigance did not include a statement on the nature of rhetorical criticism. Yet in 1954, Marie Hochmuth Nichols introduced volume three with an essay on "The Criticism of Rhetoric."[5]

A useful starting point for one who wishes to develop an approach to rhetorical criticism is the examination of the articles and books published since Wichelns's essay, and particularly since the publication of *Speech Criticism*. Few writers claim to provide a complete understanding of the practice of rhetorical criticism but their writings provide a basis for understanding the variety of critical approaches and indicate that rhetorical criticism in the field of speech communication is diverse in its practices.

However, there does seem to be a relatively limited number of problems which have concerned these writers. The answers provided to them help to define the approaches to rhetorical criticism. The purpose of this essay is to clarify these problems and answers. Although the essay reveals some of my biases, it does not argue for a particular point of view. Rather, it clarifies some of the options a rhetorical critic has in defining his approach. This essay deals with eight questions, the answers to which will provide a fair outline of each critic's approach. In general, these questions investigate the broader issues of how one defines the rhetorical act, understands the interrelations among its constituents, and identifies the bases for judging it.

The first three questions ask for a basic definition of rhetorical criticism, the nature of the object examined, and the relative importance of the variables in the rhetorical act. The next four questions look at four factors (effect, intent, morality, and rationality) which may serve as bases for judgment. The final question is one of pluralism versus monism in method.

1. *What is the relative importance of the material the critic seeks to examine and the method he chooses?* Walter Fisher speaks clearly for a number of writers who argue that material, not method, is the central defining characteristic of rhetorical criticism: "The most critical question in rhetorical criticism is not, in my judgment, what method is most appropriate and useful in the analysis and evaluation of speeches, but what is our concept of speech as an object of criticism."[6] A related position is taken by Lloyd F. Bitzer but his notion of material contains an interesting difference. For him the subject matter of rhetoric is a "rhetorical discourse" or a "rhetorical work." "Rhetorical and non-rhetorical discourse" can be differentiated. But "rhetorical discourse" is for Bitzer broader than message. It is "the situation which generates it" which gives "rhetorical discourse . . . its character-as-rhetorical."[7] In Bitzer's view, some messages are nonrhetorical and some situations which produce no messages are rhetorical.

Other writers respond differently to this question. For them rhetorical criticism is not defined by the material or even the situation. Like the "Committee on the Advancement and Refinement of Rhetorical Criticism" of the National Conference on Rhetoric, they emphasize "the nature of the critic's inquiry" rather than "the materials studied."[8]

In actual practice, the division between those who emphasize material and situation and those who emphasize method is not as clear-cut as I have thus far portrayed it. A number of theorists make no clear distinction between material and method. Certainly Herbert Wichelns and Lester Thonssen and A. Craig Baird, while primarily concerned with outlining a method of rhetorical criticism, limit the notion of rhetorical materials. For them, a "rhetorical act" is associated with a "speaking performance." Wichelns considers written forms of persuasion such as editorials and pamphlets suitable for critical examination but bases his approach to criticism on the unique characteristics of the subject matter "oratory."[9] Donald C. Bryant notes that "rhetoric is method not subject," but also limits subject to "fundamental rhetorical situations." "What makes a situation rhetorical," he says, "is the focus upon accomplishing something predetermined and directional with an audience."[10]

Thus one approach to rhetorical criticism accepts any criticism of an event which is defined broadly or narrowly as rhetorical; another insists upon a particular method of criticism which can be applied to any event. The first might accept as rhetorical criticism a discussion of the design of the chairs at a national political convention while the second might accept the examination of a football game in rhetorical terms as rhetorical criticism. Along the spectrum a wide variety of approaches may be distinguished. Some believe that there are different kinds of rhetorical acts, each of which requires a different rhetorical method. They believe, in Wayne Brockriede's words, that method must "be adjusted to meet the dynamics of rhetorical practices."[11] That point of view will be discussed later in this essay under the question of pluralism versus monism.

Coordinated with the question posed here—to what extent an approach to rhetorical criticism should be defined in terms of material or method—is the question of which materials are most appropriate.

2. *What materials does the critic find appropriate for rhetorical criticism?* Because rhetoric began in ancient times as the rationale of oratory and because our profession in modern times arose from an interest in public speaking there is a strong tendency to think of speeches (even more narrowly, formal public addresses) as synonymous with rhetoric. Wichelns titled his article "The Literary Criticism of Oratory." Thonssen and Baird's *Speech Criticism* reflects the public-speaking orientation of much rhetorical criticism. For example, Albert Crofts says that the rhetorical critic's "primary limitation is that he must focus on public speaking, *per se.*"[12]

Many writers broaden the appropriate subject matter to include written as well as spoken messages,[13] including even nonverbal communication.[14] The report of the "Committee on the Advancement and Refinement of Rhetorical Criticism" of the National Conference on Rhetoric asserts:

> . . . rhetorical criticism may be applied to any human act, process, product, or artifact which, in the critic's view, may formulate, sustain,

or modify attention, perceptions, attitudes, or behavior. . . . The rhetorical critic has the freedom to pursue his study of subjects with suasory potential or persuasive effects in whatever setting he may find them, ranging from rock music and put-ons, to architecture and public forums, to ballet and international politics.[15]

Even this broad statement of appropriate materials limits rhetorical criticism to "subjects with suasory potential or persuasive effects." Virtually every writer imposes some limitations, if not on the basis of materials, then on some other ground. Some limitation would seem essential since the critic cannot say everything about everything. And rhetorical criticism, if accepted to be any comment about any thing, would lose any distinctive characteristics. Rhetorical criticism *per se* would then have no significance. Perhaps more important limitations than those on the nature of the material studied are the limits placed on rhetorical criticism by emphasizing for study certain variables in the rhetorical act.

3. *Which variables in the rhetorical act are most important in defining the critic's approach?* Even the propagators of the most completely method-oriented critical approaches acknowledge that rhetorical criticism deals with a communication situation for which gross variables can be identified. As a minimum, the four (source, message, environment, critic) identified in Lawrence Rosenfield's "Anatomy of Criticial Discourse"[16] should be acceptable. Rosenfield makes message the essential variable. He asserts that "the rhetorical critic not only fastens his observation to M [message] ; he does so in the conviction that the message is fundamental to an appreciation of the entire event."[17] The emphasis on message limits the critic's alternatives. It rules out, for instance, a critic's judgment about the general character of the source or his comments about the relationship between the source and the environment. Comments which note that people voted for Eisenhower because they knew he was a great man do not qualify as rhetorical criticism under Rosenfield's restriction.

From this insistence that message is the essential variable Rosenfield constructs six *rhetorical* foci: (SM) Source-Message, (ME) Message-Environment, (MC) Message-Critic, (SME) Source-Message-Environment, (SMC) Source-Message-Critic, and (MEC) Message-Environment-Critic. Thus it is the interaction of message with one or more of the other variables which defines each focus. Since Rosenfield has reviewed the foci rather carefully I will deal with them in the next few paragraphs only generally in terms of their source, environment, and critic emphases.

There are some who assert that source is as central as message to the criticism of the rhetorical act. It is not surprising that a concern with ghostwriting should lead Ernest Bormann to write: "Indeed, so common is the practice [of ghostwriting] today, that the first question a critic of contemporary public address ought to ask himself when he contemplates a research project is . . . 'I wonder who wrote it for him?' For the rhetorical critic this question is not an expression of idle curiosity but an important criterion for evaluating the difficulty and worth of his project."[18] Awareness of ghostwriting is clearly related to a source-message—oriented criticism and the emphasis may, as it does in Bormann's case, make such critics seem significantly less concerned about environment.[19]

Others, while not specifically interested in ghostwriting, also find that the source of the message is one of the central factors in their critical approaches.[20] Brockriede provides an interesting comparison between classical and contemporary rhetorical acts. In part he says that the latter are more complex and consequently "The contemporary student who wants to develop an Aristotelian approach to rhetoric . . . must concern himself with the interaction of speaker and audience as well as with the discourse itself. He must describe how speakers relate to their various audiences in status. Such observations, and others, when systematized in a meaningful way, may explain how ideas are adjusted to people and people to ideas."[21] Quite clearly, in his reexamination of the rhetorical act he attributes to the source an importance equal to environment and even message.

To other writers source is relatively unimportant. For them information about the nature and purpose of the source is, perhaps, interesting but not central to understanding a rhetorical act. They prefer a message-environment focus.[22] They are by far the largest group of writers from the field of speech communication, an understandable situation in view of the effects orientation which has been pervasive since Wichelns.

On the other hand, the message-critic focus[23] is practiced less among critics from speech communication. It is, of course, a quite respectable position in literary criticism. In such a focus the critic acts as the receiver and responds to the message as a sensitive and perceptive observer. There is less concern with an attempt to secure detachment from the object under examination than in the case of some source- and environment-oriented approaches. The message-critic focus is not the only one, however, where the critic admits to active involvement. Rosenfield's M-E-C focus clearly indicates that the critic is either unable or unwilling to function with complete detachment. Such a critic looks for the relationship between message and environment, as he sees it, and does not try to achieve the complete objectivity the M-E critic attempts.

No matter how introspective a M-C, a M-E-C, or a S-M-E-C critic may be, he does focus on a message and his relation to it. Such a position is quite distinct from the claim that any comment about any aspect of the situation is worthwhile rhetorical criticism.[24] There is an increasing number of writers, however, who desire a broader base of criticism even within a message focus.

They acknowledge that one cannot say everything, that time, space, and emphasis impose limitations on the criticism. But they argue for pluralism wherein emphasis may shift depending upon the nature of the rhetorical act or the inclination of the critic. The question of pluralism will be examined later.

Thus far we have addressed three questions which help to define the nature of a critical approach: the role of method and material in defining rhetorical criticism, the nature of the subjects of rhetorical criticism, and the relative importance of potential variables in the critical act. The next four questions deal with problems which define the critic's basis of judgment.

4. *What significance and definition does the critic give to effect in his approach?* Rhetorical criticism, says Wichelns, "is not concerned with permanence, nor yet with beauty. It is concerned with effect. It regards a speech as a communication to a specific audience, and holds its business to be the analysis and appreciation of the orator's method of imparting his ideas to his hearers."[25] This statement has been the focus of what well may be the most important modern controversy in rhetorical criticism.

Its resolution is complicated by the confusion between effect and intent. While Wichelns's statement is about effect, his concern for "the orator's method of imparting his ideas" implies that knowing the speaker's intent is essential to understanding the effect of the message. Much confusion has resulted because writers who object to so judging a message have frequently assumed that intent was the natural handmaiden of effect. Says Robert Scott, "If we take the criterion of *effect* in its extreme, the perfect criticism might result from discovering, perhaps in his diary, the speaker's statement of his *intent* and then unearthing direct evidence, perhaps a nice shift-of-opinion ballot, of the audience's response. The supreme judgment of the speech could be made without reading the speech."[26] Effect and intent need not be linked as we shall see below in section five.

Even when we do not confuse effect with intent, the problem is a major one. Many since Wichelns have argued for,[27] and others have reacted against, effect as a standard of judgment.[28] The arguments against judging by effect have been cogent and are not easily brushed aside. Numerous attempts have been made to justify criteria for judging the effect of a message on receivers.

Everyone seems agreed that judging a message by its effect does not mean that the most effective person rhetorically is the one who won. Richard Nixon was not necessarily a more effective communicator than Hubert Humphrey or George McGovern in the presidential elections of 1968 and 1972 because he got more votes. Human decisions are not based on rhetoric alone. Rhetoric is often overshadowed by events the communicator cannot control, such as the sudden British-French move against Egypt in the last moments of the 1956 presidential campaign. Similarly, other messages may be as influential or more influential than those under examination. Political oratory, for instance, may not be as important in election results as stories spread by word of mouth, endorsements, written propaganda, or newspaper editorials.

Some writers have taken the position that the effects of communication need not be immediate. It may very well be that the real effects occur later as new facts come to light making persuasive what was not so before. John Lee Jellicorse argues that "emphasis on immediate audiences is an accidental product of persuasion's long association with oral discourse." He claims that "while concern for results is inherent in rhetorical criticism, concern for *immediate* audience is not inherent."[29]

Thomas R. Nilsen also extends effect to include the influence of a message beyond the immediate occasion: "The evaluation of effect," he says, "should be a judgment about the contribution the speech makes to, or the influence it exerts in furthering, the purposes of the society upon which it has its impact."[30] In a later statement he sees effect including "what the speech indirectly implies, for man and the society in which he lives."[31] Thus, any assessment of effect for Nilsen includes all judgments which deal with the social consequences of the rhetorical act no matter how far removed from the immediate proposal. It would not be a long step from Nilsen's position to the point of viewing long-range aesthetic criteria which can never be completely divorced from social action as standards for effect.

In any event, it is clear that much of the energy spent attacking the application of the effect of messages as a criterion for rhetorical criticism has been misspent because no theorist since Wichelns has insisted that the rhetorical value of a message is determined only by its immediate effect on immediate receivers. "Effect" can be immediate or long range, physical or philosophical, tentative or complete.

The current need is not to question Wichelns's original immediate effect standard. That has been thoroughly done. The central problem is a satisfactory limitation of its scope. If effect is a criterion it must be clearly differentiated from other standards of evaluation. To say that the scope of effect criteria ranges from immediate audience responses to a critic's long-range aesthetic responses is to say precious little; such a broad use of the term has little meaning.

Another alternative to careful definition is to question effect altogether. What may a rhetorical critic say about the effectiveness of a message which by the effect standard seems a failure, but which some critics find outstanding? Abraham Lincoln's "Gettysburg Address" has been identified as a speech which cannot be explained by effect criteria.[32] Edwin Black's discussion of the Coatesville address is surely a more obvious case. John Jay Chapman went to Coatesville to speak against a lynching he had read about a year earlier, hired a hall, and delivered a speech to three people—a friend, an old black woman, and a local spy. The speech was found "strange and moving" by Edmund Wilson in 1938, twenty-six years after it was delivered.[33]

One could say that the Coatesville address had an effect on the friend, the old black woman, and the spy, but few would count that as a significant effect. One could also look for long-range social effects but, at least from the evidence Black gives, there probably are none. One could also say it had no immediate or long-range effect of any social consequence and that, although it is interesting, it has no rhetorical significance. Effects criteria, however, cannot comfortably be stretched to the point where one says that the Coatesville address was effective because it had an effect on Edmund Wilson. Such a view merely supports Message-Critic criticism. To call it effect makes effect a meaningless term with unlimited scope. One would be better off either to declare such materials not *rhetorically* significant or to drop effect criteria.

In sum, effectiveness as a standard for a critical approach remains a central concept in the literature of speech communication. It cannot be dismissed lightly but if it is to be useful its weaknesses must be examined and its scope defined carefully. If it is to be dropped its replacement must be carefully thought out. With or without effect criteria, the role of the intent of the source must be considered.

5. *What significance does the critic give to intent in his approach?* Intent as a standard for literary criticism has been seriously questioned under the rubric of the "intentional fallacy."[34] For scholars from the field of speech communication, the most influential literary critic is, of course, Kenneth Burke, who questioned intent as a standard of rhetorical criticism with the statement that "the key term for the 'old' rhetoric was 'persuasion' and its stress was upon deliberate design. The key term for the 'new' rhetoric would be 'identification' which can include a partially unconscious factor in appeal."[35] Nilsen's statement is stronger. "Certainly, the effects a speech *has* are more important to society than the effects it was or is *intended to have*."[36] Such a position is clearly compatible with critics who emphasize the relationship of message and environment. For them, knowledge of the source's intent, or even who the source is, is an interesting, perhaps useful, but not essential piece of information.

But much critical theory is oriented to intent.[37] Why is it questioned? Because, its detractors say, of the difficulties of knowing the speaker's intent and because messages may have unintended effects the critic finds worthy of note.

There are cases wherein a person has clearly specified his intent for a given message, made decisions consciously to fulfill it, and left evidence about both the intent and the method of fulfillment. It is always possible, of course, that such statements are in error or even deliberately misleading. Then the source-oriented critic must examine the available evidence with great care to develop some assurance that the person's statements about his intent were accurate or that his friends recorded him correctly. The critic rarely can be sure. He deals in probabilities and makes the best argument he can for his judgment. His problem in dealing with intent is perhaps no more difficult than evaluating effects, beauty, form, social value, or any other criteria of evaluation.

But the problem of arguing a person's intent is even more complex than that of ferreting out possibly inaccurate statements of intent. Many message senders, perhaps most, leave little direct evidence of their intent. The critic is frequently forced to judge intent not from external evidence but from internal analysis as when the critic observes that the form which Shakespeare gave to Mark Antony's speech for Caesar clearly indicates that Shakespeare's Antony intended to foment rebellion.

There is another and perhaps more serious difficulty with intent. What do we say of the message with a significant effect unintended by the source? William Jennings Bryan intended his "definition of a business man" to be his most important argument in his speech to the Chicago convention, but it received little immediate attention.[38] He also noted that he did not realize until after the speech that he has used the crown of thorns and cross of gold metaphors.[39] Bryan's various explanations are confusing, but for our purposes, they make it clear that to judge by the intent leads to the judgment that the speech was less effective than most critics believe.

Despite difficulties intent is a significant question. It is particularly important for the critic who regards the source of the message to be central to his critical system. It would seem, however, that one ought to be able to separate intent and effect. What the source of the message intended to say could be compared to what he actually said without concern for the effect of the message on receivers, just as its effect can be studied without concern for intent. However, no writer that I have examined concerns himself with this relationship.

6. *To what extent does the critic make moral judgments of the rhetorical act?* A standard notion about rhetorical criticism is that the rhetorical critic must do more than analyze the rhetorical act; he must judge. The moral position has strong adherents who in one way or another argue that moral judgments are not only acceptable but necessary. Some are as tentative as Brockriede's comment that "one's theory of rhetoric must be comprehensive enough to permit the practitioner and critic various moral points of view, for as Professor Bryant points out, attempts to define rhetoric lead 'almost at once into questions of morals and ethics.' " Others are as sharp and dramatic as Richard Murphy's assertion that "there is no great speech on the values of holding fellow humans as slaves."[40]

Other theorists specifically rule out moral judgment as a function of rhetorical criticism. Richard Rieke and James Golden, recognizing the widely used pejorative sense of the term "rhetoric," note that "one man's reality is another man's rhetoric."[41] Jellicorse says that the critic may make a moral judgment but that in so doing he is not functioning as a rhetorical critic.[42] Grube, in discussing ancient criticism, identified the "moral fallacy" for which "the rhetoricians were not to blame." That fallacy, he says, is "the insistence that a good poem is morally good, that the artist is responsible for the moral effect of his work."[43]

If the critic's judgment is to be moral as well as technical, what standards of morality shall obtain? Those of the society at the time of the message? The social standard of the critic's day? The critic's personal moral standard? Shall the critic judge the morality of what the communicator intended to do? Of what resulted? Of what the message implied apart from either intent or effect?

Some writers who see the rhetorical critic as a moral agent expect him to define his standards by those of the society. While not specifically oriented to the critic, the most important work in this regard is Karl R. Wallace's "The Substance of Rhetoric: Good Reasons." "Good reasons" form the content of any message, are statements "offered in support of an *ought* proposition or a value-judgment," and provide for "a plan of *topoi* in the language of ethics and morals." They are "to some extent fixed by human nature and to a very large extent by generally accepted principles and practices which make social life, as we understand it, possible."[44] It is clear that such a standard, while rooted in the society, would not be quickly or lightly changed. Once discovered, "good reasons" would be expected to stand as a society's ethical foundation for some time. No writer I know evaluates the morality of a message or its author on the temporary value standards of the society. Such a position would be no more than judging by immediate effectiveness.

The acknowledgment that there is a substance to rhetoric in the values, or "good reasons," of the society and that these are fundamentally moral statements does not necessarily lead to moral judgment in rhetorical criticism. Edward Steele, for instance, makes societal values the center of his rhetorical system but he takes an amoral point of view. For him, "rhetorical analysis becomes, indeed, a social science technique, discovering the new, verifying the uncertain, affirming the established."[45]

The conflict between moral and amoral criticism has been sharp. Parke Burgess has observed that the amoral view has been caused by "the justified fear that moralistic criticism or theory would virtually bury the strategic function of rhetoric from critical sight." Burgess calls for a "metamoral" criticism. Like Wallace, he sees moral choice as an essential part of the strategic choices to be made by the communicator. Such criticism would concern itself with "a functional unity two distinct but interacting dimensions . . . the strategic and the moral," and thus avoids both "superficial and bland" strategic analysis and "moralistic outbursts."[46]

The argument for and against amoral criticism is not an exclusively modern concern. It relates to ancient thought as well. Everett Lee Hunt points out that Aristotle's rhetorical system was "largely detached from . . . morality." J. Robert Olian, on the contrary, argues that Aristotle meant to postulate an ethical system. Although that system was concerned with the means of being effective with an audience, he says, it was directed at an aristocratic audience which knew the standard values of the society. Thus, to be effective the speaker would need to accommodate the ethical system of that audience.[47]

A question which has been with us since antiquity is not likely to be solved soon. But the critic must decide whether he will or will not make a moral judgment of a rhetorical act. Linked to his decision will be another question not soon to be solved: the role of rationality.

7. *What significance does the critic give to rationality in his approach?* The idea that rationality is superior to irrationality, that reasoning is somehow superior to emotion, is an accepted value in our society. It is virtually impossible to find a speaker or writer who says that he is irrational. Thus, in our society an almost inherent moral (or value) judgment to be made about any communication would seem to be one about the extent to which it succeeds or fails to meet some standard of rationality.

Traditionally, rationality has been considered one of the essential standards of rhetorical evaluation and many recent writers have restated and refurbished that criterion.[48] But these and other authors have avoided the unsophisticated notion that rationality is some form of logical demonstration separated from receiver value and motive and from source credibility. Wallace, for instance, argues that "the word *reason* [in the term "good reason"] indicates that the process of proof is a rational one and can be used to cover such traditional forms of reasoning as deduction and induction, the syllogism, generalization, analogy, causation, and correlation." He also claims that in a rhetorical theory with "good reasons" as its base, "any distinctions that modern rhetoric may be trying to maintain between logical, ethical, and emotional modes of proof would immediately become unreal and useless, except for purposes of historical criticism."[49] Thus, one can be as wedded to rationality as Wallace without the routine application of classical forms and classifications.

Black attacks a large segment of contemporary criticism for its excessive concern with the rationality of the message and argues that there are circumstances wherein to assume rationality is to misconstrue the essential nature of the rhetorical act.[50] Interestingly, Mills and Petrie, whose scholarship is perhaps likely to be more closely identified with argumentation than any of the writers mentioned here, are at least as severe as Black when they say, "while defending logical argumentation as *one* of the means of persuasion and as one of the legitimate tools for the analysis of rhetorical argumentation, we feel no obligation to assume that man is only, or even essentially, rational."[51]

A standard of rationality has, perhaps, been confused with a standard of formal logical validity. The literature of rhetorical theory and criticism is thorough in denying that to be rhetorically rational a message must be formally logical by some standard of logical demonstration. Most modern theorists who maintain the defense of rationality in rhetoric look for movement from value system to conclusion. Whether one sees this traditionally through enthymeme and example, or by the use of Stephen Toulmin's model, or by other models, it is considerably broader than narrowly defined logical validity.[52] There is a rationality behind black militancy or white student revolt, a rationally oriented critic might argue, even though it may escape a middle-aged, middle-class American critic. The danger, says Black, is that in some situations the rational system will be stretched to the point where it is no longer useful.

> If we posit that the state of moral anarchy and spiritual dispossession that has erupted at periods in modern history, and will erupt again, itself is material for enthymematic premises, then we can redeem the enthymeme as a true and adequate account. But this redemption will have been gained at considerable expense to the precision of the enthymematic system. . . . We can, of course, augment the list of potential enthymematic premises to include states of mind, but in so doing we would render the system of enthymematic analysis less precise, more remote from the world of linguistic action, and less useful, therefore, as a critical instrument.[53]

But what is the substitute for rationality as a standard of evaluation? If even the more liberal designations of rationality, such as Wallace's, are, as Black argues, unable to account adequately for some rhetorical acts, what will replace them? To call for a nonrational standard of critical judgment is so fundamentally antagonistic to our value system that most critics would find it incomprehensible. Such a standard, if accepted as part of a critical approach, would surely make most of what has been discussed in this essay useless. There is an underlying assumption of rationality in the concept of a carefully thought out approach to rhetorical criticism.

There may be implications for the critic in Robert Scott's statement that "rhetoric may be viewed not as a matter of giving effectiveness to truth but of creating truth."[54] If rhetoric is epistemic, as Scott states and others imply, then a new point of view may be developed for rhetorical criticism. A critical system developed from such a point of view would care not for judgments made about rational and irrational rhetoric or moral, immoral, and amoral rhetoric. It would concern itself, I imagine, with determining how certain strategic decisions of the sender of the message (whether intended or not) influenced the creation of ideas which were unique to that situation or that class of situations. All the questions raised in this essay would need to be reexamined in this new light and critical judgment would be less oriented toward "good and bad" and more oriented toward "why?"

While Scott's point is provocative, it is not yet operational for critics. It may be worthwhile to examine and test such a basic view but for the time being it is little more than an interesting thought. There are, however, some major latter day attempts to liberalize rhetorical criticism in the movement toward pluralism in method.

8. *To what extent does the rhetorical critic use different methods for different forms, periods, and circumstances of rhetorical acts?* While Herbert Wichelns, in an effort to differentiate literary criticism from his idea of rhetorical criticism, could define a single set of parameters for criticism, few since 1925 have followed him in searching for a single approach.[55] Indeed much of the writing about criticism, either openly or by implication, argues for a pluralistic approach.[56] Karlyn Kohrs Campbell sees "the third stage of critical analysis" as one in which "the critic selects or creates a system of criticism" so that for her, it would seem, the real standards for criticism are those which are applied to the selection of a critical approach.[57] Edwin Black objects to a large body of contemporary criticism which he sees as following one approach. He postulates a limited number of rhetorical situations and responses and implies that a limited number of critical approaches might be developed to meet them.[58]

Black's classifications of discourse along a continuum based upon intensity of conviction suggests a different standard for each category of discourse. Thus, he sees exhortative and argumentative discourses as having basic differences in their "latent power to affect human beings."[59] In the last paragraph of his book, Black calls for no standard of criticism "in our present state of knowledge," but only for "an orientation, together with taste and intelligence."[60] But the pages which precede this statement leave little doubt that Black believes that a limited number of types of discourse will be found, each of which may be dealt with by its own approach.

Black looks most carefully at the "genre of argumentation" and notes that by examining it in various contexts we can learn more about it. A genre, then, is not only freed of immediate receiver effectiveness; the study of it will provide insight across time and presumably across societies:

> Rather than attempt to gauge the effect of a single discourse on its immediate audience . . . we have instead sought to discern the effects of the whole process of argument, and we have in consequence seen these effects as sequential: different at different stages of the argumentative process. We have assumed the single discourse to be part of a historic process of argument, one that, in the case of some subjects, has never

really ended, but has instead passed into new phases. In viewing specimens of argument, our account has only arrested this process at given moments in its development.[61]

An environment-oriented critic might well develop pluralistic approaches based upon the social and economic factors in a rhetorical act. Several of the current writers on black rhetoric claim that there are special problems of dealing with it critically and thus illustrate one facet of this point of view.[62] Robert T. Oliver's argument that we must develop a different "rhetoric" for each of the foreign cultures we study is another.[63]

Sectional differences within the United States which some claim differentiate rhetorical acts might also imply different approaches. Waldo Braden, basing his case on his examination of Southern speakers, argues for care before defining regional differences in rhetoric.[64] Anthony Hillbruner, on the other hand, finds a distinctive character in Western public address.[65] For him, American public address is in reality a study in regional public address.[66] Each region, Hillbruner says, requires its own critical approach.[67]

Herbert Simons argues that "the standard tools of rhetorical criticism are ill-suited for unravelling the complexity of discourse in social movements or for capturing its grand flow" and argues for a separate critical approach for dealing with movements as opposed to the examination of "particular speeches."[68]

Leland Griffin has called on critics to "judge the discourse in terms of the theories of rhetoric and public opinion indigenous to the times."[69] Black complains that while "for many purposes there can be no quarrel with Griffin's historically relative frame of critical reference" such a practice would make it difficult to see patterns in rhetorical movements over periods of time if one had to adapt different concepts of "pattern" or "form" in different periods.[70] A fundamental point of disagreement between Black and Griffin can be easily understood. One argues for the similarity of genre over time. The other argues for a difference between one period of time and another, a difference requiring that judgments be based on the standards of the society at the time of a given rhetorical act. The important contribution of both Black and Griffin is that each attempts to clarify a basis for differences in critical approach rather than merely exhorting pluralism.

Earlier we examined various foci of criticism and noted that the critical emphasis would differ depending upon the focus chosen. A source-oriented criticism concerned with determining and evaluating authorship in ghostwriting would not seem applicable in other foci. Psychoanalytic methods and standards of evaluation are more useful for source than for environment-oriented criticism.

Differences of time, place, and circumstance are also very real. There may also be differences of genre. But whether such differences require different critical approaches to examine them, or how flexible a single approach must be to deal with them, is an open question worthy of serious consideration.

In this essay I have examined a substantial number of statements on the nature of rhetorical criticism. These statements, directly or by implication, attack a number of problems which are important to the development of an approach to rhetorical criticism. The eight problems discussed here appear to be the most persistent ones and various positions have been identified within each of them.

Much of the writing on rhetorical criticism has been responsive; that is, it has been in opposition to some practice with which the writer disagreed. For this reason and others, much of the writing has also been fragmentary. There is little which has attempted full explication of an approach to rhetorical criticism.

The field is ready for some more comprehensive statements of approach. While the eight problems discussed here should not be examined mechanically, nor do they constitute a complete list of the questions and responses necessary, I advance them as a starting place. Hopefully, they will provide the critic with some means for examining his own thought and explaining his approach to others.

1. Marie Hochmuth Nichols, *Rhetoric and Criticism* (Baton Rouge: Louisiana State University Press, 1963), p. 106.

2. *Ibid.*, p. 66. Herbert Wichelns, "The Literary Criticism of Oratory," in *The Rhetorical Idiom*, ed. Donald C. Bryant (Ithaca, N.Y.: Cornell University Press, 1958), pp. 5–42; also in *Studies in Rhetoric and Public Speaking in Honor of James Albert Winans* (New York: Century, 1925), pp. 181–216. In addition to Professor Nichols many others have expressed a preference for a systematic approach to criticism. Cf. Samuel L. Becker, "Rhetorical Studies for the Contemporary World," *The Prospect of Rhetoric*, eds. Lloyd F. Bitzer and Edwin Black (Englewood Cliffs, N.J.: Prentice-Hall, 1971), p. 22; Edwin Black, *Rhetorical Criticism: A Study in Method* (New York: Macmillan, 1965), p. 2; Wayne E. Brockriede, "Toward a Contemporary Aristotelian Theory of Rhetoric," *Quarterly Journal of Speech*, 52 (1966), 33–40; Wayne Brockriede, "Trends in the Study of Rhetoric: Toward a Blending of Criticism and Science," *The Prospect of Rhetoric*, pp. 123–139; James L. Golden and Richard D. Rieke, *The Rhetoric of Black Americans* (Columbus, Ohio: Charles E. Merrill, 1971), p. 35; Lawrence W. Rosenfield, "The Anatomy of Critical Discourse," *Speech Monographs*, 35 (1968), 50–69.

3. There are well over ten times as many articles on the theory of criticism in national and regional journals of speech communication from 1946 to the present than there were from the founding of the *Quarterly Journal of Public Speaking* in 1915 until 1946. There have been at least a dozen speech communication books published since 1950 which theorize about rhetorical criticism.

4. Lester Thonssen and A. Craig Baird, *Speech Criticism* (New York: Ronald Press, 1948). All citations are from the first edition. The second edition by Thonssen, Baird, and Waldo W. Braden maintains the approach of the first.

5. William N. Brigance, ed., *A History and Criticism of American Public Address,*

volumes I and II (New York: McGraw Hill, 1943); and volume III, ed. Marie Hochmuth [Nichols] (New York: Longmans, Green, 1955), pp. 1–23.

6. Walter Fisher, "Method in Rhetorical Criticism," *Southern Speech Journal*, 35 (1969), 104–105. Cf. John Waite Bowers and Donovan J. Ochs, *The Rhetoric of Agitation and Control* (Reading, Mass.: Addison-Wesley, 1971), p. 2; Karlyn Kohrs Campbell, *Critiques of Contemporary Rhetoric* (Belmont, Calif.: Wadsworth, 1972), p. 2; Anthony Hillbruner, "Creativity and Contemporary Criticism," *Western Speech*, 24 (1960), 5–11; Mark Klyn, "Toward a Pluralistic Rhetorical Criticism," in *Essays on Rhetorical Criticism*, ed. Thomas R. Nilsen (New York: Random House, 1968), pp. 147–151; Marie Hochmuth [Nichols], "The Criticism of Rhetoric," *A History and Criticism of American Public Address*, III, 5; Otis M. Walter, "On the Varieties of Rhetorical Criticism," in *Essays on Rhetorical Criticism*, p. 161.

7. Lloyd F. Bitzer, "The Rhetorical Situation," *Philosophy and Rhetoric*, 1 (1968), 3.

8. *The Prospect of Rhetoric*, eds. Bitzer and Black, p. 220. Cf. Barnet Baskerville, "The Critical Method in Speech," *Central States Speech Journal*, 4 (1953), 1; Wayne Brockriede, "Toward a Contemporary Aristotelian Theory of Rhetoric," p. 38; Donald C. Bryant, "Rhetoric: Its Function and Scope," *Quarterly Journal of Speech*, 39 (1953), 406; Albert Crofts, "The Functions of Rhetorical Criticism," *Quarterly Journal of Speech*, 42 (1956), 287; John Lee Jellicorse, review of *Rhetorical Criticism: A Study in Method*, by Edwin Black, *Quarterly Journal of Speech*, 51 (1965), 340.

9. Thonssen and Baird, *Speech Criticism*, p. 5; Wichelns, "Literary Criticism," pp. 40–41.

10. Bryant, "Rhetoric: Its Function and Scope," pp. 406, 411.

11. Brockriede, "Toward a Contemporary Aristotelian Theory of Rhetoric," p. 38.

12. Crofts, "Functions of Rhetorical Criticism," p. 283. Cf. Ernest G. Bormann, *Theory and Research in the Communicative Arts* (New York: Holt, Rinehart and Winston, 1965), p. 226; Martin Maloney, "Some New Directions in Rhetorical Criticism," *Central States Speech Journal*, 4 (1953), 1; Loren Reid, "The Perils of Rhetorical Criticism," *Quarterly Journal of Speech*, 30 (1944), 417; Phillip K. Tompkins, "Rhetorical Criticism: Wrong Medium?," *Central States Speech Journal*, 13 (1962), 9; Walter, "Varieties of Rhetorical Criticism," p. 159; Ernest Wrage, "The Ideal Critic," *Central States Speech Journal*, 8 (1957), 20–21. Worthy of note here is Carroll Arnold's position that while rhetoric is not limited to the oral there is a significant distinctiveness to the condition of "orality." "Oral Rhetoric, Rhetoric and Literature," *Philosophy and Rhetoric*, 1 (1968), 191–210. Such distinctiveness might very well imply a different method for looking at spoken rhetoric than at other forms.

13. Brockriede, "Toward a Contemporary Aristotelian Theory of Rhetoric," p. 36; Brockriede, "Dimensions of the Concept of Rhetoric," *Quarterly Journal of Speech*, 54 (1968), 1; Bryant, "Rhetoric: Its Function and Scope," p. 407; Campbell, *Critiques*, p. 2; Dennis Day, "Persuasion and the Concept of Identification," *Quarterly Journal of Speech*, 46 (1960), 271; Fisher, "Method in Rhetorical Criticism," p. 105; Leland Griffin, "The Rhetoric of Historical Movements," *Quarterly Journal of Speech*, 38 (1952), 187; Hoyt H. Hudson, "The Field of Rhetoric," in *Historical Studies of Rhetoric and Rhetoricians*, ed. Raymond F. Howes (Ithaca, N.Y.: Cornell University Press, 1961), p. 13; Jellicorse, review of Black's *Rhetorical Criticism*, p. 340; Richard Murphy, "The Speech as a Literary Genre," *Quarterly Journal of Speech*, 44 (1958), 123; Hochmuth [Nichols], "The Criticism of Rhetoric," p. 8, and *Rhetoric and Criticism*, p. 69; Arthur L. Smith, *The Rhetoric of Black Revolution* (Boston: Allyn and Bacon, 1969), pp. 1–2; Donald L. Torrance, "A Philosophy of Rhetoric from Bertrand Russell," *Quarterly Journal of Speech*, 45 (1959), 153.

14. Bowers and Ochs, *Rhetoric of Agitation and Control*, p. 6; Robert L. Scott and Wayne Brockriede, *The Rhetoric of Black Power* (New York: Harper and Row, 1969), pp. 2–3; Robert L. Scott and Barnard L. Brock, *Methods of Rhetorical Criticism* (New York: Harper and Row, 1972), p. 7. Bryant ("Rhetoric: Its Function and Scope," p. 405) accepts nonverbal signs only "when they are organized in a matrix of verbal discourse. . . ." Baskerville makes an argument similar to Bryant's. Barnet Baskerville, "Rhetorical Criticism, 1971: Retrospect, Prospect, Introspect," *Southern Speech Communication Journal*, 37 (1971), 116.

15. Bitzer and Black, *Prospect of Rhetoric*, pp. 220–221.

16. Rosenfield, "Anatomy of Critical Discourse," pp. 50–69. Incidentally, Professor Rosenfield's terminology tells us something of the status of rhetorical criticism as a science. It is now at the anatomy stage. It is, in effect, where medicine was until the late nineteenth century. It is defining bone, cartilage, and muscle with origins and insertions. There is no point to arguments that rhetorical criticism can or cannot be a science like physics. That cannot be known because the field is nowhere near that stage of scientific development. There is promising evidence, however, that a reasonable number of theorists have recently ceased to use leeches.

17. *Ibid.*, p. 58.

18. Ernest Bormann, "Ghostwriting and the Rhetorical Critic," *Quarterly Journal of Speech*, 46 (1960), 284–285. Cf. Robert Ray, "Ghostwriting in Presidential Campaigns," *Today's Speech*, 4 (1956), 15.

19. Bormann, "Ghostwriting," pp. 286–287.

20. Campbell, *Critiques*, p. 11; Hochmuth [Nichols], "The Criticism of Rhetoric," p. 9; Walter, "Varieties of Rhetorical Criticism," p. 164; Wichelns, "Literary Criticism of Oratory," p. 36.

21. Brockriede, "Toward a Contemporary Aristotelian Theory of Rhetoric," p. 37.

22. Crofts, "Functions of Rhetorical Criticism," p. 286; Charles Lomas, *The Agitator in American Society* (Englewood Cliffs, N.J.: Prentice Hall, 1968), p. 22; Marie Hochmuth [Nichols], "Kenneth Burke and the 'New Rhetoric,' " *Quarterly Journal of Speech*, 38 (1952), 138; Thomas R. Nilsen, "Criticism and Social Consequences," *Quarterly Journal of Speech*, 42 (1956), 175; W. Charles Redding, "Extrinsic and Intrinsic Criticism," in *Essays on Rhetorical Criticism*, ed. Thomas R. Nilsen (New York: Random House, 1968), p. 118; Malcolm Sillars, "Rhetoric as Act," *Quarterly Journal of Speech*, 50 (1964), 284; Craig R. Smith, "Actuality and Potentiality: The Essence of Criticism," *Philosophy and Rhetoric*, 3 (1970), 136; Edward Steele, "Social Values, the Enthymeme and Speech Criticism," *Western Speech*, 26 (1962), 74; Ernest Wrage, "Public Address: A Study in Social and Intellectual History," *Quarterly Journal of Speech*, 33 (1947), 454.

23. Linnea Ratcliff, "Rhetorical Criticism: An Alternate Perspective," *Southern Speech Communication Journal*, 37 (1971), 134–135.

24. Jerry Hendrix, "An Introductory Prognosis," in "Rhetorical Criticism: Prognoses for the Seventies—A Symposium," *Southern Speech Journal*, 36 (1970), 103.

25. Wichelns, "Literary Criticism of Oratory," p. 35.

26. Robert L. Scott, review of *Rhetorical Criticism: A Study in Method*, by Edwin Black, *Quarterly Journal of Speech*, 51 (1965), 336, italics added.

27. Waldo W. Braden, "A Prognosis," in "Rhetorical Criticism: Prognoses for the Seventies—A Symposium," *Southern Speech Journal*, 36 (1970), 106; Bryant, "Rhetoric: Its Function and Scope," p. 415; Robert S. Cathcart, *Post Communication* (New York: Bobbs-Merrill, 1966), p. 1; Fisher, "Method in Rhetorical Criticism," p. 107; Jellicorse, review of Black's *Rhetorical Criticism*, pp. 340–341; Lawrence H. Mouat, "An Approach to Rhetorical Criticism," *The Rhetorical Idiom*, ed. Donald C. Bryant (Ithaca,

N.Y.: Cornell University Press, 1958), p. 165; Hochmuth [Nichols], "Kenneth Burke and the 'New Rhetoric,' " p. 134; Nilsen, "Criticism and Social Consequences," p. 175; Sillars, "Rhetoric as Act," pp. 277–284; Wayne Thompson, "Contemporary Public Address, a Problem in Criticism," *Quarterly Journal of Speech*, 40 (1954), 26; Thonssen and Baird, *Speech Criticism*, p. 9; Tompkins, "Rhetorical Criticism: Wrong Medium?," p. 90.

28. Black, *Rhetorical Criticism*, p. 44; Campbell, *Critiques*, pp. 22–23; George Dell, "Philosophic Judgments in Contemporary Rhetorical Criticism," *Western Speech*, 30 (1966), 22; Lomas, *The Agitator*, p. 21; Richard Murphy, "Speech as a Literary Genre," p. 122; Hochmuth [Nichols], "The Criticism of Rhetoric," p. 13, and *Rhetoric and Criticism*, p. 78; Wayland Maxfield Parrish, "The Study of Speeches," *American Speeches*, eds. Wayland Maxfield Parrish and Marie Hochmuth [Nichols] (New York: Longmans, Green, 1954), p. 7.

29. Jellicorse, review of Black's *Rhetorical Criticism*, pp. 340–341. Cf. Cathcart, *Post Communication*, p. 1; Thonssen and Baird, *Speech Criticism*, pp. 458–459.

30. Nilsen, "Criticism and Social Consequences," p. 176.

31. Nilsen, *Essays on Rhetorical Criticism*, p. 87.

32. Walter, "Varieties of Rhetorical Criticism," pp. 164–165.

33. Black, *Rhetorical Criticism*, pp. 78–90.

34. W. K. Wimsatt, Jr., and Monroe K. Beardsley, "The Intentional Fallacy," *The Verbal Icon* (Lexington: University of Kentucky Press, 1954), pp. 3–18.

35. Kenneth Burke, "Rhetoric—Old and New," *Journal of General Education*, 5 (1951), 203.

36. Nilsen, "Criticism and Social Consequences," p. 175. Cf. Nilsen, *Essays on Rhetorical Criticism*, p. 87; Walter Fisher, "A Motive View of Communication," *Quarterly Journal of Speech*, 56 (1970), 139.

37. Baskerville, "The Critical Method in Speech," p. 4; Braden, "A Prognosis," p. 106; Campbell, *Critiques*, p. 2; Cathcart, *Post Communication*, pp. 9–10; Griffin, "Rhetoric," p. 187; Jellicorse, review of Black's *Rhetorical Criticism*, p. 341; Hochmuth [Nichols], "The Criticism of Rhetoric," p. 9; Craig R. Smith, "Actuality and Potentiality," p. 137; Wichelns, "Literary Criticism of Oratory," p. 39; Donald E. Williams, "The Rhetorical Critic: His *Raison D'Etre*," *Southern Speech Journal*, 36 (1970), 113.

38. William Jennings Bryan and Mary Baird Bryan, *The Memoirs of William Jennings Bryan* (Chicago: John C. Winston, 1925), p. 104.

39. William Jennings Bryan, *The First Battle* (Chicago: W. B. Conkey, 1896), p. 206.

40. Brockriede, "Toward a Contemporary Aristotelian Theory of Rhetoric," p. 38; Murphy, "The Speech as a Literary Genre," p. 120. Cf. A. Craig Baird, "Speech and the 'New' Philosophies," *Central States Speech Journal*, 13 (1962), 245; Baskerville, "The Critical Method in Speech," p. 3; Bryant, "Rhetoric: Its Function and Scope," p. 403; Campbell, *Critiques*, p. 22; Crofts, "Functions of Rhetorical Criticism," p. 290; Richard Johannesen, "Richard Weaver's View of Rhetoric and Criticism," *Southern Speech Journal*, 32 (1966), 137; Hochmuth Nichols, *Rhetoric and Criticism*, pp. 70–72; Wrage, "The Ideal Critic," pp. 22–23.

41. Rieke and Golden, *Rhetoric of Black Americans*, pp. 34–35.

42. Jellicorse, review of Black's *Rhetorical Criticism*, p. 341.

43. G. M. A. Grube, "Rhetoric and Literary Criticism," *Quarterly Journal of Speech*, 42 (1956), 339–344.

44. Karl R. Wallace, "The Substance of Rhetoric: Good Reasons," *Quarterly Journal of Speech*, 49 (1963), 247–248.

45. Steele, "Social Values," p. 418.

46. Parke G. Burgess, "The Rhetoric of Moral Conflict: Two Critical Dimensions," *Quarterly Journal of Speech*, 56 (1970), 120–130; Robert L. Scott and Donald K. Smith, "The Rhetoric of Confrontation," *Quarterly Journal of Speech*, 55 (1969), 1–8.

47. Everett Lee Hunt, "Plato and Aristotle on Rhetoric and Rhetoricians," *Historical Studies of Rhetoric and Rhetoricians*, ed. Raymond F. Howes, p. 56; J. Robert Olian, "The Intended Uses of Aristotle's Rhetoric," *Speech Monographs*, 35 (1968), 137–148.

48. Baird, "Speech and the 'New' Philosophies," pp. 241–246; Bryant, "Rhetoric: Its Function and Scope," p. 414; Johannesen, "Richard Weaver's View," p. 138; Karl R. Wallace, "Rhetoric and Advising," *Southern Speech Journal*, 29 (1964), 280.

49. Wallace, "The Substance of Rhetoric: Good Reasons," pp. 248–249.

50. Black, *Rhetorical Criticism*, p. 131. Cf. Campbell, *Critiques of Contemporary Rhetoric*, p. 6, and "The Rhetoric of Radical Black Nationalism: A Case Study in Self Conscious Criticism," *Central States Speech Journal*, 22 (1971), 154–156; Eugene Knepprath and Theodore Clevenger, Jr., "Reasoned Discourse and Motive Appeal in Selected Political Speeches," *Quarterly Journal of Speech*, 51 (1965), 154; Donald Salper, "The Imaginative Component of Rhetoric," *Quarterly Journal of Speech*, 51 (1965), 307–310.

51. Glen E. Mills and Hugh G. Petrie, "The Role of Logic in Rhetoric," *Quarterly Journal of Speech*, 54 (1968), 260.

52. Lloyd F. Bitzer, "Aristotle's Enthymeme Revisited," *Quarterly Journal of Speech*, 45 (1959), 399–408; Charles S. Mudd, "The Enthymeme and Logical Validity," *Quarterly Journal of Speech*, 45 (1959), 409–414; James H. McBurney, " The Place of the Enthymeme in Rhetorical Theory," *Speech Monographs*, 3 (1936), 49–74; Stephen E. Toulmin, *The Uses of Argument* (Cambridge: Cambridge University Press, 1958); Earl W. Wiley, "The Enthymeme: Idiom of Persuasion," *Quarterly Journal of Speech*, 42 (1956), 19–24.

53. Black, *Rhetorical Criticism*, p. 127.

54. Robert Scott, "On Viewing Rhetoric as Epistemic," *Central States Speech Journal*, 18 (1967), 13.

55. Brockriede, "Toward a Contemporary Aristotelian Theory of Rhetoric," p. 38; Mouat, "An Approach," p. 165; Wichelns, "Literary Criticism of Oratory," pp. 7–8.

56. Barnett Baskerville, "Selected Writings on the Criticism of Public Address, Addendum, 1967," in *Essays on Rhetorical Criticism*, ed. Thomas R. Nilsen, pp. 189–190; Crofts, "Functions of Rhetorical Criticism," p. 287; Anthony Hillbruner, "Criticism as Persuasion," p. 262; Scott and Brock, *Methods of Rhetorical Criticism*, p. 404.

57. Campbell, *Critiques of Contemporary Rhetoric*, pp. 21–23.

58. Black, *Rhetorical Criticism*, pp. 132–177.

59. *Ibid.*, p. 133.

60. *Ibid.*, p. 177.

61. *Ibid.*, p. 177.

62. Campbell, "The Rhetoric of Radical Black Nationalism: A Case Study in Self Conscious Criticism," pp. 151–160; Golden and Rieke, *Rhetoric of Black Americans*, p. 38.

63. Robert T. Oliver, "Culture and Communication," *Vital Speeches of the Day* (September 15, 1963), pp. 721–724.

64. Waldo W. Braden, "Southern Oratory Reconsidered: A Search for an Image," *Southern Speech Journal*, 29 (1964), 303–315.

65. Anthony Hillbruner, "Area Studies in Rhetorical Criticism," in *Landmarks in Western Oratory*, ed. David H. Grover (Laramie: University of Wyoming Press, 1968), pp. 5–11.

66. Anthony Hillbruner, "Rhetoric, Region and Social Science," *Central States Speech Journal*, 21 (1970), 172.

67. *Ibid.*, p. 174.

68. Herbert W. Simons, "Requirements, Problems and Strategies: A Theory of Persuasion for Social Movements," *Quarterly Journal of Speech*, 56 (1970), 2. Cf. Robert S. Cathcart, "New Approaches to the Study of Movements: Defining Movements Rhetorically," *Western Speech*, 36 (1972), 82.

69. Griffin, "Rhetoric," p. 187. Cf. John M. Ericson, "Rhetorical Criticism: How to Evaluate," in *Demosthenes on the Crown*, ed. James J. Murphy (New York: Random House, 1967), p. 128.

70. Black, "Rhetorical Criticism," p. 21.

Communication and Human Response:
A Heuristic View

DAVID B. STROTHER

> In the dialogue one discovers how different are the ways that lead to the light of faith, and how it is possible to make them converge on the same goal. Even if these ways are divergent, they can become complementary by forcing our reasoning process out of the worn paths and by obliging it to deepen its research, to find fresh expressions.
>
> Pope Paul VI

From ancient times to the present day, the study of man has been the study of talk. Human society is described by Kenneth Boulding as an "edifice spun out of the tenuous webs of conversation,"[1] creating what George Gordon calls an "awesome but elementary self-truth: little that man does as a social creature is not communication."[2] Whatever progress Homo sapiens have achieved, then, in formulating and building a societal structure may be attributable to their ability to communicate with one another. Conversely, the imperfections which remain may well occupy the attention of some forty-three disciplines devoted to the study of communication[3] which seek in their own ways to interpret human behavior, and to facilitate that interpretation by strengthening, where possible, societal structure.

The disciplines often work at cross-purposes because they either cannot communicate with each other or do not desire to communicate. Human society, of course, is the momentary loser if scholars from one discipline take it upon themselves to repair a particular societal deficiency when scholars from other disciplines with whom they do not communicate are in a position to render valuable assistance.

Fortunately, there are indications of a growing awareness that while many of these disciplines are artificially divided by subject-matter niches, they share common concerns. Scholars in speech, for example, increasingly appropriate knowledge from experimental and clinical psychologists, historians, political scientists, and classicists. Hopefully, scholars from other areas find material of appropriative value in speech literature, as well.

A very real disciplinary chasm occurs, however, not in the artificiality of subject-matter concerns, but in the methodologies employed to discover knowledge. These methodologies are of two forms. The first is phenomeno-logical, experiential, or that "free-wheeling speculative tradition" which, according to Anatol Rapoport, "has dominated the thinking of social philoso-phers from Plato and Aristotle to our own day."[4] It sired Darwin, Huxley, and Keynes, and a reasonable case may be made for its claim on Winans, Wichelns, and Woolbert.[5] Its premises and conclusions may appear less reliable, and yet they contain remarkable plausibility because they fall within the sense experiences of others. The second may be called experimental or quantitative where conclusions may appear more reliable because the experi-menter has carefully accounted for and placed controls on the variables. Abraham Maslow simply calls them two great philosophic orientations, the humanistic and mechanistic.[6]

In approaching the "third revolution" of theoretical development in communications, that is, the view of human communication as *dialogue,*[7] it will become increasingly necessary to close the chasm dividing the two methodologies so that one day, in the words of Harold Larrabee, "Man the meditative knower and man the zealous doer can become man the intelligent artist in living, by a flexible balance of thought by action, and of action by thought."[8]

Matson and Montagu describe the "second communications revolution"[9] as a "triumph of scientific *theory* and human engineering" which, "with its intricately elaborate logical theory of information and communication—has come to be deeply and disturbingly felt in nearly every department of the social sciences and humanities."[10] The traditional manner of approaching teaching and research in rhetoric became no less immune to its influence than were other disciplines. The rhetorician began to re-examine remnants of the "first revolution," the view of human communication as a monologous act of a speaker addressing an audience, and decided that greater insights would be gained by placing human communication within a mathematical formula. I propose, then to examine the assumptions of the "second revolution" to observe how they might be honed to prepare the groundwork for the challenges of the "third."

While some consider Norbert Wiener and Ernest Dichter as heroes of the "second revolution,"[11] a reasonable case could be built for including with them the names of Claude Shannon and Warren Weaver. The Shannon model[12] was extended to include implications for the study of human behavior by Warren Weaver[13] to produce an impact of staggering proportions. Known variously as the information theory model, the "telephone company" model, or simply the communication model, it sired numerous other models. Ronald L. Smith, in fact, diagrams a lineal descent of specific models from the Shannon and Weaver paradigm.[14] Alfred G. Smith, in his popular volume of readings on *Communication and Culture*, indicates that all of the selections included in the book were "directly or indirectly informed by it."[15] The construct is simple and the terminology catching. It consists of a *source*, an *encoder*, a *message*, a *channel*, a *decoder*, and a *receiver*. Almost immediately, Norbert Wiener appended the idea of feedback.[16] Although the physical scientist and engineer have produced some very useful innovations in electronic communication, its impact on the behavioral sciences may have now outlived its usefulness.

As numerous texts in speech will confirm, a great strength of the mechanistic approach is the vividness of detail used in describing human communication. Consider a typical occurrence—two persons involved in a conversation. By employing the information theory model, the explanation would probably come out something like this: the *sender* wants to affect the behavior of the *receiver* in some way, and he therefore *encodes messages* designed to consummate the desired behavior change. The receiver *decodes* and reacts to the messages by accepting the sender's ideas, rejecting them, or withholding judgment. To signify his reaction, the receiver encodes *feedback* messages, verbal and nonverbal, and directs them toward the sender who has now assumed a receiver role. Depending upon conditions in the room, the linguistic abilities of the receivers, their preconceived values, attitudes, and knowledge, the messages either get through or they are impeded by noise, problems in coding, or differences in attitudes.

Such an approach to the analysis of communication is clear, concise, and plausible. If one wishes to speak in those terms, so be it, although it lacks the innovativeness many attribute to it. David K. Berlo viewed it as similar to the Aristotelian model of speech, speaker, and audience.[17] If one chooses to reject Aristotle's paradigm for the information theory paradigm, he does so for terminological reasons. If he rejects Aristotle because his works are not useful for contemporary quantitative research, then he must also reject information theory because of its similarity with the Aristotelian and sophistic models which, according to Matson and Montagu, are "inherently *monological* and directive."[18]

Not only should the information theory model be reconsidered because of its simplicity; more important, it should be re-examined because it treats human communication behavior in a mechanistic way, assembling and disassembling it as if it were an inanimate machine. Three problems emerge.

First, in its terms of analysis such a model contains the suggestion that a participant may be purposive to an unrealistic degree in the process of communication. The suffix "er" in *sender, receiver,* and *encoder, decoder* is a tacit indication that purposiveness or goal-direction may be assumed in the model. Communication behavior *is* goal-directed, but sending, receiving, encoding, and decoding are not specifications of a communicator's goal, nor should they be objectives instrumental to his goals (so far as the communicator is aware). In real life, it appears likely that speakers are more aware of the process when they are preparing to give a speech than when they actually present it; and further, parties to an informal conversation almost never think in terms of process. Instead a participant is usually unaware of any of these activities. As West, Ansberry, and Carr observe, "Normally, the purpose to express an idea or want finds automatic fulfillment—grammatical or ungrammatical, logical or illogical—without conscious selection of specific neuromuscular patterns of response."[19] Too often, research scholars or teachers reveal their purposiveness or goals by designating explicitly or implicitly the function of the participants, thus producing within them a consciousness which probably causes communication to deviate to an "unnatural" course. To the experimentalist whose concern is with "messages, their antecedents, and their consequences,"[20] the conclusions from his experimental observations would appear to contain biases which are seldom, if ever, explained.[21]

A second misleading feature of the mechanistic approach is the implicit assumption that communication situations are time-bound to beginnings and endings. It implies that the sender assumes a dominant role, and, as such, initiates communication at a consciously observable point in time. This dominance presumably manifests itself until at a given point in time he chooses to close discourse. Even the circular process during communication, which is stressed by most theorists, is analyzed not only within the confines of an event with a beginning and an end, but also in terms of a time order sequence with certain elements *bound to follow* certain others. For example, scholars who have adopted the information theory approach discuss feedback only as a receiver's response to a source's message. The source, in turn, adapts the message to modify feedback.[22] Thus, in a typical paradigm, antecedents and consequences may be isolated as fixed points in time. Once isolated, they can be observed and their effects measured. Unfortunately, they are fixed by the observer to enable him to measure the things he wants to measure using the instruments he wants to use, and frequently attaining the results he wants to attain.

The third objection follows from the first two. In mechanistic models, the place of behavior modification is not clear. Some theorists maintain that feedback includes whatever changes in behavior occur from communication. Others believe that behavior modification takes place after the process of communication has run its course. Still others contend that sending, receiving, encoding, and decoding all involve behavior modification in some way. None of these explanations appears entirely congruent with reality. The "feeling" of having participated in a conversation involves modification of behavior. As Lee Thayer has noted, "People react (even reliably and predictably) to far more than words or symbols as such. And they react in far more than purely cognitive ways. A general feeling of uneasiness about someone or some situation is often a major determinant of our behavior in those situations."[23] All responses to social stimuli are instances of behavior modification, and the terms of analysis in a mechanistic model are inadequate for categorizing realistic communicative behavior.

Although these problems have been illustrated within the context of an information theory explanation of human communication, it should be clear that any model which treats communication as a mechanistic process or event is liable to the same difficulties. Further, with whatever paradigm experimentalists adopt, it should be clear that the paradigm will largely determine their conclusions. That scientists have divided up communication and examined its parts has created an inability to see much of anything else. As Darnell has remarked: "Such self-induced blindness is the more dangerous because it seems to lead first to denial of significance and then to the denial of the existence of things not seen."[24]

At this point, were a typical information theory paradigm placed into the context of person-to-person communication, it would emerge something like this. A source encodes a message to a receiver who decodes it; the receiver encodes feedback to the source who decodes it, but the source actually becomes a receiver while the receiver becomes the source. The source acknowledges the feedback by encoding feed-forward, which is actually the message. But since the source is actually a receiver, he encodes feedback rather than feed-forward. The complexity and absurdity of such description necessitates that components be isolated. For purposes of explanation, this may be feasible, but for experimental purposes such isolation can disastrously distort. If one seeks to conduct an experiment on source credibility, for example, he must assume a monologous stance—that the sender is somehow predominant because of the space he occupies, or because he has been accorded the right to relay messages verbally while others have not; they become receivers whose nonverbal messages are discounted for purposes of the experiment. For purposes of control, the experimenter designates an arbitrary beginning and ending, letting randomness account for what might have preceded or followed the actual experiment. If he conducts the experiment at different times, he assumes that his stance, wardrobe, location, and instructions will have no influence on the outcome. Although the experimenter knows that communication is an on-going process, he has no choice but to observe only a segment of it and liken it to the way people really behave.

At this juncture, it would be an act of cowardice to demure in proposing some salient features of the "third communications revolution." Those features must *not* be limited to instances in which one *intends* to affect another in some way, they must *not* be viewed as isolated events in time, and they must take into account the fact that human communication encompasses much more than ideas and thoughts. People communicate with each other because they innately desire to integrate themselves socially through *mutual understanding*. Meerloo articulates its challenge by stating that "mutual understanding is the result of maximal communication through mutual empathy. It can approximately be reached through means of manifold tools of communication, of which semantic language is only one."[25] Its occasion may be likened to conversation, and its medium the *message bit*, herein defined as the *sum total of verbal and nonverbal cues*. In the presence of another person, "all that I am and all that I do affects mutual understanding." Stated another way, *behavioral cues, whether verbal or nonverbal, constitute the communicative or dialogical act which has as its ultimate objective understanding; behavioral changes are frequent and inseparable*.

In the "third communications revolution" there are only individuals responding to each other, weaving threads of mutual understanding so intimate that the feelings and thoughts of one readily become the feelings and thoughts of all—void of specific method, technique, or format. Although physical or social conditions will modify the manner in which "message bits" are shared by respondents, there are no assigned roles and "dialogue." Thus, the "public speaker" who has a social obligation to rely largely on verbal cues and the "audience member" who is obligated to use nonverbal cues are consciously or unconsciously role-playing in a situation necessitated by social or physical expediency. Neither is sender or receiver; both are respondents seeking to engage in "dialogue" in spite of the situational constraints. The emergence of mutual understanding, however, is contingent upon the degree to which behaviors tend to meld with one another—when the respondents emit mutually pleasing behavioral cues.

The diagram on p. 95 represents symbolically what may happen in selected phases of dialogue. At the points where the three circles, representing respondents, intersect, there is behavioral congruity or mutual understanding. Only within the context of the "message bit" can congruity or incongruity be observed, however.

It should be obvious from the diagram that the "phase" determines the degree to which congruous behavior manifests itself. In conversation, mutual understanding seems more likely to occur than in either the lecture or polemic phases. It should be equally obvious that the fewer congruous behavioral cues, as in the polemic phase, the less likely the chances of mutual understanding among all parties to a dispute. Behavioral cues may also be

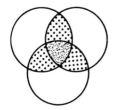

CONVERSATION PHASE

about equal amounts of interaction

each respondent deeply "involved"

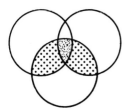

LECTURE PHASE

one respondent deeply involved and dominant in terms of amount of interaction

other respondents not interacting a great deal with each other

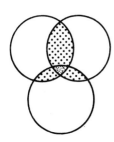

POLEMIC PHASE

two respondents dominate the events—other respondent relatively uninvolved

DIAGRAM 1

judged by their intensity or degree of overtness. A respondent may emit few behavioral cues, but they are of such intensity that other respondents can feed upon them, and reciprocate in a similar fashion; conversely, the behavioral cues may not only be few in number but of such low intensity as to prohibit mutual understanding. *When such a phenomenon occurs, communication may be said to have been disrupted.* Disruption, though, may be a positive force causing respondents to repair their "message bits" so they may interact to a greater degree toward mutual understanding. It becomes negative or even pathological when a respondent discharges behavioral cues which are consistently antagonistic and lack the adhesiveness necessary for behavioral congruity with another respondent. Antagonism may be both the cause and the symptom of social alienation resulting in sustained impairment of communication.[26]

Such a conceptualization has numerous philosophical and practical ramifications. It declares that there is an innate desire in people to want to get

along with each other through the "sharing of meaning" to achieve mutual
understanding, although it does not rule out occasions when people intentionally emit antagonistic behaviors to undermine mutual understanding. It
implicitly suggests that consistently antagonistic behaviors should be observed
to determine what the motives are which cause one to want to produce
short-circuits in the communicative act. It suggests that possible behavioral
congruence may also spark cognitive understanding—that similar actions lead
to similar thoughts. It suggests that the emphasis and frequency given to the
verbal systems by society have led Barnlund to correctly conclude that it is
"tempting to believe verbal signs are the only means, or at least the principal
ones, by which men express their ideas and feeling";[27] that nonverbal cues
should therefore be codified, systematized, and integrated into courses of
study since they are part of the "message bit." It even goes so far as to
suggest that institutions in society which rely mainly upon verbal portions of
a "message bit" may be assuming too little responsibility for advancing the
cause of mutual understanding. Oaths, contracts, statutes, proclamations, and
depositions may appear to be necessary for social control, but would they
not, by the terms of this conceptualization, be communicationless? It asks for
more theories or predictive generalizations, such as those advanced by
Raymond A. Bauer,[28] to provide a broader underpinning. It pleads for the
humanist to ignite the vital spark of originality—that "capacity to explore
imaginatively new and undreamed-of possibilities in search of ideas 'not yet
wordable,' and fuse old elements in novel combinations."[29] It urges the
scientist to refine his methodologies so they may account more responsibly
for process in human communication. Thayer appears convinced that "Scientifically, we know much less about human communication than we do about
animal husbandry—this in spite of the fact that our lives are infinitely more
affected by communication than by genetics of a particular breed of hogs.
Yet we do have conceptually superior ways of understanding and practicing
human communication."[30] Finally, it exhorts scholars of both methodological disciplines to view human society as the consequence of the individual's
attempt to communicate.

The uniqueness of this conceptualization is not in its originality, but in the
lack of it. Berlo, for example, tapped the fringes of "dialogue" with his
discussion of "process" and "interaction" in communication.[31] Methodologi-
cally, however, they have yet to be cast into a mold of sufficient sturdiness to
yield mutual understanding among the disciplines. That is the challenge of the
"third communications revolution," and if there is redeeming value to this
essay it is summarized by Rapoport who declares that "The social scientist
needs even more imagination. He should be familiar with the creative products of humanity, and he must be sensitized to values, his own and those of
the others. He cannot build scientific theories from concepts generated by
imagination and empathy; but imagination and empathy will help him in his

groping for concepts and variables, foundations on which significant and cumulative social theory can be built while such groping goes on."[32]

The author is indebted to Professor Edward McGlone of Wayne State University who collaborated with him on earlier drafts of this essay, and whose contributions are still much in evidence.

1. Kenneth Boulding, *The Image* (Ann Arbor: Univeristy of Michigan Press, 1956), p. 45.

2. George Gordon, *Persuasion: The Theory and Practice of Manipulative Communication* (New York: Hastings House, 1971), p. 7.

3. Jurgen Reusch, "Clinical Science and Communication Theory" in *The Human Dialogue*, eds. W. Matson and Ashly Montagu (New York: Free Press, 1967), pp. 52–54.

4. Anatol Rapoport, "Methodology in the Physical, Biological and Social Sciences" in *Global Systems Dynamics: International Symposium, Charlottesville, Va., 1969*, ed. E. O. Attinger (New York: Wiley-Interscience, 1970), p. 20.

5. The author is aware that in James A. Winans's book, *Public Speaking* (New York: Century Co., 1917), thirty works by twenty psychologists are cited. Added to these are forty-three separate references to James and Titchener. Winans, nevertheless, takes an imaginative, "free-wheeling" leap to make attention theory a theory of persuasion. Woolbert, a behavioral psychologist, is not above imaginative flights, as illustrated in his theory of polarization. See C. H. Woolbert, "The Audience," *Social Review Monographs*, 21 (1916), 36–54.

6. Abraham Maslow, *The Psychology of Science* (New York: Harper and Row, 1966), p. 3.

7. "Introduction: The Unfinished Revolution" in Matson and Montagu, eds., *The Human Dialogue*, p. 3. See also Richard L. Johannesen, "The Emerging Concept of Communication as Dialogue," *Quarterly Journal of Speech*, 57 (December, 1971), 373–382. For purposes of this essay, the author agrees with Johannesen who considers dialogue to represent "more of a communication attitude, principle, or orientation than a specific method, technique, or format." There is no reason why methods, techniques, or formats cannot ultimately evolve, however. In fact, some already have in psychiatry and psychotherapy.

8. Harold Larrabee, *Reliable Knowledge* (Boston: Houghton-Mifflin, 1945), p. 80.

9. Gordon, *Persuasion*, p. 6. Gordon believes the term "communications" is adequate to describe various conceptualizations contained (either quantitatively or qualitatively) within the seven categories of the "so-called 'Communication Process.' " Undoubtedly, the plural form is a misnomer in referring to the "third communications revolution."

10. Matson and Montagu, eds., *The Human Dialogue*, p. 2.

11. *Ibid.*

12. See Claude E. Shannon, *The Mathematical Theory of Communication* (Urbana: University of Illinois Press, 1949). Other selected sources on information theory are Robert Ash, *Information Theory* (New York: Interscience Publishers, 1965), and Robert G. Gallager, *Information Theory and Reliable Information* (New York: John Wiley and Sons, 1968).

13. A very clear statement by Warren Weaver appears in "The Mathematics of Communication" in Alfred G. Smith, ed., *Communication and Culture* (New York: Holt, Rinehart and Winston, 1966), pp. 15–24.

14. Ronald L. Smith, *General Models of Communication* (Lafayette, Ind.: Communication Research Center, 1962).

15. Smith, "Introduction," *Communication and Culture*, p. 8.

16. See Norbert Wiener, "Cybernetics" in Smith, *Communication and Culture*, pp. 25–35.

17. David K. Berlo, *The Process of Communication* (New York: Holt, Rinehart and Winston, 1960), p. 29. In his effort to be "consistent with current theory and research in the behavioral sciences," Berlo presents the communication model introduced by Shannon. The model, he states, is similar to Aristotle's and possesses "great similarities," with other contemporary models.

18. Matson and Montagu, eds., *The Human Dialogue*, p. 3.

19. Robert West, Merle Ansberry, and Anna Carr, *The Rehabilitation of Speech*, 3rd ed. (New York: Harper and Row, 1957), p. 254.

20. Robert J. Kibler and Larry L. Barker, eds., *Conceptual Frontiers in Speech Communication* (New York: Speech Association of America, 1969), p. 34.

21. See Robert Rosenthal, *Experimenter Effects in Behavioral Research* (New York: Appleton-Century-Crofts, 1966).

22. A "speaker's" response to his audience is usually called "feed-forward" by information theorists.

23. Lee Thayer, *Communication and Communication Systems* (Homewood, Ill.: Richard D. Irwin, 1968), p. 15.

24. Donald K. Darnell, "Toward a Reconceptualization of Communication," *The Journal of Communication*, 21 (March, 1971), 6.

25. Joost A. M. Meerloo, "Conversation and Communication" in Matson and Montagu, eds., *The Human Dialogue*, p. 143.

26. See Dennis R. Smith, "The Fallacy of the 'Communication Breakdown,' " *Quarterly Journal of Speech*, 56 (December, 1970), 345.

27. Dean C. Barnlund, ed., *Interpersonal Communication: Survey and Studies* (Boston: Houghton Mifflin, 1968), p. 511.

28. Raymond A. Bauer, "Brainwashing, Psychology or Demonology," *Journal of Social Issues*, 13 (1957), 41.

29. Larrabee, *Reliable Knowledge*, p. 172.

30. Thayer, *Communication and Communication Systems*, p. 5.

31. See David Berlo in Smith, ed., *Communication and Culture*, p. 24. "If we accept the concept of process, we view events and relationships as dynamic, on-going, ever-changing, continuous. When we label something as a process, we also mean that it does not have *a* beginning, *an* end, a fixed sequence of events. It is not static, at rest. It is moving. The ingredients within a process interact; each affects all of the others." Mr. Berlo was at the threshold of discovery, until he lapsed into mechanistic description.

32. Rapoport in Attinger, ed., *Global Systems Dynamics*, p. 26.

Dialogue and Rhetoric

ROBERT L. SCOTT

Manipulation, power relationships, superordination, subordination, control, and domination are at violent odds with the I-thou mystique.

Kenneth Keniston [1]

James Reston's column of April 20, 1969, "An Irreverent Dialogue on Relevancy," [2] is an excellent comment on the powerful sway of contemporary social jargon. The comment lies in the ironic demonstration of the degree to which the terms have been robbed of any substantial meaning. Perhaps the main thrust of the irony lies in the apparent fact that the popular power of the word "dialogue" to arouse positive responses from a multitude of people seems to have grown precisely in proportion to its being scrubbed clean of content. Interestingly a church in Minneapolis (like many others in many other places, I am sure) began several years ago to feature in its order of service a "dialogue" immediately following the sermon (which became "the contemporary word"). All this feature means is that the congregation is invited to ask questions of the minister or to make comments for a very few minutes. Recently someone sensed that the label for that section of the service needed a verbal push, and it has become dialogue-feedback-discussion.

In spite of all its comic manifestations, we sense that perhaps something fresh is in the atmosphere of our communication. Something as pervasive as that suggested by the occasional paper published by the Center for the Study of Democratic Institutions, "The Civilization of the Dialogue." [3]

Part of the attraction of "dialogue" for those professionally interested in communication may grow out of a weariness, perhaps tinctured with fear, with the push-pull click-click engineering models of human symbolic interaction. The assumptions of much contemporary study of communication, which line up well with those of old rhetoric, lead us to an uncritical acceptance of efficiency as a value orientation. Energy out should come as close as possible to equaling energy in. We may talk of the *process*, but productivity per se is taken as a sufficient measure of the efficacy of the process.

All of this, however, implies *control*—another powerful term of engineering. But as with the power to control our physical environment, we are beginning to suspect that sheer productivity may not be a sufficient measure of human good. What may be productive in one sense is polluting in another. Just as it is now easy to imagine a highly productive electrical energy plant polluting rivers and air, it is possible to imagine a highly productive communication system, one perhaps with the *barriers* reduced close to the zero point, polluting human relations. Given the uncritical assumption of productivity as a criterion, which seems to me nearly the same as saying given a high degree of control, brain-washing appears to be as laudable an instance of good communication as it is possible to cite.

In his challenging book, *The Identity of Man*, J. Bronowski centers on the question: what, if anything, makes man different from the machine? His answer seems to come down to this: the test of the efficient machine is that part of its product can be fed back into the system as instructions for the functioning of the system. To do so its product must be made perfectly regular. Man's experiences can never be fully coded to place on a punched card or magnetic tape to be fed back in as instructions which will infallibly make a product. In short, the system which is man is not fully formal.[4]

The point at issue here is close to the one that Henry W. Johnstone, Jr., makes when he argues that man is not simply a *communicating* animal but is a *persuading* animal.[5] By *communicating*, he seems to mean simply the giving of instructions. If one assumes that another simply needs to be and can be instructed, one assumes, first, that he is in control of the situation; second, that the circumstances are such that the information to be communicated is clear and need not be questioned; and third, that the other is not only capable of responding to the clear instructions but has no choice but to receive them and carry them out. Another's failure on the latter score would indicate his inferiority, which is to say, that the machine has a defective part. *Communication*, in the limited sense that Johnstone seems to be using the word, is machine-like. One might say that communication as information-giving is a situation in which the roles, goals, and instruments are clearly recognized and accepted by all parties. But to say that man is a persuading and persuaded animal, to use Johnstone's language further, is to recognize that the roles, goals, and even instruments, are not clearly recognized and accepted. It is to relinquish control of the situation, or rather, it is to treat the situation of interpersonal relations as in some important sense undefined and seek definition in symbolic interaction.

If there is a prevalent fear of control such as might be labeled "the engineering of consent," there is a countervailing fear of chaos. Even the spector of pollution, whether environmental or human, may be seen from one angle as a lack of control. It is symbolic disintegration that Jurgen Ruesch fears and brilliantly argues in his essay, "The Social Control of Symbolic Systems."[6] What we often feel as the blight of the mass media may be symptomatic of the loss of control of ourselves that we sense in our inability to respond as individuals with individuals. We seem to be confronted on every side with groups of others, sensing most vigorously the *gaps* between them and us, which may be simply to say that the symbols that seem to unite them are puzzling and unattainable to us. From our painful awarenesses of apartness, threatening in themselves as well as in what may lie behind them, arises the incantation—communicate! Our motivation in such situations is not likely to be simply an impulse to control the behavior of others, for we feel that we have lost control of ourselves.

The human dilemma in which we find ourselves entangled lies with the attraction-peril of community or regimentation on one side and the attraction-peril of individuality or anarchy on the other. The constant problem of maintaining a balance that will allow individuality within community without tumbling either into regimentation or anarchy seems especially intense today. The intensity of this human problem accounts for the almost hysterical energy we have directed to the elaboration of certain social symbols. The major thrust of this effort might be captured in such a sentence as, "We must commit ourselves to an involvement in relevant dialogue."

The impulse and the vocabulary are easily lampooned. Perhaps I have at least flirted with mocking the notion of "dialogue." The temptation, often yielded to, and the resilience of the concept in the face of ridicule both testify to a palpable value more and more widely shared.

Although I find the value suggested by "dialogue" well worth taking seriously, it seems to me impossible to stipulate a very precise meaning for the procedure suggested by the word. There is, however, something in the concept of dialogue that stands as a challenge to the old idea of rhetoric. Old rhetoric suggests a unidirectional control that threatens to become the sort of manipulation rejected as tending toward regimentation rather than community. Our impulse in the face of that threat may be to say in effect, "Let there be no rhetoric! Let there be dialogue instead!" What we are probably saying is, "Let us relinquish one way of attempting to control through the use of symbols for another way." Since I would define rhetoric as symbolic efforts to shape human means-ends relations, I would draw the tentative conclusion that the value inherent in the contemporary demand for *dialogue* is a thrust toward enlarging the concept of rhetoric to come closer to encompassing the verbal interactions engendered by the human dilemma. The point is not so much to relinquish the old rhetoric as to see its limitations and, especially, to see the potentialities of different rhetorical thrusts.

The rhetoric suggested by Aristotle's famous definition[7] and by his treatment of the topoi is a moderate rhetoric. It is one that presupposes a society in which values are well shared and social roles, stable. Cooperation, the ultimate end of all rhetoric, is defined in the frame of moderate rhetoric as moving others toward intermediate goals which are consistent with the generally accepted societal ends.

In seeking to induce others to cooperate, the moderate rhetorician assumes that some values held by others are consistent with the goals he recommends. On the other hand, those he seeks to persuade will exhibit some belief and behavioral tendencies which he wishes to repress; if they did not, no effort to persuade would be necessary. The rhetorician assumes that some of the values of others will be inconsistent with these tendencies. By identifying himself with the interests of those he wishes to persuade, the moderate rhetorician will seek to demonstrate the consistency of his goals with shared values and the inconsistency of contrary beliefs or behaviors with these or other values.[8] Clearly in this description of moderate rhetoric, which I take to be quite ordinary, the features that make it highly rational are apparent.[9]

There is an implication in moderate rhetoric that may not be apparent, that is, that the persuader is superior to the one persuaded. His superior position allows him to identify the consistencies and inconsistencies of shared values and to recommend belief and action on the basis of these. He chooses the goals that mediate between the positions in which both the persuader and persuadee find themselves and the common societal goals that both accept.

The superiority implicit in the fundamental relationship implied in moderate rhetoric need not be that of oppressive authoritarianism, although that is the direction in which its abuse tends. The superiority may lie in a commonly recognized institution for which the rhetorician gives voice. Or it may be attached to a role which is instrumental to established social ends. In short, it may be the sort of superiority consistent with democratic ideals.

In describing moderate rhetoric, I have tried to use a set of terms which will be helpful in constructing a model of three contrasting rhetorics: the moderate, the militant, and the agonistic-transcendent. Each has its characteristic voice, and each works through the seeking out of consistencies and inconsistencies in the value structures of those who interact. But each works differently and, although the ultimate goal of all rhetoric is cooperation, the cooperation toward which each works is of a different sort.

The great difficulty with a neat chart, of course, is that it suggests some sort of a natural structure with starting places carrying step by step through some sort of chronological or special order. No one ought to strain his

A definition of *rhetoric*: Symbolic efforts to shape human means-ends relations				
Ideal types	Voice	Means		Ends
		Value structures	Fundamental process	
moderate	superior to inferior	consistencies and inconsistencies	identifies	move the other
militant	inferior to superior	consistencies and inconsistencies	confronts	polarize self and others
agonistic-transcendent	equals	consistencies and inconsistencies	identifies and confronts	revalue values self and others

Two senses of "means-ends" are involved. *First*, the overarching social structure of general goals, more or less well agreed upon, and ways of reaching those goals, which tend to be set as values. Of course, values become ends or goals also. But this means-ends reversal is commonly recognized in using the terms. *Second*, the functioning of rhetoric within the overarching social structure, i.e., the instruments (means) and aims (sorts of cooperation sought). The ambiguity is made necessary by the reciprocity of the two senses. Rhetoric will affect the structure and the structure itself becomes instrumental in the rhetoric.

Means←Ends. *Moderate.* Within the confines of accepted relationships adjustment is sought. One who initiates moderate rhetoric assumes a superior grasp of these relationships which suggests that he move the other.

Means→Ends. *Militant.* Rejection of previously accepted relationships. One who initiates assumes an unfair exploitation which makes him, and those with whom he identifies, inferior. Since reversal is his aim, he seeks to polarize himself and the other.

Means←→Ends. *Agonistic-Transcendent.* An open attempt to revalue fundamental relationships. Since both a test and a leap are necessary, equality of participation is necessary also.

credulity for a moment in attempting to see such order in the relationships among these ideal types of rhetoric. I call them *ideal* types to stress the arbitrariness of the abstract categories. Surely the rhetorical propensities which I see coalescing around these points of focus may shade into a great variety of forms.

Fundamentally, however, all rhetoric assumes that humans responding in a social context have built value orientations, that these value orientations do not form perfectly consistent structures for any individual, and that each individual constantly revises his value orientations, although seldom drastically. These orientations provide the means of rhetoric.

With Donald K. Smith, I have attempted to describe the basic impulses of militant rhetoric, concentrating on the disposition of the militant speaker or writer to confront.[10] To say that the voice characterizing militant rhetoric is that of the inferior to the superior is not to make some sort of ultimate judgment. The relationship is in terms of the dominant values and the roles springing therefrom. The militant is apt to forge the signs of his established inferiority into fresh, defiant symbols. If he can shift the perceptions of the situation, these may become symbols of superiority. "The last shall be first!" cried Frantz Fanon with shrewd insight and sharp historical irony.[11] And in America his voice, at once mocking and confident, is echoed in scores of symbols developed by blacks for blacks, symbols which leave white liberals writhing in guilt and envy.

Thoroughly militant rhetoric assumes that adherents to new beliefs and movements will come. Gaining these adherents is secondary, and even derivative, to a more fundamental sort of cooperation sought—the response from others that will polarize the militant and those most closely identified with the established order. Such polarization is necessary if the voice that seeks reversal is to sound authentic. Although to be authentically militant may be a prime aim, such an aim does *not* suggest that the militant is merely self-serving, insincere in whatever his interpretation of the situation may be. He will highlight some alleged inconsistency in values held by himself and the others, or, even more likely, he will claim that some well agreed upon value is held falsely by the others.[12] But whereas the moderate rhetorician with a similar interpretation will seek to reduce the distance between himself and others, the militant will seek to fix the gulf or even to widen it. The moderate assumes that fundamentally what-is is good. Needed changes are subordinate and dominant values are consistent with these. The militant assumes that fundamentally what-is is bad. Values consistent with established social relationships are worthless.

There is a rhetoric which is much like the militant in sizing up the situation in which people seek order and advantage, but the voice of and cooperation sought by agonistic-transcendent rhetoric is quite different. Looking upon others as equal is radical in a surprising way. It is radical because it is rare and difficult. Agonistic-transcendent rhetoric is addressed to others, but if the others are truly seen as equal, then the rhetorician may in addressing others address himself. Further, the disposition that leads him to see others as equal, and to seek himself in the responses of others with whom he identifies, is that of uncertainty. He seeks something new, but what he seeks is not some tangible goal as much as the means to goals. He may concern himself with many of the same goals that moderate or militant rhetoricians seek in various circumstances, but, aware of the consistencies and inconsistencies of the value orientations he shares with others, he strives to test the relevant values. Inconsistency in the structure of values is only momentarily important to the moderate or the militant. Ideally, either is confident of his goals. When the goals themselves seem unsatisfactory, a thinker may turn to the structure of values which has sent him seeking. Speaking to an end then becomes secondary to understanding, if possible, the flaw in the structure of values which may account for some deep dissatisfaction.

I call this sort of rhetoric *agonistic* because it is, as the Greek root suggests, a contest. It is a contest that involves a grave risk; the risk of the self that resides in a value structure. I call this sort of rhetoric *transcendent* since if it locates fresh values, it is apt to do so by a leap, which is to say that the person so involved will face some contradiction in values which cannot be resolved logically. Some part of the structure must be abandoned, not simply repressed momentarily, and the void filled by willing an emphatic embracing of some other value.

Although a person might quite ordinarily be moderate or even militant and well aware of his stance, few probably take on the agonistic-transcendent task with a high degree of consciousness. Although it may be an ideal category standing separate from other sorts of rhetoric in the abstract, in actuality it is better viewed as ever potential in seeking to address others. In short, a person may sense an uneasiness in his tasks as a moderate or militant rhetorician which may be accounted for by the potentiality of agonistic-transcendent rhetoric in the circumstances. Perhaps the agonistic-transcendent act may prepare the way for clearer militant or moderate verbal actions.

All of this is not to say that the agonistic-transcendent is subordinate to the other ideal types. For just as the agonistic-transcendent may be preparatory, clearly an individual who has been thoroughly committed to a moderate or a militant stance may abandon his stance. Further, a successful militant is faced with becoming moderate if he is to adapt to the shifting value orientations of those he has affected and with whom he will probably wish to continue to interact. Questions of sequence of the ideal types or subordination of any to others cannot be answered apart from specific cases, and even then the answers will probably be in significant part arbitrary.

Nonetheless, the agonistic-transcendent, because of its function of testing, tempts us to see it peculiarly as a starting point. Although such rhetoric may be a test and a starting point for individuals, it is not merely the sort of private, prior decision-making which we often characterize as preceding moderate rhetoric, or militant, for that matter. This is not to say that solitary thinking may not indeed precede speaking, or that agonistic-transcendent rhetoric is a sort of passionate, thoughtless bursting forth of speech. An impromptu eloquence may flow from a militant or even a moderate stance.

The testing characteristic of agonistic-transcendent rhetoric comes in the shift from using consistencies and inconsistencies in shared value structures to resolving those inconsistencies. Although a specific resolution may seem highly logical, if it is to have value content, it cannot be completely so. Part of the resolution lies in the commitment and recommendation of an individual who says in effect, "I resolve to live by this value," and, further, since he must live with others, he adds, "and so should you." Thus the conflict must be resolved, at least in part, rhetorically. In human affairs, the willingness of others affirms the value of what we will.

Quite often humans behave as if the willingness of others is not at all germane. Some religiously oriented say they accept the Truth of God which has nothing to do with human will for its efficacy. Again, some scientifically oriented say that they accept the Truth derived by Objective Method which has nothing to do with human will for its efficacy. But allow me two observations. (1) Neither of these positions are quite what they seem at first glance. Both are most apt to assert the independence from the will of others precisely when it is the resistance of others which brings the question to issue. (2) Both the religiously and scientifically oriented tend strongly to seek adherents. Innovators in both propose reformations. What is to be reformed is highly value laden in that men and women live by what is being reformed and cannot put it aside lightly.[13]

As an illustration, the rhetoric of Jesus as recorded in the New Testament seems consistently to be a militant rhetoric in a moderate guise. Militant, because it continually confronts—inferior to superior, polarizing, seeking reversal. Paul's words characterize the movement from the beginning: "My brothers, think what sort of people you are, whom God has called. Few of you are men of wisdom, by any human standard; few are powerful or highly born. Yet to shame the wise, God has chosen what the world counts folly, and to shame what is strong, God has chosen what the world counts weakness. He has chosen things low and contemptible, mere nothings, to overthrow the existing order" (I Cor. 1:26–28).[14] Jesus' rhetoric seems moderate, because it continually identifies with well-established values. From the beginning to the end of his ministry, Jesus appealed to the Law and to the prophets. When confronted by those who would *test* him, as Mark puts it several times, Jesus asked questions such as, "Do not the Scriptures say?" and "What did Moses command you?" In his first great sermon he said, "Do not suppose that I have come to abolish the Law and the prophets; I did not come to abolish, but to complete" (Matthew 5:17–18). But of course, that which needs completing is in some vital way insufficient.

A strong and continuing thread in his rhetoric is Jesus' effort to revalue values. Perhaps the great instance of agonistic-transcendent rhetoric would be in the dialogue of Jesus and Satan in the wilderness. But the New Testament account of this confrontation is scant. The Sermon on the Mount, on the other hand, gives us ample material for analysis and thought.

The centuries that have intervened with their histories between us and the event make the words of the sermon echo dogmatically. But we must remember that then, as Matthew concludes his account, the people were astounded by the note of authority (7:28–29). The teaching and voice were fresh for them.

Much of the teaching can be paraphrased, "The letter of the Law is not enough." For us this is a cliché. And that fact may testify to the constant need to revalue values. Anyone reading the Gospels, reverently or not, must be convinced that the teaching was relevant to the times. The repeated identifying and confronting characteristic of the Sermon on the Mount shows the way to new values through old, for example: "You have learned that our forefathers were told, 'Do not commit murder; anyone who commits murder must be brought to judgement.' But what I tell you is this: Anyone who nurses anger against his brother must be brought to judgement. If he abuses his brother he must answer for it to the court; if he sneers at him he will have to answer for it in the fires of hell" (Matthew 5:20–22). The tension throughout is that of the spiritual against the material. The way is pictured as the remote and difficult as against the immediate and easy. What is at stake is not simply the goal but the way to the goal. Of course one alone could travel the way, but then should he not simply travel it in silence? Revaluing values is a double valuation. It always has the nature of a pledge which reminds us of Buber's I-Thou. To be valid, it must be reciprocal.

Through the pledge, the speaker binds himself as well as seeks to bind others. Probably the most difficult part of the Sermon on the Mount is the passage that demands that the old concept of justice be revalued:

> You have learned that they were told, "An eye for an eye and a tooth for a tooth." But what I tell you is this: Do not set yourself against the man who wrongs you. If someone slaps you on the right cheek, turn and offer him your left. If a man wants to sue you for your shirt, let him have your coat as well. If a man in authority makes you go one mile, go with him two. Give when you are asked to give; and do not turn your back on a man who wants to borrow.
>
> You have learned that they were told, "Love your neighbor, hate your enemy." But what I tell you is this; Love your enemies and pray for your persecutors; only so can you be children of your heavenly Father, who makes his sun rise on good and bad alike, and sends the rain on the honest and dishonest. If you love only those who love you, what reward can you expect? Surely the taxgatherers do as much as that. And if you greet only your brothers, what is there extraordinary about that? Even the heathen do as much. You must therefore be all goodness, just as your heavenly Father is all good (Matthew 5:38–48).

The carrying out of the pledge made in the beginning of his ministry is seen in the Passion of its end. The value of forbearance is demonstrated as binding on the one who spoke it—binding in the garden, before Pilate, and on the cross. But a pledge cannot be fulfilled by one party. The agony of Jesus was not simply in his relationship to God. As such, it would be purely private and the Sermon on the Mount, and his teachings generally, would remain empty. Jesus claimed fulfillment of the Law and the prophets, a fulfillment that necessitated belief on the part of others. Without this belief, encompassing both understanding of and faith in the message, the pledge and sacrifice would amount to absurdity. The doubt to be transcended was not simply that of the speaker in some truth considered objectively, but doubt in the value of communicating, of risking his pledge with others.

With moderate rhetoric, we are well acquainted. We are becoming better acquainted with militant rhetoric. It is time for rhetoricians to cease assuming that the agonistic-transcendent impulses obviously present in human communication must be poetic, or dramatic, or philosophic, or purely ritualistic. All of these labels may be appropriate, but the rhetorical label is appropriate also, if I am right in seeing rhetoric as symbolic efforts to shape human means-ends relations, and if, indeed, the ideal types are shifting aspects of one thing.

There is a shifting sense of dialogue permeating each of the ideal types, lending to each its legitimacy in human affairs.

Moderate rhetoric idealizes whatever system of agreed upon means and ends happens to be in force. Recognizing the potentialities of identifying the interests of various individuals, it values interchange as a means of adjustment, that is, of adjusting individuals to the system and of monitoring the system to maximize its efficient functioning. Since constant adjustment is assumed necessary, change is possible through a gradual evolution of values.

Militant rhetoric maximizes whatever contradictions are present in the system of agreed upon means and ends. Recognizing potentialities in reversing existing orders, it values interchange as a means of contrasting the interests of various individuals or groups. Confrontation is necessary to demonstrate the unbridgeable gulf that things-as-they-are fixes between those who ought to be part of a corporate whole. If one believes that the gulf is indeed unbridgeable under established conditions, then change is possible through a revolutionary reversal of value priorities.

Agonistic-transcendent rhetoric both idealizes existing values and maximizes their contradictions. Recognizing the potentialities of identification and yet accepting the necessity of confrontation, neither adjustment nor reversal is adequate to a change of values. Only a leap will suffice. Such a leap is possible only on the foundation of accepted values and is meaningful only if it becomes a bridge for others. To provide both the foundation to begin and the participation to complete the action, open interchange is mandatory.

There are, of course, moderate, militant, and agonistic-transcendent impulses which are not legitimized by dialogue. Then the moderate voice becomes simply the proclamation of rigid authority; the militant voice calls only for the violent annihilation of that authority; and the agonistic-transcendent voice chants merely private incantation. These are the limits of rhetoric.

1. Kenneth Keniston, *The Young Radicals: Notes on Committed Youth* (New York: Harcourt, Brace and World, 1968), p. 280.

2. *Minneapolis Sunday Tribune*, April 20, 1969, p. 2C.

3. An occasional paper published by the Center for the Study of Democratic Institutions, Santa Barbara, Calif., December, 1968. The essays in this publication, taken as a whole, are a good example of the vagueness and attractiveness of the term "dialogue." All the papers stem from John Wilkinson's "The Civilization of the Dialogue" in which the key term seems to come down to toleration of variant opinion and openness to talk. In addition, Wilkinson's paper is a bad-tempered evaluation of much of contemporary American education and politics as not exemplifying the vague value of "dialogue." Harrop A. Freeman in "The Legal Dialogue" comes as close as any of the participants to defining the term: "dialogue is a stated or accepted procedure of examining diverse points of view as a means of arriving at Truth" (p. 13).

4. J. Bronowski, *The Identity of Man* (New York: American Museum Science Books, 1966), *passim.*

5. Henry W. Johnstone, Jr., "The Relevance of Rhetoric to Philosophy and of Philosophy to Rhetoric," *The Quarterly Journal of Speech*, 52 (February, 1966), 41–46. Obviously I am arguing from Johnstone's terms and may not be arguing as he would.

6. Jurgen Ruesch, "The Social Control of Symbolic Systems," *The Journal of Communication*, 17 (December, 1967), 276–301.

7. "The faculty of observing in any given case the available means of persuasion." Aristotle, *Rhetoric*, 1355b, 25–26, W. Rhys Roberts translation.

8. See Theodore Clevenger, Jr., *Audience Analysis* (Indianapolis, Ind.: Bobbs-Merrill, 1966), p. 114.

9. Cf. Edwin Black's argument that logos dominates neo-Aristotelian rhetoric. See his *Rhetorical Criticism* (New York: Macmillan, 1965), chap. 5, esp. pp. 114–117.

10. Robert L. Scott and Donald K. Smith, "The Rhetoric of Confrontation," *The Quarterly Journal of Speech*, 55 (February, 1969), 1–8.

11. Frantz Fanon, *The Wretched of the Earth*, trans. Constance Farrington (New York: Grove Press, 1963), p. 30.

12. See Robert L. Scott, "The Conservative Voice in Radical Rhetoric: A Common Response to Division," *Speech Monographs*, 40 (June, 1973), 123–135.

13. The history of science demonstrates this statement as well as any other part of human history. See, for example, Thomas S. Kuhn, *The Structure of Scientific Revolutions* (Chicago: The University of Chicago Press, 1962).

14. This, and all subsequent, quotations of the New Testament are taken from *The New English Bible* (Oxford University Press and Cambridge University Press, 1961).

PART II
Communication and Rhetorical Study:
The Behavioral Perspective

Communication Theory and Theater:
An Exercise in Relationship

MARTIN COBIN

My present concern, as a theater theorist, is with communication theory. Theater scholars who have been attracted to communication theory, as well as those who have been repulsed by it, have often confused communication theory with behavioral methods. This confusion among theater scholars is a consequence of two factors: the emphasis placed on behavioral methods by most of the communication theorists with whom theater scholars come into contact; and the failure of many who identify themselves as communication scholars to differentiate theory and methods.

I want to probe the way theater theorists have reacted to both communication theory and behavioral methods to see how such scholars do relate and could better relate to communication theory. I want also to account for the seeming indifference of communication scholars to artistic communication in general and theatrical communication in particular. The apparent indifference reflects diverse backgrounds of academic training and lack of clarity (at times) as to the distinction between theory and methods; the result is that communication theory and theater art are viewed as altogether separate fields of study. My intention in this essay is (1) to encourage the theater scholar to become involved (as beneficiary and as contributor) in communication scholarship and (2) to encourage the communication scholar to recognize the need for a focus on artistic communication (with theater art providing, perhaps, the easiest and most rewarding place to begin).

In the 1970s, theater scholarship (possibly comparable to literary scholarship at the same point of time and to rhetorical scholarship at mid-century) is simultaneously accepting and rejecting concepts of communication theory and behavioral methods. Attitudes in the academic theater community vary greatly. The Conference on Theatre Research, essentially a three-part series held in 1965 and 1966, paid attention to behavioral science in relation to the possibilities for experimental research in the theater.[1] In the course of paying attention to these matters, the suggestion given to behavioral scientists by one member of this scholarly gathering was that they "keep their bloody hands off the theatre," although the proceedings indicate a divergence of learned opinion on the matter.[2] The editor of the major scholarly journal of what is now the American Theatre Association (then called the American Educational Theatre Association, or AETA) saw fit to reflect the interest in behavioral research by including an article on the subject in the May, 1965, issue.[3] That this truly reflected a professional interest within the field is documented by the existence within AETA, then as now, of the experimental research project. Significant, however, is the dearth of articles reporting on either communication theory or experimental research within the *Educational Theatre Journal* between the illuminating article of 1965 and the present; also significant is the fact that the "illuminator" is not a "theater" scholar.

Some insight may also be obtained from the apparent contradiction between the desire of many theater scholars to shy away from the "communication" label and the consistent use of "The Theatre as a Means of Communication" to designate one of the major classifications in the annual *Educational Theatre Journal* report on "Doctoral Projects in Progress in Theatre Arts." What may be particularly relevant here is the inclusion within this category of such subclassifications as directing, acting, visual arts, music, dance, architecture, administration, playwriting, translations, production, and reader's theater; and the separate designation of such other major classifications as "The Drama," "The Theatre in Its Social Function," and such "Related Means of Communication" as motion pictures and the broadcast media. Apparently scholars within theater often differ from one another as well as from scholars in other fields in their perceptions of communication.

The lack of relationship between theater and communication is also evident in the perceptions of many (certainly not all) whose scholarly focus is on communication. A theater scholar desiring to benefit from the work of communication scholars will derive little encouragement, for example, if he begins with *Methods of Research in Communication.*[4] Here he will find an early statement of three objectives: "to help students acquire the knowledge and skills to design and conduct experimental research . . . to acquaint potential researchers with the various methods and instruments available . . . to suggest new areas of research."[5] He will be forced to probe long and carefully, however, before he finds the single reference to an actual investigation dealing with the theater in what is, even here, a shared and rather brief billing: "Some recent research has involved changing the seating arrangement of members in an audience to see if it makes them react differently to speakers and theatrical productions."[6] The significance of this book to the theater scholar is not only its lack of attention to theater but also its total identification of communication research with experimental techniques.

This all-absorbing concern with communication from the point of view of the behavioral scientist does not always produce an exclusive focus on experimental research; but because of the degree to which this focus permeates the field of communication theory an artificial sense of division has been created between the communication scholar and the theater scholar. For theater scholars there have been two unfortunate consequences. Many have equated communication with behavioral research, noted their own involvement in a virile field of activity with a long tradition of productive scholarship using nonbehavioral methods, and concluded that communication and theater are unrelated. Many others have been sensitive to their own lack of enthusiasm for behavioral methods, recognized the communicative dimensions of theatrical activity, and concluded that communication and theater were related in ways that could be comprehended independent of what was taking place in the field of communication scholarship. The first consequence is probably reflected in the "keep your bloody hands off" attitude; the second in the willingness to suggest that "communication" would more closely relate to "A New Design for an Outdoor Theatre," "An Evaluation of Actor Training Programs in Selected Universities and Colleges in the U.S.," or "The Management of Sara Bernhardt's American Tours," than it would relate to "Violence in Contemporary British Drama as a Projection of Philosophic Rebellion," "Polish Drama: Interplay between Politics and Drama," or "Playwrights and Playwriting of Modern Chinese Communist Drama."[7]

Many communication scholars have concentrated their activity on areas they considered relatively more open to behavioral research methods. The potential of these methods has been perceived, often, as much on the basis of the investigator's background as in response to the unique limitations and capabilities of the investigative methods. In any case, the concentration may well be self-defeating in its impact if it is allowed to continue too long. For example, despite the inclusion of materials of considerable interest to a theater scholar in the recent Sereno and Mortensen collection of readings,[8] even a glance at the table of contents of this work clearly indicates no overt concern with theater or—which is far worse—with any other art form. Theorists can focus on any subdivision within their discipline they choose, of course (although such limitations may reasonably be expected to be reflected in the titles of their publications), but I am moved to consider the implications of this particular omission in its relation to the avowed objectives described by the editors in their introductory chapter, "A Framework for Communication Theory."

The readings in this book are designed to provide a core of foundational concepts and a theoretical framework for studying the nature and process of human communication. The topics are broadly based and comprehensive in scope. The readings focus on the inner workings of communication, the common denominators which underlie all modes of human interaction. Gaining an understanding of the dynamics involved in human interaction requires some insight into what happens when people communicate, a recognition of the forces which interact to produce complex communicative events, and an understanding of what is known about the effects of major variables as they influence specified communicative outcomes. The topics, in other words, do not deal with particular modes of interaction such as rumor, conversation, markings on a wall, speeches and the like. The focus is rather upon the nature and function of the major determinants of communicative acts.[9]

I admit that lights on a stage or the scripts of plays are no more appropriate subjects for investigation than are markings on a wall or speeches; but how are scholars to focus "upon the nature and function of the major determinants of communicative acts" and on "the common denominators which underlie all modes of human interaction" without "some insight into what happens when people communicate" *artistically*, without "a recognition of the forces which interact to produce complex communicative events" *of an artistic nature*, and without "an understanding of what is known about the effects of major variables as they influence specified communicative outcomes" *in the theater or other arts?* In brief, *how can scholars build a meaningful communication theory on data so restricted in scope as to reflect no major concern with investigations of artistic communication?* How can they seek common denominators underlying "all modes of human interaction" when they have no denominators derived from artistic interaction?

If theater and communication scholars alike can accept the actuality and the value of the communication researcher's emphasis on behavioral science without identifying communication theory exclusively with behavioral science, they may see with greater clarity two elements sometimes partially obscured. First, communication scholarship can be defined in relation to its focus on an area of knowledge rather than on its manipulation of specific research techniques (the techniques having value only as they contribute to the knowledge). Second, theater scholarship is not apt to benefit richly from the fruits of communication scholarship unless theater scholars are involved in the applications. Regarding the application of behavioral research methods to one instance of theater scholarship, Clevenger has pointed out that "only the technique comes from behavioral science. The variables and the hypothesis are uniquely theatrical."[10] In addition, he reminds us, "Long experience has taught the behaviorist that his methods give satisfactory answers only to questions which can be translated into behavioral terms. His methods are useless—indeed, they are pernicious—when misapplied to other types of questions."[11] Theater scholars, particularly, need to realize more fully that (1) *some* questions about artistic communication *can* be translated into behavioral terms and (2) *those that cannot* be so translated may, nevertheless, be examined—quite meaningfully and helpfully—from the standpoint of communication theory. Surprisingly, perhaps, more evidence seems available to support the former assertion[12] than the latter.

A comment by Becker is particularly relevant at this point: "I believe that we err if we simply cast our fishing line about in the ponds of other disciplines to discover what research techniques we might snag that we can somehow apply to our field. We ought to start by asking *precisely* what it is we want to know or to understand and then devise or borrow tools that help us to find answers to *our* questions and achieve understanding of *our* concepts."[13] The relevance of this statement to the present discussion derives from the ability of a theater scholar to so define what it is *he* wants to know or understand and to so formulate *his* questions and *his* concepts as to lead him to the awareness that *as a theater scholar* he is concerned with communication theory. Given this awareness, theater scholarship can proceed by relating a variety of theoretical theater constructs to communication theory constructs not normally associated with the theater. The utility of such a process for the theater scholar can be tested by determining what it stimulates in the way of intuitive insights, ways of looking at specific practices or periods, hypothetical statements of relationship, and enlarged fields of investigation.

For some, however, even the possibility of such a process may require demonstration. What follows, then, is a simple exercise in applying communication theory constructs not normally associated with the theater to a specific problem of peculiar interest to theater students. Admittedly the exercise may appear rather arbitrary and artificial both in conception and restrictiveness. It should serve, however, as an appropriate test and demonstration; the exercise will be carried out, therefore, no further than is necessary to provide such a test and demonstration.

The specific problem selected as being clearly of interest to students of the theater is that of developing a theoretical framework for increasing our understanding and appreciation of the traditional Asian theater. The communication theory constructs utilized will be taken from a widely known work in the field of organizational communication by Lee Thayer.[14] A meaningful rationale lies behind this combination of selections. Those of us in the Occident can approach Oriental theater with a greater degree of objectivity than is apt to be the case in our approach to any theater problem within our own tradition. Additionally, if our search for understanding requires us to bridge from one culture to another, we may find it particularly useful to look upon the art form we examine as part of a complex communication system (such as an organization) rather than as a specific communicative act. If the problem is of theatrical interest (regardless of how interesting to any specific person) and if the constructs are taken from a theoretical work on communication (regardless of how representative or expert in the judgment of any specific individual), the requirements are met for an exercise that will provide the desired test and demonstration.

One final word of caution may be in order. This exercise of applying constructs necessarily involves the frequent use of communication terms as substitutes for theater terms or at least for terms with which theater scholars are more familiar. Communication scholars should not infer from this that theater scholars have no means of dealing with these concepts; indeed, communication scholars must be sensitive to possible distortions created in the attempt to match one set of terms with another set of concepts. Theater scholars, on the other hand, should not jump to the conclusion that familiar ideas are simply being expressed in novel (and often awkward) ways; the need rather is to remain open to any instances in which novel ideas about familiar elements are stimulated by the different conceptions that accompany (and in other contexts give rise to) these unfamiliar terms.

For present purposes I shall confine my consideration of traditional "Asian theater" to the theaters of those countries that have experienced the fullest theatrical development: India, China, and Japan.[15] Since these theaters differ from one country to another and there are differences within each country, the label "Asian theater" must be accepted as dealing with commonalities.[16] I will also consider "traditional" theater as one handed on through time by a society striving to preserve values and procedures from the past. Such a view is consistent with anthropological[17] and sociological[18] usage and guards against fallaciously equating the traditional with the past—a fallacy we cannot afford when dealing with traditional theater forms that are in large measure contemporaneous.

The Occidental seeking to appreciate and enjoy Oriental traditional theater finds himself beset by many difficulties beyond the linguistic one. The American who has become capable of responding enthusiastically to operas presented in languages he does not understand (a capability not shared by most Americans even when the language is English) is frequently disturbed in seeking a comparable enthusiasm for Oriental theater, by what he perceives to be ear-rending sounds, agonizingly slow movements, boring repetitiveness, interminable interruptions in the story, and incomprehensible situations or motivations. Yet he is told by some American theater scholars that this is an exciting, dynamic, sophisticated theater[19] and that traditional forms still command a significant following.[20] Help is needed to bridge the gap between where the Occidental theatergoer finds himself as a consequence of his own tradition and experiences and where he would like to be when he seeks to appreciate Asian theater. This help may be provided by considering such concepts as *aesthetic meaning, social function, and theatrical intensity.*[21]

Use of the term *aesthetic meaning*, simply implies that the pleasurable response involved in an art experience can be described, for the member of a theater audience in this case, as a response to the symbolic behavior of the artists. The behavior is symbolic because its impact derives not merely from itself but from its referents. The hand gesture of the Indian dancer, the color patterns of a Peking Opera "painted-face" make-up, the position and movement of the Kabuki actor's fan, are symbols or "event-data" offered on the assumption that the audience members will achieve the necessary "transformation of event-data into information."[22] But to the extent that "communication always occurs in the receiver,"[23] the transformation, the perceived meaning, the response, will vary from one audience member to another. In short, the aesthetic meaning will differ from one audience member to another not because of any deficiencies of the artist but as a simple consequence of the nature of the communicative process. The artist finds himself, therefore, seeking not so much to project a meaning or an aesthetic impact inherent in his material or himself but rather to limit the range of response variations among those he strives to stimulate. The audience member desiring stimulation, in turn, seeks not so much to achieve an awareness of the artist's "true and single" message as to maximize his own capacity to be responsive within a fairly narrow range to the implications of the artistic symbolism.

What is of special importance here is that such implications are derived in large measure from the wider contexts or worlds within which artist and audience live. If "the world and our conceptions of it co-determine each other,"[24] the range of responses will become narrowed to the degree that the various audience members live in similar worlds; and the range will seem satisfactory to the artist(s) or critic(s) to the degree that these worlds are similar to the world(s) of the artist(s) or critic(s). Left to their own devices, human beings confronting the variety of experiences and circumstances of a normal lifetime would seem doomed to fail in any attempt to shape similar worlds for themselves. To get a similarity of worlds close enough—that is, a range of responses sufficiently limited to satisfy the artist and critic—would seem like an impossibility. As Thayer suggests, "the purpose of a human organization is to accomplish ends which are otherwise impossible,"[25] however, and the human organization we designate as a *culture* or a *society* does, in fact, tend to shape and limit the circumstances of human life so as to create a certain similarity in the worlds of its members.

This shaping and limiting is intensified when the society is traditional—not only because it takes place and works its effects over a longer period of time and through a greater number of generations but also because of the reinforcement it provides to the desirability of perpetuating familiar patterns. Any student of theater can readily assert his clear recognition (shared by his predecessors for centuries) that a theater art must be understood in relation to its cultural context. In actuality, however, the assertion is far more evident than is the recognition. Many students of theater read (and are encouraged to read) nothing but theater books. A surprising number of theater people understand English history only as it has come to them in the works of Shakespeare. Of those who would learn about Asian theater far too many are content with a glossary of names, dates, and technical terms (particularly if well illustrated)—exhibiting a point of view akin to those who might accept the memorization of a dictionary as providing sufficient mastery of a foreign language. In practical production activities numerous directors and actors (perhaps a majority) will ascribe lack of the proper aesthetic impact—as *they* have defined it—to the inadequacies of the audience; many critics will clarify the "meaning" the audience failed to appreciate; and designers often assume their own sensitivity to color, line, and mass as being either similar to the sensitivities of most other people (an assumption not usually based on real evidence) or else similar to those members of the audience possessing good taste ("good" meaning comparable to their own and implying no studied concern for the tastes of those not so blessed).

Before proceeding further I would pause to reflect on how the discussion has just progressed from a shift in terminology to reconceptualizations and possible insights. The theater scholar undoubtedly strained at the translation of "symbolic gestures, make-up, and movement" into "transformation of event-data into information" and the communication scholar should recognize that something was lost in the translation. What was gained, however, was a casting of the theatrical activity into the communication framework and, as a consequence, a view of the activity in communicative dimensions. This resulted in a focus on individual response differences as a natural and unavoidable part of the interaction process in the theater. Such a focus may seem "common sense" when identified but it is not common in the theater where the normal emphasis is on stimulus rather than response and where even ambiguity is conceived generally as the consequence of a deliberate decision on the part of the artist (playwright, director, designer, actor) to project multiple meanings. With this focus on response differences, the possibility was suggested of viewing audience behavior as variations within a conditioned range of responses and the cultural or social context was seen as a conditioning mechanism—with traditional cultures or societies recognized as being particularly strong in their conditioning impact. This line of thought has led to a perception of the importance of social context quite different from that of most theater scholars and practitioners who feel more at home in the "allied" fields of art, literature, and philosophy than in the "more remote" fields of history, social psychology, and sociology.

If clarity regarding *aesthetic meaning* is not merely the result of asserting the significance of cultural context but reflects a more profound theoretical acceptance of the concept that communication occurs in a receiver who responds within the communication situation on the basis of his conceptions of the world in which he lives, what are the implications for the Occidental student of Asian theater? Since the theater production strives to narrow the range of variation in the aesthetic responses, it should be useful to inquire into the methods by which this narrowing occurs in traditional Asian theater. Three factors come to mind. One already suggested is the rigid structuring of a society that limits the experiences and shapes the knowledge and attitudes of its members. This is a factor a theater cannot control but can exploit. Those who would understand such exploitation must determine the nature of the experiences, knowledge, and attitudes fostered by a particular society. Those who would share the responses of the audience in such a theater must achieve a capacity to play the role of being limited by just such experiences, knowledge, and attitudes. A study of the theater itself will provide a valuable key to these elements but it is not sufficient. The assumptions made within the theater will be often incomprehensible, at best vague, and at times misleading to one who comes merely as an outsider.[26] For example, nothing within the play itself indicates why separated lovers of a Bunraku or Kabuki play commit suicide rather than simply defy their parents or go off to set up housekeeping in another village. Lacking this understanding, the plot seems contrived and the characters unsympathetic—perceptions obviously not shared by the deeply moved Japanese audience.

A second factor is conditioning through social reinforcement—which the theater can do in its own right. The traditional theater of Asia repeats not only plays but production techniques. The newcomer in the audience is conditioned by the response behavior of those around him, is reinforced by the frequent experience of very similar responses, and in turn repeats these responses as part of later audiences conditioning other newcomers. The Kabuki scene that will be interrupted by the "nick-of-time" appearance of the death-defying hero grows in emotional excitement only partly because of its own internal conflicts; the tensions within the audience grow in intensity out of all proportion to what is happening on the stage because everyone knows the interruption that will come. The awesome hush as thousands wait, the riveted attention on the area where the bridge from the stage out into the audience disappears from view (behind the curtain at the back of the auditorium or out of sight under a projecting balcony), the sense of excitement that fills the theater when the rattle of rings on rod indicates the whipping aside of the curtain, the sighs and shouts of satisfaction from the audience when the voice of strong, courageous manhood calls out, "Wait a moment!" are all products of conditioning.[27] Here again intellectual comprehension is not sufficient. The serious student of Asian theater has no alternative but to participate in the conditioning process to the point of being, himself, conditioned.

A third factor meriting consideration is the bypassing of distracting symbolism. This dominates a great deal of Oriental art and is obviously a significant part of Western art, although not common to the theater; in Asian theater it is widespread and particularly apparent in the dance. The bypassing process consists simply (in the description of it) of dealing directly with an artist's response rather than with the object or situation that triggered the response. The artist's response of serenity or terror to a landscape or seascape, for example, does not lead him to stimulate comparable responses of serenity or terror by bringing (as a person) the viewer to the scene or (as an artist) the scene to the viewer. In either case, with communication a function of the receiver, the artist has relatively little control over the response. The artist has more control over the response if (through his art) he brings to the viewer the serenity or terror itself—borrowing from his own perceptions of the reality only such elements as he considers useful in symbolizing not the scene but his response to the scene. This process is greatly facilitated by the evolution of conventions that provide clarity. Such conventions, of course, run counter to the concern for realism that has marked the development of the Western theater tradition through most of its history. The same concern for (or at least interest in) realism is apparent in Asian theater[28] but the traditional forms have vigorously maintained the artistic validity of the nonrealistic[29] and there has never been any reluctance to mix the realistic and the nonrealistic. For the Western student of Asian theater this creates a clear necessity to learn the conventions and to exercise an imaginative flexibility for which his past theatrical experiences may not have prepared him.

The *social function* of theater is manifold and will be considered here only in part. The sense of "togetherness" derived from the interaction between audience and artists and among members of an audience gives to the theater participant a greater consciousness of community, perhaps, than he can achieve from any other art. Some people, indeed, derive from the theater more than from any other aspect of their lives a feeling of relatedness, of kinship, of group identity. Most students of theater would express this as involving shared emotions, of having a good (or sad) time together. On a sophisticated level the theater student can explore audience facilitation and intensification. Another approach (perhaps provocative because it leads to less familiar areas) is available through a consideration of "integration." Certain passages from Thayer are particularly relevant here. After indicating the human need to stabilize the relationship between the self-concept and the world-concept, he suggests three levels at which this relationship is sought. At the intrapersonal level the individual achieves "the integration and perpetuation of his psychological system" as a consequence of confirming "established (or desired) state relationships" with what he can perceive of his environment. At the interpersonal level individuals establish relationships and maintain them to the degree that the behavior facilitated by these relationships is perceived "in some mutually acceptable way." At the organizational level the "integrative functions are provided in part by bureaucratization, proceduralization, institutionalization, etc." and "the necessary integrative mechanisms become imbedded in" the "literature, art, folklore . . . and institutional practices."

Particularly pertinent to the theater is the concept that "whatever it is that the members of large social systems separately partake of in common is a potential vehicle for the integrative functions of communication which in turn link them together culturally."[30] In this sense the theater serves as the housing for an "integrative mechanism" providing, especially if the theater is traditional, the necessary "proceduralization" and "institutionalization." The traditional Asian theater, then, may open up more readily to the student who approaches it with an awareness of its identity as a social institution with a social function. This particular social institution, because of its formal organization and its overt commitment to procedures, may be expected to carry out vigorously the task any social institution must undertake as a simple consequence of its identity—the perpetuation of the value system of the society that creates and nourishes it. The implications of this view of theater for the general theater student are obvious. Among them is the theoretical assertion (readily open to investigation and testing) that the theater is essentially conservative; that "theaters of revolt" cannot really exist; and that what theater historians and critics often describe by such "activist" terms are the social institutions of subcultures, committed to perpetuating the value system of the subculture, and so overwhelmingly narrow in their appeal (communicatively involving almost no "outside people") as to be not so much attitude-changing as reinforcing and even ritualistic. Another implication of this view of the particularly institutional nature of theater is that the student of traditional Asian theater should not be overly concerned about what may seem at first to be some sort of "social deficiency"; the theater student rather than the traditional artist may have misperceived the theater's potential for social protest.[31]

Another concept to be touched upon with profit is that of *theatrical intensity*. Theatrical artists of all traditions strive not only for a communicative relationship with an audience but for the involvement of the audience in this relationship to a maximum degree. A common way to refer to this is to speak of seeking an impact at as high a level of intensity as possible. Asian traditional theater may be distinguished by, or better understood through a consideration of, the extremely high priority it gives to the achievement of intensity—as evidenced by the price it pays and the methods it employs. In this regard, thinking of communication in a "game" sense may be profitable: "Intercommunication is a universal, pervasive game, in which statements arbitrarily representing states of our separate existences, are offered and accepted (or not). Our willingness to accept the conventional meanings of words is our entry fee into the game. If each participant follows the rules of the game, we say they 'communicate with' each other."[32] Thayer's observation is particularly applicable if (1) we include in our understanding of the term "words" any element in the rich vocabulary of the theater: gesture, posture, music, light, color, and the like, and (2) we recognize "statements" as being *any* manifestation of the "states" of our existences and not merely those that are verbal, linguistic utterances.

To the extent that the vocabulary employed to achieve the manifestation is both *highly* conventional and unlike our normal, already learned vocabulary, the entry fee into the game is a high one; in this sense, the traditional Asian theater "player" must pay a much higher price than those who play most other theater games. The high cost of this theater's commitment to intensity, however, is even more obvious and expensive in the restrictions placed on the performers: "The intangible 'dues' that one 'pays' to belong to any organization, are basically, his abdication of certain degrees of freedom to choose, to determine more or less independently when and how to behave, etc. To belong to any organization, an individual must give up certain choices that he might make about the what, the when, the how, the how much, etc., of his task—or of his role-related behavior. This is his organizational contract."[33] The unwillingness or the inability to sign such a "contract" is precisely the reason some artists of high literary talent have avoided writing for the theater or failed in their attempts to do so. In forms as traditional as those under consideration in Asia, the "contract" is particularly demanding and places tremendous limitations on the performing artist. The demands are so pervasive and clear that the theaters tend to be director-free; each performer seeks to shape his artistic behavior by doing what has been handed down to him from past generations in ways also handed down from past generations. The result is a discipline far more demanding of time, concentration, and personal commitment than most theater artists of the Occident are accustomed to (or even, perhaps, capable of)[34] and a limitation upon "degrees of freedom" many Occidental artists interpret as a lack of creativity. In short, theater artists trained in the European and American traditions would frequently refuse to pay the dues involved even if membership were offered.

We can better understand the motivation for paying this high price (and rid ourselves of the mistaken notion that traditional arts are not creative) by considering the compensatory reward—intensity. The psychological factors of attention are such that human beings, including theater audiences, will focus more on the novel than on the familiar provided the novel is perceived within a framework that facilitates relating it to something meaningful. To what does an audience attend in a theater situation where almost everything is familiar as a consequence of many previous repetitions? On the other hand, on what does a performer focus in a theater situation where most of what he performs has been so frequently repeated as to be automatic? As suggested earlier, vivification is derived from the build-up and satisfaction of anticipations based on familiarity with the material. More significantly, however, this theater situation provides an opportunity for a sharpness of focus never possible in our modern theaters. The actor wastes no time on gaining insights and polishing techniques that are part of what he has already brought to the role many times in the past. The audience member wastes no energies trying to puzzle out character motivations or plot complications nor in seeking to guess the outcome before it is revealed. The performer's focus is much less on what to do than on doing it as well as possible. The audience's focus is much less on satisfying curiosity as to what will happen than on being saturated in the happening of it. The concept of saturation may describe the performer's activity also since, obviously, his focus on "doing well" is advanced far beyond the level of conscious attention to technique.

Such a situation would seem to maximize the potential for intense experiences. Within such a situation, also, the artistic and human sensitivities and expressive talents that necessarily distinguish one artist from another—and the human (as opposed to machine) nature of the artist that necessarily distinguishes one performance from another by the same artist—will result in subtle changes. Within these subtleties lies the creative genius of the artist of the traditional Asian theater. Because they are presented to an audience familiar with all the norms from which the deviations are made, they can be tremendously powerful in their impact. The implication of this for the student of traditional Asian theater is that he cannot possibly assess or even perceive the variation until he has become familiar with the norms. In a purely artistic (as distinguished from scholarly) sense a traditional art cannot be properly experienced except by those who—at least in the role of "game-player"—can place themselves within the tradition. For this, too, a price must be paid.

The expressed purpose of this exploration was to demonstrate the possibility of relating theoretical communication constructs to theoretical theater constructs. Such a relationship having been made, the focus would necessarily change if the exploration continued beyond this point. The motivation for the exploration was to persuade but, in the last analysis, it is the reader who must determine whether anything new was stimulated in the way of intuitive insights, ways of looking at specific practices, testable hypotheses, or areas for further investigation. I can make this determination for myself, of course; there may be merit in identifying a few of the elements stimulated in my own thinking. I am moved, for example, to reject the typical method of teaching theater history (relatively independent of social and cultural context). I consider it helpful to look at the development of the appreciation of a particular theater period as a process of seeking to share the limitations of experience, knowledge, and attitudes that shaped the responses of the audiences of that period. I find numerous hypotheses that merit testing through quite diverse methods. I could hypothesize—as already mentioned— that so-called "theaters of revolt" are basically reinforcing agencies committed to the already formulated value system of a subculture. I could also hypothesize—to provide a quite different example—that a successful costume designer has taste preferences regarding color, line, and style closely akin to the taste preferences of a large majority of the people among whom he is considered successful. I am attracted by the value of investigating further the degree to which enthusiasts of traditional performing arts are sensitive to variations in the performance. For me, in other words, an exploration of the relationship between theater and communication is stimulating and fruitful. My realization of this impels me to emphasize the need to go beyond the unavoidably artificial mechanisms of the exercise just concluded. The real need is for an increasing number of theater scholars to develop a sound orientation to communication theory and for an increasing number of communication scholars to develop an active concern for artistic communication.

1. Special Issue, "Conference on Theatre Research," *Educational Theatre Journal*, 19, 2A (June, 1967). See papers by Norman Frederiksen and George Gunkle.

2. *Ibid.*, p. 245.

3. Theodore Clevenger, Jr., "Behavioral Research in Theatre," *Educational Theatre Journal*, 17 (May, 1965), 118–121.

4. *Methods of Research in Communications*, eds. Philip Emmert and William D. Brooks (Boston: Houghton Mifflin, 1970).

5. *Ibid.*, p. vii.

6. *Ibid.*, p. 352.

7. "Doctoral Projects in Progress in Theatre Arts, 1969," *Educational Theatre Journal*, 21 (May, 1969), 214–219.

8. *Foundations of Communication Theory*, eds. Kenneth K. Sereno and C. David Mortensen (New York: Harper and Row, 1970).

9. *Ibid.*, p. 3.

10. Clevenger, "Behavioral Research in Theater," p. 118.

11. *Ibid.*, p. 119.

12. See studies cited in the Clevenger article, for example.

13. Samuel L. Becker, "Experimental Studies in Oral Interpretation: A Critique," *Western Speech*, 33 (Fall, 1969), 275.

14. Lee Thayer, *Communication and Communication Systems* (Homewood, Ill.: Richard D. Irwin, Inc., 1968).

15. This is the general perception of Asian theater scholars and is reflected in the "Prefatory Note" of Henry W. Wells, *The Classical Drama of the Orient* (New York: Asia Publishing House, 1965).

16. Any examination of such theatrical forms as Sanskrit, Yakshagana, Yüan, K'un-chu'ü, Noh, or Kabuki will demonstrate the appropriateness of such plural labels as "theaters of India," "theaters of China," "theaters of Japan," to say nothing of the "theaters of Asia" that are here treated in a generic sense.

17. See A. L. Kroeber, *Anthropology: Culture Patterns and Processes* (New York: Harbinger Books, 1963), pp. 61, 219.

18. Joseph S. Roucek and Roland L. Warren, *Sociology, an Introduction* (Totowa, N.J.: Littlefield Adams, 1965), p. 175.

19. See Leonard C. Pronko on "Freedom and Tradition in the Kabuki Actor's Art," *Educational Theatre Journal*, 21 (May, 1969), 139–146.

20. See particularly pages 159–160 of Martin Cobin, "Traditional Theater and Modern Television in Japan," *Educational Theatre Journal*, 21 (May, 1969), 156–170.

21. The concepts merit being developed at great length but this is not necessary for present purposes. The labels are arbitrary and have no currency beyond the limits of this discussion.

22. Thayer, *Communication and Communication Systems*, p. 17.

23. *Ibid.*, p. 113.

24. *Ibid.*, p. 112.

25. *Ibid.*, p. 96. Admittedly the organization enables people to perform "specialized tasks" possibly accentuating differences but the "fit together" of these tasks provides a commonality of identity, goal, and values.

26. Relevant to this is the Japanese designation of foreigners as *gaijin* (outside people).

27. A partial comparison can be drawn to the experience of seeing a well-liked film for the second or third time; here, too, knowledge and anticipation of what is about to occur often colors the response to preceding scenes.

28. Note the "refinements" of the puppets in Japanese Bunraku.

29. This is obvious in the battle scenes of Kabuki, the narrative and dance elements in Noh and in Indian folk theater, and the staging techniques of Peking opera.

30. Thayer, *Communication and Communication Systems*, pp. 240–242.

31. The proper orientation on this point may well be essential to an appreciation of the "agit-prop" theater of China; few outcries against this theater's methods of changing attitudes will be heard from those who do not consider its main objective to be the changing of attitudes. As Thayer, *ibid.*, p. 137, expresses it, "how one measures communication effectiveness will largely determine what he attempts to communicate—and how he goes about it."

32. *Ibid.*, p. 90.

33. *Ibid.*, p. 97.

34. The Peking opera actor, for example, typically trains intensively (the concentration being such that he is normally equipped to enter no other walk of life when his schooling is finished) for about eight years, starting at the age of eight.

Speech Communication Experimentation and a Problem of Uncertainty

J. DONALD RAGSDALE

Introduction

Most scholars today regard Wilhelm Wundt as the first experimental psychologist. As Edwin Boring put it, "We call him the 'founder' of experimental psychology . . . [for] he promoted the idea of psychology as an independent science and . . . he is the senior among 'psychologists.' "[1] Wundt's *Beiträge zur Theorie der Sinneswahrnehmung*, published between 1858 and 1862, has "some claim to being the beginning of experimental psychology."[2] Yet nearly a century earlier, a critique by no less a thinker than Immanuel Kant appeared which struck at the very possibility of an experimental psychology. Chiefly through a comparison to physics and chemistry, Kant argued that psychology could not claim to be a science in the strictest sense. Among other things, Kant had grave doubts about subjecting human beings to the experimentation appropriate for scientific purposes. "Observation in itself," said Kant, "changes and distorts the condition of the observed subject."[3]

What is striking about this statement is less its wisdom than its prescience. It was not until 1927 that Werner Heisenberg formulated his famous, and analogous, "principle of uncertainty" for physics.[4] It was later still that such a principle gained wide recognition in psychology and in the social and behavioral sciences generally, chiefly as the result of the work of such men as Martin Orne and Donald Campbell. Comparatively little has appeared in print dealing with a principle of uncertainty in speech communication experimentation. The purpose of this essay, therefore, is to explore one of the major problems posed by the operation of such a principle in speech communication experimentation, to suggest some solutions to it, and to evaluate some of the legal and ethical problems posed by these solutions.

Problems Posed by a Principle of Uncertainty

Immanuel Kant's concern about the distortion of experimental subjects by the very act of observation did not extend to the nonbehavioral sciences. As Werner Heisenberg was later to show, however, the nature of the universe may make it impossible to avoid this distortion regardless of the nature of the observed. In his well-known example, Heisenberg postulated a hypothetical microscope so powerful as to enable an electron to be seen. He then proposed a situation in which a physicist tries to determine the position and velocity of a moving electron with this device. In order for the physicist now to illuminate the electron, he must use gamma radiation, since an electron is smaller than the wave length either of regular light or of X rays. It is at just this point, Heisenberg noted, that a serious problem arises. In harmony with the photoelectric effect, one would predict that a light wave, and therefore certainly a higher-frequency gamma ray, would deflect a moving electron. Hence, the act of observing its position alters the velocity of the electron. Heisenberg was able to show that another effect also applied. As one measures its velocity more accurately, the electron's position becomes more uncertain.[5] It appears, therefore, that regardless of the refinements of his observational techniques, man may be confronted with an irreducible amount of uncertainty in his universe.

The problem of uncertainty in the social and behavioral sciences, although different from that in Heisenberg's world of subatomic phenomena,[6] is acute. There are, first, no measuring instruments so refined as the electron microscope, and, second, human behavior is simply not as predictable as physical behavior. "It has long been recognized," writes Martin Orne, "that certain differences will exist between the types of experiments conducted in the physical sciences and those in the behavioral sciences because the former investigates a universe of inanimate objects and forces, whereas the latter deals with animate, often thinking, conscious subjects."[7] Experimentation with human subjects, to be sure, has grown extraordinarily in this century, and this growth is closely correlated with the development of refined statistical methods, experimental designs, and measuring instruments. Even with human subjects, it is now possible to handle cogently large amounts of complex data and to control many variables which might otherwise influence the variables under study. Unfortunately, it is at just the juncture where a reasonable degree of control has been achieved by the experimenter that there emerges the even more formidable and perhaps ultimately insolvable problem of uncertainty suggested by Kant. *In the very attempt to exercise control over irrelevant variables, the experimenter may change his subjects' behavior in important, but unknown, ways.*

As Orne notes, it is quite improper to assume that any human is "a *passive responder* to stimuli."[8] Indeed, "one of the basic characteristics of the human being is that he will ascribe purpose and meaning even in the absence of purpose and meaning."[9] Orne also points to the rather high status enjoyed by experimentation in the eyes of most potential subjects and reasons that, in an experimental situation, a human subject may well see "it as his task to ascertain the true purpose of the experiment and respond in a manner which will support the hypotheses being tested."[10] *Reactivity effects* is the usual designation for such inductions. It should be emphasized, of course, that they need not only have the purpose of supporting the experimenter's hypotheses but of denying them as well. Clearly, neither purpose is desirable, but to make matters worse behavioral scientists have such little understanding of reactivity effects that they are as yet unable to relate either purpose to specific circumstances except in quite limited instances.

Reactivity effects are but one of a number of variables which contribute to experimental invalidity and, hence, to uncertain outcomes. One group of such variables is most likely to affect the *internal validity* of an experiment. Internal validity has to do with whether or not the experimenter's treatments had any effect on his subjects. Variables such as fatigue on the part of a subject, unreliability on the part of a judge in an evaluative task, and learning by a subject which may transfer from one testing situation to another are examples of sources of internal invalidity. Reactivity effects belong to a second group of variables which is most likely to affect the *external validity* or generalizability of an experiment. Other such variables are sampling effects and the levels of confidence attained in statistical tests.[11]

One type of reactivity effect stems from the *role-selection* kind of behavior[12] which Orne believes typifies most research situations. He relates the following amusing example of such behavior: "A number of casual acquaintances were asked whether they would do the experimenter a favor; on their acquiescence, they were asked to perform five push-ups. Their response tended to be amazement, incredulity and the question 'Why?' Another similar group of individuals were asked whether they would take part in an experiment of brief duration. When they agreed to do so, they too were asked to perform five push-ups. Their typical response was 'Where?' "[13] Aware that he is a participant in a scientific study and, perhaps further, that a respected institution, a university say, has provided facilities and funds to support the research, a subject may actively seek to give the experimenter "what he is looking for." The problem, of course, is that the subject has usually been given so little information about the nature of the study in an effort to prevent his induction of its purposes that even his best guess has only a chance probability of being correct. If the experimenter has deliberately deceived his subjects, then their guesses are even less likely to be correct.

Even if these guesses were correct, it would be undesirable for the subject to alter his behavior to "please" the experimenter. If the subject does this, the findings of the experiment can only be generalized to other such experimental situations. Perhaps, on the other hand, the subject chooses to guess the experimenter's intent with a view toward wrecking the study. Obviously, experimenters can only rarely know in which if either of these behaviors their subjects are indulging.

A few years ago, the writer administered two forms of a semantic differential to a group of international students from Central and South America. The two forms were the same except that the first one was in Spanish and the second was in English. During the administration of the second form, several of the students asked if they were expected to give responses which were the same as they gave on the first form. They were assured that their responses on the two forms need not bear any relationship to each other. In conversation after the testing session, however, the students' remarks made it apparent that they had not fully believed these assurances. The similarity between the two forms and their previous experiences with testing made it difficult to believe otherwise. As Orne says, "it becomes an empirical issue to study under what circumstances, in what kind of experimental contexts, and with what kind of subject populations, demand characteristics become significant in determining the behavior of subjects in experimental situations."[14]

Another reactivity effect is a type of *regression* stemming from the effects of measurement on the variable under scrutiny. These effects are perhaps best illustrated in a methodological study by William Brooks.[15] In comparing the effects of two different experimental designs for measuring attitudes, Brooks found that, in the one utilizing a pretest, followed by a persuasive speech treatment, then by a posttest, attitude shift of any kind appeared to be *inhibited*. In the design which did not utilize a pretest, an attitude shift in favor of the position advocated in the treatment speech occurred which was significant beyond the .01 level of confidence. This kind of regression effect is one of the oldest and best-documented sources of uncertainty in the research literature.[16]

In speech communication situations, it may be possible to explain pretest effects on attitudes as a commitment phenomenon. When a subject marks an attitude scale prior to hearing a speech dealing with that attitude, he commits himself and thus makes any shift of attitude less likely than it might otherwise have been.[17] Whatever the explanation, however, some uncertainty must remain. There might be experimental treatment variables, for example, which also inhibit attitude change, and the effects of these would be confounded with the regression effects. In addition, the pretest variable might interact in some situations with the role-selection variable to *foster* attitude change. As recent issues of the professional journals in speech communication indicate, however, the use of pretests has by no means ended. An examination of volumes 35 and 36 of *Speech Monographs*, for example, reveals that all of the eleven research studies dealing with attitude change utilized a pretest.

A final, although by no means the only other, reactivity effect results from the *response set*. The writer's most frequent experiences with this phenomenon involve the occasional subject who always marks the center position on a semantic differential scale or who patterns his markings by systematically alternating between the two most extreme positions.[18] Another, and fortunately rarer, "subject" is the student who patterns his responses in some fashion on a multiple choice examination.[19] To one who has encountered such response sets, however, little emphasis needs to be placed on the problem of uncertainty which they pose. In even the most obvious instances, there is a small trace of doubt left as the experimenter discards the suspect data.

Solutions to the Problem of Reactivity Effects

While research proceeds, as it should, on the nature and significance of reactivity effects and other sources of both internal and external invalidity, there is, in the meantime, an urgent need for avoiding or minimizing the uncertainty which is associated with these variables. The most promising techniques yet advanced for accomplishing these purposes appear to be so-called unobtrusive or nonreactive measures. The use of measures which are made without a subject's awareness makes it much more feasible to conduct the remainder of an experiment unobtrusively, although it is no guarantee of the latter. All of these measures, then, eliminate the subject's awareness that he is being tested and minimize his awareness of anything at all unusual at work. For those readers who are fans of the mystery novel, especially of the Sherlock Holmes variety, several examples of unobtrusive "measurement" will come immediately to mind. Webb and his colleagues relate the following instance:

> The singular Sherlock Holmes had been reunited with his old friend, Dr. Watson . . . and both walked to Watson's newly acquired office. The practice was located in a duplex of two physician's suites, both of which has [sic] been for sale. No doubt sucking on his calabash, Holmes summarily told Watson that he had made a wise choice in purchasing the practice that he did, rather than the one on the other side of the duplex. The data? The steps were more worn on Watson's side than on his competitor's.[20]

Holmes was using a *physical trace*, in particular an indication of *erosion*, on which to base his compliment.[21] Other physical traces might indicate *accretion*, as in the familiar case of the accumulation of trivia in a home the longer a family occupies it. In speech communication experimentation, one might count the number of signs, placards, and the like which are left on the ground after political speeches in order to estimate the size of the audiences or perhaps the aggressiveness of the different events' organizers. One might also survey the television repair shops in a community to determine which tuning strips, in the receivers being repaired, show the greatest amount of wear as an index of network viewing preferences.

It is obvious, though, that such measures as these are by no means unequivocal or fully adequate. More people at a political rally might keep their signs if a march is scheduled following the speech than if a speaker is whistle-stopping, and factors such as the age of a receiver and the quality of the contacts obviously influence tuning-strip wear. Moreover, physical traces are rather gross indicators even of the phenomena for which they are appropriate. It is very difficult, for example, to imagine a discriminating physical trace measure of attitude. Although physical traces are certainly unobtrusive or nonreactive, they are fortunately not necessarily more so than some other measures. As Webb and his colleagues note, "physical-evidence data are off the main track for most psychological and sociological research."[22]

A second type of unobtrusive measure is the use of *archives*.[23] Historians and speech critics, of course, use archives as sources of data. The analysis of speeches themselves is a use of archives. Experimenters may utilize such public records as census reports, birth notices, voting returns, employment statistics, consumer price indexes, and so on as means of classification or sampling. In studies of radio listening, televison viewing, and advertising effectiveness, there is a particularly widespread use of such demographic data. Archival evidence may also be the measure of effectiveness for experimental treatments. The voting records of a precinct in which a persuasive speaking campaign was conducted might be compared, for example, to a similar one in which a house-to-house doorbell-ringing campaign was pursued. With such a measure as voting records would afford, it should be quite easy to keep experimental treatments disguised. The use of archival, as well as of physical trace data, might have the desirable additional effect of removing speech communication experimentation from the relatively confining environs of the university classroom. Again, however, archives do not yield wholly unequivocal or adequate data, even though they eliminate reactivity effects. Although less so than physical traces, they are also off the main track for most social and behavioral research.

Two other types of unobtrusive measures, *simple observation* and *contrived observation*, appear to be the most appropriate techniques for the needs of social and behavioral research.[24] A speech clinician may obtain a record of a child's phoneme substitutions simply by asking the child to tell about his most exciting experience. The writer has analyzed the classroom speeches and group discussions of university students in an effort to determine whether or not the two different situations affect the frequency and the type of hesitations which occur in them.[25] In these examples, the measures themselves are quite different. In the one case, the measure is a phoneme inventory, while in the other it is a tabulation of nonfluencies. The avenue of measurement, simple observation, is the same in both however. In the first example, the observer must be careful to disguise the fact that a record of some sort is being made in order to insure that the measure is nonreactive. This may be accomplished with a small hand counter, by placing the child out of the line of vision of the observer's pencil and paper notations, and so on. In the second case, the use of a tape recorder to facilitate the observation was, in a sense, obtrusive, but the students were accustomed both to oral performances and to being tape recorded.

Simple observation is somewhat more likely to produce reactivity effects than either physical trace or archival methods. More attention, therefore, must be given to insuring its unobtrusiveness. This is rather a modest price to pay for a substantial increase in the validity and the adequacy of measurement over the previously discussed techniques. In view of the rather extensive controversy over the apparent disparity between attitude change and behavior change and the speech communication experimenter's nearly exclusive concern with the former, perhaps the wider use of simple observation would serve also to correct a certain scholarly myopia.

Perhaps the most extreme type of unobtrusive measure is contrived observation. It exemplifies the most rigorous attempt to guard against reactivity stemming from measurement. The element which distinguishes contrived observation from simple observation is the use of hidden measuring instruments. The most notorious examples of such instrumentation are perhaps the "bugging" of a diplomat's hotel suite with concealed microphones, telephone wiretapping, and the "candid camera" of television program fame. The writer recently directed a doctoral dissertation which illustrates the use of contrived observation in a speech communication experiment.[26] The experimenter was interested in the degree to which university student public speakers exhibit linguistic nonimmediacy[27] when speaking extemporaneously before three kinds of audiences. The independent variables of education status and speaker awareness of audience composition were used in selecting an audience of all peers, one of peers and superiors with no warning to the speakers that the latter would be present, and one of peers and superiors with prior warning. A videotape recorder was concealed from the speakers' and the audiences' view, and each experimental treatment was recorded in full. Later, typescripts of each speech were analyzed by the experimenter for several kinds of linguistic nonimmediacy. The hidden instrumentation made it possible for the entire experiment to be conducted without the knowledge of either the speakers or their audiences. It also freed the experimenter from the duress, as in some types of simple observation, of keeping his notes or recording surreptitiously throughout the experiment.

Contrived observation is likely to call more upon an experimenter's ingenuity and financial resources than most of the other nonreactive measures. Furthermore, it may often require the cooperation of confederates, each of whom is a potential "leak" of information which is crucial to keeping the experiment unobtrusive. In the experiment on linguistic nonimmediacy, confederates were required to operate the videotape recorder. Contrived observation does, though, seem to have the greatest potential for overcoming the effects of reactivity and for avoiding the problems of equivocal and inadequate data. "As the experimenter's activity increases," say Webb and his colleagues, however, "and he achieves the gains of finer measurement and control, the price paid is the increased risk of being caught,"[28] and that is certainly a risk not lightly to be taken.

In speech communication experimentation, especially, but also in social and behavioral research generally, the use of unobtrusive measures is in its infancy. This is partially because of a lack of widespread awareness of the problems of reactivity but perhaps more so because of the state of the art in the development of such measures. At this point there simply are no very good unobtrusive measures of such crucial variables as personality, attitude, source credibility, and the like available. With some of the unobtrusive measures which are available, such as the counts of nonfluencies mentioned earlier, some question remains about the temporal reliability of the observer's judgment among other things. With counts of signs and placards left at the site of a political rally, one might well question the validity of the measure. Aware of all of the problems such as these, the most prolific advocates of nonreactive research stress the need to use several measures for each variable: "Once a proposition has been confirmed by two or more independent measurement processes, the uncertainty of its interpretation is greatly reduced. The most persuasive evidence comes through a triangulation of measurement processes."[29] Even where the experimenter feels that his only recourse is to use a reactive measure, he can often supplement it with one or more nonreactive ones. It may happen that the measures agree. Where they do not, the differences will be virtually as important as each individual finding, even where it is impossible to discern the causes of the differences.

Legal and Ethical Problems of Unobtrusive Measures

Some of the legal and ethical problems associated with nonreactive research in the social and behavioral sciences are as important for the experimenter as the strategic problems discussed above, however. For the nonexperimenter, these problems may well be of paramount importance. There has long been a tradition in speech communication of ethical sensibility, and one would expect this tradition to be as relevant to method as it is to theory. Recognizing such an expectation, Webb and his colleagues write: "Some readers will find none of the [unobtrusive] methods objectionable, others may find virtually all of them open to question. . . . We do not feel able at this point to prepare a compelling ethical resolution of these complex issues. Nonetheless, we recognize the need of such a resolution. . . ."[30] Probably few speech communication experimenters would endorse research methods which are supported by a questionable ethic, even to reduce an abhorrent uncertainty.

Although it is most often only tacitly admitted by experimenters, social and behavioral research of all kinds comes close to infringing upon a subject's right to privacy as it seeks to minimize uncertainty. With anything less than full disclosure of the nature and purpose of his research, the experimenter may obtain information which even a voluntary subject would not otherwise provide. Edward Shils believes that even the most apparently harmless social and behavioral research technique, the interview, probably often violates a subject's right to privacy. Even though few interviews could be conducted without an agreement with the interviewee, seldom do researchers disclose the intent of their study except in the vaguest of terms. Sometimes, interviewers "deliberately falsify their roles . . . and tell less than the whole truth or something quite other than the truth in order to avoid arousing resistance to the disclosure of the information sought."[31] It is rather unlikely that these techniques do any palpable harm to an interviewee. Moreover most people would not be very sensitive to the ethical issues which they raise. For Shils, however, individual self-determination is hindered by such tactics, and this makes them quite unacceptable in most cases. "The mere existence of consent," he argues, "does not exempt the social scientist from the moral obligations of respect for another's privacy."[32] From a pragmatic viewpoint, the use of such deception as this may also create, if indeed it has not already created, another source of uncertainty. Orne writes:

> This problem [of role-selection] is implicitly recognized in the large number of psychological studies which attempt to conceal the true purpose of the experiment from the subject in the hope of thereby obtaining more reliable data. This maneuver on the part of psychologists is so widely known in the college population that even if a psychologist is honest with the subject, more often than not he will be distrusted. As one subject pithily put it, "Psychologists always lie!" This bit of paranoia has some support in reality.[33]

Unobtrusive measures, to be sure, help to eliminate this kind of reactivity effect, but they may not obviate Shils's argument against deception, which the subject's remark above underscores. Although they are invaluable in solving problems of uncertainty, unobtrusive measures may only aggravate the problem of deception. Some of them, especially contrived observation, may also raise the ominous specter of an omniscient Big Brother. In order to evaluate the contribution of unobtrusive measures to these problems, one must begin with an examination of the basis of the right to privacy in a democratic society.

It was Vance Packard who, in 1964, brought to the attention of the general public many of the problems of diminishing privacy in the United States.[34] Although its evidence was largely anecdotal, his book was a convincing testament that ours is a naked society or is rapidly becoming one. To give greater import to this observation, Packard noted the American Civil Liberties Union's statement that " 'a hallmark of totalitarian societies is that the people are apprehensive of being overheard or spied upon.' "[35] Constitutionally, an American's right to privacy is guaranteed in the Bill of Rights, principally by the Fourth and, to a lesser extent, by the Fifth Amendment. The Fourth Amendment gives protection "against unreasonable searches and seizures." The Fifth Amendment exempts a person from being "compelled in any criminal case to be a witness against himself" and from being "deprived of life, liberty, or property, without due process of law." Unfortunately, these amendments have never been so liberally interpreted as to be especially relevant to the more subtle aspects of privacy. They have brought about the search warrant and have limited the use of such means of gathering evidence as wiretapping. The Supreme Court, however, has frequently favored the right of the public to protection from criminals rather than the individual's right to privacy when questionable means of gathering evidence have been at issue before it. "From a libertarian's viewpoint," says Packard, "the Supreme Court's record here has been discouraging."[36] This is a curious phenomenon, indeed, in view of the Court's decisions in some other areas, notably in cases involving the taking of confessions and the admissibility of evidence.

With a rather equivocal position on the use of such electronic means as the wiretap and the hidden microphone, one cannot reasonably expect Supreme Court decisions to furnish principles with which to judge the experimenter's use of unobtrusive measures. To make matters worse, there is also no unequivocal statutory basis for such a judgment. Packard remarks that "in general the legal checks are in a state of lamentable confusion, vagueness, or neglect" and that "one judge has described the state of the law of privacy, for example, as 'still that of a haystack in a hurricane.' "[37] If there are principles for judging nonreactive research methods, then they will most probably be found in the ethical values of society.

In a totalitarian society, of course, it would be pointless to discuss infringements of privacy, even though nonreactive rsearch methods know no societal boundaries. It may also be that, even among free societies, cultural differences would call for minor modifications, or qualifications, of a set of principles for judging research methods. In general, though, the ethical values of a democratic society should suffice for the present analysis, and Edward Shils is one of the most libertarian advocates of their use in judging any research method. Shils writes that "the ethical values affected by contemporary social research are vague and difficult to formulate precisely," but "they refer mainly to human dignity, the autonomy of individual judgment and action, and the maintenance of privacy."[38] He reasons that "the respect for privacy rests on the appreciation of human dignity, with its high evaluation of individual self-determination, free from the bonds of prejudice, passion, and superstition."[39] As stated earlier, Shils sees most deception as an interference with an individual's self-determination. "Most social scientists," write Webb and his colleagues, "would find this position too extreme. . . . Nevertheless, Shils' position specifies some of the dangers to the citizen and social science of an unconscionable invasion of privacy."[40] Whether Shils's viewpoint would be widely endorsed or not may be a quite relevant question. Since it is such an extreme view, however, a discussion of the ethics of unobtrusive measurement based on it may be instructive.

In actuality, Shils's position is not so categorical as it appears on first glance. He recognizes that "the respect for human dignity and individuality shares an historical comradeship with the freedom of scientific inquiry, which is *equally precious* to modern liberalism."[41] Shils also writes that "Where principles are in conflict, only the exercise of reasonable judgment, following reflective consideration of the issues is in order."[42] When he later argues that "the interviewer is obliged to explain to his interviewee not only his own personal goal, e.g., to complete a thesis, but also the cognitive intention," then, Shils is promulgating "a guiding principle" rather than "a specific stipulation."[43] His view is really quite similar to the one expressed by Alan Westin: "American society wants both statistical data *and* privacy. Ever since the Constitution was written, our efforts to secure both order and liberty have been successful when we have found ways to grant authority to Government but to control it with the standards, operating procedures and review mechanisms that protect individual rights."[44] The American Psychological Association's position on the use of deception is also not essentially different from Shils's view. By this association's standards, "the psychologist is justified in withholding information from or giving misinformation to research subjects only when in his judgment this is clearly required by his research problem."[45] Deception, therefore, is not irredeemably wrong even by Shils's standards.

Unobtrusive measures, of course, obviate the need for the sort of deception under discussion by eliminating the subject's awareness that he is participating in an experiment. The very elimination of this awareness, however, contains in it an element of deception or violation of privacy. In this regard, it may be helpful to keep in mind the customary distinction between an individual's public life and his private one. Certainly, it cannot be considered a significant invasion of privacy to record the passage of one's automobile along a city street or to count, each decade, the number of people who are living in his home. Similarly, it should not be considered an infringement of one's right to privacy to videotape record his public addresses. It seems rather unlikely that such practices as these would prevent either "autonomy of individual judgment and action" or "individual self-determination" any more so than does everyday social intercourse. As a social being, one could hardly avoid being noticed by his fellows. Shils also recognizes that "observation which takes place in public or in settings in which the participants conventionally or knowingly accept the responsibility for the public character of their actions and expressions . . . is different from observation which seeks to enter the private sphere unknown to the actor."[46]

The records, even of a person's public actions, however, should not be treated in such a way as to lead to infringements of the right to privacy. The photographer, in most cases, must obtain a model release if he intends to publish an identifiable photograph of someone. Similarly, it is and should undoubtedly continue to be a convention that the data obtained in an experiment must be conveyed anonymously to the academic community or to the public, except in unusual circumstances. The American Psychological Association's code of ethics requires that "the identity of research subjects must not be revealed without explicit permission."[47] As Westin remarks, "we must recognize that the individual's right to limit the circulation of personal information about himself is a vital part of his right to privacy."[48]

Some techniques of unobtrusive measurement clearly make it easy to observe an individual's private life, and social scientists are aware that they can go too far in intruding on privacy. Webb and his colleagues write that "Recording deliberations in a jury room or hiding under beds to record pillow talk are techniques which have led to moral revulsion on the part of large numbers of professionals."[49] In speech communication research it would not be especially difficult to devise an experiment utilizing an unobtrusive network of wiretaps. If unobtrusive instruments are utilized, they may not long remain secret and the potential effects on the public are serious. Whether in a jury room or in a laboratory, public knowledge of such unobtrusive invasions of privacy is likely to provoke suspicion and modify behavior. Yet participants in deliberations must be able to discuss cases openly and vote according to their consciences.

The results of experimentation are normally reported in one form or another. If the reports modify the future behavior of persons in such situations as those under study, then the findings may be empty and ethically questionable. At the least, they are uncertain. If experimenters fail unmistakably to oppose unobtrusive observation of private life, they run the very real risks of tarnishing their reputations and of making empty and unethical generalizations from their findings. It may be necessary in extreme cases to use unobtrusive measures and to infringe upon privacy, for example, to protect the public from criminals. But it is doubtful that important research activities would be curtailed or hampered by such opposition to unobtrusive measures.

In the absence of legal standards, the experimenter's own ethical sensibility is society's only safeguard against the misuse of unobtrusive measures. Perhaps this is the most desirable state of affairs. Few laws, after all, could prevent the activities of a determined and unscrupulous investigator. Oliver Wendell Holmes, moreover, wrote that "general propositions do not decide concrete cases" and that "decisions will depend on a judgment or intuition more subtle than any articulate major premise."[50] It would be sad, indeed, to be forced into the admission that experimenters who could use such sophisticated strategic tools as unobtrusive measures could not be judicious in that use.

Conclusion

In 1908, Edward Bradford Titchener wrote, "Kant told us, . . . that psychology could never rise to the rank of an experimental science, because psychological observation interferes with its own object."[51] This interference, as has been seen, introduces into the experimental situation an element of uncertainty. Except in limited instances, the effects of interference are unpredictable. While men such as Martin Orne are conducting research with the goal of explaining these effects, others are arguing that unobtrusive measurement, which is done without a subject's awareness, will solve the problem of uncertainty caused by reactivity effects by avoiding its cause. Nonreactive research, however, raises a question of ethics. While there appear to be no Constitutional or statutory restrictions which would preclude such research, the possibility that a subject's privacy might be invaded could make it a questionable practice. If the use of unobtrusive measures is confined to public behavior and if, further, the data obtained from it is kept anonymous or identified only with the subject's permission, then it does not seem to be necessary that nonreactive research infringe upon an individual's right to privacy. Although they serve the lofty aims of science and are aided by public confidence in the institutions which they typically represent, social and behavioral researchers would do well not to select their methodologies for strategic reasons only. Should they do so, they may find that their future choices will be restricted, not by society's ethical standards, but by the law. If the scientist's values "are not thought to measure up to the values of the community . . . it is probable that . . . judges will, themselves, seek to devise the necessary standards to give effect to the community's values."[52]

1. Edwin G. Boring, *A History of Experimental Psychology*, 2nd ed. (New York: Appleton-Century-Crofts, 1950), p. 316.

2. *Ibid.*, p. 320.

3. Immanuel Kant, *Metaphysiche Anfangsgründe der Naturwissenschaft*, in Immanuel Kant, *Sämmtliche Werke*, eds. Karl Rosenkranz and Friedrich Wilhelm Schubert, IV (Leipzig: L. Voss, 1838), 310–311. My translation of *"die Beobachtung an sich schon den Zustand des beobachteten Gegenstandes alterirt und verstellt."*

4. W. Heisenberg, *"Über den anschaulichen Inhalt der quantentheoretischen Kinematik und Mechanik," Zeitschrift für Physik*, 43 (May 31, 1927), 172–198.

5. Werner Heisenberg, *Physics and Philosophy: The Revolution in Modern Science* (New York: Harper, 1958), pp. 44–48, and his *The Physical Principles of the Quantum Theory*, trans. Carl Eckart and Frank C. Hoyt (New York: Dover, 1950), pp. 20–30.

6. For some time following its dissemination, Heisenberg's principle was sometimes discussed without proper regard for its limitations, primarily to the phenomena of quantum mechanics. For an especially relevant antidote for such discussions, see Ivan D. London, "Psychology and Heisenberg's Principle of Indeterminacy," *Psychological Review*, 52 (May, 1945), 162–168. The reader may also wish to pursue Heisenberg's analysis of "The Relation of Quantum Theory to Other Parts of Natural Science," in Heisenberg, *Physics and Philosophy*, pp. 93–109.

7. Martin T. Orne, "On the Social Psychology of the Psychological Experiment: With Particular Reference to Demand Characteristics and Their Implications," *American Psychologist*, 17 (November, 1962), 776–783.

8. *Ibid.*, p. 776.

9. *Ibid.*, p. 780.

10. *Ibid.*, p. 779. Orne uses the phrase *"demand characteristics of the experimental situation"* to refer to "the totality of cues which convey an experimental hypothesis to the subject."

11. Cf. Donald T. Campbell and Julian C. Stanley, *Experimental and Quasi-Experimental Designs for Research* (Chicago: Rand McNally, 1966), pp. 5–6.

12. Eugene J. Webb, Donald T. Campbell, Richard D. Schwartz, and Lee Sechrest, *Unobtrusive Measures: Nonreactive Research in the Social Sciences* (Chicago: Rand McNally, 1966), pp. 16–18.

13. Orne, "On the Social Psychology of the Psychological Experiment," p. 777.

14. *Ibid.*, p. 779.

15. William D. Brooks, "Effects of a Persuasive Message upon Attitudes: A Methodological Comparison of an Offset Before-After Design with a Pre-test-Post-test Design," *Journal of Communication*, 16 (September, 1966), 180–188. Cf. William D. Brooks and Larry K. Hannah, "Pretest Effects of the STEP Listening Test," *Speech Monographs*, 36 (March, 1969), 66–67.

16. Webb, *et al.*, *Unobtrusive Measures*, pp. 18–19.

17. Cf. Carolyn W. Sherif, Muzafer Sherif, and Roger E. Nebergall, *Attitude and Attitude Change: The Social Judgment-Involvement Approach* (Philadelphia, Pa.: Saunders, 1965), pp. 219–246.

18. Cf. Charles E. Osgood, George J. Suci, and Percy H. Tannenbaum, *The Measurement of Meaning* (Urbana: University of Illinois Press, 1957), pp. 226–236.

19. See Lee J. Cronbach, "Response Sets and Test Validity," *Educational and Psychological Measurement*, 6 (Winter, 1946), 475–494.

20. Webb, *et al.*, *Unobtrusive Measures*, p. 35.

21. *Ibid.*

22. *Ibid.*, p. 52.

23. *Ibid.*, p. 53.

24. *Ibid.*, pp. 112, 142.

25. J. Donald Ragsdale, "Influences of Sex, Situation, and Category Differences on Nonfluencies," *Central States Speech Journal*, 20 (Winter, 1969), 310–311.

26. Richard Lane Conville, Jr., "Linguistic Non-Immediacy in the Public Speaking Situation" (Ph.D. dissertation, Louisiana State, 1970).

27. In general, linguistic nonimmediacy refers to the social and personal distance cues evidenced in language. The use of such terms as "the speaker" instead of "I" is a simple example.

28. Webb, *et al.*, *Unobtrusive Measures*, p. 170.

29. *Ibid.*, p. 3.

30. *Ibid.*, pp. v–vi.

31. Edward A. Shils, "Social Inquiry and the Autonomy of the Individual," in *The Human Meaning of the Social Sciences*, ed. Daniel Lerner (Cleveland, Ohio: Meridian Books, 1959), p. 123.

32. *Ibid.*, p. 124.

33. Orne, "On the Social Psychology," pp. 778–779.

34. Vance Packard, *The Naked Society* (New York: D. McKay, 1964).

35. *Ibid.*, p. 11.

36. *Ibid.*, p. 316. Cf. pp. 305–319.

37. *Ibid.*, p. 14.

38. Shils, "Social Inquiry," p. 117.

39. *Ibid.*, pp. 120–121.

40. Webb, *et al.*, *Unobtrusive Measures*, p. vi.

41. Shils, "Social Inquiry," p. 121. My italics.

42. *Ibid.*

43. *Ibid.*, p. 127.

44. Alan Westin, "The Snooping Machine," *Playboy*, 15 (May, 1968), 157.

45. *Ethical Standards of Psychologists* (Washington, D.C.: American Psychological Association, 1953), p. 122.

46. Shils, "Social Inquiry," p. 130.

47. American Psychological Association, *Ethical Standards*, p. 123.

48. Westin, "Snooping Machine," p. 157.

49. Webb, *et al.*, *Unobtrusive Measures*, pp. vi–vii.

50. Oliver Wendell Holmes, "The Lochner Dissent," in *Private Life and Public Order: The Context of Modern Public Policy*, ed. Theodore J. Lowi (New York: Norton, 1968), p. 124.

51. Edward Bradford Titchener, *Lectures on the Elementary Psychology of Feeling and Attention* (New York: Macmillan, 1908), p. 174.

52. Oscar M. Ruebhausen, quoted in Dael Wolfle, "The Use of Human Subjects," *Science*, 159 (February 23, 1968), 831.

Relative Ease in Comprehending Yes/No Questions

JOSEPH A. DeVITO

Occupying a unique and important position in the study of speech communication is the psychology of language.[1] Recent developments in linguistics and psychology have provided new and significant insight into language and language behavior, reflected most clearly in the changes in the research questions being asked and in the research methodologies employed to answer them.

One of the most fruitful areas of research within this general field is that concerned with differential responses to sentences of varying syntactic structure. Studies exploring the relative ease of comprehending active as opposed to passive sentences,[2] the effects of grammatical transformations on recall[3] and speed of understanding,[4] and the influence of syntactic structure on learning[5] characterize this area of psycholinguistic investigation,[6] called by some researchers, experimental psycholinguistics.[7]

Miller and McNeill in their review of psycholinguistics put the issue clearly: "Psycholinguistic studies of how we understand complicated sentences obviously border on some of the most important practical problems of communication and education. . . . It is no virtue of these experiments that their results are not more immediately useful; future studies will almost certainly be more concerned with practical applications."[8]

The present study follows this general strategy, that is, utilizes syntactic structure as the independent variable, but centers on questions, a class of sentences that has been the focus of little empirical research. That which has been done has been concerned with children's developmental patterns in the course of language acquisition.[9] More specifically, the concern here is with the relative ease of understanding questions of different transformations. Before reporting the experiment, however, some general properties of questions need to be considered.

Some Properties of Questions

Owen Thomas, working within a generative grammar framework, classifies questions into five basic types depending upon the linguistic unit being questioned.[10] For example, given the sentence, "The young debater argued logically," five general kinds of questions may be generated, each of which queries a different element in the sentence:

(1) Who argued logically? (Nominal element questioned)
(2) What did the young debater do? (Verb)
(3) How did the young debater argue? (Adverb)
(4) What kind of debater argued logically? (Adjective)
(5) Did the young debater argue logically? (Sentence)

The present study focuses on questions similar to type (5), that is, questions that query the entire sentence. Such questions are generally referred to as yes/no questions, since they call for a *yes* or a *no* answer.

In this study nine ways of asking a yes/no question are investigated. One set of questions used in the present study is presented in Table 1. In addition to these nine possibilities other structures are permissible in English. For example, questions (5) and (7) may be made emphatic by the addition of the morpheme *do*: "The circle does follow the square, doesn't it?" and "The circle does follow the square?" In some situations the question "The circle the square follows?" would also be considered grammatical.[11] These nine question types, then, are not exhaustive but rather are representative of the varied ways of asking yes/no questions and, at the same time, seem to be the most common in English.

On the right of Table 1, the structural properties of these questions relevant to the hypotheses tested in this study are included. Special note

TABLE 1

	Structural Properties			
Transformation Types	Active Passive	Affirmative Negative	Nontag Tag	Neutral Loaded
1. Does the circle follow the square?	Active	Affirmative	Nontag	Neutral
2. Doesn't the circle follow the square?	Active	Negative	Nontag	Loaded
3. Isn't the square followed by the circle?	Passive	Negative	Nontag	Loaded
4. Is the square followed by the circle?	Passive	Affirmative	Nontag	Neutral
5. The circle follows the square, doesn't it?	Active	Affirmative	Tag	Loaded
6. The circle doesn't follow the square, does it?	Active	Negative	Tag	Loaded
7. The circle follows the square?	Active	Affirmative	Nontag	Neutral
8. The square is followed by the circle, isn't it?	Passive	Affirmative	Tag	Loaded
9. The square isn't followed by the circle, is it?	Passive	Negative	Tag	Loaded

should be made concerning the classification of affirmative and negative questions, the nature of tags, and the basis for the distinctions between neutral and loaded questions.

A question was considered negative only if it contained the negative marker in the main clause. Thus, although questions (5) and (8) contain the negative morpheme *n't* they were not considered negative since their main clause was affirmative. This procedure follows the generally accepted linguistic classifications and is particularly appropriate here since the negative or affirmative nature of the tag is, as explained below and in the Results and Discussion section, easily predictable.

Tag questions are those that contain, in addition to the principal clause, an added phrase that repeats the question in different form. These phrases are literally tagged to the main part of the question. The affirmative or negative nature of the tag is almost always predictable on the basis of the main verb. When the main verb is affirmative the tag is negative and when the main verb is negative the tag is affirmative. Though rare, a tag question may be affirmative in both the main clause and the tag; for example, the baiting kind of question, "The circle follows the square, does it?" Questions including negatives in both the main clause and the tag, however, are not permissible in English. The question, "The circle doesn't follow the square, doesn't it?" for example, is ungrammatical. Thus, in tag questions with an affirmative in the main clause the negative in the tag is highly, though not totally, redundant. In tag questions with a negative in the main clause the affirmative in the tag is totally redundant.

By a loaded question is meant a question that specifies the answer the questioner wants to receive or expects. Questions containing an affirmative in the main clause and a negative tag (Questions 5 and 8) and those containing a negative in the main clause and no tag (Questions 2 and 3) expect a *yes* answer. Questions containing a negative in the main clause and an affirmative tag (Questions 6 and 9) expect a *no* answer. Questions containing an affirmative in the main clause and no tag (Questions 1 and 6) are neutral, that is, are not loaded in the direction of either *yes* or *no*. Questions of type (7) constitute the one case that appears to cause some problems in determining the expected answer. Of these "echo" questions, Owen Thomas says that they have "a rising inflection as if the person speaking were incredulous."[12] This observation, however, seems to demand qualification. With certain intonation patterns (for example, [2]the circle follows the [4]square[3]↑ or [2]the circle[3-4] follows the square [3-4]↑) incredulity seems signaled, as Thomas observes, and here a *no* answer seems expected.[13] However, with other intonation patterns (for example, [2]the circle follows the [3]square[3]→) neither *yes* nor *no* seems expected. Questions of type (7) were recorded with the latter intonation contour and henceforth will be considered as neutral.

Because these several transformations vary in their structural properties and because they set up different expectations in the mind of the listener, differential cognitive processing and behavioral responses to these questions should be anticipated. In order to determine whether these varied transformations actually do lead to different responses the following experiment was conducted.

Experimental Investigation

Methods and Procedures

Twelve statements of the form "The circle follows the square" were composed and each transformed into nine different types of yes/no questions, illustrated in Table 1. Four of these statements included references to two figures (for example, "The circle follows the square?"); and four included references to four figures (for example, "The circle and the square follow the triangle and the star?"). Six of the statements utilized the verb "follow" and six utilized the verb "precede." These particular verbs were chosen because they permit the sentences to be transformed into the nine yes/no questions investigated. Sentences containing the verb to be such as "The circle is to the right of the square" and sentences of the form "The circle comes before the square" cannot be transformed in the same ways as sentences with the verbs "follow" and "precede."

In all, then, there were 108 questions; each of the nine transformation types was represented twelve times. The questions were randomized and recorded on tape.

Next, 108 diagrams were composed. Each diagram contained the figures referred to in the taped questions and were arranged accordingly. Thus, if the first question was "The circle and the triangle are not followed by the square, are they?" then the first diagram would contain a circle, a triangle, and a square. Half the diagrams were arranged so that the correct answer would be yes and half were arranged so that the correct answer would be no. The order of questions to be correctly answered yes and those to be correctly answered no was randomized. These 108 diagrams were placed in a looseleaf notebook to permit easy turning of pages.

The test questions were recorded at 3 3/4 speed and played to the subjects at 7 1/2.[14] This was done to insure a relatively difficult task. Had the questions been played at normal speed relatively few if any errors would have occurred.

Each of the twenty subjects (faculty members and advanced undergraduate and graduate students) was tested individually. The pertinent instructions were as follows:

On this tape there are 108 questions which are to be answered with a simple *yes* or *no*. Do not say *right* or *wrong* or *I don't know* or anything but *yes* or *no*. In this test booklet there are 108 pages of diagrams all of which are numbered. The test questions all refer to the relative placement of the diagrams on these pages. As the tape plays please answer each question and keep turning the pages to keep up with the questions. I will record your responses. If you wish to omit answering a question just say nothing. I will follow your answers and record them on this answer sheet. This tape was recorded at 3 3/4 speed but will be played at 7 1/2. Thus, the questions will be asked very rapidly. Do you have any questions?

Hypotheses

Four directional hypotheses were formulated. It was predicted that the number of errors (taken as the measure of difficulty) would be greater for (1) passive (Questions 3, 4, 8, and 9) than for active (1, 2, 5, and 6) questions; (2) negative (2, 3, 6, and 9) than for affirmative (1, 4, 5, and 8) questions; (3) loaded (2, 3, 5, 6, 8, and 9) than for neutral (1, 4, and 7) questions; and (4) tag (5, 6, 8, and 9) than for nontag (1, 2, 3, and 4) questions. Because it was desirable to have the questions differing on only one variable, questions of type (7) were only included in the analysis of neutral versus loaded questions.

Justification for these hypotheses comes from linguistic theory as well as from previous experimental findings. That passive questions will be more difficult (and hence would involve more errors) than active questions seems logical since passives are linguistically the more complex structures. The surface structure (roughly, the graphic or phonetic representation) of passive sentences is more removed from their deep structure (roughly, the abstract representation which conveys the meaning) than is true for active sentences.[15] If, as linguistic theory holds, sentences are understood on the basis of their deep structure, then it is reasonable to expect that sentences whose surface structure more closely resembles their deep structure will be easier to process than those sentences whose surface structure is more removed from their deep structure. Previous experimental findings on the relative ease of comprehending active as opposed to passive sentences have shown that passives are in fact more difficult to understand.[16] It seems reasonable, therefore, to expect that the same relationship will hold for questions as well.

Negative questions should be more difficult than affirmative ones because the negative involve an added transformation which the listener must process in order to understand the question.[17] The negative questions present the listener with one additional bit of linguistic information that must be taken into account in understanding or decoding the questions. Previous experimental findings demonstrating that negative information is more difficult to understand than positive would also lead to the direction predicted here.[18]

Loaded questions should be more difficult to understand than those which are phrased in a neutral manner. In answering questions of the type used in this study it is necessary, with loaded questions, first to divorce oneself from the expected answer and then to determine if the question is to be answered *yes* or *no*. There is probably a psychological set to give the answer the questioner expects since this seems to be the habitual pattern in answering questions throughout life. Here, however, this psychological set has to be broken down which would lead to added difficulty in sentence processing.

Tag questions would involve greater difficulty than nontag questions since they, like negatives, involve an added bit of information that must be processed by the listener. Also, however, tag questions are all loaded questions and consequently would involve, in addition, the difficulty peculiar to loaded questions.

Additional evidence for these hypotheses may be derived from the developmental pattern observed in children. If we assume that the child acquires the more simple structures first and only later those which are linguistically more complex, we have, in one sense, an index of complexity based simply on the temporal pattern of language acquisition. The evidence which has been accumulated on this topic, although far from complete, would support the hypotheses formulated here.[19]

Results and Discussion

The results pertaining to these four hypotheses are presented in Table 2. As can be seen all four hypotheses were confirmed at statistically significant levels.[20] (1) Passive questions are more difficult to understand than active ones ($p < .001$). This result, as already implied, is consistent with previous research findings about statements. Although no frequency data are available on these nine question transformations it seems reasonable to suppose that the passive forms are the less common. Questions are statements addressed directly to the listener; they are, in the classification of Rudolf Flesch, "personal sentences."[21] Because they are direct, the indirect passive form seems inappropriate and perhaps for this reason is seldom used. The implication here is that transformation types which occur frequently are easier to process than those which occur less frequently.

The principal reason for the greater difficulty of passive questions, however, seems due to the differences in the surface and deep structures of these differing transformations. Some psycholinguistic theorists have argued that sentences are understood on the basis of their deep structure and that when decoding a sentence the listener reduces the sentence to a basic form (roughly, a simple, active, affirmative, declarative sentence) with a notation pertaining to the transformations.[22] Thus, the passive question would be reduced to "the circle follows the square" plus the notation that the sentence is a question and a passive. Understanding the active sentence requires the

TABLE 2
Comparisons of Errors for Different Transformations

Transformation Type	Mean	t[a]	p
Passives (3, 4, 8, 9)	21.65	5.51	< .001
Actives (1, 2, 5, 6)	13.65		
Negatives (2, 3, 6, 9)	18.65	2.33	< .025
Affirmatives (1, 4, 5, 8)	16.40		
Loaded (2, 3, 5, 6, 8, 9)	4.55[b]	4.00	< .001
Neutral (1, 4, 7)	3.61[b]		
Tags (5, 6, 8, 9)	19.00	4.03	< .001
Nontags (1, 2, 3, 4)	16.20		

[a]One-tailed t-test for correlated means. d.f. = 19
[b]Since the number of questions in each category was not equal, the mean number of errors per question rather than per class of questions was computed here.

same basic processing except that the passive transformation is not involved and this simplifies its decoding. Put differently, understanding passive questions involves more information that must be processed than is the case in understanding active questions. As already observed, active statements and questions have surface and deep structures which are more similar than are the surface and deep structures of passive statements and questions. Consequently, in decoding, it is necessary to process more information in order to derive the deep structure (from which the meaning is obtained) from passive than from active statements.

(2) Negative questions are more difficult to understand than affirmatives (p < .025). As already noted negative questions were considered such if they contained a negative in their main clause. That the negative in the tag does not pose any great decoding problems seems clear from the results and also from an information theory analysis of these transformation types. Specifically, in questions that are affirmative in the main clause and contain a tag the negative marker in the tag is almost totally redundant and hence easily predictable. That is, if the main clause is affirmative the tag is almost always negative. If the main clause is negative the tag must be affirmative (see questions 6 and 9 in Table 1). Because of this redundancy the negative or affirmative nature of the tag probably adds little to the information that must be taken into account in order to process the question.

The same general argument applied to passive versus active questions seems capable of explaining the greater difficulty for negatives as opposed to affirmatives. If the deep structure of the sentence is in the affirmative, then in order to process a negative sentence the decoder must take into account more information than he would in the case of an affirmative sentence. That is, in decoding the negative question he must derive its deep structure which is affirmative and also retain the notation that the question is negative.

(3) Loaded questions are more difficult to understand than neutral questions (p < .001). This result is perhaps easiest to appreciate intuitively. Loaded questions present the decoder with a double task. As with neutral questions the sentence must be processed but the added task, in loaded questions, is to divorce oneself from the expected answer.

To the question "Does the circle follow the square?" the answer would be simply *yes* or *no*. However, a simple *yes* or *no* seems intuitively unsatisfying for loaded questions. Thus, to the question "The circle doesn't follow the square, does it?" the answer *yes, it does* or *no, it does not* seems more natural since it provides an answer not only to the basic question (by *yes* or *no*) but also to the expected answer (by *it does* or *it does not*). The added information that must be taken into account presents increased difficulty in answering such questions.

(4) Tag questions are more difficult to understand than nontag questions (p < .001). Although the affirmative or negative nature of the tag does not seem significant, the presence or absence of the tag does influence ease of understanding.

Again, the degree of similarity of the deep and surface structure of tag versus nontag questions seems to provide a reasonable explanation for the greater difficulty of tag questions. If the deep structure of sentences resembles the simple, active, affirmative, declarative form, then the tag questions have to be broken down into component sentences in the decoding process which naturally leads to greater difficulty. For example, in the question "The circle doesn't follow the square, does it?" the structural analysis would have to be something like "The circle doesn't follow the square" and "The circle does follow the square." This second sentence would then have to be transformed for the form "does it" to be derived. A deletion transformation (*follow the square* → ϕ), substitution transformation (*the circle* → *it*), and permutation transformation (*it does* → *does it*) would be necessary to derive the surface structure form, *does it*. Put differently, tag questions contain more than one sentence and consequently they involve more information that must be processed than questions containing only one basic sentence.

Also, since all tag questions are loaded questions they involve the added problems peculiar to these latter transformation types.

If loaded-tag questions are more difficult than neutral-nontag questions, as these results demonstrate, then it should also follow that loaded-nontag questions would be less difficult than loaded-tag questions. This hypothesis is confirmed at the .005 level ($t = 2.96$).

Summary and Conclusions

In this study the relative ease of comprehending yes/no questions of nine transformation types was investigated. Comparisons were made on the basis of active versus passive, affirmative versus negative, neutral versus loaded, and nontag versus tag questions. Each of the four hypotheses formulated was confirmed at statistically significant levels. Active, affirmative, neutral, and nontag questions proved easier to understand than their passive, negative, loaded, and tag counterparts.

The results of this study as well as those of numerous others clearly support the distinctions and the formulations currently being argued by generative grammarians. Each of the directions hypothesized in this study, for example, was derived solely on the basis of linguistic theory. A few decades ago linguistic theory said very little about speakers and listeners; linguists were then content to treat language as a purely abstract system removed from any considerations of behavioral correlates. The influence of generative grammar has resulted in significant and healthy changes in emphasis, culminating perhaps in Noam Chomsky's recent characterization of linguistics as a branch of cognitive psychology.[23]

It should be emphasized, however, that these results, while supporting the distinctions made in generative grammar, do not support or refute the theory of mind or cognition which many generative grammarians have defended.[24] Nor do they refute or support the simplest behavioristic view such as proposed by B. F. Skinner or the mediational behaviorism of Charles E. Osgood with which most generative grammarians find themselves at odds. Conceivably these results could be explained solely on the basis of the relative frequency of occurrence of these different transformations; those questions that proved easiest may well be the most frequent in speech. A simple S-R theory could then explain the results.

Furthermore, the results of such studies contribute substantially toward a theory of stylistics, especially when viewed from a prescriptive point of view. Stylistic prescriptions are by their very nature receiver-oriented. That is, they function to guide the speaker/writer to create messages which will have the desired effects upon listeners/readers. The findings reported here and those of the numerous studies conducted in this general area, should be direct inputs into any prescriptive stylistic theory.

Operating within the constraints imposed by language structure as well as those imposed by content considerations, the communicator has various degrees of freedom, that is, choices, for example, in the words and sentence structures selected.[25] If these choices, which are the essence of style, are to produce desired effects, they must be guided by a theory of stylistics which has as part of its data results from psycholinguistic experiments in sentence processing.

Advice on stylistic matters has, for the most part, been based on the insights of rhetoricians and the practice of successful or effective speakers. Although these sources of advice should always be considered, the results from controlled experiments cannot be ignored but rather should be given priority. More generally: if a theory of rhetoric or speech communication seeks to describe and ultimately explain and predict relationships between language and behavior, then it is precisely controlled experiments, derived from a sound theory of language structure, which are best going to provide the information needed for formulating such principles.

1. See, for example, Joseph A. DeVito, *The Psychology of Speech and Language: An Introduction to Psycholinguistics* (New York: Random House, 1970). The relationship between psycholinguistics and other areas of language study is more fully covered in DeVito, "Psycholinguistics and General Semantics: Some Conceptual 'Problems' and 'Resolutions' " in *Research Designs in General Semantics*, ed. Kenneth O. Johnson (New York: Gordon and Breach, 1974) and in DeVito, *Psycholinguistics* (Indianapolis, Ind.: Bobbs-Merrill, 1971).

2. Joseph A. DeVito, "Some Psycholinguistic Aspects of Active and Passive Sentences," *Quarterly Journal of Speech*, 55 (December, 1969), 401–406.

3. Jacques Mehler, "Some Effects of Grammatical Transformations on the Recall of English Sentences," *Journal of Verbal Learning and Verbal Behavior*, 2 (August, 1963), 346–351.

4. Philip B. Gough, "Grammatical Transformations and Speed of Understanding," *Journal of Verbal Learning and Verbal Behavior*, 4 (April, 1965), 107–111.

5. William Epstein, "The Influence of Syntactical Structure on Learning," *American Journal of Psychology*, 74 (March, 1961), 80–85, and "A Further Study of the Influence of Syntatical Structure on Learning," *American Journal of Psychology*, 75 (March, 1962), 121–126.

6. For reviews of this area see Jerry Fodor and Merrill Garrett, "Some Reflections on Competence and Performance," in *Psycholinguistic Papers*, eds. J. Lyons and R. J. Wales (Chicago: Aldine, 1966), pp. 135–154, and also their "Psychological Theories and Linguistic Constructs," in *Verbal Behavior and General Behavior Theory*, eds. Theodore R. Dixon and David L. Horton (Englewood Cliffs, N.J.: Prentice-Hall, 1968), pp. 451–477; and Philip B. Gough, "Experimental Psycholinguistics," in *A Survey of Linguistic Science*, ed. William Orr Dingwall (College Park, Md.: University of Maryland, 1971), pp. 252–292.

7. George A. Miller and David McNeill, "Psycholinguistics," in G. Lindzey and E. Aronson, eds., *The Handbook of Social Psychology*, III (2nd ed.: Reading, Mass.: Addison-Wesley, 1969), pp. 699–713. A characterization of this literature is provided by DeVito, *Psycholinguistics*.

8. Miller and McNeill, "Psycholinguistics," p. 709.

9. See Ursula Bellugi, "The Development of Interrogative Structures in Children's

Speech," in *The Development of Language Functions*, ed. Klaus F. Riegel (Ann Arbor, Mich.: Center for Human Growth and Development, 1965), pp. 103–137; Roger Brown, "The Development of Wh Questions in Child Speech," *Journal of Verbal Learning and Verbal Behavior*, 7 (April, 1968), 279–290; Edward S. Klima and Ursula Bellugi, "Syntactic Regularities in the Speech of Children," in *Psycholinguistic Papers*, pp. 181–208.

10. Owen Thomas, *Transformational Grammar and the Teacher of English* (New York: Holt, Rinehart and Winston, 1965), pp. 177–190.

11. Although this seems at variance with accepted usage, a more familiar example, with this same structure, indicates that such a transformation does in fact occur in English; consider, for example, the incredulously intoned question, "The final examination the student failed?"

12. Thomas, *Transformational Grammar and the Teacher of English*, p. 23.

13. The linguistic notation used here and throughout is standard. See, for example, DeVito, *The Psychology of Speech and Language*, pp. 27–56.

14. Results of recent studies on speeded-up speech indicate that intelligibility is not adversely affected when the rate is doubled. Cf., for example, Emerson Foulke, "Listening Comprehension as a Function of Word Rate," *Journal of Communication*, 18 (September, 1968), 198–206, and Ronald H. Reid, "Grammatical Complexity and Comprehension of Compressed Speech," *Journal of Communication*, 18 (September, 1968), 236–242. The only influence the speed-up had was to reduce the time available for processing the sentences.

15. See Noam Chomsky, *Aspects of the Theory of Syntax* (Cambridge, Mass.: M.I.T. Press, 1965), pp. 103–106, and Kinsuke Hasegawa, "The Passive Construction in English," *Language*, 44 (June, 1968), 230–242.

16. DeVito, "Some Psycholinguistic Aspects of Active and Passive Sentences."

17. On negative as opposed to affirmative constructions, see Edward S. Klima, "Negation in English," in *The Structure of Language: Readings in the Philosophy of Language*, eds. Jerry A. Fodor and Jerrold J. Katz (Englewood Cliffs, N.J.: Prentice-Hall, 1964), pp. 246–323, and Thomas, *Transformational Grammar and the Teacher of English*, pp. 190–192.

18. Carl I. Hovland and Walter Weiss, "Transmission of Information Concerning Concepts through Positive and Negative Instances," *Journal of Experimental Psychology*, 45 (March, 1953), 175–182; P. C. Wason, "The Processing of Positive and Negative Information," *Quarterly Journal of Experimental Psychology*, 11 (May, 1959), 92–107, and "Response to Affirmative and Negative Binary Statements," *British Journal of Psychology*, 52 (May, 1961), 133–142.

19. See, for example, Paula Menyuk, *Sentences Children Use* (Cambridge, Mass.: M.I.T. Press, 1969); Roger Brown, *Social Psychology* (New York: Free Press, 1965), pp. 246–349; Susan M. Ervin-Tripp, "Language Development," in *Review of Child Development Research*, I (New York: Russell Sage Foundation, 1966), pp. 55–105, for excellent reviews of research findings. Also see those references cited in footnote 6 for data pertaining particularly to questions.

20. Although directional hypotheses were set up and consequently a one-tailed test used, the statistical significance of these results would not be altered had null hypotheses and a two-tailed test been used. The only change in the significance levels would be for affirmative versus negative questions; here p would be $< .05$ instead of $< .025$ as noted in Table 2.

21. Rudolf Flesch, "A New Readability Yardstick," *Journal of Applied Psychology*, 32 (June, 1948), 221–233.

22. For evidence and argument in support of this view see George A. Miller, "Some

Psychological Studies of Grammar," *American Psychologist*, 17 (November, 1962), 748–762, and Garrett and Fodor, "Psychological Theories and Linguistic Constructs." For an opposing view see Charles E. Osgood, "Toward a Wedding of Insufficiencies," in *Verbal Behavior and General Behavior Theory*, eds. Theodore R. Dixon and David L. Horton (Englewood Cliffs, N.J.: Prentice-Hall, 1968), pp. 495–519.

23. Noam Chomsky, *Language and Mind* (New York: Harcourt, Brace, Jovanovich, 1968), p. 1.

24. On this point see Osgood, "Toward a Wedding of Insufficiencies."

25. This concept of style is developed more fully in DeVito, "Style and Stylistics: An Attempt at Definition," *Quarterly Journal of Speech*, 53 (October, 1967), 248–255.

The Interaction of Refutation Type, Involvement, and Authoritativeness

VERNON E. CRONEN

The Speech communication field has long manifested an interest in the processes of decision-making through public debate. This enduring interest has not, however, found frequent expression in the behavioral study of those variables that are unique to public debate. The purpose of this study is to investigate one kind of choice that a speaker may make when refuting a prior speaker's argument. The choice studied here is whether to devote a given amount of time to counter argument or to fallacy exposure. The significance of this choice, of course, must be understood in light of other crucial variables in the rhetorical situation. Listeners make judgments about the authoritativeness of each debater and they bring to the situation their prior judgments about the subject. Listeners may find the subject matter important or trivial. They may agree or disagree with the position taken by either speaker. Thus, the variables of refutational method, authoritativeness, prior attitudes, and involvement are among the most obvious constituents of rhetorical situations in which opposing communicators face a common audience. These variables provide a useful starting place for behavioral research.

This study is designed to answer two general questions: (1) For purposes of refutation, is fallacy exposure or counter argument the more desirable choice? (2) Under what specific conditions of speaker authoritativeness, audience involvement, and prior audience attitudes is fallacy exposure or counter argument more effective? It must be stressed that these questions are *not* posed with reference to tournament debate. The concern here is for public debate where an audience hears contrary or contradictory messages.

Theoretical Bases

To date there has been no behavioral research relevant to the choice of fallacy exposure or counter argument. Thus, it is necessary to provide a general theoretical structure that can serve to generate specific hypotheses and research questions.

Before considering the specific variables manipulated in this study, let us posit three assumptions descriptive of human listeners. First, listeners' beliefs are patterned in sets and are hierarchically arranged.[1] The notion of patterned sets of beliefs is common to summation and balance theories.[2] The central idea is that attitude toward a superordinate concept is a function of those subordinate beliefs that the individual holds about it. Quite simply, attitude toward "Indians" is determined by one's beliefs about Indians and the valences of those beliefs. The notion of hierarchically arranged sets of beliefs is also a common conception in theories of attitude.[3] The assumption of hierarchical arrangement assigns major importance to the position of beliefs within the hierarchy. Daniel Katz says "the centrality of an attitude refers to its role as part of a value system which is closely related to the individual's self concept."[4] Some beliefs and their associated valences are simply more important than others. As Sherif and Cantril point out, an individual is reluctant to change beliefs centrally positioned in his cognitive hierarchy because they bear more closely upon his self-concept.[5]

The second assumption is the existence of a general tendency toward cognitive consistency. The statement does not imply that man is totally rational; it simply recognizes a human need to "make sense" out of one's environment.[6] No man has a perfectly consistent cognitive system and individuals differ in their need for cognitive consistency.[7] The consistency that people seek includes two tendencies according to research conducted by William McGuire. There is both a tendency for "a person's beliefs (expectations) on related issues to be in accord with each other in the pattern required by the rules of formal logic," and a tendency for a person's beliefs on a given issue to be in accord with his desires about it.[8] The need for consistency is related to the hierarchical conception of cognitions. Sherif and Cantril say "it is the intensity with which an attitude is held, the degree of ego-involvement it has for the individual, that in large part determines the consistency of opinion."[9] The more involving the beliefs, the greater the need for consistency among them.

The third assumption is that listeners may defend against inconsistency without re-evaluating concepts. The term "re-evaluation" indicates the behavior by which an individual changes the valence of a given concept to make it consistent with his associated beliefs. If, however, the concept under "assault" from contrary information is an involving one, then one defense against having to re-evaluate the concept is to consciously or unconsciously misperceive the discrepant information, a defensive behavior well documented in the literature.[10] Another defense is "cognitive isolation." McGuire says that one type of response to discrepant information is "the cognitive

isolation of these opinions from one another by logic-tight compartmentaliza-
tion."[11] This behavior does not really eliminate inconsistency but rather
provides a reordering of cognitions so that discrepant cognitions do not
conflict with an involving attitude.

To proceed to a consideration of the specific independent variables
manipulated in this study, refutation is, in the broadest sense, the objection a
communicator raises to a conclusion presented in another communication. In
this study the primary focus is on the comparison of two types of refutation:
fallacy exposure and counter argument. Fallacy exposure is refutation in
which a communicator explains that a unit of proof fails "some" test of
formal validity. Counter argument is refutation in which a communicator
adduces a new body of proof to reach a conclusion contrary or contradictory
to the position he wishes to negate. The importance of this distinction can be
illuminated by reference to our assumptions about listeners.

Counter arguments allow a communicator to change attitudes about a
concept by adding new beliefs to the listener's set of beliefs. Let us suppose
that a hypothetical listener has two negative beliefs about the concept
"Nixon." In counter argument a communicator might provide many positively valenced beliefs about the concept. If a sufficient number of positive
beliefs are added to the listener's cognitive set, then the listener's attitude
must shift in a positive direction in order to maintain cognitive consistency.[12] Thus, through counter argument one *might* shift attitude from
positive to negative if a sufficient number of new beliefs can be added to the
listener's cognitive set.

From a "logical" point of view the potential of fallacy exposure seems
more limited. While fallacy exposure provides reason for rejecting a belief
learned in a prior communication, it provides no logical basis for adopting a
strong attitude contrary to the refuted position.

Essentially, to show that a given belief about a concept was developed
illogically is to attempt to remove that belief from the listener's cognitive set.
Fallacy exposure thus removes beliefs from a set and seems not to have
potential for moving attitude beyond neutral to a contrary position.

This "logical" limitation on the impact of fallacy exposure may, however,
be offset by other considerations. Fallacy exposure can make it difficult for
the listener to employ "cognitive isolation" as a defense. The assumption of
cognitive organization into patterned sets does not imply that any specific
belief elements are in communication, but it does imply, says Rokeach, that
the potential for communication exists.[13] McGuire found that by making
inconsistent beliefs salient within a short time interval he could sensitize
subjects to their compartmentalized inconsistencies and produce change in
the direction of attitudinal consistency.[14] An additional argument for the
superiority of fallacy exposure over counter argument is that the latter is

dependent upon the proper interpretation of dissonant information and is thus more susceptible to "cognitive distortion." Fallacy exposure is based on making salient cognitions that are *already present* in the auditor's cognitive system.

In public debate it is necessary to consider the initial attitude of the audience toward the topic, and the degree of involvement the audience has with it. There is reason to expect that initial attitude and involvement will interact with the choice of refutation type. As noted earlier, increased involvement causes a heightened need for consistency. When a speaker takes a stand consistent with prevailing audience attitudes on an involving topic he might be well advised to use fallacy exposure if he can, because it has the effect of *eliminating*, not merely counter balancing, dissonant information. If our perception of sources is a function of the rewards they provide, then behavior that eliminates inconsistent information on an involving topic may be a rewarding behavior that improves perception of the speaker's authoritativeness. It must be cautioned, however, that a flood of new attitude-consistent beliefs induced by counter argument might reduce the discrepant beliefs to seeming insignificance, thereby providing the same reward in the form of reducing inconsistency. The superiority of fallacy exposure when taking the popular side of an involving issue thus rests on highly tentative speculation.

Prior research on speaker authoritativeness makes possible somewhat more confident predictions about the probable effects of this variable. Much research supports the conclusion that a highly authoritative speaker is more successful than a less authoritative speaker in efforts to establish new conclusions.[15] McCroskey stresses the importance of authoritativeness for the establishment of new beliefs in the listener's cognitive set. He says "for the very low *ethos* source, evidence would serve no persuasive purpose. The audience would reject perfectly valid evidence because of the person presenting it."[16] Thus, in general, speakers low in authoritativeness who seek to change auditors' attitudes toward some concept should probably choose fallacy exposure, and highly authoritative speakers should probably choose counter argument.

The choice of refutation strategy should also affect the relative authoritativeness of debaters. The inability to reason soundly should reflect adversely on ratings of speaker authoritativeness. As McBurney and Wrage put the matter, "no one wishes to be informed or advised by an incompetent."[17] In public debate the employment of fallacy exposure may have a dual effect. First, it may demonstrate the reasoning ability of the speaker who employs it, thus increasing his own authoritativeness. Second, it may discredit the reasoning ability of the speaker under attack, thus decreasing his authoritativeness. Hence, the use of fallacy exposure by a speaker perceived low in authoritativeness should reduce the disparity in perceived authoritativeness between himself and another speaker. Since authoritativeness is important for the establishment of new beliefs, authoritativeness and refutation type may interact during a message to increase or diminish a speaker's ability to establish new beliefs.

In this study refutation type, audience attitudes and involvement, and speaker authoritativeness function as independent variables. Their main and interactive effects are measured on two dependent variables. The first is attitude toward a conclusion. Here we are concerned with the effect of the independent variables on attitude toward a specific fallacious conclusion drawn by the first of two speakers. The second dependent variable is the relative authoritativeness of two speakers. Here our concern is with how the choice of refutation type (a) assists an unauthoritative speaker in diminishing the perceived *difference* between his authoritativeness and that of his opponent, and (b) allows a highly authoritative speaker to establish or increase the difference between his authoritativeness and that of his opponent.

Research Questions and Predictions

The assumptions offered about the cognitive systems of listeners and the discussion of the independent variables in light of those assumptions allow us to generate the following research questions and hypotheses.

1. Main effects. Because no substantial theoretical reasons can be offered for preferring the logical to the psychological basis of prediction, no specific hypotheses as to the main effect of refutation type on attitude can be offered. Hence, the following general research question about the main effect of refutation type: *Is fallacy exposure or counter argument generally the more desirable choice as measured by attitude toward the specific conclusion in dispute?* Because fallacy exposure implied both sound reasoning ability of the speaker employing it and defects in the reasoning ability of the speaker against whom it is used, the following prediction is made: *Fallacy exposure is significantly superior to counter argument as means of enhancing the relative position of the responding speaker with respect to perceived authoritativeness;*

2. Two-way interactions. Fallacy exposure seems less dependent on the authoritativeness of the speaker presenting it. Thus, fallacy exposure should be useful for assisting an unauthoritative speaker to overcome the perceived difference between his authoritativeness and that of his opponent and for attacking a conclusion. Therefore, it is reasonable to expect an interaction between authoritativeness and refutation type. The following predictions are advanced:

(a) *The choice of fallacy exposure over counter argument will be especially significant for enhancing the relative position of the responding speaker with respect to perceived authoritativeness when the initial speaker is high in authoritativeness and the responding speaker is low in authoritativeness.*

(b) *When a speaker low in authoritativeness responds to a speaker who is high in authoritativeness, the responding speaker will evoke an attitude significantly more favorable to his position on the conclusion being debated if he uses fallacy exposure instead of counter argument.*

Because of the highly tentative nature of our theoretical treatment of the involvement variable no specific hypotheses are advanced. Instead, we pose two general research questions:

(a) *Will fallacy exposure or counter argument be the preferable alternative for enhancing the relative authoritativeness of the responding speaker when the responding speaker takes the popular side of an involving issue?*

(b) *Will fallacy exposure or counter argument be the preferable alternative for changing attitude when the responding speaker takes the popular side of an involving issue?*

Validating the Independent Variables

A number of procedures were required prior to the conduct of the main experiment in order to operationalize and control the dependent variables.

Validating the Refutation Variable

To operationalize the conditions of fallacy exposure and counter argument a short message was prepared in support of each experimental proposition. Each message led to a conclusion supporting the proposition and each contained a logical fallacy in a deductive argument. Two forms of refutational messages were prepared for each of the messages containing fallacies. In one form, the proposition and the argument's conclusion were denied and a single argument was presented reaching a conclusion opposite that reached in the first message. The fallacy exposure counter message contained three elements: (1) A denial of the proposition and the conclusion of the fallacy, (2) an explanation of the fallacy, and (3) a simplified example of the type of fallacy committed. A panel of four faculty members judged the messages for equivalence.

In order to know whether the *act* of exposing fallacies made a difference, it was necessary to know whether the fallacies contained in the initial messages *required* exposure. To determine this the fallacious messages were pretested. No subject in the pretest found the fallacies in any message (N=31).

Validating the Authoritativeness Variable

The fallacious messages and refutative responses used in this study were presented by speakers possessing different degrees of initial authoritativeness. Three conditions of authoritativeness were validated: (1) First speaker high in authoritativeness, responding speaker also high in authoritativeness. (2) First

TABLE 1
Authoritativeness Pilot Study

HIGH AUTHORITATIVENESS "Mr. Miller"	$\bar{X}$ = 32.60	N = 30
HIGH AUTHORITATIVENESS "Mr. Drummond"	$\bar{X}$ = 34.41	N = 31
LOW AUTHORITATIVENESS "Mr. Seymore"	$\bar{X}$ = 16. 77	N = 27

Miller, Drummond, and Seymore are fictitious names used in the pretest and main experiment to identify the speakers.

speaker high in authoritativeness, responding speaker low in authoritativeness. (3) First speaker low in authoritativeness, responding speaker high in authoritativeness.

Establishing speakers representing these conditions of initial authoritativeness necessitated another pretest. In this pretest initial authoritativeness was established by manipulating a recorded chairman's introduction and the speaker's delivery.[18] The study established two high and one low authoritativeness speakers. Both high condition speakers differed from the low beyond the .0005 level of confidence.

Validating the Involvement-Attitude Variable

The messages presented to subjects also had to be based on propositions that evoked different initial audience attitudes and audience involvement. Propositions were sought that could represent three configurations of involvement and initial attitude: (1) propositions toward which attitude was favorable and which were involving, (2) propositions toward which attitude was unfavorable and which were involving, (3) propositions toward which attitude was neutral and which were not involving. A pilot study using forty-one undergraduate subjects yielded two propositions for each of these three conditions. The Fulton ego-involvement scales[19] and Likert scales were the dependent measures. One tailed t-tests were employed. The high involvement proposition differed significantly from low involvement (P < .005). Favorable propositions differed significantly from unfavorable (P< .005).

Main Experimental Procedures

The subjects for the main experiment were 736 lower division students enrolled in courses offered by the departments of speech, theatre, and agriculture at the University of Illinois. Classes studying argumentation and debate were not used. Whole classes were randomly assigned to the eighteen cells of the main design. Subjects were told that the audio tape recordings they were to hear were cuttings from a full tape of a debate held before a campus group.

Subjects indicated their reactions to the speakers and their messages on two measuring instruments. Authoritativeness was measured by McCroskey's authoritativeness scales.[20] To conveniently analyze the relative position of the two speakers each subject's ratings of the first speaker were summed as were his ratings of the responding speakers. A spread score was assigned to reflect the *difference* between ratings of the two speakers. A simple seven-place strongly-agree-to-strongly-disagree scale was used to assess attitude. The scale was used only to assess attitude toward the specific fallacious conclusion reached.[21]

The study involved a $2 \times 3 \times 3 \times 2$ design. The last factor of "2" represents the topic variable and indicates that two topics exist to test each condition. Since the topic variable exists in every condition it is a fully nested variable. The design is unbalanced because there is an unequal number of subjects in each condition. Subjects in each cell were exposed to only one set of experimental conditions. For example, classes in a given cell might hear only the "regulated women's hours" topic, and only a highly authoritative first speaker answered by the fallacy exposure speech of an unauthoritative speaker.

This design was also employed because it afforded the investigation of a number of three-way interaction predictions. The theoretical bases of the three-way predictions and results, however, are considerations beyond the scope of this essay.

Results

The results of this study are presented from the perspective of the responding speaker who had the option to select the type of refutation.

The responding speaker's goal with respect to the dependent variable attitude is always to *lower* auditor's ratings of the previous speaker's conclusion. For example, a mean attitude score of 2.00 would indicate greater success for the responding speaker than would a mean attitude score of 5.00. The former score indicates that the speaker was more successful in attacking the conclusion of his opponent.

Discussion of results on the dependent variable authoritativeness is also presented from the perspective of the responding speaker. Results for authoritativeness indicate the *relative* authoritativeness of the responding speaker vis-à-vis his opponent. If the responding speaker is initially low in authoritativeness, his goal is to *reduce* the perceived *difference* between his own and his opponent's authoritativeness. If a speaker is initially high in authoritativeness, his goal is to create or to increase the perceived difference between his own and his opponent's authoritativeness. For example, a mean authoritativeness rating of −6.00 would indicate that the responding speaker was perceived to be lower than his opponent in authoritativeness. A mean score of +1.00 would indicate that the responding speaker was perceived to be somewhat higher than his opponent in authoritativeness.

Appropriate null-hypotheses were formulated and tested for significance at the .05 level. Tables 2 and 3 summarize the values obtained by analysis of variance for the two dependent variables. For convenience, mean differences are reported in separate tables appropriate to the discussion of specific hypotheses.

The first general research question posed was: Is fallacy exposure or counter argument generally the more desirable choice as measured by attitude toward the specific conclusion in dispute? The nonsignificant F ratio for the main effect of refutation (A) shown in Table 2 indicates that there are insufficient grounds for rejecting the null-hypothesis. Thus, the data provided by this study give us no reason to believe fallacy exposure to be *generally* more effective than counter argument for attacking a specific conclusion.

The first research hypothesis put forward in the study was: Fallacy exposure is significantly superior to counter argument as a means of enhancing the relative position of the responding speaker with respect to

TABLE 2
Analysis of Variance for Dependent Variable Attitude

Source	df	SS	MS	F Ratio	Prob.
A (Refutation Type)	1	0.446	0.446	0.002	0.96134
B (Authoritativeness)	2	0.538	0.269	14.164	0.00000
C (Involvement attitude)	2	0.398	0.199	104.704	0.00000
D (Topic)	1	0.166	0.166	8.740	0.00322
A × B	2	0.297	0.148	7.814	0.00044
A × C	2	0.249	0.124	0.656	0.51940
A × D	1	0.723	0.723	3.806	0.05146
B × C	4	0.429	0.107	0.565	0.68819
B × D	2	0.173	0.867	0.457	0.63356
C × D	2	0.263	0.131	69.237	0.00000
A × B × C	4	0.626	0.157	0.825	0.50968
A × B × D	2	0.117	0.585	3.082	0.04648
A × C × D	2	0.253	0.127	6.666	0.00136
B × C × D	4	0.448	0.112	5.906	0.00011
A × B × C × D	4	0.174	0.436	2.297	0.05767
E (Subjects)	704	0.134	0.190		

TABLE 3
Analysis of Variance for Dependent Variable Authoritativeness

Source	df	SS	MS	F Ratio	Prob.
A (Refutation type)	1	0.801	0.801	12.512	0.00043
B (Authoritativeness)	2	0.230	0.115	179.977	0.00000
C (Involvement-attitude)	2	0.652	0.326	5.093	0.00637
D (Topic)	1	0.444	0.444	0.694	0.40508
A × B	2	0.109	0.544	8.504	0.00022
A × C	2	0.514	0.257	4.014	0.01849
A × D	1	0.892	0.892	13.935	0.00020
B × C	4	0.874	0.218	3.414	0.00890
B × D	2	0.476	0.238	3.718	0.02477
C × D	2	0.254	0.127	19.835	0.00000
A × B × C	4	0.260	0.649	1.014	0.39911
A × B × D	2	0.177	0.886	1.385	0.25102
A × C × D	2	0.186	0.930	0.145	0.86473
B × C × D	4	0.191	0.478	7.476	0.00001
A × B × C × D	4	0.740	0.185	2.890	0.02163
E (Subjects)	704	0.450	0.640		

perceived authoritativeness. The significant F-ratio for the main effect of refutation type on the responding speaker's authoritativeness provides support for the research hypothesis, (counter argument: $\bar{x} = +0.260$; fallacy exposure: $\bar{x} = +2.495$; $p < .0004$). Thus the null-hypothesis was rejected.

The second research hypothesis was: The choice of fallacy exposure over counter argument will be especially significant for enhancing the relative position of the responding speaker with respect to perceived authoritativeness when the initial speaker is high in authoritativeness and the responding speaker low in authoritativeness. The data provide strong support for rejecting the null-hypothesis in favor of this research hypothesis ($f = 8.50$, $p < .0002$). To clarify the nature of the interaction between refutation type and initial authoritativeness on the dependent variable of relative authoritativeness, we will examine it graphically. Table 4 shows that in the confrontation of two speakers both high in initial authoritativeness (H vs H) the use of fallacy exposure produced a mean difference of +2.194. That is, the responding speaker was perceived to be slightly higher in authoritativeness than his opponent. When using counter argument the two speakers were perceived to be almost identical in authoritativeness ($\bar{x} = +0.407$).

When a speaker high in initial authoritativeness was answered by a speaker low in initial authoritativeness (H vs L) the impact of refutation type was far more significant. As shown in the graph when the responding speaker used fallacy exposure the mean difference in perceived authoritativeness was only

TABLE 4
Authoritativeness Ratings: A × B

GROUP MEANS*

	H vs. H	H vs. L	L vs. H
Fallacy exposure	+2.194[c]	−2.648[a]	+8.304[b]
Counter argument	+0.407[c]	8.320[b]	+8.575[b]

*Groups with different superscripts differ beyond .05, assessed with Tukey's HSD test.

INTERACTION GRAPH

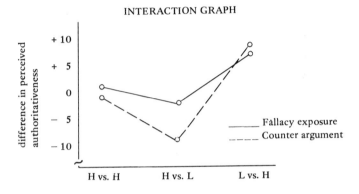

−2.648. When the respondent low in initial authoritativeness used counter argument against a highly authoritative opponent the mean difference between them was −8.320. For the high authoritativeness speaker the choice of refutation type had no impact when responding to a low authoritativeness speaker (L vs H).

The third research hypothesis was also supported. When a speaker low in authoritativeness responds to a speaker who is high in authoritativeness, the responding speaker will evoke attitudes significantly more favorable to his position if he uses fallacy exposure instead of counter argument. The significant F ratio for the A x B interaction (p < .0004) provides sufficient grounds for rejecting the null-hypothesis. Again, the choice of refutation type is most important when a speaker low in initial authoritativeness answers a speaker of initially high authoritativeness (H vs L). Speakers of low authoritativeness were thus more successful in attacking a specific conclusion with fallacy exposure.

The data suggest an answer to one of the two research questions about the interaction of refutation and involvement. Fallacy exposure was superior for increasing relative authoritativeness when the responding speaker took the *popular* side of an involving issue (I-P). The choice had no impact when the

TABLE 5
Attitude Ratings: A X B

GROUP MEANS*

	H vs. H	H vs. L	L vs. H
Fallacy exposure	3.888[b]	3.918[b]	3.555[b]
Counter argument	3.522[b]	4.400[a]	3.299[b]

*Groups with different superscripts differ beyond .05, assessed with Tukey's HSD test.

INTERACTION GRAPH

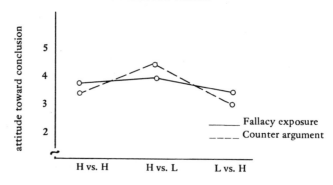

responding speaker had the *unpopular* side of an involving issue (I-UP), or when the responding speaker advocated a position on an issue toward which the audience was neutral and uninvolved (UI-Neut). The significant F-ratio for the A X C interaction justifies rejection of the null-hypothesis (F = 4.01, p < .01). The data thus support the tentative speculation offered earlier: That on involving issues the speaker provides the partisan listener with greater reward by using fallacy exposure because this method *eliminates* dissonant beliefs while counter arguments leave the listener with dissonant beliefs in his cognitive set. The effect was only suspected to be present on involving issues since increased involvement entails increased need for consistency.

The nonsignificant F ratio for the interaction of refutation and involvement (A X C) on the dependent variable attitude means that the data provide no justification for believing fallacy exposure or counter argument to be the preferable choice for changing attitude when the responding speaker takes the popular side of an involving issue.

One highly disturbing result is the existence of significant main and interactive effects for the nested variable "topic." This means that some uncontrolled variable in one or more messages had a significant effect. An examination of mean scores showed that the topics did not differ systemati-

TABLE 6
Authoritativeness Ratings: A X C

GROUP MEANS*

	Inv.-Unpop.	Inv.-Pop.	Uninv.-Neutral
Counter argument	$+0.432^b$	$+0.186^b$	$+0.141^b$
Fallacy exposure	$+0.282^b$	$+4.933^a$	$+1.422^b$

*Groups with different superscripts differ beyond .05, assessed with Tukey's HSD test.

INTERACTION GRAPH

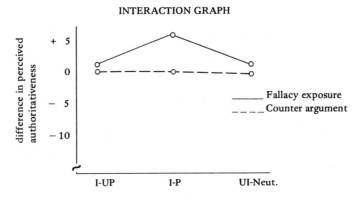

cally. That is, it cannot be concluded that some of the topics generally worked as predicted and other topics generally did not. Because the topics do not differ systematically, it is also possible that a *different* topic variable interacted in each condition. It must be concluded that a fuller understanding of the interaction of the independent variables in this study will only be possible in light of the influence of other message variables.

Three-way interactions were not significant except for those involving the nested variable.

Discussion

The purpose of this study was to investigate certain behavioral dimensions of public debate. These conclusions are especially important when we consider their impact in the context of an entire public debate. Three of the conclusions indicate that the method of refutation used to answer a preceding speaker has important bearing on the relative authoritativeness of the two communicators. These three conclusions were:

(1) Fallacy exposure, rather than counter argument, is the *generally* more effective type of refutation for enhancing the position of a responding

speaker with respect to his relative authoritativeness. However, as noted, this does not hold in all conditions.

(2) It is especially important when a speaker low in authoritativeness responds to a speaker who is high in authoritativeness, that the responding speaker should use fallacy exposure to decrease the perceived difference between his authoritativeness and that of his opponent.

(3) Fallacy exposure is preferable to counter argument for enhancing the relative authoritativeness of the responding speaker when the responding speaker takes the popular side of an involving issue.

Fallacy exposure, unlike counter argument, is not dependent on the acceptance and proper perception of new data concerning the proposition. The acceptability of data is dependent on perceptions of the communicator. Thus, a speaker may improve his relative authoritativeness by using fallacy exposure early in the message thereby enhancing his ability to utilize counter arguments *at a later time*. This is especially important for speakers perceived low in authoritativeness because of their delivery and prior reputation. The authoritativeness developed through fallacy exposure has special impact for situations in which the speaker takes the popular side of an involving issue as shown by conclusion there. In such situations the responding speaker can enhance authoritativeness through fallacy exposure and thus enhance his ability to develop counter arguments.

The fourth conclusion of this study indicates that in certain conditions the choice of refutation type may affect the attitude toward a conclusion. The fourth conclusion may be stated as follows:

(4) When a speaker low in authoritativeness responds to a speaker who is high in authoritativeness, the responding speaker should choose fallacy exposure instead of counter argument to more effectively attack the conclusion in dispute.

Papageorgis and McGuire found that the resistance to subsequent discrepant messages was increased by exposing listeners to a prior refutation even when the subsequent message contained none of the arguments refuted in the first message.[22] This evidence suggests that some refutational techniques may produce a halo effect. That is, auditors draw the rather sensible conclusion that a given position weak in certain respects may also be weak in other respects. If Papageorgis and McGuire's results are proven relevant to the variables contained in this study, there is additional reason for a speaker who is low in authoritativeness to expose a fallacy early in his presentation in order to call into question the validity of his opponent's other arguments later in the debate.

This study offers indirect evidence of the value of those general assumptions upon which it was based. Assumptions concerning cognitive sets and hierarchy, cognitive consistency needs, and defenses against inconsistency together generated useful predictions and questions when applied to a new area of research.

Recommendations

Obviously, a great deal of additional research is needed to understand the behavioral effects of techniques of refutation. The following recommendations might prove fruitful:

1. A descriptive study should be conducted to isolate variables that cause the significant AxBxCxD interaction. It is possible that the key is not in the construction of the messages but in the personal goals that auditors associate with different topics. If, for example, a listener's goal is to find useful and novel arguments to use on his peers, the listener will not be impressed or rewarded by hearing the exposure of a fallacious argument he does not anticipate. The importance of listener goals has implications beyond the study of argumentation and should be pursued.

2. The halo effect of refutation should be tested with varying types of refutation and differing levels of involvement and authoritativeness. It is important to know if specific means of refutation produce a halo effect and under what conditions. McGuire's research did not differentiate among types of refutation, involvement levels, or levels of source authoritativeness.

3. Finally, it would be interesting to know if the impact of fallacy exposure is generated by real understanding of fallacies. It is possible that influence is generated by the speaker's use of a vocabulary associated with formal logic and the listener's desire to appear sophisticated in the use of reason. This question could be studied experimentally by composing logically sound messages and pseudo-exposure messages that employ terminology associated with formal logic.

1. This assumption is central to most theorists of attitude formation and change.

2. Lynn R. Anderson, "Prediction of Attitude from Congruity, Summation, and Logarithm Formulae for the Evaluation of Complex Stimuli," *Journal of Social Psychology*, 81 (1970), 37–49.

3. See, for example, Daniel Katz, "The Function Approach to the Study of Attitudes," *Public Opinion Quarterly*, 24 (Summer, 1960), 163–204; and Milton Rokeach, "The Role of Values in Public Opinion Research," *Public Opinion Quarterly*, 32 (Winter, 1968–69), 550.

4. Katz, "Function Approach," p. 169.

5. Muzafer Sherif and Hadley Cantril, *The Psychology of Ego-Involvements* (New York: Wiley and Sons, 1947), p. 131.

6. Milton Rokeach, *The Open and Closed Mind* (New York: Basic Books, 1960), p. 33.

7. *Ibid.*; and Arthur R. Cohen, *Attitude Change and Social Influence* (New York: Basic Books, 1964), p. 48.

8. William McGuire, "A Syllogistic Analysis of Cognitive Relationships," in *Attitude Organization and Change*, eds. Carl I. Hovland and Milton J. Rosenberg (New Haven, Conn.: Yale University Press, 1960), p. 66.

9. Sherif and Cantril, *Psychology of Ego-Involvements*, p. 134.

10. See, for example, J. M. Levine and G. Murphy, "The Learning and Forgetting of Controversial Material," *Journal of Abnormal and Social Psychology*, 38 (October, 1943), 507–517; and Albert Hasdorf and Hadley Cantril, "They Saw a Game: A Case Study," *Journal of Abnormal and Social Psychology*, 49 (January, 1954), 129–134.

11. McGuire, "A Syllogistic Analysis," p. 98.

12. This prediction would hold for both balance and summation theory conceptions.

13. Rokeach, *The Open and Closed Mind*, pp. 33–37.

14. McGuire, "A Syllogistic Analysis," pp. 65–111.

15. Most of the older studies of source credibility testify to this conclusion and there is no need to review this literature here.

16. James C. McCroskey, *Studies of the Effects of Evidence in Persuasive Communication*, Michigan State University, Speech Communication Laboratory Report SCRL 4-67, December, 1967, p. 59.

17. James H. McBurney and Ernest J. Wrage, *The Art of Good Speech* (New York: Prentice-Hall, 1953), p. 43.

18. The utility of these means of manipulation is provided by the work of Haiman and Miller and Hewgill. See Franklyn S. Haiman, "An Experimental Study of the Effects of Ethos in Public Speaking," *Speech Monographs*, 16 (September, 1949), 190–202; and Gerald R. Miller and Murray A. Hewgill, "The Effects of Variation in Nonfluency on Audience Ratings of Source Credibility," *The Quarterly Journal of Speech*, 50 (February, 1964), 36–44.

19. These scales were derived by Robert B. Fulton in his dissertation "Attitude Change: A Homeostatic Model of the Listener" (Ph.D. dissertation, Department of Communications, University of Illinois, 1967). The scales were developed by Fulton from the work of Charles D. Ward, "Attitude and Involvement in Absolute Judgment of Attitude Statements," *Journal of Personality and Social Psychology*, 4 (November, 1966), 465–476. The rationale for the use of these sclaes is presented in Timothy Meyer and Vernon Cronen, "Agnew Meets the Student Dissenters: An Experimental Study of Ego-Involvement and Argumentation," *Journal of Communication*, 22 (September, 1972), 263–272.

20. James C. McCroskey, "Scales for the Measurement of Ethos," *Speech Monographs*, 33 (March, 1966), 65–72.

21. More sophisticated measures were of course available. The decision to use this simple device was based on the need to reduce in-class administration time.

22. Demetrius Papageorgias and William J. McGuire, "The Generality of Immunity to Persuasion Produced by Pre-Exposure to Weakened Counterarguments," *Journal of Abnormal and Social Psychology*, 62 (September, 1961), 475–481.

Influence of Two Impromptu
Public-Speaking Tasks
on the Heart Rates of Young Adults

THEODORE CLEVENGER, JR.

In agreement with other theorists, Donald C. Bryant and Karl R. Wallace identify nervousness, worry, and tension as normal accompaniments of public speaking.[1] Until recently, however, very little has been known about the pattern of arousal within the individual speaking experience. Primitive technology made it impossible to answer objectively such questions as: Is arousal highest before, during, or after the speech? Can we identify specific points in the unfolding speech experience where anxiety for most speakers is especially high or low? Do arousal mechanisms (such as anticipation and adaptation) revealed in other anxiety-provoking tasks also apply to the speaking experience? Is there a general pattern, or does each speaker respond differently? Do some speakers fail to show any arousal at all?

With the advent of microminiaturized electronic circuitry in the 1960s, it became possible to manufacture very small, lightweight telemetry systems for unobtrusively measuring physiological changes in freely moving subjects. Using such a system, Clevenger, Motley, and Carlile studied heart rates in a group of students delivering prepared speeches near the end of a semester of training in public speaking.[2] Their results were striking. Every speaker showed substantial increments in heart rate, even though speaking to a small, familiar audience after considerable training and experience. Moreover, although students showed much individual variation in absolute heart-rate levels, almost all of them evidenced the same general pattern of arousal through the speaking experience. This pattern was characterized by four stages: (1) *anticipatory activation*, defined as an increment in heart rate as the time for speaking approached, (2) *confrontation reaction*, defined as a further upward surge in heart rate very shortly after facing the audience, (3) *adapta-*

tion, defined as a gradual decrement in heart rate during the speech so that arousal at the end was lower than at the beginning, and, (4) *release*, defined as a further drop in heart rate very shortly after the end of the speech. The composite five-second average heart rate for all subjects is presented in Figure 1.

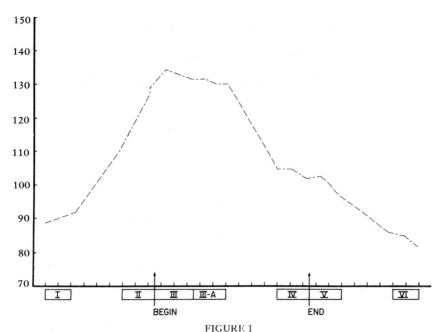

FIGURE 1
Average Mean Heart Rates
During Critical Intervals, for Prepared Speakers

This first experiment left unanswered a number of questions that might occur to both the anxiety theorist and the speech teacher, among which are the following: (1) Would the same pattern of heart rate changes characterize other speaking tasks carried out in a different setting? (2) Would the absolute heart rates be different for subjects operating under different motivational sets? In the experiment that we report here, students made an impromptu speech rather than a prepared one; they spoke to a very small audience in a highly informal setting; half of them knew that they were to receive class grades based on the speech performance, while the other half knew that they would not be graded.

Subjects

Subjects for this study were twenty-four young adult males enrolled in an undergraduate psychology of oral communication course at the Florida State

University. All were sophomores or juniors, all were between nineteen and twenty-one years of age, all had taken at least one performance course in speech in either high school or college, and all had previously made public speeches outside the classroom. In an extensive self-evaluation questionnaire completed at the beginning of the term, two months prior to this experiment, none of these subjects identified "stage fright" as a serious impediment to their speaking in public, and none reported a tendency to avoid public speaking for any reason. All were in good health and had no known history of cardiovascular disorder.

Experimental Procedures

The subjects were divided at random into four groups of six subjects each. Students in the first and third groups were given assignment sheets describing the impromptu speech task, concluding with notice that the quality of the speech would be evaluated and the assigned grade averaged with the student's other work in determining the term grade in the course. The second and fourth groups received the same assignment sheet, except they were told that the purpose of the assignment was to obtain a sample of each student's verbal behavior, which he would subsequently transcribe and analyze. It was expected that this difference in instructions would lead to a higher motivational level for the students who were to be graded. Groups 1 and 2 spoke on the first day, groups 3 and 4 on the second.

The setting for the experiment was quite informal. In a 12' X 14' room with items of equipment unrelated to the experiment arranged on benches along two of the walls, the subject spoke from behind a table facing the instructor and four other students. The five listeners were seated in informally arranged desk chairs facing the speaker.

Each student knew the order of speaking and his place in it. As his name was called, he moved toward the table from behind which he would talk. *En route*, the instructor announced orally two questions from which the speaker chose one as the topic for his speech. When he reached the table and confronted the audience, he was to begin speaking immediately. Most subjects allowed a silence of two or three seconds to elapse before actually starting to talk. Speaking time ranged from a low of 2 minutes to a high of 2 1/2 minutes with a median speaking time of about 2 minutes 10 seconds.

Apparatus

Electrical activity from the heart was picked up by small contact electrodes held in place on the surface of the chest by adhesive washers. Leads from these electrodes were plugged into a miniature FM transmitter, also affixed to the subject's body by adhesive. Being small (32 X 25 X 16 mm) and light in weight (18 grams), the transmitter was invisible under clothing and stayed in place without discomfort to the subject.

Information from the transmitter was telemetered to an FM receiver located less than 20' distant in an adjacent room. Received heart signals were passed to a Physiograph "Six" via shielded cable. The physiograph unit housed a timing pulse generator, an amplifier, a heart-rate indicator, and a strip chart recorder, which produced a graphic record of the time intervals between heart beats. Heart rates were read visually from these strip charts, using a specially constructed calibration rule.

Subjects reported that the apparatus was unobtrusive, caused no discomfort, did not impede their movements in any way, and in their concentration upon the impending speech performance was forgotten soon after being attached.

Measurements

Each subject's record was divided into consecutive 5-second intervals using the beginning and the end of the speech as reference points. Twenty-one 5-second intervals for each speaker form the basis of this report: 15 seconds ending 3 minutes before the beginning of the speech (period I), 45 seconds beginning 15 seconds prior to the start of the speech and ending 30 seconds after the beginning of the speech (periods II, III, and IIIA), 30 seconds beginning 15 seconds before the end of the speech and ending 15 seconds after the end of the speech (periods IV and V), and 15 seconds beginning 3 minutes after the end of the speech (period VI). The reader may find this selection easier to visualize by referring to Figure 1.

For each 5-second interval the mean heart rate was calculated by averaging the fastest single beat and the slowest single beat. The graphs of average mean heart rate are based on these geometric means.

To test for anticipatory activation, confrontation reaction, adaptation and release, comparisons were made between 15 second averages based on intervals as described below. Each 15-second average was obtained by taking the arithmetic average of the mean heart rates for three successive 5-second intervals.

Results

A glance at Figure 2 shows that the pattern of heart rate change in both the graded and the ungraded was remarkably similar. Before proceeding to differences between the two groups, let us first examine the common pattern. In spite of the different speaking conditions, do the subjects of this experiment show the same heart rate patterns as the subjects of our earlier study?

If we observe the 15 seconds ending 3 minutes before the start of the speech (period I), we find some evidence of early anticipatory activation. For

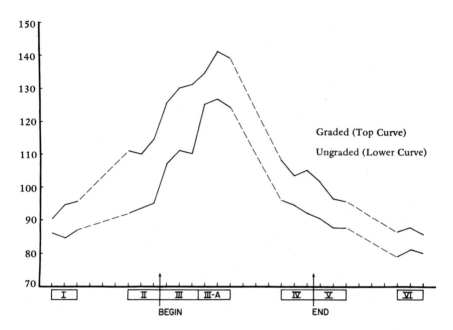

FIGURE 2
Average Mean Heart Rates
During Critical Intervals, for Two Groups of Impromptu Speakers

the ungraded speech group the mean heart rate during this interval was 86.2 beats per minute, for the graded group it was 93.5 bpm. Both of these heart rates are well above resting normal for young adults (about 65–75 bpm). Thus, although we have no individual baseline data against which to compare these pre-speech heart rates, it seems reasonably safe to conclude that three minutes before the beginning of the speech these subjects were, on the average, experiencing some anticipatory activation.

As the moment of speaking approached, this effect became markedly accentuated. In the 15 seconds just prior to the start of the speech (period II), heart rates rose to an average of 93.5 in the ungraded group and 111.8 in the graded group. These increases in activation just prior to the start of the speech evidence significant anticipatory activation.

For all subjects, activation reached its peak shortly after facing the audience and beginning to speak. For the first 15 seconds of the speech (period III), heart rate in the ungraded group rose to an average of 109.2, and for the graded group to 129.2 bpm. Peak heart rate rose to a momentary high in both groups some 25 seconds into the speech (during period III-A), with the ungraded group rising to a mean of 126.5 beats per minute and the graded group to a remarkable high of 140.5 bpm. These further increments in heart rate, occurring on top of a notable anticipatory activation in both groups, constitute evidence of a strong confrontation reaction in both the graded and the ungraded groups.

If we next compare mean heart rates during the first 15 seconds of the speech (period III) with comparable figures for the last 15 seconds (period IV), we find clear indications of adaptation. The ungraded group dropped to 94.6 bpm at the end of the speech, and the graded group dropped to 105.3 bpm. Thus, during the 2 minutes of the impromptu speech, heart rates adapted substantially in both groups.

Post-speech relaxation is revealed first in the immediate release phenomenon that can be seen when we compare heart rates during the last 15 seconds of the speech (period IV) with those during the next 15 seconds, immediately after the end of the speech (period V). Ungraded subjects dropped to an average of 88.4 bpm, and graded subjects dropped to 97.5 bpm.

Once begun, this relaxation trend continued for some time. Three minutes after the end of the speech (period VI), the average heart rate for the ungraded group had dropped to 81.8, for the graded group it had dropped to 86.4 bpm, providing evidence for further release of tension well after the end of the speech performance. Since these figures remain well above resting normal, some measure of residual tension probably persisted for at least several minutes longer.

Certainly the data in Figure 2 seem to provide ample evidence for the occurrence of anticipatory activation, confrontation reaction, adaptation, and release for both of these groups of subjects in response to impromptu speaking; but are the differences in heart rate from period to period significant? Employing a Type I Mixed Analysis of Variance design, the differences among periods I, II, III, IV, V, and VI produced an F value of 65.752 which, with 5 and 110 degrees of freedom, is significant well beyond the .001 probability level. Moreover, when each of the successive changes was tested for significance, all five produced t values significant at or beyond the .01 level.[3]

Granted that the differences on the whole were significant, to what extent did individual subjects experience the pattern of anticipatory activation, confrontation reaction, adaptation, and release? A subject was held to experience anticipatory activation if his heart rate was higher in Period II than in Period I, to experience confrontation reaction if his heart rate was higher in Period III than in Period II, to experience adaptation if his heart rate was lower in Period IV than in Period III-A, and to experience release if his heart rate was lower in Period V than in Period IV.

Using these definitions, twenty of the subjects experienced anticipatory activation. (Of the four who did not show anticipatory activation, two

TABLE 1
Analysis of Variance

Source	df	SS	MS	F
Between Subj.	23	26106		
B	1	4830	4830	4.995
error (b)	22	21271	966.9	
Within Subj.	120	29992	3708.4	
A	5	18542	1049	65.752
AB	5	5245	56.4	1.860
error (w)	110	6205		

showed no change and two showed a small drop in heart rate just prior to the speech.) Twenty-two subjects showed confrontation reaction. (Of the two who did not, one showed no change and the other showed a slight drop in heart rate during the first fifteen seconds after beginning to speak.) Twenty-one subjects underwent adaptation. (Of the three who did not, one showed no change and two showed a slight increase in heart rate at the end of the speech.) Twenty-two subjects showed evidence of release. (Both of the remaining two showed evidence of slight heart rate increment immediately after the end of the speech.) In short, the overwhelming majority of individual subjects showed evidence of each of the four critical changes in heart rate. Using the sign test, all period-to-period comparisons for individual subjects were significant at the .001 probability level.[4]

Of the eleven individual discrepancies from the predicted pattern, only two occurred in the graded speech group. All of the remaining discrepancies occurred in the ungraded group. The commonest discrepancy pattern, which occurred in three ungraded subjects, was failure to show either anticipatory activation or adaptation. These subjects did, however, show confrontation reaction and release. Their heart-rate pattern, therefore, resembled a plateau which rose immediately as they began to speak, remained high through the speech, and dropped immediately as their performance ended.

Thus far, we have not taken special note of differences between the graded and the ungraded speakers, yet the graphs in Figure 2 suggest that heart rates for the group who expected to be graded on their performance were higher on the average than heart rates for subjects who expected not to be graded. In fact, the analysis of variance yielded an F-value of 4.995 for the difference between the two groups. With 1 and 22 degrees of freedom this difference is significant at the .05 probability level. The graded speakers were significantly more aroused.

Granted that the graded and the ungraded groups differ in their average levels of activation, the two charts tend to run parallel to one another; throughout the speaking experience, as one group increases the other tends to increase, where one declines the other tends to do likewise. Any substantial departure from such parallelism would be reflected in the interaction term of the analysis of variance. As Table 1 shows, the interaction F of 1.860 (df = 5, 110) falls short of significance, confirming that the patterns of heart rate increase and decrease at the critical points during the speech performance do not differ significantly between graded and ungraded speakers.

Conclusions

The data in this experiment show that anticipatory activation, confrontation reaction, adaptation, and release are not confined to the prepared classroom speech; in the experiment reported here we have seen that this activation pattern characterizes the informal impromptu speech as well. On the average, the pattern is the same whether the student expects to be graded or not, although for students not subject to evaluation pressure, the average level of activation is significantly lower and individual deviations from one or more of the characteristic critical changes are more frequent.

When we compare the heart rates of these impromptu speakers with those of prepared speakers in the earlier study, we see some interesting differences of detail.

To facilitate the comparison, Figure 3 shows the results of the first experiment (Figure 1) superimposed on the results of the second (Figure 2). It can be seen that anticipatory activation and confrontation reaction for the subjects of the first experiment, making a graded, prepared speech to twenty-five or so peers, would fall just about midway between the graded and the ungraded groups of this experiment, if Periods II through III-A were shifted 15 or 20 seconds to the right. Until shortly before the speech, activation for the subjects in Experiment 1 ran roughly halfway between the two groups of Experiment 2; however, beginning about 15 seconds before the speech, the subjects of Experiment 1 experienced more rapid increases in heart rate than either group in Experiment 2, achieving peak activation during the first 5 or 10 seconds of the speech, after which a slow adaptation process began. Subjects in Experiment 2, however, continued to increase heart rates for an additional 20 seconds, with the graded group eventually achieving a very high peak activation 20 seconds later.

Examining the results for Periods IV and V, it appears that by the end of the speech, activation for the Experiment 1 subjects is about equal to that of the graded group in Experiment 2, and well above that for the ungraded group. When we remember that subjects in Experiment 2 spoke to a very small audience in a highly informal setting, it seems reasonable to conclude

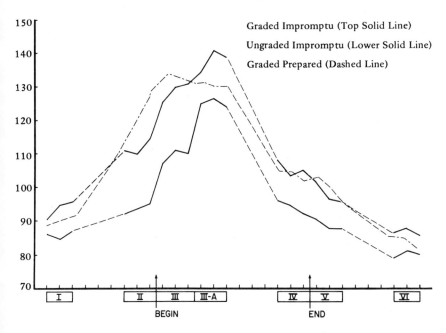

FIGURE 3
Average Mean Heart Rates
During Critical Intervals, for Three Groups of Speakers

that impromptu speaking was inherently more stressful for these students than making a prepared speech.

Although it is always risky to combine results from different experiments, it is tempting to speculate that: (1) immediately prior to the speech, the impromptu speaking task elicits higher levels of anticipatory activation than the prepared speech but (2) confrontation reaction is more pronounced for the impromptu speech; (3) impromptu speaking is, all things considered, more stressful to the student than making a prepared speech, but (4) the stressfulness of the impromptu task may be offset to some degree by staging the speech in an informal, very-small-audience setting; (5) a graded speech performance is, all things considered, more stressful than an ungraded one, and moreover, (6) the effects of grade pressure coupled with an impromptu assignment are sufficient to more than offset whatever reduction in arousal is gained by staging the speech in an informal setting before a very small audience of known peers.

If these speculations are confirmed by further research, they have important implications not only for teachers of public speaking, but for all who are concerned with the study or control of performance anxiety.

1. Donald C. Bryant and Karl R. Wallace, *Fundamentals of Public Speaking* (New York: Appleton-Century-Crofts, 1969), pp. 240–245.

2. Theodore Clevenger, Jr., Michael T. Motley, and Lawrence Carlile, "Changes of Heart Rate During Classroom Public Speaking," *Psychophysiology*, (in press).

3. E. F. Lindquist, *Design and Analysis of Experiments in Psychology and Education* (Boston: Houghton Mifflin, 1953), pp. 90–96.

4. Sidney Siegel, *Nonparametric Statistics for the Behavioral Sciences* (New York: McGraw-Hill, 1956), pp. 68–75.

PART III
Studies in American Political Communication

John Foster Dulles: A New Rhetoric
Justifies an Old Policy

WAYNE BROCKRIEDE

In the spring of 1952 John Foster Dulles, the man who had been slated to become Thomas Dewey's secretary of state in 1944 and 1948, selected a presidential candidate to support and formulated two foreign policy proposals. In May, after talking with General Dwight D. Eisenhower in Paris, he decided to support Ike's candidacy, although he would not announce that support until the weekend before the convention. The two proposals, also in May, appeared in *Life* magazine under the title "A Policy of Boldness"[1] and argued that American foreign policy should move from containment to liberation and from counterforce to instant retaliation.

Since 1947 the primary goal of the Truman administration had been to contain communism by the application of counterforce wherever necessary. The containment policy had been applied on three notable occasions: military aid to Greece and Turkey to prevent the development of communist governments in those countries; a massive airlift of supplies into West Berlin when the corridor to that city had been closed by the communists; and, at greater cost of lives and money, United States leadership of a United Nations police action to prevent a communist takeover in South Korea. But even before the shooting that made the conflict in Korea a hot war, the struggle in Europe had taken on the nomenclature of war. Undergirding the containment policy was an anticommunist ideology that identified communism as the enemy. As troubles throughout the world continued in the late forties and early fifties, a heightened fear of a worldwide monolithic communist conspiracy was accompanied by a rhetorical escalation but by no change in policy.

In the *Life* article, in the foreign policy plank of the Republican party platform, and in speeches Dulles and Eisenhower made during the campaign, the Republicans challenged directly the appropriateness of the goal of containment and contended that the goal should be to liberate the "captive nations" of Eastern Europe and Asia.

Less than two years later, this time as secretary of state, John Foster Dulles, in a speech on January 12, 1954, before the council on foreign relations in New York City, restated his second proposal by announcing that the administration had decided to place less reliance on local defense to meet communist aggression and to depend more on a capacity to "retaliate instantly by means and at places of our choosing,"[2] that is, to depend more on strategic nuclear weapons.

Both statements were presented as major new policy changes. One ostensibly changed the dominant goal from containment to liberation. The other ostensibly changed the dominant strategy from cautious counterforce to massive retaliation. An examination of the discourses that argued for and against these proposals will suggest that liberation and massive retaliation functioned not as new policies but as rhetorical justification for old policies.[3]

I

The article in *Life* and conversations with the two leading candidates, General Eisenhower and Senator Robert Taft, earned John Foster Dulles the assignment of writing the foreign policy plank of the Republican platform. Dulles featured the concept of liberation in the following statement which was accepted by the Republican convention:

> We shall again make liberty into a beacon light of hope that will penetrate the dark places. That program will give the Voice of America a real function. It will mark the end of the negative, futile and immoral policy of "containment" which abandons countless human beings to a despotism and Godless terrorism which in turn enables the rules [sic] to forge the captives into a weapon for our destruction. . . .
>
> The policies we espouse will revive the contagious liberating influences which are inherent in freedom. They will inevitably set up strains and stresses within the captive world which will make the rulers impotent to continue in their monstrous ways and mark the beginning of their end.
>
> Our nation will become again the dynamic, moral and spiritual force which was the despair of despots and the hope of the oppressed.[4]

Dulles had caught hold of the imbalance in the administration's policy of containment and its anticommunist ideological justification. The cautious, defensive language of the former was badly outstripped by the demands of the latter. If the symbols of World War II were remembered and sounded in the making of the Truman doctrine in 1947, then the heady rhetoric of "carrying the war to the enemy" would have to find its 1952 counterpart.

But planks in political party platforms are not widely read. If liberation versus containment were to become a major issue of the campaign, as Dulles was to predict that it would,[5] the candidate had to project it. He did, in a speech on August 25, 1952, in New York City, to an appropriate audience, the American Legion Eisenhower stated:

> Now let America, saddened by the tragedy of lost opportunity, etch in its memory the roll of countries once independent now suffocating under this Russian pall. [He specifies Latvia, Estonia, Poland, East Germany, East Austria, Czechoslovakia, Albania, Bulgaria, and Rumania.] . . .
>
> All these people are blood kin to us. How many people today live in a great fear that never again shall they hear from a mother, a grandfather, a brother or a cousin? Dare we rest while these millions of our kinsmen remain in slavery? I can almost hear your answer.
>
> The American conscience can never know peace until these people are restored again to being masters of their own fate. . . . [He then calls the roll in Asia and specifies China, Tibet, Inner Mongolia, northern Korea, northern Japan, and the northern half of Indochina as captive nations which were once friendly to the United States.]
>
> Again I can hear you say the conscience of America shall never be free until these people have opportunity to choose their own paths. . . . [He then talks of the United States' peril, of Soviet strength, and of the need for the United States to become militarily and economically strong.]
>
> We can never rest—and we must so inform all the world, including the Kremlin—that until the enslaved nations of the world have in the fullness of freedom the right to choose their own path, that then, and then only, can we say that there is a possible way of living peacefully and permanently with communism in this world.
>
> We must tell the Kremlin that never shall we desist in our aid to every man and woman of those shackled lands who seeks refuge with us, any man who keeps burning among his own people the flame of freedom or who is dedicated to the liberation of his fellows. . . .[6]

The rather heavy-handed identification of kin and traditions reminds one that this rhetoric functioned in a political campaign, designed in part to gather votes. What vote-getting values lay in a message like this one? First, the lingering police action in Korea had produced a deep feeling of frustration. David S. McLellan argues that "the war in Korea had become a catalyst for many things that Americans found painful and intolerable about the Cold War." He concluded that Americans "were not accustomed to a style of combat that seemed devoid of honor, moral significance, or the satisfying goal of victory."[7] The new doctrine of liberation was "in tune with the popular mood of impatience with the cold war in Europe and the hot war in Korea"[8] and provided "a romantic outlet for impatience and frustration."[9]

Second, the doctrine of liberation appealed directly for the votes of foreign-born persons in large American cities and hence constituted a kind of "liberation of ethnic Americans from Democratic containment."[10] Certainly the Republican leaders were not unaware that traditionally Americans of East European descent composed much of the broad support the Democratic party could depend on in the industrial northeastern states. A policy of containment was scarcely commensurate with the sentiment fired by the talk of struggling against communist domination. If these voters felt fear and horror of a new totalitarianism replacing the fascism that had engulfed their homelands, then the thought of liberation was apt to be appealing to them.[11] General Eisenhower's message to the American Legion addressed these voters directly.

Third, whereas containment connoted a policy aimed at dealing in a political way with an opposing state, liberation connoted a pronouncement aimed at dealing in a rhetorical way with an opposing ideology. Dulles's authorship of the foreign policy plank in the Republican platform pits the "dynamic, moral and spiritual force" of freedom against the "despotism and Godless terrorism" of communism. The anticommunist ideology President Harry S. Truman had unleashed to develop support for the proposal to send military aid to Greece and Turkey in 1947 had burgeoned into a religious crusade for freedom. Edmund Stillman and William Pfaff stress the religious motif in their analysis of the change in mood: "Our early postwar policy had been primarily *political*—limited and pragmatic; our evangelism influenced but did not lead our actions. After Korea our outraged moral sense ruled, and we were no longer content to contain this evil; it had to be extirpated. Calvinists that as a nation we are, we saw depravity manifest in the world, and we, the elect, had to combat it."[12] Those voters who saw anticommunism within religious contexts would predictably support enthusiastically the idea that American policy must aim at liberating captive peoples, and would approve of a party and a candidate who represented a bold and dynamic force against a Godless ideology.

The Democrats tried to counter the appeal. Speeches against liberation were made by candidate Adlai Stevenson and by Secretary of State Dean Acheson. The leading opponent, though, was President Harry S. Truman, whose first antiliberation speech, presented on September 2 in Parkersburg, West Virginia, initiated the three leading arguments Democrats were to advance during the campaign:

> Maybe the Republicans don't realize this, but the people who are on the spot in Europe know very well that talk of liberation under present circumstances is war talk. That is why these Republican statements have caused so much concern among our friends in Europe. After all, our Allies there have signed up with us for combined defense of freedom. They have not signed up to join in a crusade for war.
> Now I am perfectly convinced—and I hope our Allies will under-

stand—that the Republicans do not intend by what they say to pledge this country to a frightful atomic war in order to roll back the Iron Curtain by force.

Yet, if they don't want war, why do they tell us they have some new and positive proposal to help the people behind the Iron Curtain? If they don't mean war, what is it they do mean? Do they mean insurrection by the satellite peoples?

Nothing could be worse than to raise false hopes of this in Eastern Europe. Nothing could be worse than to incite uprisings that can only end by giving a new crop of victims to the Soviet executioners. All Europeans know quite well that insurrection in the Soviet borderland these days could only be successful with armed support from the outside world.

If the Republicans don't mean to give that armed support—and I feel sure they don't—then they are trying to deceive their fellow-citizens at home and playing cruel, gutter politics with the lives of countless good men and women behind the Iron Curtain.

If the Republicans don't mean war or insurrection, what do they mean? Well, I'll tell you. They are trying to get votes and they don't care how they get them.[13]

No one put Truman's concluding argument that liberation was a political ploy quite so bluntly or so repeatedly during the campaign as did the President. Adlai Stevenson, on November 1 in Chicago, though, called the liberation proposal "irresponsible politics" to raise the hopes "of those of us with families and close friends behind the edges of the Iron Curtain."[14] No one, of course, could prove that the primary motive of Eisenhower and Dulles's call for liberation was to secure votes. And one may wonder if Americans would find novel or take seriously a charge that an opponent was playing politics.

A second argument, that liberation frightened European allies, was demonstrated by reports of concern coming from European capitals. Harold Callender reported from Paris that liberation "amazed and alarmed" Europeans.[15] The *Manchester Guardian* said that the Eisenhower who spoke to the American Legion was not the "prudent general" the British used to know but "St. Ike the crusader against the Communist dragon."[16] Again, Adlai Stevenson reinforced Truman's criticism that a crusade for liberation would frighten West Europe when, in a speech in Brooklyn, October 31, he claimed that the proposal had damaged the general personally and, more important, had damaged Europe's "funded capital of confidence in American stability and judgment which we have so carefully built up in the postwar years."[17] But liberating people for freedom from communism doubtless must have seemed more persuasive to many voters than retaining British or French approbation.

From the point of view of rational evaluation of policy consequences, the third argument was the most fundamental. It took the form of a dilemma: Either liberation would increase the risk of war, or it would prove ineffectual.

The initial criticism of Democrats keyed on the danger of war. Although President Truman seemed incredulous that anyone would risk atomic war, he pointedly emphasized that liberation risked war. Secretary of State Dean Acheson, on September 11, in a speech to the International Association of Machinists, also warned against liberation on this basis: "If through impatience or imprudence, we are urged to try to bring . . . [liberation] about by force . . . this advice would be neither realistic nor responsible. If this is what is meant by being more 'positive,' then it is in fact a positive prescription for disaster."[18] General Eisenhower in his American Legion speech, as D. F. Fleming observed, went "about as far as words could go in encouraging rebellion in Eastern Europe" even though he stopped just "short of an outright pledge to send armed aid."[19]

Through September and early October both Eisenhower and Dulles insisted that liberation could and should come peacefully. Dulles, in a statement designed to reply directly to Truman's criticism, contended that it was "absurd to suggest that General Eisenhower anticipates invoking wholesale insurrections by unarmed slaves. . . . There are countless peaceful ways by which the task of the Russian despots can be made so unbearably difficult that they will renounce their rule."[20] Dulles did not specify here any peaceful methods, although he mentioned several in other speeches—for example, repudiation of the Yalta Agreement that permitted Russian domination of Eastern Europe, propaganda programs, and the encouragement of work slowdowns and sabotage. Neither in this statement nor in any others did Dulles or Eisenhower go beyond *asserting* that liberation could be consummated *peacefully* in any of these ways.

Although the Democrats did not press far the implausibility of peaceful liberation, journalists then and historians later recognized it. Hans J. Morgenthau reported that the *London Economist* saw as early as August 30, less than a week after the American Legion address, that liberation "applied to Eastern Europe—and Asia—means either the risk of war or it means nothing."[21] Elmer Davis once described liberation as a policy of "you throw off your chains, and we'll give three cheers."[22] Neither the Republicans, nor presumably many American voters, understood the depth of the Soviet anxiety for security, which committed them to maintaining their influence in Eastern Europe. From the vantage point of 1975 that reveals not only the Soviet use of heavy armor in Hungary in 1956 but also the pouring of troops across the border of Czechoslovakia in 1968, the prospect of liberation as a dramatic and peaceful fulfillment of American policy seems ludicrous. But even before Hungary many commentators were highly skeptical.

The issue of liberation versus containment gradually diminished in importance as the question of what to do in Korea dominated discussions of foreign policy. On October 24 Eisenhower culminated the shift in emphasis by declaring, "I shall go to Korea." Although he never explained what he would do other than to go there, and although both Truman and Stevenson asked repeatedly for an explanation, the simple, undeveloped statement gave the Eisenhower campaign a mighty impetus. The extent to which liberation had declined in importance is suggested when Eisenhower, in a speech on November 1, made what he called a "brief summary of the pledges that I have made during this campaign." Liberation was not among them.[23]

The last enunciation of the liberation doctrine came during the early weeks of the new Eisenhower administration. In his State of the Union message on February 2, 1953, President Eisenhower called for a repudiation of the Yalta Agreement.[24] The new secretary of state, John Foster Dulles, had earlier called once more for liberating the captive nations. In a Senate Foreign Relations Committee hearing on January 15 he had asserted that "these people who are enslaved are people who deserve to be free," and he had reiterated his belief that liberation could be brought about peacefully.[25]

What were the consequences of the calls for liberation? The aggressive anticommunist proposals and justifications probably helped the new administration get and hold popular approval and congressional support. Although no one claims that liberation was a decisive factor in the 1952 campaign, Dulles's projection of a "bold new policy" may have created for the American public "the image of himself as a staunch and dynamic fighter against communism"[26] and of the doctrine of liberation as "a new, forceful, aggressive foreign policy."[27] Dulles's biographer, John R. Beal, contends that Dulles made a deliberate effort to gain and maintain popular support, that he held the theory that "foreign policy, no matter how wise and sound, could not succeed in a democratic republic unless the mass of people understood it and supported it."[28] Furthermore, Dulles from the very beginning of his tenure as secretary of state enjoyed excellent relations with Congress,[29] and the liberation proposal was surely popular with many congressmen.

For many Americans and their representatives the doctrine of liberation was altogether compatible with an anticommunist ideology which in the 1950s had emerged as the leading criterion by which to determine and judge foreign policy. The strong talk about liberation was so appealing because it helped fulfill an appetite created by cold-war rhetoric. Stalemate seemed the most hopeful outcome of containment, and stalemate was not what the ideology of total victory over communism promised. Americans needed a symbol that would renew their faith in the ability of this country to make its ideals ascendant.

But the rhetoric of liberation did not alter policy. Although Eisenhower and Dulles talked liberation, they pursued containment.[30] They made a passing gesture in the direction of repudiating the Yalta Agreement,[31] and Dulles "would, at least in a perfunctory way, ask the bureaucracy under him

to see what could be done to liberate the satellites by psychological devices."[32] But nothing happened. The futility was demonstrated dramatically
by the absence of American action during the Hungarian revolt. Norman A.
Graebner sums up well that demonstration: "In admitting at the moment of
greatest urgency that Hungary's independence was not required by the
security interests of the United States, American officials rendered the
concept of liberation a mockery."[33]

After the Hungarian revolt was quelled, the usefulness of calls for liberation was over. The gross disparity between rhetorical pronouncements and
actual policy had been exposed. Louis L. Gerson describes the final resting-
place of the campaign for liberation:

> The denouement to liberation came after the death of Dulles when
> Congress on July 17, 1959, passed the so-called Captive Nations Resolu-
> tion, asking the President to designate the third week in July as Captive
> Nations Week and "to issue a similar proclamation each year until such
> time as freedom and independence shall have been achieved for all the
> captive nations of the world." This resolution . . . was added to the long
> list of other national proclamations designating days, weeks, or months
> to honor veterans, mothers, crippled children, athletes. and just about
> anything.[34]

The doctrine of liberation, which had never become a policy, had also lost its
appeal as a rhetorical justification for containment.

II

On January 12, 1954, John Foster Dulles presented what high government
sources termed "the most important speech that Mr. Dulles has ever made or
is ever likely to make."[35] In the speech the secretary of state enunciated
what he said was a "new policy decision" by the National Security Council
and what was to become known popularly as the policy of "massive retaliation."

But the proposal was not born in 1954. On May 5, 1952, in a speech to
the French National Political Science Institute in Paris, John Foster Dulles
had argued the need for fighting the enemy at "times and places of our own
choosing."[36] Dulles developed the argument also in the same month in his
article in *Life* magazine. He stated:

> Obviously, we cannot build a 20,000-mile Maginot Line or match
> the Red armies, man for man, gun for gun and tank for tank at any
> particular time or place their general staff selects. To attempt that
> would mean real strength nowhere and bankruptcy everywhere.
> *There is one solution and only one: that is for the free world to
> develop the will and organize the means to retaliate instantly against*

open aggression by Red armies, so that, if it occurred anywhere, we could and would strike back where it hurts, by means of our choosing.[37]

The initial draft of a national defense plank in the Republican platform had included the doctrine of retaliation. C. L. Sulzberger reported that "General Eisenhower objected violently to this. He instructed John Foster Dulles . . . to have mention of retaliation stricken from the projected platform."[38] But the idea appeared in at least two Republican campaign speeches. In his August 25 speech to the American Legion, General Eisenhower "spoke of haunting the Kremlin with nightmares of punishment that could be visited by the 'retaliatory readiness' of powerful American forces."[39] On October 4 Dulles, at Rochester, New York, placed retaliation in the service of deterrence with these words: "Are we planning to create a military establishment able, at any moment, to fight successfully by air, by sea and by land; in Asia, Africa and Europe; in the Arctic and in the tropics? If so, we are bound to be economically ruined. . . . Our primary objective is, not to fight wars, but to prevent wars. The best way to prevent armed aggression is to possess the power to strike at the heart of aggression."[40]

But these early statements that the United States must develop a capacity for instant and massive retaliation, made primarily by a presidential candidate's foreign policy advisor, did not generate as much excitement or controversy as did the later pronouncements of a policy decision by a secretary of state. On January 12, 1954, after a brief introduction in which Dulles recognized the merit of many emergency decisions the Democrats had made, he continued:

Emergency measures—however good for the emergency—do not necessarily make good permanent policies. Emergency policies are clostly [sic]; they are superficial and they imply that the enemy has the initiative. They cannot be depended upon to serve our long-time interests. . . . [Dulles discusses the importance of long-range policy and relates it to national security.]

We need allies and we need collective security. And our purpose is to have them, but to have them on a basis which is more effective and on a basis which is less costly. How do we do this? The way to do this is to place more reliance upon community deterrent power, and less dependence upon local defensive power.

This is accepted practice so far as our local communities are concerned. We keep locks on the doors of our homes; but we do not have armed guards in every home. We rely principally on a community security system so well equipped to catch and punish any who break in and steal that, in fact, would-be aggressors are generally deterred. That is the modern way of getting maximum protection at bearable cost.

What the Eisenhower Administration seeks is a similar international security system. We want for ourselves and for others a maximum deterrent at bearable cost.

Local defense will always be important. But there is no local defense which alone will contain the mighty land power of the Communist world. Local defense must be reinforced by the further deterrent of massive retaliatory power.

A potential aggressor must know that he cannot always prescribe the battle conditions that suit him. Otherwise, for example, a potential aggressor who is glutted with manpower might be tempted to attack in confidence that resistance would be confined to manpower. He might be tempted to attack in places where his superiority was decisive.

The way to deter aggression is for the free community to be willing and able to respond vigorously at places and with means of its own choosing.

Now, so long as our basic concepts in these respects were unclear, our military leaders could not be selective in building our military power. If the enemy could pick his time and his place and his method of warfare—and if our policy was to remain the traditional one of meeting aggression by direct and local opposition—then we had to be ready to fight in the Arctic and in the tropics, in Asia, in the Near East and in Europe; by sea, by land and by air; by old weapons and by new weapons.

The total cost of our security efforts, at home and abroad, was over $50,000,000,000 per annum, and involved, for 1953, a projected budgetary deficit of $9,000,000,000; and for 1954 a projected deficit of $11,000,000,000.

This was on top of taxes comparable to wartime taxes and the dollar was depreciating in its effective value. And our allies were similarly weighed down. This could not be continued for long without grave budgetary, economic and social consequences.

But before military planning could be changed the President and his advisers, represented by the National Security Council, had to take some basic policy decisions. This has been done.

And the basic decision was as I indicated to depend primarily upon a great capacity to retaliate instantly by means and at places of our choosing. And now the Department of Defense and the Joint Chiefs of Staff can shape our military establishment to fit what is our policy instead of having to try to be ready to meet the enemy's many choices. And that permits of a selection of military means instead of a multiplication of means. And as a result it is now possible to get, and to share, more security at less cost.

Now let us see how this concept has been practically applied to foreign policy. . . . [Dulles applies the concept to Korea, to Indochina, to Okinawa, to NATO—with special attention to West Germany, and to foreign assistance programs. He concludes by voicing the belief that the appeal and resources of freedom are irresistible and will ultimately triumph.] [41]

What are the appeals of this speech? First, it continues the Dulles campaign to project himself and his conduct of foreign affairs as positive and aggressive, an image that interacted favorably with the anticommunist ideology of this country. Such an image was reinforced by Vice President Richard M. Nixon, who, in answer to Dulles's critics, exclaimed, "Isn't it wonderful that finally we have a Secretary of State who isn't taken in by the communists, who stands up to them."[42]

Second, the aggressiveness had a more immediate goal. The Indochinese insurgents, with the support of the Chinese communists, were at the point of ousting the French. Louis Gerson asserts that the Chinese would not "miss his meaning" in the speech of January 12, that they would know that Dulles had threatened them "with massive retaliation."[43]

Third, a greater reliance on strategic weapons and less stress on conventional weapons would, as Dulles contended, be less expensive. The government could hardly justify reducing the effort to develop nuclear weapons—even for such a prize as balancing the budget. But the policy of massive retaliation could permit less cost for conventional preparedness. As Hans J. Morgenthau indicated, this speech of 3,500 words contained no fewer than fifteen references to the advantage of economy.[44] That the administration probably considered the cost criterion is suggested by President Eisenhower's announcement nine days after Dulles's speech that military spending had been cut by $4 billion.[45]

The argument for economy was consistent with what the public had come to associate with Republican administrations. If a policy of liberation was congruent with the ideology of anticommunism, then the greater effort it implied placed a concomitant burden on the administration—meeting the tension entailed by the governmental spending. Although calls for extraordinary sacrifice are common, Dulles and Eisenhower suggested another solution in 1954. Since the Cold War had become so much a matter of threats, making the biggest threat possible seemed quite natural.

The day after Dulles spoke President Eisenhower told newsmen that he did not need to "elucidate" what Dulles had said.[46] After that, the speech appears to have been on its way toward being forgotten. That no immediate criticism of the speech or policy was heard may be attributed in part to American familiarity with the language of the Cold War. The speech in which the policy is articulated is filled with references to aggression, both direct and implied. Nothing had become more commonplace in the context of deterring aggression than the threat of retaliation. Americans had long since become used to calling such bellicose language the stuff of peaceful intentions, as Dulles had done in the last paragraph of his speech.

Louis Gerson comments on the favorable timing of the Dulles speech when it was presented and explains also why severe criticism ultimately developed. After the speech, Gerson points out, "a series of sensational events dramatized the phrase 'massive retaliation.' " These events included "some hair-raising revelations of thermonuclear explosions carried out by the United States at Eniwetok in November, 1952. . . . The world had scarcely assimilated this fact when the United States on March 1, 1954, detonated a huge hydrogen bomb, the destructiveness of which far exceeded the expectations of scientists who had developed it. . . . When all this information became public there was a great to-do, a flood of polemics."[47]

The two leading polemicists included one domestic critic, Adlai Stevenson, and one representative of the Allies, Lester Pearson, Canada's secretary of state for external affairs and later, in 1957, winner of a Nobel peace prize. Stevenson criticized the policy because it had not been formulated through bipartisan machinery. Indeed, although Dulles attributed the decision to the National Security Council, the speech which pronounced it, according to Louis J. Halle, had been written entirely by Dulles, and "apparently with only one exception even the members of his immediate professional staff in the State Department did not know about it until it was delivered and published."[48] Stevenson and others criticized the policy as constituting false economy. Chester Bowles, former ambassador to India, complained that the administration had started "with a *budget* decision and attempted to fit our foreign policy to it." Bowles contended that "broad, patient, positive policies . . . are not to be found in a budgetary bargain basement."[49]

But the two most searching critiques were developed by Stevenson and Pearson. Adlai Stevenson criticized massive retaliation primarily because American choice of action had been limited by the policy. On March 6, 1954, in a speech to the Southeastern Democratic Conference in Miami Beach, Florida, Stevenson contended that

> there has been . . . little public curiosity about such a genuine concern as the "new look" in national defense and foreign policy. I had hoped that there might be a resumption in this Administration of the bipartisanship of President Truman's administration when Secretary Dulles and many other prominent Republicans, including the President himself, served in important roles.
>
> At all events, without the benefit of bipartisanship, the Administration has recently unveiled this "new look." It has been presented to us as a program of more for our money, a "bigger bang for a buck," national security in the large economy size. . . .
>
> All this means, if it means anything, is that if the Communists try another Korea we will retaliate by dropping atom bombs on Moscow or Peiping or wherever we choose—or else we will concede the loss of another Korea—and presumably other countries after that—as "normal" in the course of events.
>
> Is this a "new look" or is it a return to the pre-1949 atomic deterrent strategy which made some sense so long as we had a monopoly of atomic weapons together with a strategic Air Force? Yet even then it didn't deter attack, and brought us to the brink of disaster in

Korea, where atom bombs were useless and we were only saved by heroic exertion to re-create conventional ground forces.

But, you say, we did not use the bomb against Russian and Chinese targets for fear of enlarging the war. Exactly, and if we should now use them in retaliation that way it would certainly mean World War III and atomic counter-retaliation. For the Russians have massive powers of retaliation with atomic weapons just as we do, and our cities are also susceptible to destruction. . . .

Instead of greater freedom of choice, does this decision to rely primarily on atomic weapons really narrow our choice as to the means and the places of retaliation? Are we leaving ourselves the grim choice of inaction or a thermonuclear holocaust? Are we, indeed, inviting Moscow and Peiping to nibble us to death?

This is the real danger. This is the real problem. Will we turn brush fires and local hostilities into major conflicts? . . .[50]

Stevenson's primary argument, that massive retaliation narrowed United States choice to inaction or thermonuclear holocaust, was also voiced by others. For example, the Thailand embassy asked the United States "whether the new policy meant that if the Communist Chinese invaded Vietnam or Thailand the United States would not offer help with ground forces but instead would bomb Peiping or Moscow."[51] Chester Bowles feared the Allies would reject the new policy: "We may be willing to accept the all-or-nothing risk of a third world war which the policy of atomic retaliation entails. But our war-weary European allies, only a few hundred miles from Soviet bases, would suffer even more grievously than we from atomic counter-attack. Suspicion that our new policy incurs unnecessary risks of a third world war may further dampen their enthusiasm for the essential task of European defense."[52]

The point of view of European Allies was well expressed by Mr. Lester Pearson, who raised a number of questions in a speech to the National Press Club in Washington, D.C. These questions were especially forceful because "it was unusual for a diplomat to criticize another nation's policies in that nation's capital."[53] In that speech Mr. Pearson stated:

The key words in this sentence, as I see it, are "instantly," "means," and "our." . . . From our point of view it is important that the "our" in the sentence I have quoted, means those who have agreed together, particularly in NATO, to work together and by collective action to prevent war or, if that should fail, to win it. Indeed, in an earlier part of his speech, Mr. Dulles himself gave that interpretation, when he said: "The way to deter aggression is for the *free community* to be willing and able to respond vigorously at places and with means of *its* own choosing."

But what effect will that have on the other words "instantly" and "means"?

Collective action means collective consultation, but that must be reconciled with the necessity for swift and effective action. This reconciliation is not easy, *within* a single government. It is even less easy between governments.[54]

The implicit dilemma is hard to answer: Either the retaliation would be instant and Allies (and Congress) could not be consulted, or retaliation would follow consultation (but not instantly).

The administration, and especially Dulles himself, tried to answer these charges. President Eisenhower reaffirmed the administration's commitment to a bipartisan approach to foreign policy—although he did not explain why Democrats had not been consulted in formulating the policy of massive retaliation. Dulles explained that he had not meant to imply that instant retaliation would be automatic but that the United States needed the "capacity for instantaneous retaliation" and that "the key to the success of this policy was to keep a potential enemy guessing about the kind of action the United States might take in any particular case"[55] —although he did not make clear what might keep an enemy from miscalculating the United States response. Dulles assured allies that "there would certainly be consultation" with the Allied nations "in most of the cases that I can conceive of"[56] —although he did not then show how retaliation could be instant. At his press conference on March 16 Dulles released copy of an article, "Policy for Security and Peace," which was to appear in the April, 1954, issue of *Foreign Affairs.*[57] The article modified and moderated the speech of January 12. Hans J. Morgenthau summarized the process of modifying the policy through response to criticism: "Lester Pearson has questioned it; Adlai Stevenson has criticized it; Vice President Nixon has defended it; Sir John Slessor has amplified it; Secretary Wilson has minimized it; Admiral Radford and his colleagues have set out to "explain" it and ended by explaining it away; President Eisenhower has stated that the new doctrine is not a new doctrine at all; Secretary Dulles has reaffirmed its newness in a somewhat more modest form."[58]

The most pronounced immediate result of the proposal of massive retaliation and the debate that followed it was confusion. James Reston claimed that even "the Republicans themselves are bound to agree that, as of this moment, the statements of the President, the Vice President, the Secretary of State and the Secretary of Defense do not give a clear picture of what the policy is."[59] But the historical critic is likely to concur with the judgment of Louis J. Halle that "the United States cannot be said to have ever had a policy of 'massive retaliation,' any more than it ever had a policy of 'liberation' as opposed to the policy of 'containment.' "[60]

Liberation had been proposed during the 1952 campaign and in the early weeks of the Eisenhower administration as the leading goal of United States foreign policy. In 1954 John Foster Dulles announced that the new strategic method of foreign policy was "to retaliate instantly by means and at places of our choosing." A curious incongruity existed between the goal of liberation and the method of instant retaliation, for that method cannot achieve that goal. An interesting implication of the rhetoric of massive retaliation is that, although it is thoroughly consistent with an anticommunist ideology, the only policy goal it could possibly support is the one Dulles had opposed—containment.

Perhaps the rhetoric of massive retaliation provided a rationale for redistributing and reducing military expenditures; for entering into additional alliances and commitments so that "definite lines [could] be drawn to make clear in advance to the enemy that his aggression would trigger a massive response by the United States"[61] —although presumably Dulles also wanted to keep the enemy guessing; and, above all, for assuring the American people and its Congress that their ideology was protected and promoted by a dynamic secretary of state who "isn't taken in by the Communists."

But the rhetorical fervor supporting anticommunism did not become policy. Massive retaliation, like liberation, remained largely at "the level of symbolic treaty or verbalizing; they were revealed as hollow by the French debacle at Dien Bien Phu in 1954, the Hungarian revolution in 1956, and the Iraqi revolution of 1958, in none of which the United States intervened."[62]

III

This analysis of Dulles's rhetoric is based chiefly on two primary proposals—liberation and massive retaliation. The conclusions appear supported also, however, by such other slogans as "unleashing Chiang Kai-shek," "positive loyalty," "agonizing reappraisal," "immoral neutralism," and "the brink of war," each of which represents language bolder than any subsequent action. What can one conclude about the rhetoric of John Foster Dulles?

First, his evangelistic advocacy of the anticommunist ideology gave him general popular and congressional support. Dulles had his performance as secretary of state evaluated not by the wisdom of his policy but by the enthusiasm of the rhetorical justification for the current United States ideology. Dulles saw the Cold War as primarily "a moral struggle" rather than as a power political struggle.[63] He told the Missouri Bar Association on September 26, 1952, "Whether we like it or not—and I like it—our people are predominantly a moral people, who believe that our nation has a great spiritual heritage to be preserved."[64] As David S. McLellan put it, Dulles "epitomized the ideological and moral fervor of the mandate that the electorate had given Eisenhower."[65] By "cultivating his own public image as the strong man of anti-Communism," Dulles could "retain the confidence and respect of the American public."[66]

Two aspects of John Foster Dulles's character and experience contributed to his ability to function well as the guardian of the anticommunist ideology: Dulles as evangelist and as advocate. The son of a minister, he was an active churchman throughout his life. A Presbyterian, he was an elder of his church from 1937 to 1959; the chairperson of a commission for the Federal Council of Churches of Christ in America, from 1940 to 1948, to study the bases of a just and durable peace; and speaker of the first assembly of the World Council of Churches in Amsterdam in 1948.[67] He was endowed with a "sense of predestination"[68] and mission to lead the anticommunist crusade.

Another important dimension was Dulles's experience as a lawyer. The situation in 1952 seemed to call for "an advocate's account of the existential circumstances by which to identify itself with righteousness and its opponent with evil."[69] Dulles was well equipped to play that role. Reputedly the most highly paid corporation lawyer in New York City,[70] Dulles as secretary of state "lived, acted, spoke, reacted, advanced, retreated, threatened, courted, summarized, analyzed, briefed, cross-examined, responded, appealed, objected, thrust, parried—like a lawyer."[71] Secretary Dulles went about "his job with the assurance of a skilled lawyer, able to develop all the elements of each side of the case, to make multiple and varying readings, and to remember the small print when it's necessary. His pronouncements . . . are usually surrounded by a haze of qualifications and provisos, of interpretations, misinterpretations, and reinterpretations."[72] Dulles was the evangelistic advocate for anticommunism more than he was the pragmatic diplomat negotiating the political interests of his country.

Second, in spite of his change-demanding rhetoric, Dulles maintained existing policies. The Dulles-Eisenhower foreign policy had an "innate conservatism."[73] Liberation and massive retaliation were symbolic appeals that did not change the fundamental United States foreign policy since 1947—containment. Paul Seabury distinguishes between the "declaratory policy" of Dulles as preacher and action policy.[74] Mr. Dulles's actions were mainly to continue the task of building an intricate system of alliances designed to confront the Soviet Union with force to counter any effort to expand its sphere aggressively. NATO was formed, before the Dulles era, in 1949; but SEATO came into being in 1954, and CENTO in 1959. These were not efforts to liberate captive nations—not in Europe, nor Asia, nor the Near East. Furthermore, in spite of militant rhetoric, Dulles was careful to preserve peace. When possible aggressive responses might have provoked war, they were not taken. This attribute was noted by Nikita Khrushchev, who told Dag Hammarskjold, secretary general of the United Nations, on the occasion of Dulles's resignation in 1959, "Dulles invented brinkmanship, but he would never step over the brink."[75]

Third, Dulles harmonized the apparent conflict between an aggressive rhetoric and a conservative policy, between what Chalmers M. Roberts termed "the two sides of the same coin"—the elements of "reckless brink-manship and of intransigent standpatism."[76] The need for such a resolution and an image of the Dulles method is pictured by Joseph Harsch:

> Mr. Dulles inherited from Mr. Acheson a public opinion which demanded bold statements of defiance against the Communist world, but which also yearned for an end to the Korean War, and release from the fear of a greater atomic war.
> The Secretary has marvelously served these conflicting desires. He has appeared to be the crusading knight bearing the cross of righteous-ness on his shield, his sword upraised against the foe and his voice calling for the charge. But if your glance descends from this stirring picture, you notice that the charger he bestrides is ambling placidly in the opposite direction.[77]

The primary mode of juggling a cautious policy with a bold statement is linguistic ambiguity. William Lee Miller insightfully contrasts the verbal behavior of the secretary with his chief: "President Eisenhower manages, despite his trouble with language, to make his larger meaning come through; Mr. Dulles manages, despite his greater facility with language, to keep his larger meaning obscure."[78] Mr. Dulles's initial gambit appears to have been to express a policy statement in language which to an immediate audience of determined anticommunists would sound satisfyingly tough but to prag-matists might sound guarded. When the language shifted too far from balance in the direction of ideological enthusiasm and alarmed critics, Mr. Dulles amended some of his statements "to meet the protests of those who thought he had gone too far."[79] In these ways he kept "the Senate war-wing happy by his public pronouncements, while quietly paving the way for a settlement with the Communist world by his actual operations."[80] The day after Dulles had resigned as secretary of state in 1959, James Reston characterized the Dulles strategy as "dualistic." Reston illustrated the claim by recalling that the Dulles-Eisenhower administration had "proclaimed a policy of 'unleashing Chiang Kai-shek' in 1953, but quietly negotiated an arrangement whereby the Nationalist leader agreed not to invade the Chinese mainland without United States support."[81] Through such linguistic strategies Mr. Dulles could pro-mote energetically the anticommunist ideology and his own image as the personification of that ideology, while preserving the cautious policy of containment and peace. Dean Acheson's phrase about Republicans who advocated liberation during the 1952 campaign seems applicable to the rhetoric of Dulles generally: He had his "hands on the horn" and his "feet on the brakes."[82]

Fourth, the rhetoric of Dulles may justly be held responsible for several instrumental effects, each of which has proved disadvantageous to the United States. One immediate consequence was that the ideological enthusiasm made patient negotiation with the communists more difficult. Whatever advantages the crusading spirit of liberation and massive retaliation may have had in relieving the tensions built up from the failure of containment to fulfill anticommunist aspirations, Dulles's rhetoric could scarcely prepare the public to accept small accommodations that might lessen the absolute sway of the Soviet Union over its immediate neighbors. For if, as Hans J. Morgenthau has observed, "the struggle between east and west is not primarily a struggle for power, but a crusade of good against evil, then . . . a negotiated settlement [is precluded]; there can be no accommodation between hostile and incompatible moral principles."[83] Given the premise that the conflict is mainly ideological, the conclusion follows logically "that there should be no negotiations at all with the Soviets and only occasional talks to let the other fellow know where you stand, and vice versa."[84]

Furthermore, when conditions change and the other fellow becomes less intractable, as the Soviet Union under Khrushchev during the late 1950s gave the impression of becoming,[85] the ideological antagonisms escalated by a hostile rhetoric would hamstring attempts to settle or minimize differences. In short, Dulles's rhetoric, perhaps appropriate for certain short-term domestic considerations, had the unfortunate effect of turning diplomacy "from its traditional function of compromise and placed [it] in the service of a worldwide crusade for freedom."[86]

Another undesirable effect of the Dulles rhetoric was to widen the distance between the United States and the USSR. Since the two nations negotiated and communicated so little, since both sides viewed their antagonist as not an opponent but as the enemy, they tended to see the other side as an abstraction and to develop distorted perceptions of the intentions and actions of the other.[87] If a harsh voice was a compensation for a soft hand, one might argue that Dulles did not need to sound the cry. Many voices were contributing to this compensation. On the other hand, the secretary of state might have helped create a counterrhetoric more nearly consistent with the sort of policy he actually pursued.

A third unfortunate result of Dulles's rhetoric is that it helped provoke the United States into making commitments which, although perhaps effective short-term maneuvers, have proved disastrous to long-term American interests. The Dulles-Eisenhower approach to rhetorical justification of anticommunism led to "a kind of reckless proliferation of American commitments far beyond the true national interest and actual national will to sustain."[88] One must question, for example, whether the political interests of the United States were served by the decision to move into the vacuum created by the departure of the French from Vietnam in 1954, a decision that unleashed a momentum that carried it to unspeakable horror. And yet the rhetorically escalated anticommunist ideology of the 1950s dictated that the

United States must fight communists wherever they were involved in conflict situations—even with means and at places of *their* choosing.

Consequently, John Foster Dulles could achieve with words what he dared not do with deeds[89] and, in the process, could satisfy many Americans that their secretary of state could stand up to the communists. But the price he paid was to limit severely, during his tenure and long after, the conduct of pragmatic diplomacy in the national interest. Since Dulles, "fully supported by President Eisenhower's unprecedented prestige, could have pursued whatever foreign policies he chose without fear of a domestic opposition," one can only agree with the judgment of Hans J. Morgenthau that "the price was unnecessarily high by far."[90]

1. *Life*, May 19, 1952, pp. 146–160.

2. *New York Times*, January 13, 1954, p. 2.

3. Although this essay on the rhetoric of John Foster Dulles, hopefully, stands alone and should not require prior reading to discover commitments to my critical method or to establish a larger context of cold-war rhetoric into which to place an examination of Dulles's discourses, such sources are available for interested readers. The present essay is an application of "dimensional criticism," focusing on the dimension of ideology as a way of seeing to what extent the Dulles rhetoric relates to United States foreign policy. This approach to criticism is sketched in my "Dimensions of the Concept of Rhetoric," *Quarterly Journal of Speech*, 54 (February, 1968), 1–12; see especially pp. 11–12. A larger view of cold-war rhetoric, of which Dulles's is a notable instance, is reflected in my book with Robert L. Scott, *Moments in the Rhetoric of the Cold War* (New York: Random House, 1970); see especially chapter 5.

4. *New York Times*, July 11, 1952, p. 8.

5. *Ibid.*, August 28, 1952, p. 12.

6. *Ibid.*, August 26, 1952, p. 12.

7. David S. McLellan, *The Cold War in Transition* (New York: Macmillan, 1966), pp. 31–32.

8. Louis L. Gerson, *John Foster Dulles*. Volume XVII in the series: *The American Secretaries of State and Their Diplomacy*, ed. Robert H. Ferrell (New York: Cooper Square Publishers, 1967), p. 86.

9. James P. Warburg, "Which Way to Liberation?," *The Annals of the American Academy of Political and Social Sciences*, 288 (July, 1953), 87.

10. Gerson, *John Foster Dulles*, p. 88.

11. See Louis J. Halle, *The Cold War as History*, (New York and Evanston: Harper and Row, 1967), p. 271, and McLellan, *Cold War in Transition*, pp. 34–35.

12. Edmund Stillman and William Pfaff, *The New Politics* (New York and Evanston: Harper and Row, 1961), p. 34. See also Max Frankel, "Can We End the Cold War?," *New York Times Magazine*, January 29, 1967, p. 58; Charles O. Lerche, Jr., *The Cold War and After* (Englewood Cliffs, N.J.: Prentice-Hall, 1965), p. 10; John Lukacs, *A History of the Cold War* (Garden City, N.Y.: Doubleday, 1961), p. 100; and Edmund Stillman, " 'Containment' Has Won, But . . .," *New York Times Magazine*, May 28, 1967, p. 76.

13. *New York Times*, September 3, 1952, p. 20.

14. *Ibid.*, November 2, 1952, p. 86.

15. *Ibid.*, September 7, 1952, p. E-3.

16. Quoted in *ibid.*, August 27, 1952, p. 15.

17. *Ibid.*, November 1, 1952, p. 14.

18. *Ibid.*, September 12, 1952, p. 12.

19. D. F. Fleming, *The Cold War and Its Origins, 1917–1960* (Garden City, N.Y.: Doubleday, 1961), p. 806.

20. *New York Times*, September 4, 1952, p. 20.

21. Quoted in Hans J. Morgenthau, "John Foster Dulles," in *An Uncertain Tradition: American Secretaries of State in the Twentieth Century*, ed. Norman A. Graebner (New York: McGraw-Hill, 1961), p. 293.

22. Quoted in William Lee Miller, "The 'Moral Force' Behind Dulles's Diplomacy," *The Reporter*, August 9, 1956, p. 20.

23. *New York Times*, November 2, 1952, p. 78.

24. *Ibid.*, February 3, 1953, p. 14.

25. "Dulles Reveals Policy on World for U.S.," *U.S. News and World Report*, January 23, 1953, p. 100.

26. Morgenthau, "John Foster Dulles," p. 293.

27. *Ibid.*, p. 296.

28. John R. Beal, *John Foster Dulles, 1888–1959* (2nd ed; New York: Harpers, 1959), p. 13.

29. Joseph C. Harsch, "John Foster Dulles: A Very Complicated Man," *Harper's Magazine*, September, 1956, p. 34.

30. Halle, *Cold War*, p. 271.

31. Miller, "The 'Moral Force' Behind Dulles's Diplomacy," p. 20.

32. Halle, *Cold War*, p. 271.

33. Norman A. Graebner, *Cold War Diplomacy: American Foreign Policy, 1945–1960* (Princeton, N.J.: D. Van Nostrand, 1962), pp. 66–67. See also Fleming, *Cold War*, pp. 809–811, 1052, and Morgenthau, "John Foster Dulles," p. 293.

34. Gerson, *John Foster Dulles*, pp. 116–117.

35. Quoted in Chester Bowles, "A Plea for Another Great Debate," *New York Times Magazine*, February 28, 1954, p. 11.

36. Quoted in Beal, *John Foster Dulles, 1888–1959*, p. 129. See also *New York Times*, May 6, 1952, p. 3.

37. John Foster Dulles, "A Policy of Boldness," *Life*, May, 1952, pp. 148–149.

38. *New York Times*, August 27, 1952, p. 15.

39. *Ibid.*

40. *Ibid.*, October 5, 1952, p. 74.

41. *Ibid.*, January 13, 1954, p. 2.

42. *Ibid.*, March 14, 1954, p. 44.

43. Gerson, *John Foster Dulles*, p. 151. See also Graebner, *Cold War Diplomacy*, p. 95.

44. Hans J. Morgenthau, "Will It Deter Aggression?," *The New Republic*, March 29, 1954, p. 14.

45. *New York Times*, January 22, 1954, p. 1.

46. *Ibid.*, January 14, 1954, p. 17.

47. Gerson, *John Foster Dulles*, pp. 147–148.

48. Halle, *Cold War*, p. 281.

49. Bowles, "A Plea for Another Great Debate," p. 26. See also Morgenthau, "Will It Deter Aggression?," p. 14.

50. *New York Times*, March 7, 1954, p. 62.

51. Cited in *New York Times*, March 16, 1954, p. 12.

52. Bowles, "A Plea for Another Great Debate," p. 24. See also Fleming, *Cold War*, p. 678.

53. *New York Times*, March 16, 1954, p. 1.

54. Lester Pearson, "Who Decides?," *The New Republic*, March 29, 1954, p. 14.

55. *New York Times*, March 17, 1954, p. 5.

56. *Ibid.*

57. John Foster Dulles, "Policy for Security and Peace," *Foreign Affairs*, 32 (April, 1954), 353–364.

58. Morgenthau, "Will It Deter Aggression?," p. 11. See also Halle, *Cold War*, p. 283.

59. James Reston, *New York Times*, March 15, 1954, p. 16.

60. Halle, *Cold War*, p. 283. See also Morgenthau, "John Foster Dulles," pp. 295, 306.

61. McLellan, *Cold War in Transition*, p. 41.

62. Edmund Stillman and William Pfaff, *Power and Impotence* (New York: Random House, 1966), p. 190.

63. McLellan, *Cold War in Transition*, pp. 36–37.

64. *New York Times*, September 27, 1952, p. 3.

65. McLellan, *Cold War in Transition*, p. 36.

66. Halle, *Cold War*, p. 272. See also Morgenthau, "John Foster Dulles," p. 296.

67. *The Spiritual Legacy of John Foster Dulles*, ed. Henry P. Van Dusen (Philadelphia, Pa.: Westminster Press, 1960), pp. 229–232.

68. Morgenthau, "John Foster Dulles," p. 292.

69. Halle, *Cold War*, p. 413.

70. Harsch, "John Foster Dulles: A Very Complicated Man," p. 28.

71. Emmet John Hughes, *The Ordeal of Power* (New York: Atheneum, 1963), p. 204.

72. Miller, " 'Moral Force,' " p. 18. See also Lukacs, *History of the Cold War*, p. 100, and Gerson, *John Foster Dulles*, p. 13.

73. Stillman and Pfaff, *Power and Impotence*, p. 178.

74. Paul Seabury, *The Rise and Decline of the Cold War* (New York: Basic Books, 1967), pp. 72–73. See also Halle, *Cold War*, pp. 288–289; Morgenthau, "John Foster Dulles," p. 306; and "End of the Dulles Epoch," *The Economist*, April 18, 1959, p. 205.

75. Quoted in Gerson, *John Foster Dulles*, p. 322.

76. Chalmers M. Roberts, "The Pious Truculence of John Foster Dulles," *The Reporter*, January 23, 1958, p. 23.

77. Harsch, "John Foster Dulles: A Very Complicated Man," p. 34. See also Graebner, *Cold War Diplomacy* p. 62.

78. Miller, " 'Moral Force,' " p. 17.

79. *New York Times*, April 16, 1959, p. 14.

80. Harsch, "John Foster Dulles: A Very Complicated Man," p. 33.

81. *New York Times*, April 16, 1959, p. 14.

82. *Ibid.*, September 12, 1952, p. 12.

83. Hans J. Morgenthau, "The Policy of the USA," *The Political Quarterly*, 22 (January–March 1951), 55–56. See also Lerche, *Cold War and After*, p. 10; Stillman and Pfaff, *Power and Impotence*, pp. 135–136; Miller, " 'Moral Force,' " p. 19; and Reinhold Niebuhr, "The Moral World of Foster Dulles," *The New Republic*, December 1, 1958, p. 8.

84. Roberts, "The Pious Truculence of John Foster Dulles," p. 22. This judgment seems warranted even though, as indicated earlier in this essay, some private negotiations

were apparently concluded in spite of contradictory public pronouncements. For example, the Eisenhower administration seems to have persuaded the Chinese Nationalists privately not to invade the mainland even though Dulles's public pronouncements suggested they might do just that—under the rhetorically exciting phrase "unleashing Chiang Kai-shek." In spite of instances like this, though, the United States and the Soviet Union would have trouble even negotiating with one another in the polarized climate that existed throughout much of the Cold War. And, even if they were to negotiate, either side would have a great deal of trouble trying to resolve real differences, like the persistent Berlin crisis, without seeming to communicate on the home front that it had sold out to the enemy. Although Eisenhower and Khrushchev were able to talk about general matters at Camp David, Maryland, in 1959, and thereby achieve a general thaw, a "Spirit of Camp David," which represented a temporary rhetorical de-escalation, they could arrive at no agreement of any kind on controversial issues.

85. Lerche, *Cold War and After*, pp. 39–40.

86. Frankel, "Can We End the Cold War?," p. 58.

87. Marshall D. Shulman, *Beyond the Cold War* (New Haven, Conn.: Yale University Press, 1966), pp. 2–3; Halle, *Cold War*, pp. 413–414; and Lerche, *Cold War and After*, pp. 11–12, 25.

88. Stillman and Pfaff, *Power and Impotence*, p. 190. See also Stillman and Pfaff, *The New Politics*, p. 39, and Graebner, *Cold War Diplomacy*, pp. 63–64.

89. Beal, *John Foster Dulles, 1888–1959*, p. 179.

90. Morgenthau, "John Foster Dulles," p. 308.

Congress and the School Prayer Issue: The Becker Crusade

CHARLES J. STEWART

The controversy over religious exercises in public schools smoldered for years before 1958 when parents of school children in New Hyde Park, New York, brought suit against the New York Board of Regents for a prayer written in 1955 and recommended for recitation each morning in the public schools of New York. The prayer read, "Almighty God, we acknowledge our dependence upon Thee, and we beg Thy blessings upon us, our parents, our teachers, and our country." The parents appealed their case until the Supreme Court reviewed it as *Engel* v. *Vitale* on June 25, 1962. The Court ruled 6 to 1 that the regents' prayer violated the establishment clause of the First Amendment to the Constitution—"Congress shall make no law respecting an establishment of religion or prohibiting the free exercise thereof. . . ."[1]

Reaction to the Supreme Court's decision was immediate and furious. The fundamentalist and Catholic pulpit, along with conservative secular and religious presses, accused the Court of outlawing God, of being atheistic, and of supporting communistic materialism. Nowhere was the Court's decision condemned with more vigor than in Congress, especially in the House of Representatives. George Andrews of Alabama remarked that the Supreme Court had "put the Negroes in the schools and now they've driven God out,"[2] while L. Mendel Rivers of South Carolina declared that the Court had "now officially stated its disbelief in the God Almighty."[3] Within twenty-four hours of the *Engel* v. *Vitale* decision, Representative Frank J. Becker of New York introduced a resolution to amend the Constitution to allow prayer in the public schools. The Court's action, according to Becker, was the "most tragic in the history of the United States."[4] Fifty-four similar resolutions were introduced before the end of the eighty-seventh Congress, but they died in committee.

Meanwhile, two other cases were in the courts: *Abington* v. *Schempp*, a case concerning a Pennsylvania statute requiring Bible reading in the public schools, and *Murray* v. *Curlett*, concerning a Baltimore school commissioners' rule authorizing the recitation of the Lord's Prayer in the Baltimore public schools. The Supreme Court considered these cases together on June 17, 1963, and decided 8 to 1 that required Bible reading and the recitation of the Lord's Prayer as specified in the statutes of Pennsylvania and Maryland also violated the First Amendment.[5] The school prayer controversy flared anew and the Court's antagonists were certain that the Justices would not stop until they had stricken every vestige of religion from American life. Representatives, who had introduced only seventeen prayer resolutions into the Eighty-eighth Congress before the June 17 decision, now began an all-out campaign to get an amendment to the House floor where they were confident of its passage.

The school prayer campaign provides an excellent opportunity to study the interaction of the persuasive efforts of dedicated spokesmen and the machinery of Congressional organization. Too often the speech historian considers the Congressman as a campaigner or as a speaker upon the House floor; forgotten are committees, pressure groups, hearings, Congressional rules and traditions, and opposing strategies and tactics. The purpose of this essay is to analyze the Becker "crusade" for a school prayer amendment by considering the many facets of persuasive efforts in Congress.

Eighty-eighth Congress—First Session

Pro-amendment forces wanted to obtain passage of an amendment that would allow prayer and Bible reading at any government-sponsored activity. Their task was not easy. Although opposition to an amendment was as yet neither organized nor vocal, the leading opponent, Emanuel Celler of New York, was the man prayer amendment enthusiasts least wanted as opposition. Celler was chairman of the House Judiciary Committee through which all proposed Constitutional amendments had to pass, and he was employing the strategy available to chairmen of House committees—delay. Not one of the seventy-two prayer resolutions submitted between the two Supreme Court decisions had even reached the hearing stage.

Chairman Celler and fellow opponents of school prayer legislation felt that time was on their side. Frank Becker of New York, the first Congressman to introduce amendments into the Eighty-seventh and Eighty-eighth Congresses and the campaign's unofficial, self-appointed leader, had announced his intention to retire after the Eighty-eighth Congress, and no other Congressman seemed inclined to continue the crusade with similar zeal. Time would also permit the creation of a viable opposition in and out of Congress. If Celler could stall long enough, the major Protestant denominations would meet in their annual conferences, and several were likely to issue statements opposing a prayer amendment. Above all, opponents of an amendment thought that, as time went on, "rational" rather than "emotional" arguments would prevail.[6] The campaign for a prayer amendment rapidly became a match between Emanuel Celler and Frank Becker, both veteran and skilled legislative tacticians.

Becker knew that he could counter Celler's strategy only by applying pressure by every means at his disposal. Delay and pressure thus became the opposing strategies for the duration of the amendment crusade. On June 19, two days following the second Supreme Court ruling, Becker made his first move. He announced from the House floor his intention to file a discharge petition (the only way to bypass a House committee).[7] Such a petition simply "discharges" a committee of its powers over a given piece of legislation—in this case Becker's House Joint Resolution 9.

The discharge petition is not an easy route, however.[8] Two hundred and eighteen representatives, more than half of the entire House, must sign a petition before it becomes effective. Congressmen can sign only while the House is in session, and all petitions die with adjournment of each Congress— a point not overlooked by delaying chairmen. A successful petition can be called up only on the second and fourth Mondays of each month and not at all during the final six meetings of a Congress. Thus, timing and speed are important.

Naturally the most difficult aspect of the discharge petition is the necessary 218 signatures. Bypassing a committee is neither popular among Congressmen nor calculated to win friends among committee chairmen. Congressmen are reluctant to sign because *they* might want to bottle up legislation at some future date, because they feel the procedure tramples on prerogatives of their peers, because they might be increasingly pressured to sign petitions, and because the result might be poor legislation. The previous five Congresses had had an average of seven petitions filed, and an average of fewer than one bill discharged and passed on to the Senate. Only two bills have ever become law by the discharge method.[9] The value of the petition lies mainly in its potential pressure on a committee.

Aware of the reluctance of Congressmen to sign discharge petitions, Becker wisely prefaced his announced intention by saying that never in his sixteen years as a state and national legislator had he introduced, signed, or voted for a discharge petition. But because of the gravity of the proposed legislation and its "spiritual" rather than "material" nature, it was time to break his career-long policy.[10] Becker's statements seemed calculated to maintain his credibility with Capitol Hill colleagues and to stress the need for a prayer amendment. Regardless of the grave nature of the issue, however, he would wait several days before officially filing the petition to give the Judiciary Committee additional time to act. Thus Becker could not be charged with undue haste, with not allowing time for committee action. The first step in the pressure strategy had taken place.

Meanwhile, other Congressmen were submitting a long list of joint resolutions calling for prayer amendments. They submitted nine on June 18, the day after the second Court decision, and added twenty-two more by July 9, when Becker rose on the House floor to announce that he had just filed discharge petition 3 with the House clerk.[11] He had waited nearly three weeks for some sign of activity in Celler's committee; now it was time to act. His speech, limited by the one minute rule, contained three brief points: that the introduction of new court cases was making the prayer situation worse each day, that he had always opposed discharge petitions until now, and that it was most urgent for Congressmen to sign the petition as soon as possible.[12]

Becker knew that he was gambling, but it seemed worth the effort. If the petition were successful, a school prayer amendment could reach the floor with time to spare. If it failed to get the required signatures, the petition might provide the needed leverage to pressure Celler to move an amendment through the Judiciary Committee. Celler did not want a prayer amendment, but above all he did not want an amendment not prepared by his committee. If Becker acquired Celler's enmity, so what; he was retiring at the end of the Eighty-eighth Congress.

Becker also announced in his July 9 speech that he wanted to meet with the other forty-seven representatives who had submitted prayer resolutions. The purpose was to write a single amendment that they could all support. Emanuel Celler was about to face a united and more determined opposition.

In succeeding weeks Becker repeated the same one minute speech several times. He cited the increasing danger to religion in America, gave reasons why it was *proper* to sign *this* petition, and urged immediate action. On July 16, he stated, "I agree that Members will not sign petitions having to do with things that are Caesar's, but I feel that when it comes to the area of Almighty God, no man can use the excuse that he does not sign discharge petitions."[13] After all, he had waited one full year for the Judiciary Committee to act. Becker aligned his position with Almighty God, an association Congressmen could not easily ignore. Becker also remarked that he had sent personal letters to each representative asking for his support and his signature. Celler and other Congressmen were now under constant pressure from amendment-supporting colleagues.

On July 25, Becker got another minute on the floor and announced that he had met with some fifty colleagues and that a bipartisan committee of six—three Republicans and three Democrats—had been selected to draw up a joint resolution. His speech had a decided bandwagon flavor. The number of "signatures are moving up gradually" he assured his listeners. He urged them to sign the petition "at the earliest possible moment" because more and more cases were appearing in the courts.[14] Becker referred to an American Civil Liberties Union suit against the "under God" phrase in the Pledge of Allegiance, and concluded, "This is not a matter of signing a discharge petition or disliking to sign a discharge petition on a piece of legislation that can come before the House at any time."

A week later, July 31, Becker was back on the floor with his "speech." Concerning the signatures on discharge petition 3, he declared, "We have quite a number now and we are getting more every day."[15] He alone, according to House rules, knew the exact number of signatures, and he was not going to reveal the number until it was impressive. Becker closed by placing into the *Congressional Record* an article from the *Catholic Free Press* that strongly urged Congressmen to sign the petition and citizens to write their Congressmen. Conservative religious and secular presses and other groups were beginning to encourage a mail campaign that eventually became one of the biggest in the history of Congress.

The month of August was good and bad for both sides in the controversy. Senate hearings on nine school prayer bills ended on August 2, and the Senate committee took no further action.[16] Although Becker had hoped for action "in that other body," he knew that all pressure and attention would now focus on the House Judiciary Committee and its chairman, Emanuel Celler. Celler was undoubtedly pleased with the lack of Senate action, but he could hardly welcome the increased pressures. On August 19 Becker announced from the floor that "the numbers [of signatures] are increasing every week."[17] Again, he did not say how many legislators had signed the petition, but repeated his justification for filing the discharge petition: "I am afraid the only way we can do it [get an amendment] is by way of the discharge petition which I dislike, but which course I feel I must take because I cannot sit idly by and wait year after year after year for legislation through the regular process to correct this tragic decision by the Supreme Court." Becker's constant plea was for fellow Congressmen to join his holy crusade—others were doing so every day. Celler remained silent on the issue.

Early in September the bipartisan committee completed its work on a school prayer amendment, and Becker had the honor of submitting it first as House Joint Resolution 693. Twenty-nine other Congressmen submitted the resolution under different numbers on the same day, September 10, 1963. The resolution read:

SECTION 1. Nothing in this Constitution shall be deemed to prohibit the offering, reading from, or listening to prayers or biblical scriptures, if participation therein is on a voluntary basis, in any governmental or public school, institution, or place.
SECTION 2. Nothing in this Constitution shall be deemed to prohibit making reference to belief in, reliance upon, or invoking the aid of

God or a Supreme Being in any governmental or public document, proceeding, activity, ceremony, school, institution, or place, or upon any coinage, currency, or obligation of the United States.

SECTION 3. Nothing in this article shall constitute an establishment of religion.

SECTION 4. This article shall be inoperative unless it shall have been ratified as an amendment to the Constitution by the legislatures of three-fourths of the several States within seven years from the date of its submission to the States by Congress.[18]

Later in the day Becker stated in the House that he had filed the new amendment and was placing it in the *Congressional Record* so all Representatives would have a copy. "All members can now sign the discharge petition knowing just what the amendment will do," he remarked.[19] In the weeks that followed, twenty-eight other Congressmen submitted the committee-prepared resolution. There is no record of how many signed the discharge petition, however.

A week after submitting House Joint Resolution 693, Becker delivered his usual speech, but stressed more than ever that the discharge petition was "the only way you are going to get a chance to act on this."[20] He spoke of new legal suits against military chaplains and the "under God" phrase in the Pledge of Allegiance, and assured his audience that the Supreme Court would outlaw both practices if it got the chance. The joint resolution, once it reached the floor and was passed, would end all threat of court action, he said. Becker was trying to frighten Celler with the discharge petition and to frighten fellow Congressmen with the spectre of imminent Court actions, but neither party showed much sign of fright. This speech seemed to reveal a sign of desperation, for Becker's campaign for a discharge petition was not producing the results he intimated.

On November 20 Becker addressed the House again—his final effort in the first session of the Eighty-eighth Congress. He announced that, during the past week, there had been a "tremendous increase in the rate of signatures."[21] For the first time he divulged the number of signatures on the discharge petition—108, or not quite half enough.

Becker's chief tactic during a four-month period was the bandwagon, claiming that "signatures are moving up gradually," that he was "getting more every day," and that "the numbers are increasing every week." Now, after a "tremendous increase in the rate," he had only 108 signatures—hardly a landslide. His bandwagon evidently gained passengers rather slowly, thus provoking serious questions about his strategy. When employing the bandwagon tactic during a controversy, do potential allies defer because they assume that adequate support is being gained? And what happens when a bandwagon does not materialize sufficiently and both friends and foes discover this fact? Does the persuader's credibility suffer? Perhaps Becker could have gained more signatures by openly admitting that the campaign was going very slowly and by presenting stronger evidence of the danger of new, more sweeping court decisions.

In his final appeal of 1963, Becker also commented on the massive volumes of mail reaching Congressional offices, the greatest in the careers of many representatives. The important fact, according to Becker, was that individual Americans were waging the mail campaign for his prayer amendment. To accentuate this point, he placed into the record a letter and petition from an eighty-seven-year-old woman who had *walked* through her neighborhood to obtain 250 signatures.[22]

During this first session of the Eighty-eighth Congress, Becker had thoroughly established his leadership of the prayer crusade. He spoke on the issue from the House floor nearly as often as all other Representatives combined, and he managed to organize a bipartisan group that produced an amendment acceptable to the majority of the Supreme Court's opposition. Although fifty-eight Congressmen submitted the new amendment under different numbers and their own names, the proposal became known nationally as the "Becker Amendment." Becker had built up enough public and congressional pressures on his reluctant colleagues to assure some action in the second session. The question remained, however: would his pressure strategy work in time to get an amendment through both chambers before adjournment in the fall of 1964? So far the majority of Congressmen were resisting Becker's major tactics: association with God and threat of more court decisions. Emanuel Celler maintained his strategy of silent delay and still led.

Eighty-eighth Congress—Second Session

The second session of the Eighty-eighth Congress convened on January 7, 1964. Chairman Celler had successfully delayed action in the Judiciary Committee for a year and a half, but pressures in and out of Congress were slowly building to the point where he and his committee would have to take some action. Thousands of letters and petitions were coming in from every state, and some nationally organized groups like Project America were becoming active in Becker's crusade. Project America provided printed letters and postcards so that all a "voter" had to do was sign and mail.[23] The postcard read: "Dear Congressman, I, as one of your voting constituents, respectfully request you to sign discharge petition No. 3 for the Becker Amendment to return the Bible to our schools. Please let me know whether or not you have signed the petition. Thank you." Congressmen could not long resist this kind of pressure, especially since 1964 was an election year. They began to warn Celler that if he did not act on prayer legislation, they would be forced to sign the discharge petition. On February 19, the House Republican Policy Committee added to Celler's problems by passing a resolution requesting Celler to hold hearings and to report a proposal at the earliest time.[24] The next day, February 20, Michael Feighan of Ohio (the ranking member of the Judiciary Committee behind Celler) submitted House Joint Resolution 930. He announced on the House floor that he had introduced the amendment, that Congressmen had been reluctant to sign the discharge petition because they feared it "would establish a precedent with which they are not in agreement," and that he would be willing to chair hearings on the proposed amendments. He trusted that hearings would be held soon.[25]

Becker continued his behind-the-scenes persuasive efforts, but did not take his campaign to the House floor until February 20—a month and a half into the second session. Time was getting desperately short, and Becker's speech reflected his frustration. Rumors of hearings had been circulating "for months and months and months," he exclaimed, still there was no apparent action in the committee.[26] "I say to the Members of this House," Becker concluded, "if you want to bring this subject to the floor of the House and get it over to the other body, in time for action to be taken at this session, the signing of discharge petition No. 3 is the only route by which we will be able to do it." "Sign the discharge petition now," he pleaded; 145 Congressmen had already done so.

On February 25 Becker was back on the floor. Discharge petition 3 had gained one more signature, and Becker cited a recent flurry of amendments—twenty-one since the second session opened—as evidence that pressures from "back home" were forcing apathetic Congressmen to join his prayer amendment campaign.[27] Twenty months had passed since the first resolutions had reached the Judiciary Committee. Too little time remained to hold committee hearings and to get Senate action before adjournment of the Eighty-eighth Congress, Becker commented. The discharge petition was the only way, for hearings now would only delay action on an amendment.

The next day Becker returned to the floor and cited a letter from Emanuel Celler. Celler had responded to a series of questions posed in a February 5 letter from Becker. The answers revealed more delay: a staff study had been completed; the study was in the page-proof stage; hearings would be held before the *full* committee; and *no date* had yet been set for the opening of hearings. "I wonder what the good gentleman means by 'very shortly,' since 10 months have passed," Becker declared.[28] This was Becker's first direct reference to Celler and it revealed a growing exasperation. Again he stressed that the discharge petition was the only way "to bring this matter before the House," and added a final plea, "I hope those who have been holding off signing, waiting for hearings, will realize this, and will sign the petition in good faith." Unfortunately for Becker, Congressmen are prone to wait great lengths of time for the "proper" Congressional machinery to function.

Pressure strategies have a way of escalating, and Becker's were no different. First he threatened a discharge petition; then he actually filed a petition; next he encouraged outside pressures; and finally he began to refer openly to his opponent, Emanuel Celler. As increasing pressures seem needed and are applied, because old ones have failed to produce the desired results, the opposition often becomes more determined than ever and potential supporters can be antagonized by the heavy-handed approach. Emanuel Celler was obviously not going to budge unless the discharge petition was on the verge of passage, and other Congressmen were obviously not being induced rapidly enough to join the prayer crusade.

Two weeks later, March 10, Frank Becker rose to announce that 160 Congressmen had now signed the petition. Concerning the ever increasing volumes of mail, he remarked, "I am sorry Members are getting so much mail complaining about it (prayer issue); on the other hand, I am very happy that the people of this nation are very much disturbed."[29] There was only one way out of the dilemma—sign the petition. Becker was constantly trying to increase the pressures on Congressmen and the Judiciary Committee.

Emanuel Celler had delayed hearings for nearly two years—long enough in the Eighty-eighth Congress to make passage of a prayer amendment highly unlikely. If he waited much longer, however, the discharge petition might enable Frank Becker to bypass his committee. Thus, on March 19 he announced that hearings before the full Judiciary Committee would commence on April 22 and that the committee would hear testimony from *all* interested parties on *all* proposed amendments. "The nature and importance of the subject require that the committee have the best thinking of all schools of thought in its consideration of the pending resolutions," he said.[30]

Becker had waited two years for hearings, and had hoped that they would be on his amendment alone, that a small subcommittee would conduct the hearings, that it would hear testimony from a limited number of Congressmen, and that the hearings would last no more than two weeks. Obviously, Celler had other plans. On March 23 Becker angrily accused Celler of devious delays, and charged that the starting date was two weeks later than he had been led to expect. "I was a little amazed," he said, that Celler would schedule the start of such important hearings on the opening day of the New York World's Fair.[31] He might have added that only an old pro could have planned so well. One hundred and sixty-one representatives had now signed his petition, and Becker declared that only a few more votes were needed to get an amendment before the House—fifty-seven would appear to be a large "few." The discharge petition was probably the only hope in April, 1964, for it was too late in the Eighty-eighth Congress to hold hearings, to get out a report, to hold debate, to send the result to the Senate, and for the Senate to act, but many pro-amendment Congressmen still would not sign the petition.

Becker and his allies had wanted hearings so they could persuade the Judiciary Committee to write and to submit to the House an amendment that would allow prayer and Bible reading at any governmentally sponsored activity. This goal was virtually impossible to achieve in the spring of 1964. The controversy was nearly two years old, and the thirty-five member committee—the immediate audience to be persuaded—was seriously divided over the prayer issue. Nine committeemen had sponsored resolutions for amending the Constitution; six of them eventually testified at the hearings.[32] The actions of chairman Celler and sharp cross-examination of witnesses by such committeemen as James C. Corman of California, Jacob H. Gilbert of New York, Roland V. Libonati of Illinois, and George F. Senner of Arizona showed the strong opposition on the committee. Witnesses also faced a problem common to many Congressional activities—failure of committee members to attend the hearings. During the first six days when most Congressmen testified, an average of only twenty of the thirty-five members were present. In addition, pro-amendment witnesses faced one of the House's best qualified committees. All but one committeemen were lawyers, and only four were freshmen in Congress. These factors coupled with the scheduled testimony of numerous pro-Supreme Court constitutional experts, clergymen, and educators meant that Congressional witnesses would have to establish arguments able to withstand strong counter persuasion. Added to these problems was the antagonism caused by the as yet unsuccessful campaign for a discharge petition and efforts to bring public and Congressional pressures upon Celler and the Judiciary Committee.

The best strategy under the circumstances might have been the following: (1) limit the number of witnesses, Congressional and otherwise, so the hearings would last only one or two weeks; (2) select witnesses because of particular competencies (education, theology, constitutional law) and prestige or power; (3) organize the testimony to avoid needless repetition of the same arguments; (4) present reasons for an amendment that could be carefully explained and substantiated; (5) avoid extreme exaggeration or oversimplification of important facets of the prayer issue; and (6) refute opposing arguments, especially those presented by anti-amendment witnesses. Frank Becker's comments before and during the hearings indicate that he would have preferred such a strategy.[33] Lack of cooperation from his colleagues, including Emanuel Celler, frustrated his desires.

Celler evidently extended invitations to nearly anyone who might want to testify, especially Congressmen. To Becker's chagrin, a great many individuals and organizations accepted the invitations. When the hearings ended on June 3—a precious month and a half later—193 witnesses (102 from Congress) had appeared before Celler's committee and another 130 had submitted written statements. Ninety-six of the 102 Congressional witnesses opposed the Supreme Court's rulings and took the opportunity to present their cases to the live audience on Capitol Hill and the watchful one back home. Other witnesses represented groups like the Children's Bible Mission, the Committee for the Preservation of Prayer and Bible Reading in the Public Schools, Project Prayer, International Christian Youth of the United States of America, and Return the Bible to the Schools Campaign; all wanted a chance to persuade the committee to act on prayer legislation. Becker could not end the long parade of witnesses, although he did complain on the House floor that he had asked for only five witnesses and a couple of weeks of hearings. He charged that Celler was scheduling hearings for only two or three days a week to delay as long as possible. The charge was justified since the eighteen day-long sessions were scattered over a month and a half. Celler had to be careful not to antagonize his Congressional colleagues and, except for Becker, he apparently succeeded. Ample opportunity to testify seemed to please pro-amendment Congressmen.[34]

When the hearings opened at 10:00 A.M. on April 22, Becker took the stand (Celler scheduled Congressional witnesses first) and testified for the entire morning session—two hours and five minutes.[35] A recurring illness prevented him from continuing his persuasive efforts at the afternoon session. Other Congressional witnesses anxiously took his place and appeared one after the other until the afternoon of the third day. Finally, B. F. Sisk of California appeared to speak against the multitude of proposed constitutional amendments; he was witness number sixty-six. Chairman Celler greeted Sisk with the comment: "We had a procession of Congressmen on the other side and I wanted to say you are very much like a breath of cool air in the heat of summer."[36] This was one of Celler's rare expressions of personal feelings, and a few days later he and Representative Sisk drew a sharp rebuttal from Congressman Steven Derounian of New York.[37] Celler did not deviate again from his strategy of silence until after the hearings ended in June. The anti-Court assault continued for another three days and twelve witnesses (including another two hours with Becker) before a second defender of the Court's decisions appeared, the first non-Congressional witness.

The great rush of Congressmen to the hearings ended on the sixth day with the score 86 (84 Congressmen, 1 clergyman, and 1 governor—George Wallace) against the prayer rulings and 6 (1 Congressman, 4 clergymen, and 1 law professor) for the rulings. Testimony at the next twelve sessions differed markedly. Fifty-four of 101 witnesses (five of twelve Congressmen and forty-nine of eighty-four law professors, clergymen, educators, and pressure group spokesmen) defended the Supreme Court's prayer decisions. This apparent evolution at the hearings had several implications for Becker's crusade. First, it suggested that the tide had begun to turn against amending the Constitution, a point Celler was to make once the hearings ended. Second, Congressional testimony stood in sharp contrast to that of other witnesses. And third, anti-amendment witnesses tended to have the last word at the hearings.

The scheduling of witnesses, Congressmen first and in random order, denied Becker any chance to organize his forces. A Congressman with seniority and influence might be bracketed between colleagues with little of either. One Congressman might deliver a forty-five minute statement and answer questions for an hour, while the next might deliver a two minute statement and answer no questions. Major reasons why Congress should overturn the Court's actions were repeated again and again with little new being added. Occasionally a witness would apologize for presenting the same arguments as his colleagues, but he would continue to do so. The major arguments and frequency of occurrence were as follows:

1. The Court's rulings were contrary to American heritage and traditions.	69 (of 96 witnesses)
2. The Court's rulings would lead to removal of all vestiges of religion from American official or governmental activities.	64
3. The Court's rulings were contrary to the desires of the vast majority of Americans.	63
4. The Court had outlawed "voluntary" prayers and Bible readings.	55
5. The Court's interpretation of the First Amendment was too narrow and wrong.	54
6. The Court's rulings were tampering with religion when it was most needed in American life.	46
7. The Court's rulings had caused confusion and religious dissension.	32

Not only did Congressional witnesses recite the same points with monotonous repetition, but they generally failed to support and to explain them adequately. For instance, Congressmen continued to cite Harvard's Law School Dean, Erwin N. Griswold, as a supporter of a prayer amendment even after he had sent a letter to Emanuel Celler saying that he had opposed the prayer decisions but was "against any amendments to the Bill of Rights."[38]

Witnesses would greatly exaggerate one point and then oversimplify the next. For example, several Congressmen charged that the Supreme Court had established atheism as the state church and that children could not mention God in a school building.[39] The highly complex issue of the "voluntary" nature of religious exercises got the reverse treatment. Whereas the Supreme Court had contended that religious practices in the schoolroom might subject the small child to unjustified psychological and social pressures, Congressmen retorted that they had attended public schools where prayers and Bible reading were part of the morning ritual and had faced no dilemma.[40] Therefore, no problem existed when the religious exercises were voluntary because a child could simply remain silent if he opposed the ritual.

Few Congressional witnesses attempted to refute arguments against amending the Constitution. Frank Becker's effort during his first appearance before the committee was perhaps the best. He conducted a point-by-point rebuttal of an article by Shad Polier, chairman of the Governing Council of the American Jewish Congress.[41] Since the majority of Congressmen testified before anti-amendment witnesses appeared before the committee, opportunities to refute specific witnesses were scarce. However, more Congressmen could have followed Becker's example and answered opposition statements that had appeared in the press. A few of the later Congressional witnesses did refute earlier testimony. For example, James C. Fulton of Pennsylvania, a Presbyterian, reacted to the statements of leading spokesmen for the United Presbyterian Church. "You see, churches are institutions," Fulton said. "In some churches there has gotten to be the feeling that their's is the only institution, and they are the only way that any person can have an approach to God."[42] More Congressmen should have devoted part of their testimony to refutation.

Hearings at this stage in the prayer controversy fitted perfectly into Emanuel Celler's strategy of delay. Valuable weeks slipped by with adjournment drawing nearer, and the very existence of hearings blunted Becker's charge that the Judiciary Committee was not acting on prayer resolutions. In addition, few Congressmen were likely to sign the discharge petition until the hearings ended and then only after waiting to see if the committee would file a report and send a resolution to the floor.

The hearings drew to a close on June 3, and the futile wait for Celler to file a report began. Frank Becker waited two weeks before taking his campaign back to the House floor on June 15. After working nearly two years to get hearings on prayer amendments, now there was no report from the committee, he declared.[43] The discharge petition needs only fifty-two signatures, Becker pleaded, and "time is running out on this session." Only five Congressmen had signed the petition since Celler announced hearings on March 19.

Becker returned to the floor on June 24 angered by remarks, attributed to Celler, that the tide of opinion was turning against amending the Constitution. Just the opposite was happening, Becker exclaimed. Celler had managed to rush the civil rights bill through his committee; "why would he not do the same for prayer, for God?," Becker asked.[44] The discharge petition was the only way to get an amendment to the floor for a vote. On July 1 he placed into the record a statement by the Open Bible Standard Churches that strongly favored a prayer amendment. According to Becker, this was adequate evidence that the tide was still in his favor.[45] Nearly a month later, July 29, he said it was "quite evident now to everyone that the chairman of the Committee on the Judiciary does not intend and will not bring in a resolution." "We need less than 50 signatures now in order to bring this to the 218 required," Becker pleaded.[46] Discharge petition 3 had picked up very few signatures since the hearings ended in June. The bandwagon had stalled.

Becker was probably correct in his claim that the tide of public opinion had not turned. What was happening in late spring and early summer, 1964, was increased vocalization of opposition views, a phenomenon that seemed to indicate a change in point-of-view. The hearings ended with the majority of noncongressional witnesses against amending the constitution. A few days later 222 of the nation's leading constitutional lawyers, including fifty-five law school deans, signed a petition against any prayer amendment.[47] Meanwhile religious groups like the Baptists, Lutherans, Presbyterians, and the National Council of Churches made their opposition public. The witnesses at the hearings, constitutional lawyers, and religious leaders were not *changing* their views but only making them known. Celler's hoped for "viable opposition" was becoming a reality; the tide of persuasive efforts had evidently changed.

The greatest blow to Becker's crusade came in June when the Supreme Court ended its term by refusing to rule on baccalaureate services, religious tests for teachers, religious programs, religious census, and showing of religious films in public schools, as well as the "In God We Trust" inscription on coins and the "under God" phrase in the Pledge of Allegiance.[48] Gone was Becker's major argument that the Supreme Court would outlaw all religious practices if not stopped by an amendment. Immediate action on prayer legislation no longer seemed so necessary.

During the long battle over a prayer amendment, Emanuel Celler had remained virtually silent, both in and out of Congress. The only time he had voluntarily mentioned the issue in the House was on March 19, 1964, when he announced the scheduling of hearings. But in early August he remarked in an Associated Press release that Congressional mail had reversed and was now running strongly against amending the First Amendment, and added: "There is not the slightest doubt, now, that Congress will never approve this amendment. The people have had a chance to learn what really is involved here and in the light of mature reflection and sober judgment they have made it clear they do not want the first amendment tampered with."[49]

Becker rose on the House floor on August 11, press clipping in hand, and delivered the strongest rebuttal and challenge of his entire campaign.[50] "Mr. Speaker, I would like to dispel some very unjustifiable claims made by the chairman of the House Judiciary Committee," he began. After citing two passages from the press release, Becker issued several challenges:

> First. My amendment does not in any way change or alter the first amendment. The Supreme Court did that.
>
> Second. I challenge the gentleman from New York, to bring an amendment to the floor of the House. If it is his contention that Congress will never approve it, then he should have no concern about bringing it to the floor for debate and vote.
>
> I know he is afraid to do this, and it is a tragedy that one man in the Congress can so block the will of the American people.
>
> I further challenge the gentleman's statement that mail is running heavily against an amendment to permit prayer and Bible reading in public schools. I have made a personal check with many Members of the House, and the results of many questionnaires sent out by Members indicate clearly that the American people are overwhelmingly in favor of such an amendment. The answers on Members' questionnaires run between 75 and 95 percent in the affirmative.
>
> I am inserting this newspaper article following my remarks, and I say to the chairman of the House Committee on the Judiciary that I am perfectly willing to have this matter come before the House and go to the people through their various State legislatures to determine the will of the American people.
>
> I challenge the gentleman from New York to do the same.

Becker ended his challenge by placing the Associated Press release into the *Congressional Record*.

Emanuel Celler, as might be expected, did not acknowledge Becker's challenges. Perhaps Becker should have challenged Celler earlier in the campaign and directed stronger attacks against Congressional opposition to a school prayer amendment. However, both tactics could have antagonized potential supporters and even strengthened the opposition.

The 1964 Presidential and Congressional campaigns were getting underway and adjournment was near. Celler could remain silent and allow time to run out. Becker's August 11 speech, the strongest of the campaign, climaxed his crusade for school prayer. Neither he nor any other Congressman addressed himself to the prayer issue again until October 3—the day the Eighty-eighth Congress adjourned. In his last speech as a Congressman, Becker first offered results of letters he had sent to Roman Catholic bishops in the United States and then delivered his epilogue: "this session comes to an end without the Congress taking any action on my constitutional amendment House Joint Resolution 693. I regret this more than I can put in words, and while I will not return to Congress next year, I shall not cease in my efforts to restore a 173-year right to the American people."[51]

Conclusion

Frank Becker led the Congressional campaign for a school prayer amendment with considerable finesse. He did succeed in uniting pro-amendment forces and helped to arouse massive public support for prayer legislation. Why, then, did he fail to secure a prayer amendment?

Many factors probably accounted for the defeat. Some Congressmen were afraid to become involved in the highly volatile controversy; others hesitated to tamper with the Bill of Rights; and still others saw the discharge of a prayer amendment as a dangerous precedent. Thus, enough Congressmen refused to sign the discharge petition, and Becker's bandwagon stalled at 178 signatures—forty short of the 218 needed.

Opposing strategies may also have been significant in Becker's defeat. The user of a pressure strategy in Congress must operate from a power position or at least be able to promise future support or opposition. Frank Becker held no important power position, while his leading opponent, Emanuel Celler, was chairman of the Judiciary Committee, a recognized power in the House of Representatives, and had served in Congress longer than Becker. In addition, Becker had announced his retirement plans and thus could not promise support or opposition. Celler intended to be around for several more years and could promise or threaten both opposition and support.

Once committed to the pressure strategy, Becker had no choice but to escalate the type and degree of pressure when desired results did not materialize. Threats from constituents, pressure groups, and fellow Congressmen might have alienated potential supporters and made the opposition more determined to resist. Also, each time Becker spoke on the issue—mainly to keep the issue alive and to add pressure on his colleagues—he ran the chance of saying something that might antagonize a possible ally. Perhaps Becker assumed that if all else failed, massive public opinion would force the House to act. No doubt many Congressmen did testify at the hearings and did sign the discharge petition because of pressures from back home. However, the majority of Congressmen waited for Judiciary Committee action—the proper channel for legislation.

Emanuel Celler's strategy of silent delay generally avoided the pitfalls of Becker's pressure strategy. Inaction does have the potential for antagonizing

Congressional colleagues, but Celler skillfully avoided delaying too long. His Committee did act, but very slowly. He provided the opposition with adequate opportunity to testify on behalf of an amendment, thereby pleasing the opposition (except Becker) and delaying beyond the point of possible legislative action. The delay strategy also provided enough time for the eventual undermining of Becker's major tactics. The Supreme Court's refusal in the spring of 1964 to hear several new "religious practices" cases struck heavily at Becker's fear tactic. For months he had predicted new Court decisions against religion in government, then his predictions were proven wrong just when his campaign desperately needed new life and support. If the Court had outlawed just one more religious practice, Becker might have won. Opposition to a prayer amendment by a number of religious organizations and the majority of religious witnesses at the hearings undoubtedly weakened the alignment of his crusade with Almighty God. Again, this happened late in the campaign when Becker desperately needed support.

Clearly the critic of Congressional rhetoric must realize that at times all of the available means of persuasion cannot overcome opposition bolstered by Congressional structure, rules, and traditions. The critic must also realize that a single speech is likely to be only a small part of the effort to create a piece of legislation. Persuasive efforts in Congress of necessity involve committees, committee chairmen, pressure groups, hearings, rules and regulations, public opinion, *and* speeches from the floor.

1. For a review of this decision see Philip B. Kurland, "The School Prayer Cases," *The Wall between Church and State*, ed. Dallin H. Oaks (Chicago: University of Chicago Press, 1963), pp. 147–150, 153–158.

2. *New York Times*, June 26, 1962, p. 1.

3. *Ibid.*, June 27, 1962, p. 20.

4. *Ibid.*

5. Kurland, "School Prayer Cases," pp. 150–152, 158–172.

6. *Congressional Quarterly Weekly Report*, May 1, 1964, p. 884, contains a discussion of the delaying tactic and what anti-amendment Congressmen hoped it would accomplish.

7. *Congressional Record*, 88th Congress, 1st Session, 1963, p. 11180.

8. *Congressional Quarterly Weekly Report*, December 6, 1963, p. 2129, discusses the nature and requirements for discharge petitions.

9. *Ibid.*, p. 2130, discusses the history of discharge petitions and why Congressmen hesitate to sign them. The two bills that became laws by the discharge route were the 1936 Wages and Hours Act and the 1960 Federal Employees Pay Raise Act.

10. *Congressional Record*, 88th Congress, 1st Session, 1963, p. 11180.

11. *Ibid.*, p. 12291.

12. *Ibid.*

13. *Ibid.*, p. 12763.

14. *Ibid.*, pp. 13343–44.

15. *Ibid.*, p. 13828.

16. *Congressional Quarterly Almanac*, 88th Congress, 2nd Session, 1964, p. 401.

17. *Congressional Record*, 88th Congress, 1st Session, 1963, p. 15295.

18. *Hearings before the Committee on the Judiciary, House of Representatives, Eighty-Eighth Congress Second Session, on Proposed Amendments to the Constitution Relating to Prayer in the Public Schools* (Washington, D.C., 1964), p. 22. Referred to hereafter as *Hearings*.

19. *Congressional Record*, 88th Congress, 1st Session, 1963, p. 16700.

20. *Ibid.*, p. 17211.

21. *Ibid.*, p. 22547.

22. *Ibid.*

23. *Congressional Quarterly Almanac*, 88th Congress, 2nd Session, 1964, p. 401.

24. *Ibid.*, and *Congressional Quarterly Weekly Report*, February 21, 1964, p. 359.

25. *Congressional Record*, 88th Congress, 2nd Session, 1964, pp. 3244–3245.

26. *Ibid.*, p. 3225.

27. *Ibid.*, p. 3537.

28. *Ibid.*, p. 3656.

29. *Ibid.*, p. 4862.

30. *Ibid.*, p. 5734.

31. *Ibid.*, p. 5883.

32. *Hearings*, Part I, pp. ii–xvi, contains a list of committee members, all prayer resolutions, and all witnesses.

33. *Congressional Record*, 88th Congress, 2nd Session, 1964, pp. 3656 and 11971–11972.

34. Ninety-six Congressmen testified for a prayer amendment and, except for Becker, no complaint was made as to the time required for the large number of witnesses at the hearings.

35. *Hearings*, Part I, pp. 211–245.

36. *Ibid.*, p. 533.

37. *Ibid.*, p. 642.

38. *Ibid.*, pp. 256–257.

39. *Ibid.*, Part II, p. 1073.

40. *Ibid.*, Part I, pp. 226, 510.

41. *Ibid.*, pp. 225–228.

42. *Ibid.*, Part II, pp. 1202–1203.

43. *Congressional Record*, 88th Congress, 2nd Session, 1964, p. 13738.

44. *Ibid.*, p. 14933.

45. *Ibid.*, p. 15599.

46. *Ibid.*, p. 17246.

47. *Congressional Quarterly Almanac*, 88th Congress, 2nd Session, 1964, p. 404.

48. *Ibid.*, pp. 309, 404.

49. *Congressional Record*, 88th Congress, 2nd Session, 1964, p. 18963.

50. *Ibid.*, pp. 18962–18963.

51. *Ibid.*, p. 24043.

John F. Kennedy at Houston, Texas, September 12, 1960

HERMANN G. STELZNER

"With such a man in office the myth of the nation would again be engaged, and the fact that he was Catholic would shiver a first existential vibration of consciousness into the mind of the White Protestant."[1] Norman Mailer's forecast illuminated an essential element in John F. Kennedy's contest for the presidency as November, 1960, approached.

Even straightforward commentators sensed the shiver. Shortly before election day, 1960, George Gallup polled the citizenry and the data reflected the tensions within the electorate over the religious issue. Gallup could not easily determine the "full impact" of the issue, concluding that it "would not be felt" much before November 7, 1960. Citizens, Gallup observed, were struggling. Some "Protestants now in the Kennedy camp" were "in conflict," and similarly "Catholics . . . now supporting Mr. Nixon" were doing so "with some misgivings."[2] Later, with the fact of Kennedy's assassination in 1963 casting dark shadows on the landscape of the collective conscience, William G. Carleton analyzed the political issues of the 1960s and judged that "only the religious . . . [issue] will loom large in history."[3]

Looking back, was the meaning of the essential element recognized? Was it made manifest and tangible for the American citizens? A touchstone for these questions is Kennedy's address before the Greater Houston Ministerial Association on September 12, 1960, two months before election day. Lawrence H. Fuchs concluded that "no President has ever made as important a speech on church-state matters" as did Kennedy in Houston.[4] Theodore Sorensen, a Kennedy advisor and speech writer, is reported to have said of the immediate occasion: "We can win or lose the election right there in Houston on Monday night."[5] Winning or losing for Sorensen referred to the immediate contest for the presidency between John F. Kennedy, the Democratic nominee, and Richard M. Nixon, the Republican. But partisan politics pale in the hindsight of the impact of a speech and an election. The observations of Mailer and Gallup and the judgments of Carleton, Fuchs, and Sorensen suggest that Kennedy's Catholicism forced the electorate to struggle with itself as it sought to give meanings and values to Kennedy's candidacy and to the larger question of the tension between religion and politics in the life of the country. Kennedy's Houston ministerial address was a political statement for support of his candidacy for the presidency, but it was also an important rhetorical act that helped to shape and give meaning to future church-state relations, which had been set in motion historically by the making of a new nation and partially worked out between 1620 and 1960, from the Puritans at Plymouth to the confrontation at Houston.

There is no reason to develop here the centrality of the religious issue in the presidential campaign of 1960.[6] Both Kennedy and Nixon felt its presence; both sought to avoid exacerbating it. Kennedy often said that the emphasis placed on his Catholicism prevented him from doing justice to far more compelling issues.[7] In his introduction to the Houston ministers, he indicated that war, hunger, ignorance, and despair transcended the religious issue: "While the so-called religious issue is necessarily and properly the chief topic here tonight, I want to emphasize from the outset that I believe that we have far more critical issues in the 1960 election. . . . The real issues . . . are not religious issues—for war and hunger and ignorance and despair know no religious issue."[8]

Kennedy's acknowledgement that the "religious issue" was "necessarily and properly the chief topic" was his formal recognition of its importance to his immediate listeners. In terming the issue "so-called," Kennedy indicated his personal view that the matter was much less central and germane to the body politic and that citizens must define and order issues and distinguish between the essential and the nonessential. His evaluation suggests a subtle rhetorical question: If a people could not grapple successfully with religious differences, however important they were, could they hope to cope with the social issues affecting the collective body politic? The tensed polarities, "chief" versus "so-called," imply that the inability to see clearly is much like blind faith and neither is a redeeming virtue for political and religious leaders or citizens.

Kennedy's introduction centered on the immediate issue and audience. But the Reverend Mr. Herbert Menza, vice-president and program chairman of the Greater Houston Ministerial Association and introducer of Kennedy to the congregation, sought in his remarks to provide a historical orientation to the topic and to establish a climate and context for Kennedy's address. "The program," he said, "had been motivated by the religious issues in the campaign—issues that are not modern." Noting that "extremists on both sides" have "tended to dominate the debate," the Reverend Mr. Menza offered a different approach: "The problem is to place it in perspective and to determine where the candidate stands in relation to that perspective."[9]

Mr. Menza's recognition of "issues that are not modern" not only anticipated some of Kennedy's specific historical allusions, but also recalls that the matter of church-state relationships has roots in American history and literature, especially in the election day sermons preached in the colonies and particularly those in Massachusetts where the tradition began in 1634 and continued until 1884. Preached by ministers chosen by civil authorities, election day sermons were treatises on the nature of the governor and the governed and of the relationship of church and state; they were opportunities "to announce the means of keeping the New England way pure and functional,"[10] and they "helped to shape the traditions of the Inaugural, Fourth of July orations, and State of the Union messages."[11] Although Kennedy's immediate concern is political, his basic theme is similar to those found in many election day sermons. In Houston, however, there was an ironic reversal of the secular and ecclesiastical roles.

Kennedy's appearance before the Houston Ministerial Association was the result of circumstances over which he had no control. In July, 1960, both Kennedy and Nixon received invitations to appear.[12] Nixon accepted but a later conflict in scheduling forced him to cancel. Kennedy did not respond immediately to the invitation; he and his advisors believed that the religious issue should be handled frankly, but to prevent backlash they planned to develop it late in the campaign.

However, events moved too rapidly. On September 7, 1960, the National Conference of Citizens for Religious Freedom, a group of 150 ministers and laymen led by the Reverend Dr. Norman Vincent Peale of New York and the Reverend Dr. Harold John Ockenga of Boston, met in Washington. The conference, called "The Peale Group" after its nationally known chairman, asserted that a Catholic President would be influenced by his church: "It is inconceivable that a Roman Catholic President would not be under extreme pressure by the hierarchy of his church to accede to its policies with respect to foreign relations in matters, including representation to the Vatican."[13] The conference further concluded that the religious issue was not created by the candidates. The "nature of the Roman Catholic Church" created it: "Finally that there is the 'religious issue' in the present political campaign is not the fault of any candidate. It is created by the nature of the Roman Catholic Church which is, in a very real sense, both a church and a temporal state."[14]

Because the "prestige of the Reverend Norman Vincent Peale had . . . given respectable leadership to ancient fear and prejudice,"[15] Kennedy decided with "considerable reluctance"[16] to accept the invitation extended by the Houston Ministerial Association. If we take him at his word, his reluctance is not easily explained. On August 25, 1960, Kennedy had received a report from the Simulatics Corporation that on the religious issue "the net worst has been done."[17] He would "not lose further from forthright and persistent attention to the religious issue, and could gain."[18] Perhaps Kennedy's hesitation resulted from his feeling that "The Peale Group" had forced him to meet the issue earlier than he had planned. Ironically, had Kennedy been able to postpone a major statement about his religion and his candidacy, the timing would have placed his statement nearer to election day, 1960, a semiceremonial day, and would have linked it even more directly to the traditional and archetypal colonial election day sermon.

In accepting the invitation Kennedy also accepted a format proposed by the Reverend Menza. Kennedy would speak to the religious issue and then answer questions put by the assembled ministers.[19] The immediate audience was considerably enlarged when it was announced that twenty Texas television stations would carry the speech live.

Thus, shortly before 9:00 P.M. on the evening of September 12, 1960, John F. Kennedy seated himself between the co-chairmen of the occasion and awaited the introduction that would present him to an audience of nearly 1,000 ministers, the majority of whom were both politically and theologically opposed to him The Reverend Mr. George Beck, a co-chairman, welcomed the audience and admonished "restraint, respect, and good conduct."[20] When asked why such an admonition was necessary, he responded briskly, "I was just afraid."[21] The co-chairmen also observed Kennedy's tensions. The candidate said little to them and "was very, very nervous."[22] Listeners, too, seemed on edge. The Reverend John W. Turnbull was present and offered explanations for the "peculiar atmosphere" of the evening:

> The peculiar atmosphere of the gathering was probably due in much larger part to the ambivalence and embarrassment that every sensitive Protestant minister present must have felt somewhere in his being. Several times Senator Kennedy expressed his gratitude for the opportunity to discuss his convictions with us, and his gratitude gave every evidence of being genuine. But most of us were not so sure that we ought to be grateful for the occasion. Too many uncomfortable thoughts assailed us. The meeting had all the earmarks of an inquisition, and we always thought we were against inquisitions.[23]

Whatever the motivations, the "existential vibration of consciousness" that Mailer believed would engage the nation if Kennedy became President seems to have been present in Houston. "Plainly hostile ground," thought *Time*.[24] A "sullen crowd"[25] of "glaring ministers,"[26] others observed. Kennedy was aware of the tensions. Before he went to meet his audience, he asked his press secretary, Pierre Salinger, "What's the mood of the ministers?" Salinger replied, "They're tired of being called bigots."[27]

Kennedy's occasional irritation at the need to explain his Catholicism and the ministers' frustrations at the charges of bigotry are but two specific reflections of the generalized feelings of large numbers of citizens during the presidential campaign of 1960. After his appearance in Houston, Kennedy himself "seemed much surer of the course the campaign would take,"[28] and within a few days of his address the Reverend Mr. Peale resigned from the National Conference of Citizens for Religious Freedom. Further, except for extremist groups, the religious question was no longer a respectable public issue. There was, then, a shift in the saliency of the issue, although as Gallup indicated the shift could not be correlated with the way the electorate would actually vote.

All participants in the rhetorical situation at Houston placed themselves in jeopardy. Kennedy, obviously, had to show that his Catholicism would not prevent him from ministering to the secular state and that his religion should not be a deterrent to initiation into the highest office of the nation. The audience, publicly assembled, risked a test of their long-standing requirements for initiation. To the extent that Kennedy succeeded, he would not only improve his chances of winning the office, but he would also provide to some listeners a certain measure of comfort and of shared ideation. For the nation, a productive climax to the archetypal situation of initiation would be an awakening, awareness, and increased perception by all citizens of the meaning of the fundamentals of American government. Thus one possible outcome of jeopardy might be the purification of secular ideals and a reordering of the criteria for initiation. The self-transcendent character of the symbolic meaning of the presidency and the government would no longer be distorted.

Although Kennedy's Houston address is political, it has marks of a Protestant sermon adapted to his needs. Kennedy's text is the oath of the presidency, but he does not announce it until he is ready to conclude, a major reversal of standard sermon form, but a necessary one because it was the text that was intensely contended. Because Kennedy could not explicate an unannounced text, he offers definitions of himself and his religion and the relationship of both to the presidency. All of his early ordering and sorting of details is directly related to his text and will ultimately be joined to it. Kennedy offers a two-part doctrine and an application of doctrine to the secular state. Woven into this structure are other resources known to the immediate audience. The relationship between Kennedy's address and a formal sermon is not a point-to-point correspondence. However, the similarities are sufficient and clear enough to be provocative to the Protestant audience largely opposed to the secular aspirations of the Catholic speaker.

Although Kennedy told his Houston audience that he did "not intend to apologize" for his religious and political views, it is clear that he understood well the need to separate the primary from the secondary facts of his candidacy. To order a proper relationship and a hierarchy of values, he explicates. "I am not," he stated, "the Catholic candidate for President. I am the Democratic Party's candidate for President who happens to be a Catholic." The verb, "happens," suggesting circumstance and appearing in a dependent clause, orders a relationship. An earlier statement also sorts and orders private and public relationships: "So it is apparently necessary for me to state once again—not what kind of Church I believe in, for that should be important only to me, but what kind of America I believe in." Kennedy happened to be a Catholic speaking to a finite group of ministers who similarly happened to be Protestants. The assembled congregation became a vessel for the feelings of the larger national audience about church-state relationships. Kennedy's explication asks if the secondary circumstantial facts cannot be set aside in the communal effort to find relationships nearer to the fundamental ideals of American government.

Kennedy's effort to make both himself and his position consistent with secular ideals is supported by two major parts of his address: his doctrine of the secular state and his application of doctrine to the practical affairs of the secular citizenry. His basic design, then, is a common ritualistic form well-known to Protestant ministers who preach Sunday sermons and to parishioners who attend them. The application to secular issues of a structure heard each Sunday by church-going Protestants is a rhetorical choice for exorcising doubts about the purity of Kennedy's vision of what the nation should be. To the extent that Kennedy enters into a union with form, he reflects commitment. To the extent that the form of a sermon invites, and even immerses, the worshipper into the text, the form becomes a fundamental dynamic in the search for meaning and understanding. The truth of anything is known only so far as we enter into union with it.

If doctrine and application of doctrine is familiar as structure, Kennedy strengthened the form by additional resources known to listeners, especially the ministerial audience. Creeds are familiar to church-goers and the immediate audience knew the Athanasian and Nicene Creeds, both of which are oral ecumenical creeds[29] and therefore not analytic but formulaic. Although the Athanasian Creed has "a remarkable grandeur and sublimity,"[30] its liturgical use "has been largely confined to the Roman and Anglican communions,"[31] partially because it contains somber and dogmatic damnatory clauses that stress the "fierce repudiation of deviationist theology."[32] It proclaims the binding necessity of unwavering belief in the Catholic faith in its entirety to achieve eternal salvation, and because such a doctrine is too narrow for the modern mind, the creed is "used in the West only on occasions."[33] The concluding section of the creed illustrates well its severe, damnatory tone: "This is the Catholic Faith: which except a man believe faithfully (truly and firmly), he cannot be saved."[34] Had Kennedy's address reflected the thought and tone of the Athanasian Creed, it is probable that the worst fears of the Houston ministry would have been confirmed.

A reading of Kennedy's Houston address reveals the thought, diction, and tone of the Nicene, not the Athanasian, Creed. Despite some differences in interpretation of fundamental concepts, the major Christian faiths subscribe to the Nicene Creed. Because objections to Kennedy's initiation into the office of presidency often centered on the degree to which he was an ecumenical candidate, it remains now to observe the doctrine-application structure of a sermon and selected features of the Nicene Creed interacting within Kennedy's address. The interaction contributes to the ordering of Kennedy's hierarchy of secular values; the ordering must be consistent with that of his listeners if his initiation is to become possible.

Kennedy's doctrine is enunciated in two inextricably interrelated parts. The first division of the doctrine is addressed to the metaphysical ends of the secular state: "what kind of America I believe in." The ethos of the secular state is posited: 'I believe in an America where the separation of church and state is absolute. . . ." "I believe in an America that is officially neither Catholic, Protestant nor Jewish. . . ." "I believe in an America where religious intolerance will someday end. . . ."

The second division of Kennedy's doctrine centers on means, on the leadership of the secular state; the means derive from and are consistent with the ends: "I believe in a President whose views on religion are his own private affair. . . ." "I would not look with favor upon a President working to subvert the First Amendment's guarantees of religious liberty. . . ." "I want a Chief Executive whose public acts are responsible to all and obligated to none. . . ."

Listeners familiar with the Nicene Creed would find suggestive similarities in Kennedy's doctrine. Viewed this way, Kennedy's statements are congenial to and congruent with the larger value system of the immediate audience. For example, the Nicene Creed begins: "I believe in one God the Father Almighty, Maker of heaven and earth, And of all things visible and invisible."[35] Unlike the Athanasian Creed, the Nicene is inclusive, not exclusive; it promotes oneness, not divisiveness. In the secular state, Kennedy insists that "no public official . . . requests or accepts instructions" from any "ecclesiastical source," mentioning specifically the Pope and the National Council of Churches. Speaking of himself, he states: "I do not speak for my church on public matters—and the church does not speak for me."

The creed continues: "And in one Lord Jesus Christ . . ." who "was crucified also for us under Pontius Pilate. . . ." A central concern of Kennedy's doctrine and application is the unity of the secular state; the well-being of citizens could not be realized in an acrimonious climate. Kennedy's concern is illuminated at least mildly with the overtones of crucifixion: "This year it may be a Catholic against whom the finger of suspicion is pointed. . . .

Today, I may be the victim—but tomorrow it may be you—until the whole fabric of our harmonious society is ripped apart at a time of great national peril." Speaking to the future, he hoped for a community where "Catholics, Protestants and Jews, both the lay and the pastoral level, will refrain from those attitudes of disdain and division which have so often marred their works in the past."

The creed concludes: "And I believe in the Holy Ghost, The Lord, and Giver of Life, Who proceedeth from the Father and the Son; Who with the Father and the Son together is worshipped and glorified." If the teachings and the spirit of the Father and the Son are heeded, then, suggests Kennedy, "religious intolerance will someday end" and the American ideal of brotherhood" will come to pass. Despite the many partitions in the secular state, it can become one in substance.

The suggestive similarities between Kennedy's doctrine and the Nicene Creed are only one sign that his appearance before the Houston Ministerial Association was a test of *his* secular orthodoxy. Another sign is the dominance of the first person singular "I." The absence in this address of the third person plural "we," the common sign of political and communal identification, is a clear indicator of the divisiveness between the speaker and his audience. Kennedy could not enter into discursive argument; he had to affirm his resolve. And his "I" statements had to be interpreted as public and communal statements, not as private or personal remarks. In short, his "I" professions must enter him into the state's witness. When a Christian recites the Nicene Creed he does not announce private opinions or speak merely as an individual. He joins with the "People of God, adding his voice to the Church's unending praise of him who brought them out of bondage."[36] Kennedy's "I believe, I believe, I believe" statements function to join him with the people and enter him into the prevailing ethos of the secular state. Kennedy's personal statements assert and solicit acceptance. Not until he is accepted and initiation consummated is "we" warranted.

Having established his doctrine, Kennedy could have immediately developed the application of the doctrine to the secular state. But he delayed the application and introduced a compact and unembellished aside, centering on his and his brother Joe's military service during World War II. Though they were Catholics, their loyalty was not then questioned any more than was the loyalty "for which our forefathers did die" in the national effort to secure the freedoms cherished by citizens. These examples are not descriptions of the manifest evils of intolerance. Rather they illustrate that in the past men of different religious affiliations had united to confront dangers to the secular state. Citing the absence of religious tests in the military history of the nation, Kennedy closed the aside with an adroit illustration from the history of Texas, referring to "the shrine I visited today—the Alamo," and reciting a litany of heroes and commoners who died, Bowie, Crockett, Fuentes, McCafferty, Bailey, Bedillio, and Carey. Because "there was no religious test there" no one knew "whether they were Catholics or not." But several Irish and Spanish surnames suggest that some might well have been.[37] Kennedy's choice of "shrine" suggests that he felt at one with the Texans. He apparently did not think that the connotations of the noun would apply to him and his religion.

The personal aside, spatially a "setting aside" consistent with early efforts to sort and order relationships, raises a question of means and ends, for in the examples the religious emotion is strongly appealed to in the guise of opposition to it. The appeal and the moral implications of it are muted by the personal context and the spatial relationship in which they are embedded. But the aside functions to underscore and to turn a disadvantage into an asset. Kennedy wisely placed in an aside this direct appeal which runs counter to his doctrine and application.

Kennedy, the "I," was central to the doctrine of the address. However, statements of belief can easily be interpreted as professions of faith rather than as confessions of faith. Kennedy's application of doctrine functions to support the doctrine as a confession. Although a doctrine can stand independent of an application, the circumstances of the rhetorical environment in Houston forced the application in which are manifested signs of Kennedy's constancy to the secular faith. "I ask you tonight . . . to judge me on the basis of fourteen years in the Congress" introduces the application. He refers to political decisions he made on the matter of an ambassador to the Vatican and on public support of parochial schools. He reaches abroad to consider the record of church-state relations in "such nations as France and Ireland," and he affirms that if elected he will decide such issues as "birth control, divorce, censorship, [and] gambling" according to the "national interest."

A public confession of faith, whether religious or secular, is a serious statement of intention, as Kennedy and his immediate and removed audiences knew. Although he did "not concede any conflict to be remotely possible," Kennedy, like other mortal men, recognized the perpetual struggle between the word and the deed and offered to "resign the office" if he could not resolve the tests he expected to experience. The offer extends the application too far. Because citizens expect a President-elect to serve his term, the offer is awkward and ought not to be taken seriously. However, because Kennedy has publicly stated his authoritative and binding doctrine which is intended to enter him into a union through initiation with his listeners, the offer suggests a commitment in depth. He will not violate the national interest in order to avoid violating his conscience.

The unusual circumstances of Kennedy's Houston address account for some of the notable differences between it and other political statements made during the campaign for the presidency. Other speeches often contain citations of literary and historical figures as well as biblical testimony.[38] Except for one specific instance to be noted shortly, the Houston address lacks direct testimony. Kennedy mentions, but does not quote, the Constitution, the Bill of Rights, and the Virginia statute of religious freedom. He was wise to avoid direct testimony which might cause an audience trained and practiced in explication to observe closely the meanings he gave to the language. From a contest in proper translation, he had little to gain. The observation applies most especially to biblical quotations. If he had chosen to use such testimony, he would have had to choose the Douay translation of his church or some version that would seem like obvious catering to Protestant opinion. Perhaps he also avoided direct testimony because he anticipated some of the interrogators in the question period following the address. Three of the seven ministers who put questions cited documents and sought responses to the citations. One minister cited lengthy quotations from *The Catholic Encyclopedia*, the *Osservatore Romano*, and a statement by Pope John XXIII from the *St. Louis Review*.[39] In these instances Kennedy responded to the questions but refused to be drawn into discussions of the meanings of the texts.

Expansive and elaborate historical and literary testimony does not illuminate the doctrine or the application. Instead Kennedy chose to make short statements about specific situations. His balanced neither-nor statements established the doctrine as the universal. For example: "No Catholic prelate would tell the President (should he be a Catholic) how to act and no Protestant minister would tell his parishioners for whom to vote" refers to an ideal, even as it embodies and balances the hypothetical argument of some persons opposed to him against the actual practices of some Protestant churchmen, specifically "The Peale Group." Referring to public officials, Kennedy indicates that they should not request or accept "instructions" from "the Pope" or "the National Council of Churches." Further, the office of the President must not be "humbled by making it the instrument of any religious group, nor tarnished by arbitrarily withholding it, its occupancy, from the members of any religious group." If it is necessary to "condemn" transgressions from doctrine, "condemn with equal fervor those nations which deny their Presidency to Protestants and those which deny it to Catholics." Doctrine transcends particulars. The repetitive pattern of counter-balanced neither-nor statements applies with equal force to all citizens of the secular state. All can agree that the doctrine of the secular state should be pure. But impurities in the application are not the fault of any group in the community.

The absence of literary and historical testimony gives the address the spare, lean, and understated quality of grace under pressure. Its absence also centers attention upon the personal statements of the "I" and leaves the single instance of testimony without competition, thereby intensifying its importance. Preparing to conclude his application and the address, Kennedy indicated that if he won the election he would fulfill "the oath of the Presidency" which was "practically identical," as even the ecumenical Athanasian and Nicene Creeds are ultimately practically identical, with the oath that "I have taken for fourteen years in the Congress." Kennedy's doctrine and application justified the choice of the presidential oath as his text and as his climax. Although the oath serves as the text for his address, precisely because it was so bitterly contended, he wisely delayed his statement of it. However in citing the oath, he risked being considered profane and blasphemous by listeners unsympathetic to him because of his religion. The act would be one of lese majesty. Yet in the presence of those who claimed the secular presidential oath unto themselves, he did what some felt he could not do or ought not be allowed to do. Rather than concluding by simply stating that his doctrine and application made him worthy of initiation into the office, Kennedy went further. He spoke the oath and the sounds of oaths tend to socialize. Kennedy could not have done more to blunt the sting of the WASP and to show that insofar as the religious issue was concerned, he was capable of ministering to the secular state.

His doctrine and application concluded, Kennedy was prepared to thrust himself into a higher order of secular relationships. The "I" and the oath become one. He could "without reservation . . . quote" the oath; and "quote" is the apt verb because until elected he could not confess to the oath. I "solemnly swear that I will faithfully execute the Office of President of the United States and will to the best of my ability preserve, protect and defend the Constitution, so help me God." The secular oath, Kennedy's text, supported by the formal structure of a sermon and sustained and intensified by a subdued analogical relationship with elements of the Nicene Creed, is the chief purificatory language in the address. Purification is a prerequisite to initiation and initiation is a prerequisite to a test of the fundamental ideals of the secular doctrine through John F. Kennedy, Catholic, Democrat, citizen, President.

Kennedy obviously went to Houston, Texas, on September 12, 1960, to seek political support for his candidacy for the presidency. Yet his appearance had larger meanings that provoked the shivers Mailer anticipated only if Kennedy were elected. Kennedy openly tested the reality of the religious base and strain in American democracy by affirming that his doctrine and application were consistent with the criteria for initiation. His subsequent election to the presidency in November, 1960, was a reaffirmation and, as with the best reaffirmations, a freshening, and an enlarging and extending of the meaning of a relationship. In this case the relationship was of church and state, of the life of an individual in relation to church, to state, and to others.

1. Norman Mailer, *The Presidential Papers* (New York: Berkeley Publishing, 1970), p. 49.

2. *New York Herald Tribune*, October 30, 1960, p. 15.

3. William G. Carleton, "Kennedy in History: An Early Appraisal," *The Antioch Review*, 24 (Fall 1964), 283.

4. Lawrence H. Fuchs, *John F. Kennedy and American Catholicism* (New York: Meredith, 1967), p. 179.

5. Cited in Theodore H. White, *The Making of the President 1960* (New York: Atheneum, 1969), p. 260.

6. The literature is extensive and the issue is probed from numerous points of view. Some materials are: "T. R. B. from Washington," *The New Republic*, September 19, 1960, p. 2; Douglass Cater, "The Protestant Issue," *The Reporter*, October 13, 1960, pp. 30–32; "Campaign: Religion Becomes an Open Issue," *U.S. News and World Report*, September 12, 1960, p. 94; Fletcher Knebel, "Democratic Forecast: A Catholic in 1960," *Look*, March 3, 1959; pp. 13–17; Elmo Roper, "The Myth of the Catholic Vote," *Saturday Review*, October 31, 1959, p. 22; John Wicklin, "Protestant and Catholic Votes Found to Offset Each Other in Kennedy's Victory," *New York Times*, November 11, 1960, p. 2.

7. See the full text of a speech, "I Am Not the Catholic Candidate for President," delivered to the American Society of Newspaper Editors, April 21, 1960, in Washington, D.C., in *U.S. News and World Report*, May 2, 1960, pp. 90–92. Also see James L. Golden, "John F. Kennedy and the 'Ghosts,' " *Quarterly Journal of Speech*, 52 (December, 1966), 351.

8. White, *Making of the President*, pp. 391–393, contains the text of the address used in this analysis. Future citations of Kennedy's remarks can be found in White and will not be footnoted. The John F. Kennedy Library in Waltham, Massachusetts, has both a reading copy of the address and an audiotape of the address as delivered.

9. The complete text of the Reverend Mr. Menza's statement appears in Deane Alwyn Kemper, "John F. Kennedy before the Greater Houston Ministerial Association, September 12, 1960: The Religious Issue," Ph.D. dissertation, Michigan State University, 1969, p. 40. Kemper's useful study includes interviews with the leaders of the Houston Ministerial Association and other participants in the events leading to Kennedy's appearance in Houston.

10. A. W. Plumstead, ed., *The Wall and the Garden: Selected Massachusetts Election Sermons, 1670–1775* (Minneapolis: University of Minnesota Press, 1968), p. 21.

11. *Ibid.*, p. 3.

12. Kemper, "John F. Kennedy," p. 13.

13. *New York Times*, September 8, 1960, p. 25. For a Kennedy analysis of these statements see Theodore C. Sorensen, *Kennedy* (New York: Harper and Row, 1965), p. 189.

14. *Ibid.*

15. White, *Making of the President*, p. 259.

16. Sorensen, *Kennedy*, p. 189.

17. Thomas B. Morgan, "The People Machine," *Harper's*, January, 1961, p. 54.

18. *Ibid.* Also see Ithiel de Sola Pool, Robert P. Abelson, and Samuel L. Popkin, *Candidates, Issues, and Strategies: A Computer Simulation of the 1960 and 1964 Presidential Elections* (Cambridge, Mass: M.I.T. Press, 1964), pp. 20–21.

19. Kemper, "John F. Kennedy," p. 30.

20. *Ibid.*, p. 39.

21. *Ibid.*

22. *Ibid.*

23. John W. Turnbull, "The Clergy Faces Mr. Kennedy," *The Reporter*, October 13, 1960, p. 33.

24. *Time*, September 26, 1960, p. 21.

25. White, *Making of the President*, p. 262.

26. Sorensen, *Kennedy*, p. 190.

27. *Time*, September 26, 1960, p. 21.

28. Evelyn Lincoln, *My Twelve Years with John F. Kennedy* (New York: D. McKay, 1965), p. 176.

29. B. A. Gerrish, ed., *The Faith of Christendom* (Cleveland, Ohio: World Publishing, 1963), p. 61.

30. Charles A. Briggs, *The Fundamental Christian Faith* (New York: Scribner, 1913), p. 285.

31. J. N. D. Kelly, *The Athanasian Creed* (New York: Harper and Row, 1964), p. 49.

32. *Ibid.*, p. 71.

33. Briggs, *Fundamental Christian Faith*, p. 285.

34. Philip Schaff, *The Creeds of Christendom* (New York: Harper, 1919), II, 70.

35. All citations from the Nicene Creed are taken from *The Book of Common Prayer* of the Protestant Episcopal church.

36. Gerrish, *Faith of Christendom*, p. 19.

37. Sorensen, *Kennedy*, p. 189, indicates that Kennedy asked him to find out how many Catholics fought and died at the Alamo. Sorensen placed a call to an aide in Washington and set him to the task. Some possible Irish-American names were secured but the religious affiliations were unknown.

38. See Donald C. Bryant, "Analysis of the Inaugural," in Donald C. Bryant and Karl R. Wallace, *Fundamentals of Public Speaking* (New York: Appleton-Century-Crofts, 1969), pp. 425–437.

39. "Remarks of Senator John F. Kennedy, Question and Answer Period, Ministerial Association of Greater Houston." Transcript released by the Democratic National Committee, Washington, D.C., September 13, 1960.

The Search for the 1972 Democratic Nomination: A Metaphorical Perspective

JANE BLANKENSHIP

"Naming," Kenneth Burke argues, is an "interpretive act" and thus a guide to act in one way or another toward the thing named.[1] This is so in part because of the "magical decree" which is "implicit in all language."[2] "If you size up a situation in the name of regimentation," as Burke points out, "you *decree* it an essence other than if you size it up in the name of planned economy."[3] Thus the "command" that one act one way rather than another is "*implicit* in the name."[4]

For Burke, words are "acts upon a scene" which in part *arise from* that scene and which in turn *shape* that scene.[5] In many respects the presidential election scene in 1972 was no different from any other. There were sleeper issues and gut issues, some of which were defused while others never caught fire, some of which were scrapped and on which some candidates waffled, white-washed, and soft-pedaled.

Candidates were still drumming up support, beating the daylights out of opponents, swallowing bitter pills, making pilgrimages, putting up straws in the wind, leaving doors open, creating sparks, sending up trial balloons, swinging into high gear, wooing the voters, tossing hats into the ring, and jumping on bandwagons.

The press continued to fuel speculation, bombard the candidates with questions, and claim to be made whipping boys.

Audiences still flocked to hear candidates, voted in beauty contests, gave candidates enough money to be called fat cats, or only enough to be called skinny cats. They observed meteoric declines, long shots, lame ducks, and changes of heart.

Others have provided a fuller political lexicon of past elections, much of which is clearly in use today.[6] This essay examines the metaphors used about and by the candidates in the print media for the democratic presidential nomination from January 1, 1971, to August 5, 1972. The analysis is based primarily on eight daily newspapers and four weeklies.[7] The metaphors, grouped in twelve categories, were selected because they were, in a loose quantitative sense, the most pervasive. Category one reflects the kinds of metaphors used the most times; category twelve, the least.[8]

These twelve categories of metaphors provide a set of "common topics" used by reporters to describe the 1972 nomination process. The examples noted under each category illustrate the "special topics" which varied with the candidate, reporter, situation, or some other element in the search for the nomination.

By examining the way the press talked about a significant part of the political process, the selection of a presidential nominee, we may be reminded that while we are using language, it is using us. Thus the way we talk *about* a political campaign may, in the end, be not merely descriptive but "prescriptive" as well.[9]

General Violence

Politics "is a brass-knuckles business," James Reston pointedly reminded us in 1972. By far the largest number of verbal and nominal metaphors could be placed under the category of general violence, even when those specifically referring to war and contact sports are excluded.[10]

The violence took many forms. Candidates "assaulted" and were assaulted, "attacked" and were attacked, "tussled," "flayed," "slapped," "jostled" each other. They "needled" and tried to "nail" each other.

By early 1971, McGovern had "already taken a few swipes at front runner Muskie. . . ." He "hit" hard at the POW issue, "jabbed" at Humphrey and Muskie on their vote to cut N.A.T.O., and offered an economic policy that would "wallop the wealthy." One "top union official" complained of McGovern campaigners: "They preach nonviolence . . . but the first chance they get they poke you in the snoot."

The candidates hammered away at each other or at the issues. Wallace "in his neo-populist style hammered away at busing." Muskie's rivals "hammered away" at his absence from a meeting of the Manchester, New Hampshire, Democratic committee. In nationally televised debates with McGovern, reviewers saw "Humphrey hammering away at . . . the issues of jobs and national security. . . ."

Everyone "blasted" everyone else. Muskie "blasted" Wallace for "practicing 'the politics of exclusion.'" A Humphrey aide forecast that Nixon would "blow" McGovern "right out of the water." And, David Broder pointed out "The Democrats . . . could not bear to wait for Miami Beach to blow their convention and their party sky-high."

The candidates cut and got cut. McCarthy "knifed into the Democratic leadership that fought him in 1968. . . ." The AFL-CIO treasurer-secretary, "privately warned that labor would 'cut Muskie to ribbons.' . . ." Humphrey accused McGovern of "cutting into the very fiber and muscle of our defense establishment. . . ."

The *effects* of such violence were clear. The 1972 campaign was a "bloody" and "suicidal" campaign. By mid-1971 many old guard Democrats "made clear they [preferred] Muskie. But after being bloodied by the party's left so often, they doubt[ed] their ability to influence [the] wild-and-wooly [New York] Democratic primary." So they worked to "prevent another blood-bath. . . ."

Just before the primaries started we were down "to the candidates whose strategy [was] either to prove themselves in the early primaries or to stand aside while the others bleed themselves in state after state. . . ." "The sudden collapse of the Muskie bandwagon," according to Evans and Novak, threatened "uncontrolled bloodletting. . . ."

Some Democrats became increasingly concerned over the possibility of "Convention Floor Blood." The Democrats, William S. White observed, "don't at all mind coming over the tube as hand-to-hand combatants, in living color." He predicted that the G.O.P. convention would be "pretty weak tea as against the gladiatorial entertainments offered by the Democrats."

With the California credentials decision the "explosion" some "feared and predicted, was triggered prematurely . . . at the Sheraton-Park Hotel, and they were . . . clearing up the blood and debris from Capitol Hill to California. . . ." After the convention there was some relief that it had taken place "without the predicted spilling of rivers of blood across millions of color TV screens. There was blood enough, but well short of the massive public carnage many had foreseen."

Two candidates used particularly violent language. George Wallace promised: "I'm Gonna Shake Their Eyeteeth Out." He talked about "sending a few shock waves" by winning some primaries. To the question "How do you think you'll be treated in Miami?," he replied: "I might get to Miami Beach and they throw me through the rooftop."

John Lindsay's language was also especially violent. When Governor Rockefeller "expressed approval of the sanitation men's terms," Lindsay "accused him of giving in to 'extortionist demands.' " He bitterly complained that his "community of New York and every community is ravaged by inflation. . . ." He said his "city was 'raped' by the state legislature in the annual budget battle. . . ."

Lindsay also was *perceived* in violent terms. Some predicted that he would "run like gangbusters" in the urban and big delegate states and that his appearance on the primary scene would send "tremors through the camp of every presidential hopeful." His encounters were described violently. Lindsay and Rockefeller were seen "stabbing at each other . . . with the vindictiveness of back-alley brawlers." At a Queens, New York, $50-a-plate dinner, Kennedy reportedly "wielded his political mace and ordered Lindsay disinvited."

Muskie, on the other hand, was often described as one who "conspicuously lacks the power to hurt, the muscle to assert against competitors." "Some politicians have an instinct for the jugular," explained one delegate, "but Muskie has an instinct for the capillaries."

Almost everybody wanted to "get back" at somebody or something. Shirley Chisholm wanted to "punch history in the face." An Ohio machinist supported McGovern because "he wants to kick them in the tail, too." A Philadelphia precinct worker explained: "People really don't like Wallace, but they want to give the Establishment a kick in the pants."

To avoid "civil war" and *fratricidal* violence, a variety of tactics were dreamed up but by April, 1972, "the Democratic fratricide [increased] in intensity and the bodies of the slain [piled] higher."

Much was made of the Democrats' "deathwish." By May, James Reston saw the Democrats "in a suicidal mood: broke, divided and . . . getting a little nasty. . . ." Wallace's campaign manager saw the platform adopted in Miami Beach as a "suicide note for November." Despite these dire predictions, Arthur Krock pointed to a "lesson" of history: "The Democratic Party is teetering again on that high, well-known window ledge, threatening to commit suicide. This posture is a cherished tradition of the oldest national political organization in the United States, and sometimes it has jumped as advertised. . . . The lesson of political history . . . is that it can quadrennially jump to apparent death in the summer and emerge miraculously resurrected in the Fall."

In 1972, the candidates did violence to each other and to the issues. The *kinds* of violence were varied and the violence was pervasive. The violent were perceived affirmatively, those candidates who "lacked the power to hurt," negatively. The general public and convention delegates alike identified mainly with those who wanted to kick some generalized "them" in the tail.

Warfare

The primaries were fought on a variety of "battlegrounds." Some claimed that the "real" battleground was the suburbs, but several famous battlefields were recalled as well. James Perry of the *Observer* wrote in June, 1971: "I do suspect that the Wallace movement crested in 1968, much as the Confederacy crested at Cemetery Ridge. It is worth remembering, though, that there was a lot of bloody business after Gettysburg." As TV zoomed in for a "beachhead" at Miami, Walter Cronkhite likened working the convention to a famous World War II battle: " 'We're not going to be able to get the guns on shore,' the general said before landing in North Africa. . . . 'We're going to have to take the Casbah with cold steel.' "

Not all the warriors used the same tactics. Harold Hughes, for a brief time a contender himself, said that Muskie was "more a conciliator and compromiser than a charge-of-the-light-brigade type. . . ." John Lindsay joined the Democratic party because he was unwilling to undertake "a 'kamikaze mission' . . ." in the increasingly conservative Republican party. Gary Hart, McGovern's campaign manager, believed Mayor Richard Daley would help against Nixon because "Daley's not a bomber. . . ."

All the generals had their troops. Reminded that as a declared candidate she would automatically be placed on the ballot in some states, Chisholm said, "I might shoot my foot soldiers into some of these states. . . ." Among McGovern's assets were "the kids" who were "his shock troops, his envelope-stuffers. . . ."

The press talked of battalions, phalanxes, and juggernauts. Describing a "grassroot's fair" for McGovern, the *Post* included in supporters "about two battalions of tiny tots. . . ." Humphrey had a "phalanx" of labor leaders "ready to do battle. . . ." However, there was talk that Humphrey would be an early casualty of "the Muskie 'juggernaut.' "

Blitzes and bombardments proved to be handy tools of war. In Ohio, McGovern waged a "massive, last-minute, radio-television blitz. . . ." McGovern's "call to share the wealth" proved to be a "soft bombshell." One shot in the "barrage" of Humphrey accusations plainly "hit" McGovern. For, according to Joseph Kraft: "The McGovern program is way out and not only on welfare."

Many of the candidates foresaw a long battle, "from the late spring primaries to a battle on the floor" of the Democratic National Convention. In *chronology* the war drama went like this: As early as July, 1971, Mayor Sam Yorty directed "the heavy artillery in his rhetoric" at Muskie and, at the same time, conducted "guerrilla warfare on Senator Henry Jackson. . . ." A "top aide" in the Muskie camp voiced public concern "that individual candidates from either wing might 'one-shot us' fatally in the early primaries. . . ." In Arizona, Evans and Novak predicted that Muskie's strength would be thinly spread while his opponents would concentrate in small areas and " 'bullet-vote' for the delegate-candidates pledged to them." Robert Haldeman's charge "that President Nixon's Vietnam critics are 'consciously' aiding the enemy set off a fusillade of counterfire from high ranking Democrats. . . ." By April, 1972, Jackson aimed "his guns directly at McGovern" in a "frontal assault on a prime plank in McGovern's candidacy."

In Virginia, McGovern backers "captured" a big bloc of delegates from Fairfax County. They set up a Texas "ambush" and went on a "foray" to the governor's conference in Houston.

Before and at Miami Beach the usual "male dominated convention [came] under fire. . . ." Most of those attending were at their first political convention and stayed, like good troops, pretty much under control. But by Thursday of the convention they finally "broke loose" like a "boot-camp Marine on 'his first weekend pass.' " There were, of course, after-the-convention letdowns, aptly described by one reporter as "the Glums of August."

The "beaten generals" who had tried to stop McGovern appeared, briefly at least, to be "politically shell-shocked." Tom Braden accurately predicted that many who lost would "turn out . . . to be good soldiers." There was even a kind of "sentimental balm" for some of the losers. As Holmes Alexander pointed out: "Two fallen warriors, George Wallace and Hubert Humphrey, are more dear to the hearts of their countrymen than when they were riding high."

Much of the violence in 1972 was patently warlike. The candidate-generals marshaled their troops in concerted attacks not only on each other but on their onlooker-constituents as well. Few, for example, were spared the propaganda barrages of the electronic media or direct mail.

Sports/Games

Picking presidential nominees, observed Jack Waugh, "is one of the great American spectator sports." The Democrats, for example, engaged in a wide variety of games: "tinker toys," "a painful game of musical chairs," "a jigsaw puzzle," "marbles," and "darts." But mostly they went to the horse races, played football, boxed, played baseball and cards, and participated in track events. They also "gambled" a lot: at dice, roulette, high stakes poker, and craps.

In June, 1971, a *Monitor* survey suggested "the real possibility of a Democratic 'horse race' before the final selection is made. . . ." A variety of name politicians endorsed Edmund Muskie's candidacy early, saying: "Fortunately for us, Muskie happens to be the best horse to ride in most states." After the Wisconsin primary, however, "Muskie's fourth-place showing . . . raised new doubts that the tiring Maine entry can go the distance."

When John Lindsay entered the race, the *Akron Beacon Journal* commented: "With the track already crowded with candidates, the reaction was 'who needs Linsay?' " Some called him the "fairest dark horse of them all" but others were more skeptical. One journalist punned prophetically: "John V. Lindsay has finally decided to change hearses in midstream."

The "stalking-horse" notion started early and hung on. Nicholas von Hoffman poked fun at its overuse: "McGovern is a stalking-horse for Kennedy and Fred Harris is a stalking-horse for McGovern, and Muskie is a

stalking-horse for Humphrey, who is probably a stalking-horse for Bayh. . . ."
With the "starters . . . at the Gate," journalists took a look at "how the
Winter book might rate candidates. . . ."

Second only to horse racing was football. Godfrey Sperling, for example,
foresaw the campaign for the Democratic nomination through the eyes of
President Nixon: "Muskie has the ball and is already approaching the goal
line. The Muskie forces have been moving forward steadily and, clearly, have
the momentum. Now comes the big test for the other team (McGovern,
Lindsay, Humphrey, Jackson, et al.). As Muskie gets closer to the goal will
they be able to hold—as did Stanford against Michigan and Miami against
Baltimore in key defensive stands that turned those recent ballgames
around?" The "game plan" proved to be easier to implement on paper than in
action and Ohio's Governor Gilligan grew upset with Muskie's campaign; he
complained: "He's in the position of a quarterback in football. If you can't
get a running game established, then, it's harder to pass, and the whole thing
comes apart."

Vice-President Agnew, himself fond of sports imagery, depicted Larry
O'Brien as testing candidates for "the quarter-back slot in a triple option
offense." Agnew continued: "George McGovern wanted to pitch out to a
trailing back—but couldn't find anyone trailing him. . . . George Wallace
found he had reported to the wrong team. Coach Larry O'Brien won't even
talk to him or show him the play book. Vance Hartke thought about using a
quarterback sneak. But unfortunately, Jack Anderson was out of town." On
another occasion, Agnew compared Hubert Humphrey to a quarterback who
"operates out of a 'moving pocket' in his policy statements on major issues."

If the game went badly enough Tom Braden speculated that Edward
Kennedy might be called off the bench:

> . . . the Democratic Party is not moving the ball. Quarterback Edmund
> Muskie is losing ground. McGovern, Lindsay, Jackson have not done as
> well as he. The crowd is yelling for Kennedy, who has been on the
> bench for two years with an injury once considered serious. The
> question is whether or not he is fit to play. . . . Perhaps that is the way
> it will end—with Kennedy brightly pointing out weaknesses from the
> sidelines, while somebody else tries to move the ball.
>
> But the political history of the last few weeks suggests that the time
> may come when the pressure is irresistible, when a party about to lose
> an election looks down its bench, and says, so to speak, "Injured or
> not, let's put in the first team."

The "first team" appeared to be necessary, because the Democrats "seemed
baffled by the broken-field running of the last three years [by the Nixon
administration and were] reduced to sputtering about used cars. . . ." The
Democrats, however, continued to ask: "would you buy a used car from this
man?"

Boxing also occupied the attention of many reporters. As early as New Hampshire, the contenders were described in "fighting" terms. For example, the candidates "like fighters aiming for points before the final bell in the last round [swung] at all kinds of targets. . . ." In Florida, a "third-spot finish for Muskie behind Wallace and Humphrey . . . wouldn't come close to a knock-out blow against Muskie." But it would raise this question: If "Ed Muskie can't deliver a knockout blow against Humphrey in Florida, can he take President Nixon in November?" Wisconsin was "round four" for George McGovern. His near tie in Ohio "was a body blow to Humphrey's claim of industrial support." In California, many journalists conceded that: "The 1972 presidential primaries are ending like the final round of an evenly matched prize-fight—two men, toe to toe, slugging it out." After California, McGovern climbed "away from the last of the prelims toward the title."

There was also time for baseball. The Wisconsin primary was like "the Fourth of July is to major league baseball—the first chance to reckon how the pennant race is shaping up." Later, at the convention, the Old Guard turned to baseball to describe their feelings. One commented, for example: "I feel like Warren Spahn must feel in Cleveland. Spahn must feel he can still pitch, and I do too, but nobody is calling me to do anything."

Wallace's first two major Michigan appearances were termed " 'double-header' triumphs. . . ." McCarthy sat "out in left field, threatening to enter the ballgame." And Ohioan Howard Metzenbaum apologized for endorsing McGovern at a Humphrey speaking engagement by saying: "I was off base and I'm prepared to admit it."

On the track, McGovern and Humphrey looked "like milers who are running close together at the midpoint of their race, with neither giving an indication of who will spurt to victory and who will falter in the stretch." All in all, the Democratic presidential primaries and caucuses seemed a puzzling decathlon: "Like the decathlon where one fellow may be better at the broad jump and another at discus-throwing, the variousness of the states gives every primary candidate at least a chance to display his talents best. But who would have thought that an all-rounder like Ed Muskie would have such trouble clearing so many hurdles?"

In explaining "Why I'm for Muskie," Harold Hughes observed: "The contest for the nomination and for the presidency is a distance run, not a 50-yard dash. . . . I am convinced that he has the staying power to maintain the pace." But by mid-April even "Boston marathoners" got weary: "Ed Muskie at this stage of the race is like one of those marathoners who torture-toed through Coolidge Corner yesterday. The grimace of pain and shortness of breath seemed just moments away from the dry heaves at Kenmore Square and whoever said running was fun?"

In addition to sports, some of the candidates also found time for cards.

Edmund Muskie's "image of Yankee integrity" was his "strong suit." "All I have is my intellect," Shirley Chisholm commented, "but that gives me some trump cards. . . ." George Wallace, the "wild card" in the primaries, found school busing to be *his* "trump card." George McGovern's "ace in the hole" was "the youth vote."

The Democrats also seemed preoccupied with gambling. Even in December, 1971, some were guessing that Muskie's toughest foe in California would probably be Hubert Humphrey, "still the favorite of the state's high-rolling contributors." Wallace was promised a "fair shake of the dice" at the convention. Humphrey likened Nixon's policy on spending money overseas to an "international crap game."

In March, Muskie said, as he autographed a sample ballot in New Hampshire, "Now that's a big lottery ticket." All along, journalists were claiming that: "One of the handicaps of the favorite . . . is that a lot of people put bets on him." In California the "stakes" were high and the game was "winner-take-all." At Democratic headquarters the "old hands . . . [hedged] their bets" on whether 50 percent of the delegates would, as the rules dictated, be women.

In 1972 the candidates engaged in a wide variety of sports and games, most of which were gladiatorial in nature. Spectators clearly outnumbered participants in the arena. Those who sat on the sidelines could view the gladiatorial fray with the full enjoyment of one who is both vicariously "bloodied" and yet left basically unscarred by the whole business. They both knew the "plays" and egged the candidates on; yet they were somewhat superior creatures who knew better than to *actually* play the game.

Natural Phenomena

"Voting tides," William Stringer suggested, "can be as unpredictable as was tropical storm Agnes." Muskie was perhaps most aware of the truth of Stringer's observation about the "ebb and flow of candidates." A Los Angeles reporter crisply put it: "I don't think Muskie can win anymore. . . . The tide is turned." When this became abundantly clear, the *Monitor* editorialized: "The tides of political fortune, always fickle, often work their meanest truth against those who deserve them least."

Announcements for a presidential try were described in terms of water. By October, 1971, Chisholm spoke of "testing the water." Some pled "openly with the Mayor [Lindsay] to jump feet first into the . . . Presidential pool." There were "oceans of speculation" about a Lindsay candidacy and some Muskie supporters also wanted an earlier announcement but Muskie still stopped "at the water's edge."

Floods, drownings, and sinkings were often predicted and often materialized. The *Observer* predicted that the media would "cover John Lindsay like he was the Johnstown Flood." Charles Snider, Wallace's campaign manager, believed that the Democratic platform "weighted the Party down with 100 tons of cement in ocean-deep water." But perhaps the most picturesque of such images involved, not the ocean, but a bay: "The nation's press does have an eastward tilt, and all of us are going to tumble into Jamaica Bay, like it or not. I advise everyone: Grab hold of anything that's nailed down, pull on your life preserver, and together we'll all sing *Nearer My God to Thee*."

In the year 1972 fires were "rekindled," "fueled," and "heated up." At least one candidate was accused of "shouting fire" in a crowded political theater, the constituents of another were seen as willing to "commit arson" for their candidate, and one called his previous presidential bid a "refining fire."

Some candidates were able to ignite "sparks"; others were luckless in that ability. None of the four candidates appearing in Wisconsin by mid-May, 1971, Bayh, Hughes, Muskie, and McGovern, "set Wisconsin Democrats on fire with enthusiasm." The Lindsay candidacy was seen by some as having potential sparkle: "What he says isn't much different from what Senator George McGovern or Senator Birch Bayh or Senator Fred Harris, or even Ed Muskie, are saying. But somehow [Lindsay] can create sparks in crowds which they leave nodding." There *was* "an opportunity for someone to catch fire in Florida and really ignite the voters. . . ." Lindsay, however, proved "fireless in Florida" and Max Lerner observed: "Even before his candidacy had taken fire, it struck many as a burned-out case."

Some saw McGovern as a man who "throws off no sparks." He was "a virtuous man but . . . no lighter of prairie fires. . . ." He delivered "the populist message with less fire but probably a great deal more substance [than Wallace] ." Kennedy, however, said of McGovern's campaign that it "has 'caught it's old fire and is on a definite upward course. A spark has been ignited, the flame is spreading and it's going to sweep across the country.' "

The candidates, fireless or not, operated on a scene in which the "fires of inflation threaten[ed] to rage out of control." And conservatives in both parties wondered, as did Henry Jackson, whether President Nixon was "using the 'smoke screen of summitry to cover up' de facto acceptance" of growing Soviet influence in the Middle East and elsewhere.

Storms, real or predicted, constantly loomed on the horizon. When Wallace "casually" let the *New York Times* know he would run in Florida, he "stole some thunder" from Muskie's formal declaration of candidacy on the same day. Wallace's decision to enter the Florida primary, in particular, threw "a cloud over the campaign of Senator Jackson. . . ." Nor were Jackson and Muskie to be the only storm watchers: "The storm signals [Wallace's strength in Florida] have not been lost on the other Democratic candidates." But long before Miami, it was clear that three "great political imponderables"—the eighteen-year-old vote, the independent vote, and taxes—plus the China-Russia diplomacy would "cloud the vision of all forecasters. . . ."

In addition to weather forecasts there were also alerts for "erosions," "avalanches," "earthquakes," and "icebergs." But despite this array of natural disasters, some "greening" did occur. Early in 1971, George McGovern took care to dig the "grass roots" and to prune the "money-tree." There was, as Tom Braden pointed out, "a dispute among money-tree experts about whether the tree shakes as vigorously for one man as it does for another. The hardhats among them think it all depends upon careful selection of the seedlings and constant pruning thereafter." The April, 1972, "flowering" of George McGovern was credited by James Kilpatrick, "in significant part to old-fashioned organization, to a methodical tilling of the soil."

The 1972 search for the nomination appeared, thus, to the media, a "natural" thing. However, that aspect of nature most seen was the violent side. Floods, drownings, brush fires, and avalanches seemed to be the lot of candidates, issues, and constituencies alike. The two candidates most often perceived as natural phenomena were George Wallace and George McGovern, both proclaimed "populist candidates." Both were perceived as disruptive natural forces, but McGovern was *also* perceived as one who "blossoms" and "flowers." The press sometimes seemed to have co-opted the McGovern campaign button metaphor, "I am a Grassroot."

Animals

By far the animal used most to describe the Democratic candidates was the ever present horse: Hubert Humphrey, the old warhorse; John Lindsay, the pale dark horse, and the like. Because most of the horse metaphors refer to horse racing, they were discussed under sports/games.

The verbal metaphors were for the most part prosaic. Muskie "crawled home" in the Florida primary. Lindsay "flushed out" other candidates and "unleashed" his Deputy Mayor Richard Aurelio on the campaign trail. Wallace "twisted tails." And, Humphrey, like the others, "corraled" votes and was "shepherded" from place to place. In 1972 the Democrats "weaseled around," "stalked," alternately "snarled" or "purred," and "flocked" or "stampeded" toward various of the candidates. If the verbal metaphors were commonplace, not so some of the nominal metaphors. Reminding us that most of the contenders were from the Senate and that only a few such as Wilbur Mills came forth from the House, one political commentator offered an explanation: "In contrast to the proud and glamorous stags that stalk the aisles of the Senate, the House of Representatives is populated mostly by prosaic and homespun men." And Mills himself provided one of the few references to the animals of antiquity when the secretary of the treasury discussed administration economic policy before the House Ways and Means Committee. He accused John Connally of "bringing into the committee room a Trojan Horse."

The description of George Wallace and Wallace's description of the political scene provided some interesting examples; for example, Wallace of his chief opponents, Humphrey and McGovern: "Everytime I trot out a li'l old bone of an issue, these big boys grab it and run off." Florida proved rich Wallace country, metaphorically, as well as in vote tally; for example, the headline proclaiming, "In Florida, Wallace Is the Big Gator." We were reminded also that "Florida loves strong men and beautiful women. If it weren't for the offshore shark (who has a beautiful lady of his own), the Jackson entry would look unbeatable here."

Of the candidates, Henry Jackson was the most persistent user of bird imagery; for example, when speaking of defense expenditures, he observed: "The ostriches say, 'let's bury our heads in the sand and leave our rear ends exposed.' . . . I say we must stand for a prudent defense posture to protect our liberty." In a variation on the theme, he compared the blind ostrich to the keen-sighted owl: " 'Ostriches and owls,' hoots Scoop. 'We are entering an age of ostriches and owls. The ostriches bury their heads in the sand and refuse to recognize the implications of what they're saying. The owls keep their eyes open, always remembering what they do today will have repercussions tomorrow.' " To this metaphorical aviary, he added yet another bird: "If you leave the offensive weapons out [of disarmament agreements], you've let the fox in the chicken coop. . . ."

Not only candidates but constituents were also perceived by the press in birdlike metaphors. Birch Bayh's supporters existed in "little nests . . . in key states" and "assorted gaggles of curious tourists" hovered around the Kennedy compound. As convention time neared, one reporter suggested that readers not forget "a whole covey of Democrats out there in the hustings . . . who [will] flock to the convention clutching a half or quarter or less of a single vote."

Senator Edward Kennedy talked of and was talked about in terms of "lemminglike" behavior. In describing the record of the Nixon administration, Kennedy observed: "it isn't just the bad results. It's the way they've gone about them—the lemminglike pursuit of clearly failing policies, the rosy picture painted of every bad development. . . ." While the senator saw a lemminglike tendency in the Nixon administration, one political observer accused Kennedy supporters of the same tendency: "Lemmings have their pell-mell stampede to the sea, penguins their wobbling and single-minded return to the rookery, salmon their upstream odyssey home to spawn. With political animals, the cycle is a more sober and calculated affair: a quadrennial flocking to presidential politics. And nowhere is the urge to be involved more sharply etched than in Camelot—the camp of Senator Edward M. Kennedy."

Domestic animals were also to have their day in the press. Deferring the full revision of the party charter was "a bone being tossed to George Meany. . . ." Muskie was declared as "clean as a houndstooth," Humphrey vowed to be no "hang-dogger," and, a victim of credentials fight challenges, Mayor Richard Daley, was left, "according to one associate, 'like a puppy curled up in a corner after a licking.' "

James Hoffa was, perhaps, the bluntest about Democratic chances in November, declaring that only Kennedy could defeat Nixon: "I don't think these other mutts have a chance." Not all were that optimistic about Kennedy's chances: "Though Americans admire underdogs, perhaps they distinguish between breeds. It may be that politicians who stubbornly fight even foolish wars against the country's alleged enemies win elections. Those who become underdogs because of their indiscretions do not win elections. It makes a kind of sense, even if you don't like it."

Bovines were not to be outdone. Edmund Muskie folksily reminded his potential contributors: "The way to keep a cow fresh is to milk her early and often." The backers, we are told, "laughed as if it didn't hurt." At the Democratic convention, we were reminded that "old bulls never quit until the young bulls run them out. The old bulls are dead, but don't forget that the young bulls eventually become old bulls too."

Not only were candidates and constituents described in animal-like metaphors, but issues as well. George Wallace insisted that issues ought to be presented simply, vowing that he would "put the hay down where the goats can get it." McGovern's socioeconomic policies were his "albatross." And, for all the "presidential politicians, the Vietnam war issue is something like chasing a greased boar at the country fair. It's hard to get hold of and no sensible man should want to get within miles of it, but once he gets in the arena he doesn't have much choice but to go after it."

In 1972, then, the Democrats displayed a veritable "zoo of creatures" to the country. Animal metaphors so proliferated that not only were "animals" being viewed, but they were being viewed by other animals who "flocked" or "stampeded" to see them. Small wonder then that the "food for thought" both viewer and viewed tossed back and forth was "bones." Perhaps on such an animal farm it was not to be unexpected that that near *mythical* creature, "the" tortoise, would emerge with the nomination.

Vehicles

Ships of several varieties sailed the 1972 Democratic seas. At a midsummer meeting, the AFL-CIO executive council expressed distrust of Lindsay as "a showboat." Kennedy described the visit of the American ping pong team to China as an "icebreaker plowing through a frozen sea" opening up "a new passage to improved relations. . . ."

Sailcraft, however, were most visible. In May, 1971, Humphrey declared, "I've got the sails up and I'm testing the water." He did, indeed, "set sail." In Little Rock, Arkansas, McGovern refused "to trim his sails on school busing or defense cuts. . . ." And Dan Walker offered this more *general* advice: "Anyone who thinks . . . McGovern plans to trim his sails . . . is in for a disappointment."

The political seas were strewn with sinking and abandoned ships. When the Michigan Democratic party left him off the guest list for a dinner, George Wallace held another, better attended dinner at the same time. "The snub," as one columnist put it, "proved somewhat like renting a deck chair on the *Titanic*." Early in the campaign "hapless survivors of ill-starred candidacies, already sunk or sinking, were being gladly welcomed aboard other campaigns." There was "only a momentary pause" for "the quietly disappearing hulks of the doomed candidacies—the Harold Hughes, Fred Harrises and Birch Bayhs. . . ." After the Massachusetts primary, "Establishment Massachusetts's politicians, for a time fighting among themselves to board the Muskie bandwagon . . . all but abandoned ship. . . ." By June, Humphrey "had to lay off some of his staff . . . and scavenge for $200,000 to stay afloat till the convention."

With the party in disarray, some thought of Kennedy as the "only port in the political hurricane now besetting the Democratic Party." Another reporter found Kennedy "restless in safe harbor" and thought he might declare his candidacy. And, when the nomination went to George McGovern, a *Monitor* editorial asked: "Was it shrewd or foolish politics for Mr. McGovern to so downgrade the once mighty bulwarks of his party?" The internecine feud that followed left McGovern and "his people . . . trying to stabilize the purists who still want to rock the boat."

Bandwagons were sometimes in fashion. From December, 1971, until the "launching" of a McGovern bandwagon in April, 1972, much of the talk focused on one particular wagon, that of Edmund Muskie. James Perry of the *Observer* denied there ever *was* a Muskie bandwagon, saying it was "more a solid old-fashioned beer wagon" delivering "on schedule."

Diesels gave way to steam engines. Contributors were "slow to board Muskie's campaign train." There was, however, an occasional "spurt of steam" for Muskie. Even at it's slowest speeds, there was a "sputter in the engine" now and then and that "rumble" continued to produce "disquiet in the camps of Muskie rivals." There was some concern about George Wallace in July because he "seemed to pick up steam the nearer he got to Miami." But it was McGovern's "little engine, which kept puffing, 'I think I can; I think I can'. . . " that made it to the station.

An occasional plane or rocket flashed through the air. *Atlantic* sighed in March that the Democratic quest for the presidency began long ago, "lost in the criss-cross of hopefuls' planes increasing the mid-air collision rush. . . ." When Muskie announced his intention of withdrawing from the primaries, a "Muskie man in the Senate" advised a reporter, "we're in a holding pattern."

In 1972, the candidates rode out to do battle in a variety of crafts, most of which were in a state of disrepair or in imminent danger of collision or sinking. Thus, there was little certainty that any candidate had constructed a craft capable of riding out the buffeting of the campaign. It seemed difficult for candidates and their supporters to distinguish between reality and appearances. What seemed to be a sleek, durable vessel turned out to be a *Titanic* or, worse still, no craft at all. What some thought were "bandwagons" were not and what most did *not* see as a bandwagon *was* one. It was, however, a near mythical craft from a children's story that emerged the most durable craft of all, a little engine that could.

Other Persons or Types of Persons

Almost all the candidates were compared with someone else and not always admiringly so; for example, Wills suggested that Eugene McCarthy had "become another Stassen." Von Hoffman saw Birch Bayh "as a kind of WASP Sammy Glick. . . ." When Hubert Humphrey offered "What this country needs is a nice man as President of the United States," Jenkins in the *New York Times Magazine* observed: "Like Willie Loman he sets great store by being well-liked."

David Broder suggested that with "his pompadour carefully fluffed to give him every possible quarter-inch of extra height," Wallace "looked just a bit like an aging musical comedy star brought back from retirement for a revival of 'Dames at Sea.' "

"Running for office—particularly the heady excitement of the big time, the Presidency" the *Observer* recorded, "is probably what [Wallace] enjoys doing most in life; he could no more pass it up than Sky Masterson could resist a bet on Don Juan as a pretty face." In Maryland, Wallace appeared to be the "sole vendor of vanilla ice cream, when everyone else is offering chocolate. With the chocolate fanciers thus divided, it is obvious that the unique vanilla vendor can hope to sell more ice cream cones than anyone else, even if he gets under 20 percent of the total market." One headline opined, "Wallace: Pied Piper of the Dissatisfied."

John Lindsay may have suffered most from comparisons. Reston called him "the Lochinvar of the late night shows. . . ." Some Democrats viewed him as a "carpetbagger." *Newsweek* reminded their readers: "Lindsay . . . came to City Hall a term and a half ago rather like Henry V to Agincourt, pledging at his inaugural not just to work the usual civic and fiscal wonders but to strike up 'new light in tired eyes and the sound of laughter in homes.' . . . Lindsay today is far less a hero at home than to the national audience he has cultivated and won as knight-errant for all urban America. His reign has been beset by crises from its very first day. . . ." Lindsay's challenge of Wallace to a TV debate in Florida prompted one reporter to suggest that was rather "like Tiny Tim asking Joe Frazier to step outside 'so we can settle this thing.' "

McGovern's "weakness" was likened to "that of Aristides: People are numbed by his liberal virtues, and are tired of hearing him called the Just." "To a round table jammed with seventy knights, clad in battered armour, he brings the Galahad Touch," declared James Kilpatrick. At least one reporter recalled McGovern's six-week campaign for the 1968 presidential nomination, saying it "seemed to confirm an image of a wildly unrealistic tilter at windmills."

When the Dixie governors "looked askance" at McGovern, the Hatfields seemed closer to "the McCoys than Senator George McGovern . . . [to] the U.S. South." By May he suddenly became "Prince Valiant" in the media. Princely or not, it was Kennedy who remained the romantic and perhaps tragic figure to some; for example, the *Globe* was reminded of Billy Budd:

> They [McGovern sympathizers] don't just plan to draft Kennedy, since he can always object to that. They plan something more severe, more like an "impressment" of the Massachusetts senator, similar to the recruiting techniques used by the British Navy before the War of 1812. . . . As Kennedy sails the seas off Cape Cod, the flotilla of the Committee for an Open Convention is hard astern, seeking his services for the journey to November. Like Billy Budd, Melville's innocent foretopman, he may be taken from his peaceful merchant vessel and placed on the deck of a man 'o war. He may go quietly or he may protest. Either way, he's bound to be impressed.

Don Oberdorfer reminded *Post* readers that a number of people had scoffed when McGovern "sat down to play, a seemingly hapless and hopeless one note Johnny from South Dakota applying for the biggest job in the nation. . . ." Also playing on the keyboard metaphor Perry recalled: "Everybody laughed when poor old clodhopping George McGovern sat down to play the piano. Nobody's laughing now: he plays with the skill of a Van Cliburn."

Newsweek recalled how "Democratic regulars" had watched McGovern's "accelerating march toward the nomination as dismally, and as helplessly, as Rome watching the advance of Attila the Hun across Europe." Even then it was Kennedy, not McGovern, who was likened to the Greek heroes: "The day Senator Edward Kennedy of Massachusetts got into the Democratic campaign was like one of those moments in the Trojan War when things had been going badly for the Greeks and then one or another of their heroes, an Achilles or an Ajax, buckled on his armour and entered the fray."

In 1972, the candidates were often not perceived as senators and congress-men running for the presidential nomination but other types of persons engaged in other trades—they were Don Juans or ice cream vendors. More often than not they were larger or smaller than life, but rarely lifelike. Thus, the campaign appeared to be populated chiefly by royalty of various courtly ranks or by characters more to be disdained or pitied than admired. Constitu-ents (when they were not masquerading as animals of several species, domes-tic and wild) were not citizens listening to campaigners' talks about issues, but, rather, buyers of ice cream easily seduced by the enticing tune of a Pied Piper marching throughout the land.

Show Biz

Vice-President Agnew agreed that the Democratic campaign was "an open book." He quipped: "I understand the author is Clifford Irving." While the press may not have agreed on the authorship of the piece, that there *was* a scenario they were sure. By May, 1971, it seemed clear "that the irrepressible Humphrey would like to write the comeback scenario of the 1970's." In mid-1971, Edmund Muskie tried out his "scenario for a front-runner" to see if it would move. An April *New Republic* cover story previewed at length, "A Scenario for Kennedy." If McGovern turned out to be a strong candidate, speculated one reporter, that "of course, would tear Mr. Kennedy's 'I am not a candidate' scenario to pieces."

Some of the candidates performed with more verve than others; for example, "John Barrymore Lindsay" gave a "bravura performance" when he announced his switch to the Democratic party. Others saw Edward Kennedy as the "number one sweater boy of politics" who at an occasion in Arkansas honoring Wilbur Mills "scattered magnolia blossoms with Rhett Butler aban-don. . . ."

As late as July some Democrats held on to "a last hope—the feverish vision of a Last Hurrah, the sweet scenario of Ted's conscription as candidate Kennedy III, followed by his conquest of the usurper in November and his coronation in January as Sovereign of the Restoration."

There were those, however, who saw the election as less heady stuff. In 1971, one reporter thought Birch Bayh would be "cast as the juvenille lead in the Democratic follies. . . ." Bayh dropped out of the race even before the play "tried out" in the primary states but the show did, in fact, go on. "The Follies Begin," Perry of the *Observer* declared in January. The Florida primary turned "out to be the most fantastic local show since Walt Disney opened in Orlando. . . ." A later version of the "show" in Wisconsin starred the "odd couple," McGovern and Wallace. By mid-June some complained that the "real McGovern" still remained "under the grease paint."

Many viewers agreed that there was "nothing quite like" a Wallace rally calling it "a country carnival, a phenomenon. . . ." The coming of George Wallace seemed to be "an event—rather like the coming of the circus in the spring." William Raspberry saw the Wallace rally as a "minstrel show" and Godfrey Sperling likened it to the "finish to a Billy Graham revival."

Shades of the old West sometimes walked the streets. "Showdowns" occurred from New York to California. Voters were tracked "along the Chisholm Trail." The *Monitor* speculated: "Lindsay may cut off Muskie at the Gap." But it took the California primary to recall two classic Western movies. A McGovern primary aide suggested: "California is the gunfight at the O. K. Corral." The *Monitor* went further back in film history: "California may have lost the crowd scene of the Republican convention, but it is almost sure to provide a 'High Noon' backdrop for a Democratic primary climax. The big scene now is the Hubert Humphrey-George McGovern 'shoot-out.' . . ."

Westerns were not the only genre for which the press had a fondness. There was, of course, one conspicuous event, that was, at first, treated like a spy-spoof, the Watergate break-in and subsequent cover-up. "Mission Incredible," first described as a "caper," a "cloak-and-dagger" affair, remained for some a "political soap opera" but became for others a "national tragedy."

The "Barnum and Bailey world of politics '72" tilted "on its axis toward the party conventions. . . ." Until the last minute, "Humphrey scorekeepers challenged McGovern's arithmetic and guessed that his Great American Dream Machine would die around the second ballot." As the convention began, the "drama" of the three Georges (McGovern, Meany, Wallace) held the Miami "stage." Some claimed that the convention "in that stalest of all tags looked like the cast of 'Hair.' " And, as the convention ended and all the rivals stood with arms around each other on the podium, the "Democrats staged a smash rock-opera version of the old party show, 'United We Stand, Divided We Fall.' . . ." McGovern, the star of that show, caused some labor leaders concern: "We're [labor] going to have a real fight. . . . The Archie Bunkers think McGovern is too radical to vote for." The question asked much earlier, after Florida: "Was it *all* Archie Bunkers?," returned to haunt the Democrats again.

The search for the 1972 Democratic nomination turned primary season into the "great American road show." First one candidate and then another "leapt center stage" in several versions of the scenario for winning. This year the writers selected not only the older more conventional forms in which to write, but also dipped into the newer forms such as the rock opera. The play had an unusually large cast calling for a variety of actor-types—glamour boys, juvenile leads, stalwart protectors of the peace, and fumbling villains. Even with so large and varied a cast, show biz remained largely a spectator phenomenon, more to be watched than participated in. The spectators could enjoy the vicarious excitement of a shoot-out in Dodge City or the super cool antics of master spies. They could laugh at the clowns and the slightly aging musical comedy stars. But *they* did not actually put on the greasepaint and thus did not feel responsible when the play proved to be a flop.

Other Categories

The first eight categories accounted for 86 percent of the metaphors cataloged in this study. But four other categories need to be mentioned: courtship; food/cookery; religion; and health/illness.[11]

The 1972 presidential swains wooed and were wooed, courted and were courted. Only reporter predilection seems to have determined who "wooed" (and was wooed) and who "courted" (and was courted). Courted *or* wooed, the South, in the end, felt like a "bride who got left at the altar."

At least one suitor, Humphrey, was affectionately chastised by David Broder for his superabundance of ardor: "Humphrey can be faulted for his excesses, but they are the excesses of a generous spirit, not an angry or embittered heart. His exaggerations are like a lover's lies—and at 61, Humphrey is still engaged in reckless love affairs with his country, and, indeed, with all of life." All in all, however, the press appears to have seen little that was glamorous or courtly about the quest for the 1972 nomination. As one columnist put it: "The question is whether in the process of the courtship the lovely and elusive prize gets so ravished and mutilated that the swains will wonder if the quest was worth it."[12]

Some judged the election to be "mostly about who gets what share of the money pie." The press saw celestial pie as largely bipartisan: "Pie-in-the-sky is a bi-partisan confection. It's a dish that Democrats and Republican candidates serve up with a flourish each presidential election year and a race between George McGovern and Richard Nixon could become a Chef's Derby."

The other Democratic dishes ranged in elegance from stew to hors d'oeuvres. When George Wallace tossed the Alabama state legislature "an impressive stew of populist legislation" it swallowed "only a spoonful." The candidates did not always manage to choose the appropriate fare for their audiences. For example, one local politician "fumed" about Lindsay's appearances in Indiana: "They wanted red meat and he's dishing up fancy hors d'oeuvres."

Consumers were warned by a variety of people; for example, Vice-President Agnew felt the contenders for the Democratic presidential nomination were only rewarding voters with " 'Leap Year lollipops' by using 'the old soak-the-rich, share-the-wealth ploy' as a campaign issue." Elizabeth Janeway's consumer advocacy took on a more bipartisan air: "it would appear that what politicians offer us is also a product to consume; plans, programs and policies cooked up in huge stainless steel vats somewhere behind the scene and marketed in convenient cans bearing a label that declares the contents are just what grandma used to make. . . . To the sellers of politics, we, the voters, are simply consumers and the chief question becomes how best to tickle our taste buds." In 1972, the "wares" of the Democratic party clearly did not "whet" the appetites of the American public.

The "Christian witness" of George McGovern and the political "conversion" of John Lindsay dominated the religious metaphors. Henry Jackson's much reprinted comment about Lindsay's switch to the Democratic party is indicative of the tone of many: "We believe in the right of redemption. But if you join the church on one Sunday you can't expect to be chairman of the board of deacons the following Sunday." Jackson proved to be more prophetic than the columnist who observed: "the ticket could be enlivened with the very newest Democrat around, one still fresh and dripping from the political baptism font, rechristened party man John Lindsay."

Lindsay, as he campaigned for the nomination, reminded one of "an attractive young Episcopal bishop from perhaps Old Greenwich, who says most of the right things and looks princely in the robes and trapping of his ecclesiastical office." If John Lindsay was likened to an Episcopal bishop, George McGovern was described in more fundamentalist terms. His "style" seemed "more like that of a Christian witness than that of [a] charismatic leader." As some McGovern Democrats sought to persuade Humphrey Democrats to join them, William Buckley provided this reminder for onlookers: "[it] isn't as simple as that Humphrey's emphases are different from McGovern's. What it is, is sacrilege. McGovernism is something of a religion. . . . It is off-putting to be asked to vote for McGovern as a religious exercise. It is one thing to seduce the Humphrey Democrat by appealing to his party loyalty or by his disapproval of Richard Nixon. It is something else to try to co-opt him into a new religious order."

Only Kennedy was persistently sanctified. One political observer noted: "Watching the summer tourists approaching Ted Kennedy in the halls of Congress is a little like watching pilgrims coming to a shrine. . . . The supplicants stand in line for pictures, autographs, or a handshake." One writer went so far as to metaphorically *deify* him: "he is a man of destiny, like it or not. And he does not want it. Deep down he is trapped in his own Gethsemane. He would like the chalice to pass. . . ."

Some came to view both the Wallace and the McGovern campaigns as "crusades." California was at once McGovern's "finest hour and the epiphany of all his larger political problems." As with most candidates, "where his cup runneth over, where he is rich beyond measure, is in a superabundance of unsolicited advice." By September, 1972, it was clear of the old pols that "they really weren't terribly eager to recruit the 1972 'sacrifical lamb' from their own kind." Thus, it was "St. George" who went out to fight "the Dragon, Richard Nixon."

The year 1972 "brought boils to the surface to be lanced." "Front runner's miseries" dominated much of the early press coverage but the "sick list" extended to most of the candidates. It is perhaps not unexpected that the author of *In Critical Condition: The Crisis in America's Health Care* would, in these press accounts, make the most metaphorical use of health/sickness. For example, Senator Kennedy saw the I.T.T. affair as "symptomatic of a disease that infects all levels of government and all parties." He assured the South that they were "no longer swallowing . . . patent Yankee medicines." And he commented on the financial community's responses to McGovern's defense of his socioeconomic policies in the California debates: "If Wall Street sneezed over George McGovern in California in 1972, it positively caught pneumonia over President Nixon's invasion of Cambodia. . . ."

Kennedy himself was seen by the press in terms of health aid to an ailing McGovern; for example, he was called a "crutch" for McGovern and was certified a "tonic" for the South Dakota senator. "Advised that he trailed in every state except two, George McGovern took a powerful tonic—with built-in side effects. The tonic is called Edward Kennedy. And McGovern now has symptoms of charisma shock."

"Fractures" accounted for many 1972 miseries. The health/illness category is inextricably associated with the violence category, for surely candidates and constituencies alike would require time and treatment to recover from so much "flaying," "rattling of eyeteeth," "sandbagging," and the like.

The actors in the 1972 election, on occasion, indulged themselves in certain religious practices. But, there was, in 1972 at least, no biz like show biz, unless it was courting, cooking, or diagnosing illnesses. It was, for the metaphor-makers at least, "a very good year."

Conclusion

In 1971 to 1972, twelve "common topics" appeared to dominate the way the press described the search for the Democratic nomination. For each of these "common topics" or essential metaphors, a variety of examples illustrate the range of "special topics" within them.

The readership of the print media sampled in this study numbered many millions of people. They were exposed to these particular common topics for at least eighteen months. One can only speculate to what extent the language describing the 1972 (or any) nomination process is "prescriptive" as well as descriptive. If Burke and others are correct in their suggestion that a "name" directs the way one acts toward the thing named, then language *is* prescriptive as well as descriptive. As he suggests, "the mere act of naming an object or situation decrees that it is to be singled out as such-and-such rather than something-other."[13] Thus, in "its essence" language is "not neutral." For as Burke argues: "Far from aiming at suspended judgment [the speech of people] is loaded with judgments. . . . Its names for objects . . . give us . . . cues as to how we should act toward these objects."[14]

There has been a serious cautionary note in this essay for, as Hermann G. Stelzner observed, metaphors "may become current coin before there is explicit recognition [Burke would suggest even 'implicit' recognition] that an *analogy* and not an identity is involved."[15] An identity may be presumed for so long that the analogy, *if* it is seen *as* an analogy, may be perceived as more exact than originally, in fact, it was. Moreover, as Marie Nichols reminds us: "Language is not an objective tool; it's symbols are not empty but freighted with the experiences of men who are its makers, and interpreted by men who bring to it the feelings and experiences of their existential selves."[16]

If "to understand ourselves, we must study our symbolic behavior,"[17] this examination may prod us to ask: What does the way the press (and the candidates as reported in the press) talked *about* the 1972 Democratic presidential nomination tell us about the way press and candidates have come to view that part of our political process? As consumers of these metaphors, we may want to go beyond that question to another question, "What do our interpretations of them tell us about *our* existential selves?" Again, Burke provides us with useful clues by reminding us that a symbol provides us with "a terminology of thoughts, actions, emotions, attitudes, for codifying a pattern of experience."[18] He points to the close relation between symbol and situation or scene. The symbol provides either an "*orienting* of a situation, or an *adjustment* to a situation," or in good Burkeian fashion, *both*.[19] Thus, symbols are linguistic encompassings of situations.

Existentially then, for the printed press, the nomination process is one in which violence is the norm rather than the exception. "Flaying" is the essential activity, whether the candidates direct it at each other or at the issues. The encounters of the candidates with one another and their tactics are, then, generally violent if not specifically warlike. Moreover the violence is multidirectional; it is directed not only at fellow candidates but at constituencies as well; for example, audiences are treated much like a people under siege. Small wonder that after more than a year of bruising battle, not only are the candidates bloodied and impotent but their constituencies as well. Thus there is little place for the careful, reflective consideration of issues during the nominating process and little will or capacity for it immediately after a campaign.

There is a gamelike nature to all of this. The "carnage" is both real and unreal. The favorite "games" (horse racing, football, and boxing) in the nomination process are "gladiatorial" in nature. They are, first of all, largely spectator sports. Few players actually get bloodied (in the one, horse racing, it is not even humans who feel the prod of the stick) and many can watch at a safe distance. Fans not only participate vicariously in the "fray" but by gambling on the outcome they add dimensions of excitement that applause and lip service alone do not generate. They are one step closer to the fray but still largely unbloodied.

Politics also often appears to be a genre of "show biz," again more to be watched than participated in. The cast, in 1971 to 1972, is still predominantly male. Some aspirants try out for their roles and occasionally one has the potential at least of stepping into the starring role without "trying out" for it.

The playbill consists more of musicals ("follies" and the like) and situation comedies (for example, the "Odd Couple") than of serious fare. But, Westerns and cloak-and-dagger "capers" occasionally are available for divertissements. When the viewer realizes that the "caper" is less the stuff of which James Bonds are made of and more the stuff of serious drama, some decide the play has run too long and move on to something else.

Scenarios prepared by campaign staffs are rewritten or discarded as the drama is played out before audiences. And, in politics as in show biz, "comebacks" are often more easily dreamed of than enacted.

The near obsession for "likenesses" is clear. Since the "roles" in the political process are either ill-defined, unconsidered, or disliked, candidates are seen "in terms of" something else. They are seen as other people—as Sammy Glicks, Willie Lomans, or as Billy Budds and Prince Valiants. The range is wide indeed, but people largely stand at either end of the continuum. Even the "piano" is only played by a "Johnny-one-note" or a Van Cliburn. Thus, our political figures seem either smaller than life or larger than life.

Often, indeed, the political scene is inhabited not by candidates but by animals of all varieties, more domestic than wild. Moreover, it is "peopled" not by a constituency carefully considering the issues but by "coveys" and "flocks" who are "corraled" or "herded" into their decisions. Thus, if one does not want to go to gladiatorial games or to the theater, one might well go to the zoo—there, again, mostly to look.

All of these proceedings are viewed, not as exceptional, but as natural. Candidacies "blossom" as readily as plants. If we are to agree with the metaphor-makers, the McGovern and Wallace candidacies seem the most "natural" for 1972.[20] Even in this category, "violent" imagery persists; for example, "drought," "washouts," or "earthquakes" are the fate of many. Still, amid all of the "avalanches" and "floods," some "greening" persists.

If this *is* the nature of the "reality" the press has constructed under the label "political process," one may pause to ask whether the political process would be greatly enriched were we to respond to it in other ways and to look for other symbols with which to "encompass" it. Such new vocabulary might reveal that we require our *candidates* to act like something more than rival quarterbacks who see their task as devising game plans and calling audibles. And we might require of *ourselves* a more thoughtful and active role in the political process.

1. For the bases of Kenneth Burke's argument see, for example, *Permanence and Change: An Anatomy of Purpose* (Indianapolis, Ind.: Bobbs-Merrill, 1965), pp. 176–191, and *Philosophy of Literary Form*, rev. ed. (New York: Vintage Books, 1941), 5–7, 121–129. *Permanence and Change* was first copyrighted in 1935; *Philosophy of Literary Form* in 1941.

2. Burke, *Philosophy of Literary Form*, p. 5.

3. *Ibid.*, p. 7.

4. Kenneth Burke, *Attitudes toward History* (Boston: Beacon Press, 1959), p. 339. First copyright, 1937.

5. Burke, *Philosophy of Literary Form*, p. vi. For a fuller discussion see Burke's later works: *A Grammar of Motives* (New York: Prentice-Hall, 1945); *A Rhetoric of Motives* (New York: Prentice-Hall, 1950); and *Language as Symbolic Action* (Berkeley: University of California Press, 1966).

6. A recent example is William Safire, *The New Language of Politics* (New York: Random House, 1968). See also Hans Sperber and Travis Trittshuch, *American Political Terms* (Detroit, Mich.: Wayne State University Press, 1962); Jack Plano and Milton Greenberg, *The American Political Dictionary* (New York: Holt, Rinehart and Winston, 1965); Wilbur W. White, *White's Political Dictionary* (New York: World Publishing, 1947).

7. The dailies were: *New York Times, Los Angeles Times, Washington Post, Christian Science Monitor, Boston Globe, Springfield (Massachusetts) Union, Akron (Ohio) Beacon Journal, Huntington (West Virginia) Herald Dispatch.* The weeklies were *National Observer, New Republic, Newsweek,* and *Time.*

8. Percentage totals for the first eight categories were: general violence (16 percent); warfare (15 percent); sports and games (15 percent); natural phenomena (14 percent); animals (9 percent); vehicles (6 percent); other types of persons (5.5 percent); and show biz (5.5 percent).

9. Even if language and conceptualization were not so intimately related, Richard Weaver's comment would approach this position in yet another way: "Language, which is . . . predicative, is for the same cause sermonic. We are all of us preachers in private or public capacities. We have no sooner uttered words, than we have given impulse to other people to look at the world, or some small part of it, in our way." "Language is Sermonic," in Roger E. Nebergall, ed., *Dimensions of Rhetorical Scholarship* (Norman: University of Oklahoma, Department of Speech, 1963), p. 62.

10. The number of metaphors cited in this paper generates 400 plus items. Even with severely abbreviated footnote form, the end result appeared so unwieldy that the decision was made simply to list the dailies which formed the basis for the classification scheme and for the statistical data. Specific citations may be obtained from the author.

11. Percentage totals for categories 9 to 12 were: food/cookery (4 percent); courtship (3 percent); religion (3 percent); and health/sickness (3 percent).

12. For a treatment of the political courtship of Hubert Humphrey and John F. Kennedy with West Virginia in 1960, see Hermann G. Stelzner, "Humphrey and Kennedy Court West Virginia, May 3, 1960," *Southern Speech Journal*, 37 (Fall, 1971), 21–33. A more general treatment of the persuader as wooer may be found in Wayne Brockriede, "Arguers as Lovers," *Philosophy and Rhetoric*, 5 (Winter, 1972), 1–11.

13. Burke, *Philosophy of Literary Form*, p. 5.

14. Burke, *Permanence and Change,* pp. 176–177.

15. Hermann G. Stelzner, "Analysis by Metaphor," *Quarterly Journal of Speech*, 51 (February, 1965), 60.

16. Marie Hochmuth Nichols, "Rhetoric and Style," in *Patterns of Literary Style*, ed. Joseph Strelka (University Park: The Pennsylvania State University Press, 1971), p. 136.

17. Karl R. Wallace, *Understanding Discourse* (Baton Rouge: Louisiana University Press, 1970), p. 5.

18. Kenneth Burke, *Counterstatement* (Berkeley: University of California Press, 1968), p. 154. Original copyright, 1931.

19. *Ibid*., p. 156. Italics added.

20. Natural phenomena was the largest single category of metaphors used by and about George McGovern in this particular press sample; of those used by and about George Wallace in the sample, natural phenomena was the second largest category. (For Wallace, general violence was the largest category; for McGovern, it was the second largest category.)

Contributors

Professor Vincent M. Bevilacqua
Department of Communication Studies
University of Massachusetts

Professor Jane Blankenship
Department of Communication Studies
University of Massachusetts

Professor Wayne Brockriede
Department of Communication
University of Colorado

Professor Theodore Clevenger, Jr.
Department of Communication
Florida State University

Professor Martin Cobin
Department of Theater and Dance
University of Colorado

Assistant Professor Vernon E. Cronen
Department of Communication Studies
University of Massachusetts

Associate Professor Ray D. Dearin
Department of Speech
Iowa State University

Assistant Professor Carolyn Castleberry Deile
Department of Management
California State University, Chico

Professor Joseph A. DeVito
Department of Communication Arts and Sciences
Queens College, CUNY

Assistant Professor James S. Measell
Department of Speech Communication
Wayne State University

Professor Roger E. Nebergall
Department of Speech Communication
University of Illinois

Associate Professor J. Donald Ragsdale
Department of Speech
Louisiana State University

Professor Robert L. Scott
Department of Speech Communication
University of Minnesota

Professor Malcolm O. Sillars
Department of Communication
University of Utah

Professor Hermann G. Stelzner
Department of Communication Studies
University of Massachusetts

Professor Charles J. Stewart
Department of Communication
Purdue University

Professor David B. Strother
Department of Speech
Washington State University

Associate Professor Joseph W. Wenzel
Department of Speech Communication
University of Illinois